OPERATION
GATEKEEPER

OPERATION GATEKEEPER

THE RISE
OF THE "ILLEGAL ALIEN"
AND THE MAKING
OF THE U.S.-MEXICO
BOUNDARY

JOSEPH NEVINS

ROUTLEDGE
New York and London

Published in 2002 by
Routledge
29 West 35th Street
New York, NY 10001

Published in Great Britain by
Routledge
11 New Fetter Lane
London EC4P 4EE

Routledge is an imprint of Taylor & Francis Group.

Library of Congress Cataloging-in-Publication Data

Nevins, Joseph.
    Operation Gatekeeper : the rise of the "illegal alien" and the making of the U.S.-Mexico
boundary / by Joseph Nevins.
        p. cm. Includes bibliographical references and index.
    ISBN 0-415-93104-5 (hb) — ISBN 0-415-93105-3 (pb)
        1. Illegal aliens—Government policy—United States. 2. Operation Gatekeeper (U.S.)
    3. Border patrols—Mexican-American Border Region. 4. United States. Immigration Border
Patrol. I. Title.
    JV6483 .N47 2001
    363.28'5'0973—dc21

                                                    2001034989
Printed on acid-free, 250-year-paper.
Manufactured in the United States of America
Design and typography: Jack Donner

2/02

Contents

Acknowledgments

Despite the single author listed on the cover, a work such as this is never an individual endeavor. It is the outgrowth of countless conversations with friends, colleagues, and critics, the mining of other people's works, and the support—material as well as moral—of many individuals. In this regard, I must thank and acknowledge many, only a small number of whom I can mention here—not least because of the limits of my memory.

Much of this book originated from my doctoral dissertation at the University of California, Los Angeles (UCLA). In this regard, I wish to acknowledge and thank the members of my dissertation committee: Mark Ellis; Gerry Hale; Raul Hinojosa-Ojeda; Michael Mann; and Joshua Muldavin. I have learned much from all of them. On numerous occasions, they constructively challenged my ideas and provided me with valuable feedback and helpful advice.

I would like to express my indebtedness especially to the two co-chairs of my committee: Mark Ellis, for his innumerable conversations, critical insights, extremely helpful comments, and bountiful moral support; and Gerry Hale, for his careful editing and, more important, for his many years of guidance and moral and political support. The dissertation was far better than it would have been without them.

The office staff of the UCLA Department of Geography—Jason Corbett, Susan Glines, and Tina Schroeter—generously put up with my myriad requests for assistance over the years. I thank them from the bottom of my heart.

I am highly appreciative of my former colleagues in the UCLA Department of Geography for helping to make my graduate career a rich experience. In this regard, I also want to recognize my fellow academic student employees at UCLA, especially those active in SAGE (the Student Association of Graduate Employees), the trade union of academic student employees.

Numerous friends helped me through the research and writing process in countless ways. They include: Kathy Beckett, Chris Brown, Clare Campbell, Nigel Chalk, Ben Forest, Lynn Fredriksson, Don Gauthier, Steve Herbert, Scott Kessler and Cheryl Lindley and their three children (Sade, Sophie, and Shane), Dave Runsten, Fred Seavey, Ben Terrall, Lisa Tsui, and Konstantin von Krusenstiern.

One of the joys of undertaking the research and writing was having the opportunity to meet a number of people who share both many of my academic interests and political concerns. In this regard, I thank Peter Andreas,

Tim Dunn, Larry Herzog, Michael Huspek, and José Palafox. At various times, they all provided me with resources, valuable criticisms, and comradeship.

A number of people helped me in Washington, D.C., while I was there conducting interviews and doing archival work. I am indebted to Kate Doyle at the National Security Archive, Robert Ellis at the National Archives, Marian Smith, the Historian of the Immigration and Naturalization Service, and Marcus Stern of Copley News Service.

In terms of my fieldwork in San Diego and Tijuana, I am most grateful to Roberto Martinez of the American Friends Service Committee, Raul Ramirez, formerly of El Centro de Apoyo al Migrante, Claudia Smith of the California Rural Legal Assistance Foundation, and all the friends at *Casa del Migrante*. I also want to thank the numerous representatives of the United States Border Patrol who provided me with documentation and helped to arrange or took me on "line tours" and "ride-alongs" on several occasions.

A postdoctoral fellowship at the Institute of International Studies (IIS) at the University of California, Berkeley during 2000–2001 provided with the space and time to put the finishing touches on the manuscript. In this regard, I want to thank Michael Watts, the head of IIS, and Susana Kaiser, my colleague in the Rockefeller Foundation-funded "Communities in Crisis" program.

While living here in Berkeley, José Palafox was of invaluable assistance on many occasions. I also want to thank Sasha Kokha of the National Network of Immigrant and Refugee Rights in Oakland for her assistance. During that time, Connie Razza provided very helpful edits and comments on some of the chapters, help for which I am very grateful.

The UCLA Graduate Division, the UCLA Latin American Center, the Comparative Immigration and Integration Program of the Center for German and European Studies at the University of California, Berkeley, the UC MEXUS (the University of California Institute for Mexico and the United States), and the Rockefeller Foundation all provided me with generous financial assistance during the course of my research and writing. I am most appreciative.

Zoltán Grossman of the Department of Geography at the University of Wisconsin–Madison made the maps contained herein. I thank him for lending his cartographic skills and for doing such a fine job on the maps.

Anonymous reviewers of the original book manuscript were most helpful in pointing out weaknesses and suggesting constructive changes. I thank them. I also want to extend my gratitude to Eric Nelson of Routledge for his suggestions for reworking the manuscript, to production editor Jeanne Shu, and to copy editor Brian Bendlin for all their help.

Finally, I thank my family for their love and support, and express my infinite gratitude to Mizue—in addition for having read and commented on many sections of the book—for her love, patience, and generosity, as well as her inspiring example.

Foreword
Mike Davis

1.

First, there are ghosts.

Long ago, in my Cold War childhood, my father and I would regularly join the gypsy army of rock hounds who, with burlap water bags hanging from their fenders, scoured California's deserts in search of uranium deposits and *Lost Dutchman* mines, as well as more modest treasures like geodes and petrified wood. Our favorite oasis was the gas station/cafe that constituted Ocotillo Wells, 90 miles east of San Diego. The proprietor was a jocular oldtimer who liked to brag that he would be reincarnated as a Gila Monster in his next life. While he and my father argued about baseball (this was the pre-Dodger golden age of the old Pacific Coast League), I would explore his collection of desert relics and cryptic detritus. In addition to ultra-violet medicine bottles, bullet-holed 1920s highway signs, and rusted mining gear, he also collected gruesome souvenirs.

On one bulletin board he had tacked up photographs of seven or eight cadavers: all of them young Mexican men he had discovered in the arroyos between Ocotillo Wells and the nearby Border. Like most eight-year-olds I was both horrified and mesmerized by the images, as well as embarrassed by my inability to stop staring at them. "It must be horrible to slowly die of thirst," I ventured. "Oh, them wetbacks didn't die of thirst," the Gila Monster laughed. "They was all shot. In the back." He pointed to unmistakable gore in several of the photos. He had some compelling reason to believe that, in fact, they had been executed by the Border Patrol.

These dead men, whom I now know to be *compañeros*, have haunted me for almost a lifetime. I don't have the slightest idea, of course, whether they were actually victims of a Border Patrol death squad, although the mere possibility was an earthquake in my moral universe. Indisputably, however, they died in a singular, sinister place of which I had no previous inkling.

I refer, of course, not to the Borrego Desert but to the Border.

Tourists and politicians often equate the Border with the steel wall (formerly a fence) that guillotines so many communities and family ties between Brownsville/Matamoros and San Diego/Tijuana. But this is to confuse the synecdoche—what Mexican-Spanish more correctly identifies as *la Linea*—with its subject. The Border is also used as a synonym for *la Frontera*, the zone of intensified daily interaction between Norteno, Chicano, and U.S. cultures which some theorists consider to be an emergent socio-cultural galaxy in its own right. This conflation of Border and *Frontera*, however, fudges the institutional specificity of the repressive apparatus(es) that leave bodies in the desert (even if they later become the bitter theme of a *corrido*).

As I discovered at the end of my innocence in 1955, the Border, *strictu senso*, is a state-sanctioned system of violence: physical, environmental, economic, and cultural. Its principal historical function, I learned later, has been the reproduction of agricultural and industrial peonage in the American Southwest (and, more lately, in border *maquiladoras* as well as more distant U.S. labor markets). It penetrates deeply into millions of lives far from the actual demarcation of national real-estate. It shapes but is manifestly distinct from *La Frontera* as cultural formation.

The Border is often compared to a dam: defending the fat suburbs of the American Dream from a deluge of Third World misery. This, of course, misunderstands the role of a dam, which is not to prevent the flow of water but to control and ration its supply. To the despair of pundits on both sides, who would prefer to see a more orderly system of gastarbeiter migration strictly controlled by economic demand, the Border is a heavy investment in the laws of Chaos: the Brownian motion of hundreds of thousands of job-and-dignity seekers modulated by nocturnal pursuit and detention camps. Realists, of course, understand that a cheap labor flux without the necessary quotient of fear and uncertainty imposed by illegality might cease to be cheap labor.

The Orwellian hypocrisy of a free-trade utopia cum police state, not surprisingly, favors epic corruption and transnational crime. How ironic that the Border, this now massive, militarized display of bounded national identity, everywhere seems to leak sovereignty: allowing the Arellano-Felix and other drug cartels to function as shadow regional governments. In more than one way, we are recalled to Pynchon's description of "The Zone" in *Gravity's Rainbow* and its lucrative symbiosis of warfare, nomadism, and noir capitalism.

2.

The Border, as Joseph Nevins constantly reminds us in this exemplary book, is also a permanent construction site. Not only walls and fences, but national identities and exclusivities are frenetic works in progress. Here also politicians and bureaucrats manufacture the self-serving myths that advance the interests of the "border control industry."

Indeed Nevins' chief thesis is that the state has not so much responded to a "crisis of illegality" as created it. "Operation Gatekeeper," for instance, is a solution to a problem that it, in fact, has largely created: the spectre of a Mexican invasion of California. To fully understand the significance (and absurdity) of this latest apotheosis of sovereignty, Nevins takes us on a tour of Border history. "Sovereignty," it turns out, is as Sovereignty does. For most of the nineteenth century, for instance, Manifest Destiny preferred an informally open border that abetted the U.S. economic penetration of northern Mexico. "Aliens" only appeared late in the day, when the Mexican Revolution threatened to cross the Rio Grande and ignite the discontents of south Texas.

This was the first "Mexican scare" and the starting-point for the Modern cycle of border control initiatives. Nevins has a superb sense for the ever deepening irony/hypocrisy of U.S. policies and the crucial role that political dramaturgy has played in their creation. At one moment, employers are pining for Mexican immigrants; at the next, they are demanding their deportation. The Eisenhower administration likes *braceros*, but abhors "wetbacks." Later, local politicians like San Diego mayor Pete Wilson, discover that the "brown peril" plays well in the same spoiled suburbs where luxury lifestyles would not survive for a day without Mexican gardeners, housecleaners and nannies. The CIA's Bill Colby and the INS's General Chapman imaginatively torque up the Second Cold War with hysterical images of the Sandinistas at the gates of Laredo. Bill Clinton attempts to steal the "illegal immigration" issue from (now governor) Pete Wilson and Proposition 187 fanatics by unilaterally militarizing the Border. Operation Gatekeeper, however, is simply gasoline on the flames of nativism. Nevins' Border, then, is the overdetermined product of both an underlying economic logic (e.g. the manipulation of a disinherited and pliable labor-supply) and an accumulation of largely ad hoc state initiatives spiced up with a lot of political theatre. He convincingly shows that economic globalization and free trade, per the model of NAFTA, tends to strengthen, not weaken, the institutional apparatus of borders, and to deepen the existential and juridical divides between "legal" and "illegal" beings. The Border may be the outcome of rational, self-interested action, but "rational border policy" is simply a fantasy, if not a sheer oxymoron.

If Nevins argues this with compelling realism, he is at the same time deeply sensitive to the human costs of the New Border represented by Gatekeeper and other high-intensity INS operations. Far from deterring undocumented immigration per se, they have simply switched its venue from the suburbs of San Diego and El Paso to deadly deserts and mountains where more than one thousand compas have perished since Gatekeeper was inaugurated. Many, in particular, have died, and will continue to die, in that same furnace-hot stretch of desert where the ghosts of my childhood wander.

Introduction

The simple fact is that we must not and we will not surrender our borders to those who wish to exploit our history of compassion and justice.

—President Bill Clinton, July 27, 1993[1]

The Vision: The U.S. Border Patrol will control the borders of the United States between the ports of entry, restoring our Nation's confidence in the integrity of the border. A well-managed border will enhance national security and safeguard our immigration heritage.

—U.S. Border Patrol, "Strategic Plan: 1994 and Beyond"[2]

Our comprehensive strategy to restore the rule of law to illegal immigration enforcement has done more in three years than was done in thirty years before.

—President Bill Clinton, August 2, 1996[3]

In March 1999, I accompanied a group of students from the University of California, Los Angeles to San Diego and Tijuana for a one-day tour of the U.S.-Mexico border region in southern California. As part of the day's activities, we visited with the U.S. Border Patrol in San Diego. Our host was a Border Patrol agent by the name of George Reyes.[4]

While waiting for the arrival of another agent to accompany us on a "line-tour" of the boundary and the Border Patrol's enforcement apparatus, Agent Reyes told us the story of an elderly Mexican man—an unauthorized immigrant—he had apprehended a few years earlier.

As is the normal procedure, George Reyes brought the man into the local Border Patrol station to process him. When asked his name, the apprehended immigrant responded "Juan Reyes." Agent Reyes next learned that the man had been born in the Mexican state of Zacatecas, just as had the agent's father, who migrated as boy to southern Texas, where his family settled.[5] George's father later became a Border Patrol agent.

Reyes then asked the name of the town in Zacatecas from which the immigrant came. It turned out that the apprendee came from the same small town where his father was born. His curiosity greatly heightened, the agent pursued further questions, ultimately revealing that his prisoner was his father's uncle.

Reyes laughed as he finished the story. "I told him that if it had been another day, I might have been able to let him go, and that I hoped that he didn't have any hard feelings. He told me that he understood that I was just doing my job."

Such a story—and the contradictions it embodies—could have taken place in many different locales along the U.S.-Mexico boundary, but it is perhaps most relevant to the section in southern California. It is in this area of the border region that one sees most vividly the practical tensions between intense transboundary social and economic ties (as represented by the migration of Juan Reyes and the presence of his relatives in south Texas) and a U.S. boundary policing apparatus significantly strengthened over the last several years. Indeed, our group had come to the border region, in part, to see the results of Operation Gatekeeper, an enhanced boundary enforcement strategy established on October 1, 1994, to reduce unauthorized migrant crossings of the U.S.-Mexico boundary into southern California. Gatekeeper is a "territorial denial" or "prevention through deterrence" strategy that attempts to thwart migrants from entering the United States (as opposed to the old strategy of apprehending migrants after they cross) through the forward deployment of Border Patrol agents and increased use of surveillance technologies and support infrastructure.[6] As a supervisory agent, George Reyes is on the front line of this operation.

Operation Gatekeeper is the pinnacle of a national strategy that has achieved historically unprecedented levels of enforcement along the U.S.-Mexico boundary. That such an effort is taking place at a time of also unprecedented levels of economic and demographic growth within the border region, one marked by rapidly intensifying transboundary socioeconomic integration—a process that many assert is making international boundaries increasingly irrelevant—makes Gatekeeper seem all the more paradoxical. This book explores the origins, meaning, and implications of Gatekeeper, and the strong political support the operation enjoys.

OPERATION GATEKEEPER

The early 1990s saw the outbreak of what would soon become a historically unparalleled level of official and public concern about the U.S. government's ability—or the lack thereof—to police the U.S.-Mexico boundary and to prevent unauthorized or "illegal" immigration from Mexico. Many public officials and political candidates, Republicans and Democrats alike, competed with one another to curry the favor of a public fearful of the social, political, and economic consequences of a southern boundary "out of control" and of what was seen by many as excessive levels of immigration. The geographical epicenter of these concerns and efforts was the state of California, whose southern boundary with Mexico, especially in the area of San Diego, was probably the gateway for the majority of unauthorized entries into the United States. The San Diego section of the boundary became a platform for politicians, government officials, and political activists in favor of immigration restriction, who were eager to communicate their messages advocating a crackdown to an increasingly anxious public. It was in this context that California voters in November 1994 overwhelmingly approved Proposition 187, which sought to deny public education (from elementary to postsecondary levels), public social services, and public health care services (with the exception of emergencies) to unauthorized immigrants. And it was in this context that the Clinton administration launched Operation Gatekeeper.

A trip today to the California-Mexico boundary in the area of the City of San Diego reveals a very different scene than one would have found at the beginning of the 1990s. What existed in terms of a boundary fence had gaping holes. Large crowds of migrants and smugglers gathered each afternoon along the boundary waiting to cross at nightfall into the United States extralegally. "Banzai runs"—when groups of unauthorized immigrants would run on the highway through the official ports of entry into the United States—were also common. Moreover, there were frequent attacks against unauthorized migrants and crimes (mostly against property) by "border bandits."[7] As a journalist from the *Los Angeles Times* portrayed the situation, "Until 1994, the San Diego sector commonly fielded fewer than one hundred [U.S. Border Patrol] agents per shift against several thousand border-crossers lining the riverbanks and canyons. The sector recorded as many as three thousand arrests on busy Sundays. Every night was a potential riot, a journey into the battle theater of the absurd. The steel fence on the river levee had not yet been built, so agents routinely used their vehicles to herd back crowds, speeding at them, churning up clouds of dust."[8] While the journalist overstates the case—the construction of the steel barrier on the river levee, for example, took place in 1991[9]—the appearance of the present-day boundary in San Diego is unquestionably radically different. As one analyst described, "the entire border along San Diego is now eerily quiet and peaceful. It's the quiet that comes from control."[10] A report in the *Los Angeles Times* on the occasion of Gatekeeper's five-year anniversary stated that "the vaunted clampdown has slashed the number of people arrested for unlawful entry in San Diego to levels not seen since Richard Nixon was president."[11] Thus, a semblance of order has replaced the image of chaos that once seemed to reign in the urbanized border region of the San Diego Sector.[12]

These changes are the outgrowth of a massive infusion of resources into the enforcement division of the U.S. Immigration and Naturalization Service (INS) over the last several years, especially along the U.S.-Mexico boundary. It has produced a dramatic increase in the number of U.S. Border Patrol agents and in the technology and infrastructure used by the Border Patrol to aid it in its mission "to secure and protect the external boundaries of the United States

[by] preventing illegal entry and detecting, interdicting and apprehending undocumented entrants, smugglers, contraband, and violators of other laws."[13] The INS budget for enforcement efforts along the southwest boundary, for example, grew from $400 million in fiscal year (FY) 1993 to $800 million in FY 1997.[14] The number of Border Patrol agents rapidly expanded from 4,200 in FY1994 to 9,212 agents at the end of FY 2000. Current plans indicate that the number of agents will reach 10,000 by 2005 and that the amount expended on boundary enforcement will reach $3 billion.[15]

Nowhere in the United States is this buildup more pronounced than along the California-Mexico boundary where Gatekeeper takes place. Prior to the implementation of Gatekeeper on October 1, 1994, for example, the San Diego Sector of the U.S. Border Patrol had 980 agents; by June 1998, it had 2,264 agents, a level it has roughly maintained until the present.[16] Meanwhile, the amount of fencing and/or walls along the border in the sector increased from nineteen to more than forty-five miles in length, the number of underground sensors rose from 448 to 1,214, and the number of infrared scopes grew from twelve to fifty-nine. At the same time, the number of INS Inspectors,[17] those responsible for working the three official ports of entry in the sector, increased from 202 to 504.[18] Underlying this growth in resources is arguably an unprecedented level of public sentiment in favor of such operations.[19]

According to the INS, the goal of Gatekeeper is "to restore integrity and safety to the nation's busiest border" and, in the words of the Attorney General's Special Representative for Southwest Border Issues, "to restore the rule of law to the California/Baja-California border."[20] As part of a larger, comprehensive INS national strategy, Gatekeeper aims at significantly increasing the ability of the U.S. authorities to control the flow of unauthorized people and goods across the U.S.-Mexico boundary.

The mainstream press, political pundits, and government officials generally characterize Operation Gatekeeper as a worthwhile and integral part of a long overdue effort by U.S. federal authorities to make serious efforts to stem the influx of unauthorized immigrants into the United States in reaction to growing public outrage over the flouting of U.S. immigration laws.[21] A 1997 U.S. government publication presents a similar analysis, arguing that the federal government, until recently, had long failed to live up to its responsibility of securing the boundaries of the United States. But the coming to power of the Clinton administration in 1993, the publication explains, resulted in dramatic changes along the U.S.-Mexico boundary.

> For too long ... the Government stood by as illegal immigration swelled. There was an understaffed and overwhelmed corps of agents and port inspectors, inadequate infrastructure and equipment, and no coherent strategy to control illegal immigration into the San Diego area. ...

When Attorney General Janet Reno visited the Southwest Border in August 1993, just months after being sworn in, she saw for herself how years of neglect had hampered the ability of the INS to do its job. The Attorney General pledged to garner the support necessary to turn things around on the border. In September 1994, she returned to San Diego with INS Commissioner Doris Meissner and the two announced the dramatic commitment of resources that would make Operation Gatekeeper a reality.[22]

While the above account is somewhat self-serving, a dramatic transformation of the San Diego border region has undoubtedly transpired since the early 1990s. This book addresses how these changes came about and what they mean, not only for the border region, but, more important, for the United States as a whole.

THE SOCIOECONOMIC AND GEOGRAPHICAL CONTEXT OF OPERATION GATEKEEPER

The emergence of Operation Gatekeeper is somewhat paradoxical in that it is occurring at a time of rapid economic and demographic growth in the border region and increased interaction and integration between the United States and Mexico. The population of the Mexico-U.S. border region, for example, is now about twelve million and is expected to grow to twenty-four million in 2020.[23] Currently, nearly 300,000 Mexican workers cross the boundary *legally* on a daily or weekly basis to work in the United States. The number of annual authorized crossings of the boundary are in the several hundreds of millions— largely between the "twin cities" that straddle the international divide. And annual transboundary financial transactions total more than $6 billion.[24]

The boundary has proven to be not only a barrier, but also a conduit that facilitates interaction between national spaces. Beginning in the 1960s, rapid industrialization and population growth have occurred in the border area.[25] With an economic output of $150 billion, the region now has an economy larger than that of Poland.[26] The implementation of the North American Free Trade Agreement (NAFTA) in 1994 seems to have only intensified the transboundary region's economic integration and growth. Trade between the United States and Mexico, for example, increased from $80 billion in 1994 to $200 billion in 2000,[27] with much of the growth in trade a result of increased production in the border region. A concrete manifestation of this intensifying binational commercial relationship is the growth in the number of trucks traversing the boundary. Such traffic has increased by 170 percent, with over 4.2 million truck crossings in 1999 alone, since the implementation of NAFTA. Two of the seven busiest ports of entry for trucks are located in California, one at Calexico and one at Otay Mesa in San Diego. Along with that of Laredo,

Texas, the one at Otay Mesa is the busiest commercial port, averaging about 2,500 commercial vehicle crossings per day.[28]

Nowhere along the boundary are integration and boundary policing as pronounced as they are in the San Diego–Tijuana region. The number of trucks passing through the three commercial ports along the California section of the boundary has more than doubled since the beginning of NAFTA—from 886,000 in 1993 to almost two million in 1999.[29] Meanwhile, the stretch of boundary between the two cities is perhaps the world's most policed international divide between two nonbelligerent countries. In addition, it is the location of the most intense economic and demographic growth of the U.S.-Mexico border region—the fastest developing border zone in the Americas, and perhaps in the world.[30]

According to some, this transboundary urban zone is the fastest growing metropolitan region in North America.[31] The current population of the combined San Diego–Tijuana area, for example, is an estimated 4 million people, and demographic projections predict that it will reach 5.7 million by the year 2020.[32] About 60 million people and 20 million cars per year now enter San Diego from Mexico through the San Ysidro port of entry, making it the busiest land crossing in the world.[33] And an estimated 40,000 people cross the border each day to work, including several thousand who manage and work in *maquiladoras* (export-oriented assembly plants) in Tijuana, but live in the San Diego area.[34] For some, such trends would seem to indicate that the California-Mexico is boundary is becoming increasingly irrelevant. Indeed, some even argue that the boundary is disappearing.[35] Most social scientists—especially geographers—have generally been more restrained in their pronouncements, but some see similar trends. Lawrence Herzog argues that "in the last four decades, the functions of international boundaries have been redefined. . . . The most obvious change has been the shift from boundaries that are heavily protected and militarized to those that are more porous, permitting cross-border social and economic interaction."[36]

Given such changes, Operation Gatekeeper would seem to be in direct contradiction to the larger-scale processes that are ostensibly making the international boundary between the United States and Mexico increasingly irrelevant. But while there is much truth to Herzog's contention, we also see an opposite trend as the U.S.-Mexico boundary shows. As the INS states, "The border is harder to cross now [for unauthorized migrants] than at any time in history."[37] On the one hand, we see a variety of methods and strategies to denationalize and/or internationalize border space; this is most obvious in the ongoing attempts to establish a barrier-free zone to the flow of goods and capital. On the other hand, we observe the employment of overt methods to control and limit the levels of certain types of interaction between the two countries. Despite the increasing integration and growing sameness (in the sense of sharing and interacting) between Tijuana and San Diego, there are efforts, as manifested by Operation Gatekeeper, with broad public support to maintain and increase difference. Interestingly enough, most San Diego residents do not believe that the two cities are growing closer together, despite significant evidence to the contrary.[38] It is in this context that the "NAFTA-ization" and growing "militarization" of the U.S.-Mexico boundary simultaneously take place.[39]

Despite proclamations suggesting the disappearance of national boundaries in the face of intensifying globalization,[40] or growing transboundary "flows,"[41] strategies such as Gatekeeper demonstrate that state regulation of boundary enforcement and immigration is growing. Undoubtedly, the division between the United States and Mexico has changed from one that was poorly policed to one that is increasingly monitored. In this sense, the U.S.-Mexico boundary is more "real" than ever. Indeed, operations similar to Gatekeeper are occurring in numerous locations along the U.S.-Mexico boundary. In addition, intensified policing efforts are taking place along a variety of international boundaries throughout the world. Other instances include the boundaries between South Africa and Mozambique, Spain (Ceuta and Melilla) and Morocco, and Germany and Poland.[42] Such efforts are part of a war of sorts by relatively wealthy countries against "illegal" or unauthorized immigrants. Yet at the same time, these same countries are increasingly opening their boundaries to the flows of capital, finance, manufactured goods, and services. Such apparently contradictory developments speak to the growing gatekeeper role played by states. This role entails maximizing the perceived benefits of globalization while "protecting" against the perceived detriments of increasing transnational flows—especially of unauthorized immigrants. State efforts to repel unauthorized immigrants are most intense along those international boundaries that separate widely divergent levels of socioeconomic development.

That said, territorial boundaries and state efforts to control the flow of people and goods have a long and varied history throughout the world. For this reason, while this book seeks to analyze phenomena and social relations uniquely associated with the U.S.-Mexico boundary and the San Diego–Tijuana region, it also links them to the larger, ever-changing context of boundaries and the modern territorial states that they help to define. Only in this manner can we fully comprehend the origins and significance of Operation Gatekeeper.

Increasing economic integration and liberalization, along with growing immigration restriction, are not simultaneous trends unique to the United States and Mexico. Similar trends have emerged between numerous territorial entities such as Malaysia and Indonesia as well as the European Union and North Africa, suggesting that what might seem to be contradictory trends are actually complementary. While Operation Gatekeeper is a manifestation of these developments, it is also quite unique in terms of its origins and implications. This book thus seeks to link the specific political-geographic context out of which Gatekeeper has emerged, as well as the operation's significance, to a broader set of social relations that manifest themselves in the contemporary global political economy.

DEFINING SOME BASIC TERMS

Before continuing, I would like to provide working definitions of some basic terms used throughout this book. First are *border, boundary,* and *frontier*— terms often used interchangeably by academics and laypersons alike. Not surprisingly, it is among political geographers where one finds the greatest efforts to distinguish between these terms, although even within this subfield of geography the distinctions between them are sometimes not sufficiently clear.[43] Outside of the discipline of geography the terms are seemingly interchangeable, with few exceptions.[44]

In this book I employ a classification that treats a *boundary* as a strict line of separation between two (at least theoretically) distinct territories, a *frontier* as a forward zone of contact with the uncontrolled or sparsely-settled,[45] and a *border* as an area of interaction and gradual division between two separate political entities.[46] That said, I acknowledge that everyday language does not conform to the categories established by political geographers[47] and that in reality, the distinctions between these terms as social and ideological phenomena remain blurry and problematic. Nevertheless, employing these clearly defined categories will allow us to appreciate better how views and practices toward territory and people have changed over the last two centuries.

Frontiers, borders, and boundaries are not merely social phenomena in a material sense. They are also "ways of seeing": metaphors for and manifestations of how we perceive the world and act within it.[48] Furthermore, the mere demarcation of a boundary and the declaration of national sovereignty do not mean the realization of the modern territorial state ideal—that is, the homogeneous institutionalization of state power over national space. Even along the U.S.-Mexico boundary, "the zonal character" of the division persists in diverse social practices and worldviews.[49] Thus, rather than seeing boundaries, frontiers, and borders as *things*, we should see them as *ideal types* that are never fully realized. In this sense, the terms describe ongoing processes of construction of different types of geographically and historically specific divisions and zones of contact between territories, ones that reflect power relations between groups and that have very real impacts on people's lives.

The modern territorial state (an entity that gradually came into existence over the last few centuries) is the primary maker of national boundaries.

Admittedly, "the state" is a messy concept, as is the category of "state actor." For purposes of simplicity, I define the (national) state as the set of institutions and actors that wield effective power over a territorially delimited political entity while claiming and seeking to achieve control over whom and what enters and leaves national territory.[50] The daily practices of all individuals inevitably help to constitute and reconstitute the state. Nevertheless, when I refer to "the state" I mean a set of institutions that make up the state apparatus, which I somewhat arbitrarily limit—at least in terms of the (U.S.) national scale—to institutions of the federal government and of the Democratic and Republican Parties. Similarly, when I employ the term "state actor," I am alluding to relatively powerful individuals or groups associated with the institutions mentioned above.[51]

The national state is the political expression of "the nation." *Nation* and *nationalism* are frequently discussed and debated terms in the social sciences and a huge body of literature has developed on the subject matter. Nevertheless, there is a consensus of sorts on the topic regarding the basic definitions of the terms.[52] A nation is a group of persons who claim that they consist of a single "people" based upon historical, cultural, and/or ideological (in the form of a shared set of principles[53]) criteria and therefore should have their own sovereign state (a nation-state) in a clearly demarcated territory that encompasses their homeland. Nationalism is the ideology and associated practices that justify, emanate from, and reproduce the nation. In the ideal, the *nation-state* is a bounded and sovereign political unit in which the members of the *nation* and the citizens of the *state* are synonymous. Neverthtless, it is not possible, nor desirable, to attempt to arrive at eternal definitions of *nation*, as we are dealing with a social construct that is historically contingent and ever changing.[54]

Finally, I need to clarify the terms I use to describe immigrants who reside in the United States without the sanction of federal authorities, terms that have long been highly politically charged and controversial. Many terms employed historically by those opposed to such immigrants—terms such as "wetbacks" and "illegal aliens"—tend to obfuscate the role that various agents and institutions in the United States have played in encouraging and/or facilitating unauthorized immigration.[55] Furthermore, such terms are often pejorative due to the images of the immigrant they suggest and the ideas of the undesirable "other" they embody. The frequently used term "illegal," for example, implies that unsanctioned immigrants are criminals.[56] Therefore, I enclose the term "illegal" in quotation marks whenever I employ it to describe immigrants who enter or are present in the United States without authorization of the federal government. I prefer to use less politically charged terms such as *unauthorized* and *extralegal* to describe unsanctioned immigrants or immigration.[57]

OPERATION GATEKEEPER: ITS ORIGINS AND MEANING

This book has two main arguments. The first of these is that Operation Gate-keeper was the outgrowth of short-term developments beginning in the 1990s that took place within a context formed by a variety of long- and medium-term political, economic, and cultural trends. These involved the making of the United States as a nation-state and the creation of the "illegal" immigrant as a putative threat to the national sociocultural and political fabric. Second, Gatekeeper's greatest significance is that it embodies the pinnacle of a histor-ical geographical process that has made the boundaries of the United States and their accompanying social practices seem increasingly normal and unproblematic, thus placing them largely beyond question.

In terms of the first main argument, we have to ask ourselves why the matter of unauthorized immigration became a "problem" of almost crisis proportions and, thus, in need of radical redress.[58] It is far too simple to argue that a growing presence of unauthorized immigrants and/or a commitment to the rule of law led to an outbreak of public and official outrage about an "out of control" boundary and a supposed "flood" of unauthorized immi-grants, ultimately culminating in the establishment of Operation Gatekeeper. As discussed earlier, Gatekeeper emerged out of a number of short-term pres-sures, as well as on account of the concrete actions of a variety of political actors. Yet while such factors were absolutely necessary for Gatekeeper to come about, they were not sufficient. This nation-state-building project, and its asso-ciated process of what we might call the "illegalization" of unauthorized entrants, required the conquest of territory and the pacification of popula-tions on both sides of the U.S.-Mexico boundary. The resulting social geographical context allowed for U.S. authorities to begin constructing the infrastructure to define the boundary (and, thus, national territory) and to enforce laws relating to immigration and transboundary trade. In doing so, the state helped to create new ways of seeing among the populations affected by these developments, involving perceptions of territory and social identities as well as associated practices. These new ways of seeing were inextricably tied to evolving and hierarchical notions and practices regarding race, class, gender, and geographic origins—especially as they related to the American "nation."

These national-level processes unfolded in differential manners in specific locales. Place-specific social geographies mediated national efforts aimed at social and territorial boundary construction. The imposition of the U.S.-Mexico boundary in the San Diego–Tijuana area had the contradictory effects of heightening the sense of difference between "Americans" and "Mexicans" while simultaneously facilitating increasing integration between Mexico and the United States.

As the U.S.–Mexico border region became more integrated into the Ameri-can national center and gained significantly greater levels of demographic and economic importance, and as transboundary social relations increased, public awareness of "the border" grew. Beginning in the early 1970s (the beginning of what I refer to as "the medium term"), national, local, and state politicians and officials played a key role in raising the profile of the boundary and its associated "problems" in the national imagination.

In a context of economic recession and a perception of rising levels of socioeconomic insecurity, images of an immigration and boundary control "crisis" resonated deeply with much of the U.S. populace. This was especially true in the early 1990s when the conservative-led "war on illegals" reached its climax, most notably in California. Opportunistic politicians and nativist organizations presented the "illegal" immigrant not only as a lawbreaker, but more importantly as a threat to national sovereignty and the American social and economic fabric. Such imagery is rooted in a long history of largely race-based anti-immigrant sentiment in California and, more generally, the United States.

The state did not simply respond to public concern with the supposed crisis of "illegal" immigration. Rather, it has helped to create the "illegal" through the construction of the boundary and the expansion of the INS's enforcement capacity. The state also played a significant role in creating the putative crisis posed by "illegals" through the rhetoric it employed to justify its efforts to bring order to the U.S.-Mexico boundary and to rid U.S. territory of those without state sanction to be within its boundaries. Combined with the power of the state to shape the collective American mind-set to distinguish between "right" and "wrong" and to appreciate the almost-sacred nature of its national boundaries, the category of "illegal" proved extremely powerful in mobilizing public support for enhanced boundary and immigration enforcement.

Gatekeeper was also in part a reaction to growing regional integration along the U.S.-Mexico boundary, a growing integration that has led to an attempt to enhance separation between the United States and Mexico, at least in terms of unauthorized immigration. Thus, in this particular instance, growing transboundary integration seems to go hand in hand with increasing nationalization of territory. But there is nothing "natural" or automatic about such a nationalist response to the challenges and/or perceived problems brought about by the changes embodied by transnational processes such as growing movement of goods and capital and immigration between Mexico and the United States. Again, it is important to understand the historical geographical backdrop as well as the short-term actions taken by various social actors that led to the response embodied by Operation Gatekeeper.

Transboundary integration involves and affects a wide array of social actors in a diversity of manners. Therefore, Operation Gatekeeper and the general securing of the boundary entail a delicate balancing act. Gatekeeper-like undertakings must try to avoid impeding the flow of (authorized) goods, services, and people between the United States and Mexico while simultaneously (at the very least) giving the impression that the boundary is under control. In this regard, Gatekeeper represents a trade-off between social actors arguing for enhanced boundary policing (e.g., immigration restriction groups, politicians, and various elements of the state apparatus) and those championing the relatively free movement of capital, goods, and people (e.g. certain sectors of the business community, elements of the state apparatus, and, in regards to the rights of migrants, various human rights groups).[59]

These same trade-offs manifest themselves along the boundary as it represents both a line of control (for unauthorized immigrants and contraband) and a gateway (for *authorized* goods, services, and people). As a result, there are serious limitations on how far U.S. authorities can go in trying to regulate transboundary flows as the political and economic costs of too much success serve to limit enforcement. In the case of drug enforcement, for example, one high-level U.S. Customs official stated, "If we examined every truck for narcotics arriving into the United States along the Southwest border. . . . Customs would back up the truck traffic bumper-to-bumper into Mexico City in just two weeks—15.8 days. . . . That's 1,177 miles of trucks, end to end."[60] Thus, it is not surprising that the overall effect of Operation Gatekeeper has been negligible in terms of reducing extralegal immigration into the United States from Mexico.

This is not to say that Operation Gatekeeper has been meaningless. Indeed, it has had many important outcomes—intended and unintended. These relate to the book's second principal argument. Perhaps most important, from the perspective of political elites, the operation has been very successful in creating the image of a secure boundary in southern California. At the same time, Gatekeeper has significantly increased the challenges associated with crossing, resulting in some ways in much greater danger for those attempting to cross without authorization. Along with the more general, geographically extensive state project of battling "illegal" immigration, it has also contributed to increased hardships for unauthorized immigrants within the U.S. interior.

To the extent that Operation Gatekeeper is merely about a change in INS strategy and the infusion of an unprecedented level of boundary enforcement–related resources, it does not represent a radical change from a long-term perspective. Rather, the operation embodies the intensification of a trend that has evolved (admittedly, in a very uneven fashion spatially and temporally) since the designation of the boundary in the aftermath of the U.S.-Mexico War (1846–1848). And because Gatekeeper embodies, in part, a long-term development—one that sped up markedly in the 1990s—its short-term importance is somewhat overstated, while its long-term significance is largely unseen.

In this regard, the greatest significance of Gatekeeper—or, more precisely, the general buildup of the boundary of which Gatekeeper is a key component—is perhaps that it represents a significant shift in American practice and thinking toward the U.S.-Mexico boundary and unauthorized immigration. This shift is one that has entailed an evolution of the U.S.-Mexico divide from a border (or a zone of transition) to a boundary (or a line of strict demarcation). In the process, the boundaries of the United States, and their accompanying social practices have come to seem increasingly normal, "natural," and beyond politics—in terms of any group-specific agenda (except that of the "nation"). This has had the effect of greatly limiting the parameters of debate within the United States about matters concerning boundary and immigration enforcement. At the same time, the U.S.-Mexico divide is today more part of Americans' geographical imagination than it has ever been—a curious development in an age of globalization that is supposedly making boundaries redundant. The accompanying increased emphasis on boundary enforcement and immigration-related illegality is an outgrowth of growing state power vis-à-vis the U.S.-Mexico divide and high levels of public acceptance of this power. In this regard, Operation Gatekeeper is a manifestation of a way of life inextricably linked to the modern territorial state at the end of the twentieth century.

In one sense, Operation Gatekeeper, by trying to limit unauthorized entries into the United States, is an effort to eliminate boundary-related illegality. Yet, at the same time, the operation helps to construct and perpetuate illegality. By attempting to enhance the INS's ability to control who crosses the boundary into the United States, Gatekeeper furthers the material and ideological institutionalization of the boundary—the existence of which is an absolutely necessary condition for the existence of immigration-related illegality and, more important, of the United States as a nation-state. While boundaries serve to delimit geographically distinct political units, they also help define and reflect a wide variety of diverse, and often divergent, social relationships—between and within localities and countries.

The interrelated development of the nation, national boundaries, and the modern territorial state, along with their associated practices and ideologies, led to the emergence of Operation Gatekeeper. But these developments only provide a very broad context for understanding the greatly heightened public concerns surrounding "illegal" immigration and an "out of control" U.S.-Mexico boundary in the early 1990s and the subsequent establishment of Gatekeeper. Concrete actions by state and nonstate actors and institutions, in the United States and Mexico and even beyond, combined with a variety of sociocultural forces, laid the foundation for the high-profile operation over a long period of time. For this reason, the next chapter examines the historical development of the U.S.-Mexico boundary, the evolution of Mexico-U.S. migration, as well as the establishment of immigration controls and boundary policing in the U.S. Southwest through the mid-1970s. These processes laid the basis for the national-scale political efforts in favor of enhanced immigration and boundary policing that ultimately resulted in the implementation of Operation Gatekeeper in southern California in 1994.

The Creation of the U.S.-Mexico Boundary and the Remaking of the United States and Mexico in the Border Region

[T]he world should be familiarized with the idea of considering our proper domain is to be the continent of North America. From the time we became an independent people, it was as much a law of nature that this should become our pretension that the Mississippi should flow to the sea. Spain had possession of our southern border and Great Britain was upon our north. It was impossible that centuries should elapse without finding their territories annexed to the United States.

—President John Quincy Adams
speaking at a cabinet meeting, 1825[1]

Miserable, inefficient Mexico—what has she to do with the great mission of peopling the New World with a noble race? Be it ours to achieve this mission!

—Walt Whitman, circa 1846[2]

A political geographical division between Mexico and the United States is inevitable as the two countries represent neighboring and distinct politicoterritorial entities. What is not given is the nature and location of that division. For that reason, we must look to history to begin to understand the process by which the U.S.-Mexico boundary, which to many seems an immutable fact of life, has come to be.

The boundary's evolution is inseparable from American nation-state building, with its intermittent territorial expansion and the associated redefinition of the boundary and its accompanying social relations. The deployment of both coercive and administrative power has characterized the process as embodied by the creation and development of the boundary as a linear divide, the subjugation of newly acquired populations, and the establishment of territorial control in the borderlands. These developments are intimately intertwined with the evolution of Mexican in-migration, and the establishment of U.S. immigration controls and boundary policing along the country's southern divide with Mexico. As the boundary as a territorial, juridical, and ideological divide progressed, it shifted from being a mere Cartesian ideal bearing little on people's lives to becoming a real, powerful material presence. At the same time, a variety of interests—both domestic and foreign—limited the ability (and desire) of the American state to achieve full control over the boundary. This phenomenon relates to the somewhat conflicting functions of the modern territorial state of "protecting" national territory from putative threats from without while trying to maximize potential benefits for domestic interests of transnational flows. Depending on the interest group and the larger socio-economic and political context, international migrant labor represents both a threat to and an opportunity for "the nation."

THE TAKING OF MEXICO AND THE REDEFINITION
OF THE U.S.-MEXICO BOUNDARY

Competing claims to territory often serve as the basis for conflict.[3] More specifically, it is the attempt to realize those claims that creates conflict.[4] It was exactly this type of competition that led to the U.S.-Mexico War in 1846–1848 that resulted, with minor changes, in the present-day boundary between the United States and Mexico.

The origins of the U.S.-Mexico boundary are to be found in the imperial competition among Spain, France, and England for "possessions" in North America. The Treaty of Paris of 1783, which marked the end of the American War of Independence, resulted in the United States inheriting the boundaries established by its English colonial overseer. The southern boundary was the thirty-first parallel, the northern boundary was basically the same as the one now shared by the United States and Canada, and the western boundary was the eastern bank of the Mississippi River. The Treaty of Paris thus resulted in a situation in which the United States shared its southern and western boundaries with Spain, and its northern and northwestern boundaries with Great Britain. While imperial Spain and France had good relations in the late eighteenth century, the rise of Napoleon Bonaparte changed this, resulting in Spain becoming essentially a client state of France. Napoleon compelled Charles IV of Spain to cede "Louisiana" to France in 1800 in return for lands in Italy. The treaty by which the transfer of territory took place obliged France to give Spain the option of reacquiring the territory if a further transfer were ever to take place. Three years later, however, Napoleon sold the vast territory to the United States for $15 million without taking Spanish opinion into consideration. France sold Louisiana out of fear that the English might take it over as the French were unable to occupy the territory (see map, appendix C). Almost immediately after the signing of the treaty, however, President Thomas Jefferson foreshadowed U.S. expansionist designs on Mexico, expressing the view that Louisiana included all lands north and east of the Rio Grande, thus laying claim to Spanish settlements such as San Antonio and Santa Fe.[5]

Jefferson's claim was a manifestation of, among other things, a much larger problem: namely, a lack of agreement among imperial France, England, and Spain over the location of the boundaries separating their territories in North

America. The exact location of the boundary between Spanish Texas and the Louisiana territory became a subject of dispute during the process of transfer of the latter from Spain to France, and then to the United States. For many years, the United States tried to convince Spain to give up Texas, offering boundaries ranging from the Sabine River (which serves as the southern part of the contemporary boundary between Texas and Louisiana) to the Rio Grande. Meanwhile, the United States invaded western Florida in 1810, taking advantage of growing instability in Spain, which Napoleon had invaded in 1808.[6] Continuing instability in Spain delayed the U.S. recognition of the Spanish government's representative to the United States until 1815. After that, Spain and the United States eventually entered into negotiations to resolve their differences over Florida and the boundary between Texas and the Louisiana Territory. The U.S invasion of eastern Florida in 1818 was intended to force Spain's hand. Under the terms of the Adams-Onis Treaty of 1819, Spain agreed to exchange East Florida and West Florida for U.S. recognition of an international boundary between Texas and Louisiana as well as monetary compensation (which Spain never received). The boundary resulting from the treaty proceeded north from the Sabine River in a nonlinear fashion to the forty-second parallel (which divides contemporary California and Oregon) and then west to the Pacific Ocean (see map, appendix C). The treaty also established a U.S. pattern of seizing territory by force and agreeing to pay for it after the fact. Yet despite U.S. gains, many Americans were unhappy that the United States had not acquired Texas as well. They argued that the true location of the boundary of Louisiana was at the Rio Grande.[7]

Such claims were significantly symptomatic of a body of thought and practice that came to be known as *Manifest Destiny,* a slogan popularized by John Sullivan, the editor of the *Democratic Review.*[8] Manifest destiny combined the ideas of Anglo-Saxon superiority with capitalist territorial expansionism, ideas which had deep roots in American political culture. As early as 1767, Benjamin Franklin had named Mexico and Cuba as territories for future expansion by what would soon be the United States of America.[9] Thomas Jefferson, among other prominent Americans, held a similar viewpoint.[10]

When Mexico gained independence from Spain in 1821, the new country thus acquired the challenge of protecting its northern border. This was especially important in terms of Texas since many in the United States still claimed Texas as part of the Louisiana Purchase, a claim Mexico, like its former colonial master, rejected. Despite the competing territorial claims, the United States extended official recognition of the Mexican Empire (which included modern-day Central America) in January 1823 due to pressure from various groups within the United States that supported independence for Spain's Latin American colonies. Two months later, however, the empire collapsed, with Central America and Chiapas seceding and many other Mexican states declaring their independence. This led to great fear in the United States and in European capitals that the Spanish monarchy would attempt to exploit the resulting instability to reassert its control over Mexico. Soon thereafter, however, Mexican authorities were able to regroup and reorganize the country, doing so in a manner that proved attractive for all components of the Mexican Empire except Central America. In this manner the United States of Mexico was born on October 4, 1823. Two months later U.S. president James Monroe declared the doctrine that bears his name, pronouncing that the Americas were off limits to European intervention and colonization and that the United States would not tolerate such activity. Although the United States did not have the resources to realize the implicit threat, "the declaration clearly demonstrated that U.S. politicians considered the entire continent a natural zone of influence."[11]

Meanwhile, Mexico had serious difficulty establishing control over Texas, a sparsely populated territory about 745 miles from Mexico City. So the government had little choice but to continue the Spanish policy of allowing American settlers into Texas. Thousands of proslavery southerners soon flocked to Texas in search of new lands for the cultivation of cotton. In 1830, however, Mexico outlawed slavery and prohibited further American immigration to Texas, infuriating American slaveholders there as well as those elements of the local Mexican elite who enjoyed the benefits of American capital flowing into the territory. Despite the immigration restrictions, Americans continued to cross extralegally into Texas. By 1835, there were about 35,000 "Americans" and only 5,000 Mexicans in the territory. It soon became clear to the Mexican government that the United States had designs on Texas and other parts of Mexico. In 1829, for example, the military commander of Mexico's eastern interior provinces warned of U.S. expansionism, noting, "The department of Texas is contiguous to the most avid nation in the world. The North Americans have conquered whatever territory adjoins them. They incite uprisings in the territory in question."[12] The relative isolation of Texas, New Mexico, and California from the population centers of Mexico, moreover, facilitated the rise of regionalist tendencies and separatist movements. During the 1820s and 1830s, nonetheless, the U.S. avoided attempts to annex Texas forcefully, instead opting for diplomatic persuasion and economic incentives—so-called dollar diplomacy.

Such efforts became redundant when Anglo-Texans, with help from American funding and volunteers, as well as from some Tejanos (at the time, Mexican nationals residing in Texas), successfully rebelled against the Mexican authorities in 1836. The newly independent Republic of Texas asked the United States to annex it in 1837, but President Andrew Jackson, while very sympathetic to the request, merely recognized its independence. Although the annexation of Texas enjoyed wide popular support, there was also opposition to it, especially from antislavery forces in the Northeast, and Jackson did not want to provoke interregional antagonisms. Thus, it was not until 1845, under the proslavery president John Tyler, that the United States annexed Texas, greatly enraging Mexico (with which relations were already bad) in the process. Furthermore, consistent with prior claims, the United States asserted that Texas' territory extended to the Rio Grande, whereas Mexico insisted that the boundary was located 150 miles to the north at the Nueces River.

In early 1846, President James Polk, also a supporter of slavery, deliberately provoked Mexico by sending U.S. troops to the Rio Grande. (From Mexico's perspective, this constituted an invasion.) Soon thereafter, skirmishes between U.S. and Mexican troops ensued, quickly resulting in full-scale war. In terms of population size, levels of economic development, and military strength, Mexico was seriously outmatched. For two years the war raged on, largely in the favor of the United States,[13] ending with the United States occupying Mexico City and the signing of the Treaty of Guadalupe Hidalgo on February 2, 1848, through which Mexico ceded half of its territory to the United States. In going to war, James Polk had had three objectives: first, to make Mexico recognize the Rio Grande as Texas' southern boundary; second (and perhaps most important), to force Mexico to cede California and New Mexico to the United States;[14] and third, to compel Mexico to give up additional territory on its northern boundary. Under the treaty's terms, the United States annexed one million square miles of Mexican land, a territory equivalent in size to that of western Europe, and absorbed 100,000 Mexican citizens and 200,000 Native Americans living in the annexed territory.[15] All or part of ten states resulted from the treaty: Texas, Arizona, New Mexico, Oklahoma, Wyoming, Colorado, Kansas, Utah, Nevada, and California.[16]

Although key to the U.S. annexation of a huge swath of what was Mexican territory, the war was the culmination of a long process by which the United States exploited political instability in what is today the Southwest. As Carlos Vélez-Ibáñez notes, "This instability, created after Mexican independence in 1821, was a result of American penetration of the region through long-distance trade and the social and cultural penetration effected by American trappers and entrepreneurs. Probably more important than either of these factors is the consistent destruction of Mexican communities and their political structure by those Americans who were involved in illegal trade with and in fact sponsored and supported raids carried out by Apaches, Comanches, Ute, and other native peoples."[17] But while it was one matter for the U.S. to exploit and foster instability in, and subsequently gain territorial concessions from Mexico, it was quite another to construct the social infrastructure to control and to "Americanize" the newly acquired territory and peoples, Mexico's unintended legacy to the new occupying power. Such a development is an obvious example of the geographical practice of territoriality, "the attempt by an individual or group to affect, influence, or control people, phenomena, and relationships, by delimiting and asserting control over a geographic area."[18] It is this process of establishing order and control over territory and the people that inhabit it that the next section examines and that the term "pacification" describes.

TERRITORIAL STATE BUILDING AND THE PACIFICATION OF THE BORDERLANDS

U.S. efforts to pacify the territory forcibly acquired from Mexico demonstrate that the construction and operation of an administrative infrastructure is also an integral part of the pacification process and remains so until significant ideological opposition to the occupying power disappears.[19] Altering Carl von Clausewitz's dictum that war is the continuation of politics by other means,[20] the case of the U.S.-Mexico border region illustrates—in terms of pacification—that political and economic administration is a continuation of war by other means.

Like any form of territoriality, pacification requires the employment of social power. Michael Mann distinguishes between two types of power: despotic and infrastructural. *Despotic power* refers to "the range of actions which the elite is empowered to undertake without routine, institutionalised negotiation with civil society groups." But, as the state's capacity to penetrate civil society grows, the state can increasingly implement its policies throughout the territory. Mann labels this *infrastructural power*.[21]

The employment of despotic power, however, is often pivotal for establishing infrastructural power due to frequent popular resistance to the extension of state power. In the case of the U.S.-Mexico borderlands, the American employment of despotic power provided the necessary first step in "pacifying" the territory in order to establish the political economic administration of the border region.

The military conquest of the territory and the institutionalization of the occupation do not mean, however, that the border region is in fact pacified. Pacification is a process, one in constant flux and one that social actors must reproduce to maintain. A pacified society may not necessarily represent stability; it may indicate merely a territorial order in which infrastructural power dominates and despotic power is deployed only occasionally to contain threats to the hegemonic order. In this sense, despotic and infrastructural powers are inextricably intertwined and key to understanding the United States' ongoing pacification project in the U.S.-Mexico border region.[22]

It took many decades for the United States to pacify the area along its southern boundary, as part of a process of bringing "order" and "civilization" to a region perceived as one of lawlessness and chaos.[23] But instability in the border region was a concern for both the United States and Mexico, often leading to tensions between the two countries following transboundary attacks by hostile parties. Article 11 of the Treaty of Guadalupe Hidalgo required the United States to prevent incursions into Mexico by native peoples because the United States was gaining territory inhabited by "savage tribes." Yet, for a number of years, the United States did not patrol its southern boundary. Its negligence not only facilitated many transboundary Indian attacks against Mexico, but also those by U.S. filibusters intent on wresting control of territory from Mexico.[24] Over the decades following the end of the war, a number of Texas-based filibusters attempted to "liberate" northeast Mexico. Simultaneously, French and American filibusters used California as a base from which to launch invasions of Sonora and Baja California. Mexico repeatedly accused the United States of not enforcing its own neutrality law requiring the federal government to prosecute anyone in the United States planning, organizing, or engaging in military expeditions against a country with which the United States was at peace.[25]

First, however, the United States and Mexico had to resolve a boundary dispute unintentionally created by the Treaty of Guadalupe Hidalgo, which relied on inaccurate maps to define the boundary of the territory of New Mexico and the Mexican states of Sonora and Chihuahua. U.S. expansionists wanted to see the boundary line as far south as possible to gain a more favorable route for a transcontinental railroad and to ensure U.S. access to the rich mines in the area of Mesilla (in present-day southern New Mexico). Tensions flared as repatriated Mexicans and Anglo-Texan and New Mexican cattle ranchers moved into Mesilla, the governors of Chihuahua and New Mexico both claiming jurisdiction over the area and threatening to send troops to enforce their claims of sovereignty.

The United States sent James Gadsden to Mexico City in 1853 to try to resolve the conflict with instructions to seek the abrogation of Article 11 of the Treaty of Guadalupe Hidalgo.[26] The United States also charged Gadsden with normalizing trade relations between the two countries, and with gaining U.S. transit rights through the Isthmus of Tehuántepec[27] to facilitate the construction of a railroad linking the Atlantic and Pacific Oceans, a project whose importance had increased significantly with the discovery of gold in California in 1848. U.S. threats to seize parts of northern Mexico militarily convinced the Mexican authorities of the wisdom of agreeing to American demands. The United States gained all that it sought, including the mineral rich areas in southern New Mexican territory. In return, the federal government promised to pay Mexico $10 million in compensation for the acquired territory and pledged mutual cooperation in suppressing filibustering activity, but the U.S. Senate removed the article relating to the latter from the treaty. Once again, the United States had won a considerable victory over Mexico.[28]

After the Civil War, American expansionists continued pursuing additional changes in the U.S.-Mexican boundary. This led to further raiding of Mexico from Texas and southern California. As the twentieth century approached, however, Mexico consolidated its holds over its northern territory, including border towns such as Nuevo Laredo and El Paso del Norte (today known as Ciudad Juárez; see map, appendix B), through significant demographic and economic growth. These changes, along with the construction of a railroad network in the border region, facilitated further development of trans-boundary ties. Combined with generous concessions granted to foreigners by the Mexican government of Porfirio Díaz, such developments helped to undermine and lessen remaining filibustering tendencies by laying the basis for greater administrative control by both Mexico and the United States over the border region.[29]

From a U.S. perspective, however, the more serious challenges in the aftermath of the Treaty of Guadalupe Hidalgo involved the subjugation of the populations gained through the war with Mexico, Mexicanos, and Native Americans. The process was violent. Violence committed by the state and nonstate actors (Anglo settlers, for example) was a common occurrence in the border region in the latter nineteenth and early twentieth centuries "as the political definitions imposed upon the region by the Treaty of Guadalupe Hidalgo of 1848 and the Gadsden Purchase of 1853 had to be continually reinforced."[30] The social cleavages underlying the violence were not only political in nature; they were also racial, ethnic, and class based.

Southern Texas was the site of the bloodiest fights as U.S. officials and Anglo settlers clashed with the now Mexican-American population. As Timothy Dunn tells us, "theft, intimidation, swindles, dubious legal challenges, and the burden of related court costs, taxes and other debts, as well as purchases" cost the Mexican-American population much of its land.[31] Mexican Americans resisted these injustices, sometimes engaging in violent rebellion. Such events lasted into the early twentieth century. Massive influx of Anglo settlers, widespread dispossession of Texas Mexicans, and some accommodation between elite Texas Mexican and Anglo families served to reduce most Texas Mexicans "to the status of landless workers dependent for their livelihood on agricultural wage labor."[32]

During this time, there was also widespread violence in the border region related to conflicts with indigenous peoples. Like the problems faced by Mexicans absorbed into the United States, the roots of the "Indian problem" lay in the creation of a line of control that restricted freedom of movement and in the socioeconomic marginalization of the Indians with the loss of their lands to white settlers.[33] Such conflicts, of course, predated the establishment of the U.S.-Mexico boundary as defined by the Guadalupe Hidalgo and Gadsden treaties. By 1830, for example, the loss of land and game brought about by Anglo immigration into the area of the Texas-Mexico boundary compelled Comanches and Kiowas to raid throughout Texas and deep into Mexico. Americans and Mexicans, usually under the guise of "pacification," frequently raided Indian territory, often killing and capturing people in the process. Between

1848 and 1853, over one thousand Mexicans in the border states of Nuevo Léon, Coahuila, and Sonora lost their lives as a result of Indians raids, most of which originated in the United States. Significantly contributing to these raids were Americans who purchased goods and captives from the Indians. The violence, attacks on Mexico by U.S.-based filibusters, and Mexican-American resistance to U.S. hegemony led to the establishment of U.S. Army posts along the boundary from the Gulf of Mexico to the Colorado River.[34] By the early 1850s, there were four thousand U.S. troops in the border area. That said, the level of U.S. forces along the boundary was insufficient given the task at hand. The cavalry, for example, the most effective U.S. military force against the Indians, never numbered more than six hundred between 1848 and 1853.[35]

Transboundary Indian raids continued through the 1850s and 1860s. Activity by both Mexican and American bandits added to the sense of lawlessness in the border region. By the early 1870s the situation in the border area had become the primary issue in Mexico-U.S. relations. The U.S. failure to secure an agreement that would have allowed authorities from both countries to cross the boundary in pursuit of marauders led it to claim the unilateral right to enter Mexican territory. Over the next two years, the United States did so about a dozen times, resulting in vociferous protests from Mexican authorities. Finally, the two countries signed an accord allowing for mutual boundary crossings in pursuit of Indians; it remained in effect from 1882 to 1886.[36] Soon thereafter, conflict between the United States and Mexico over Indian transboundary incursions largely disappeared with the elimination or the relocation of "troublesome" indigenous groups to reservations, increasingly effective administrative and military control of the border, and decreasing political and economic isolation of the borderlands from the centers of their respective countries.[37]

The deployment of despotic power resulted in a largely pacified U.S.-Mexico border region (except in times of the Mexican Revolution, 1910–1920).[38] By the early twentieth century, major geographically extensive challenges to U.S. control of the border area were phenomena of the past. Still, the pacification flowing from infrastructural power, the kind necessary to control the flow of goods and people across the international divide, was almost totally absent. Such a situation speaks both to the insufficiency of U.S. state capacity during the period as well as to conflicting state functions and competing interests. The question of how to realize effective immigration control—most notably along the U.S.-Mexico boundary—remained unsolved.

PACIFICATION THROUGH INFRASTRUCTURAL POWER: SECURITY VERSUS OPPORTUNITY

The modern territorial state provides both security and opportunity.[39] It provides security in the sense that it defines territory; moreover, the resources mobilized to protect the territory provide a certain stability. And it provides opportunity in working to maximize the economic benefits realized by domestic interests in a competitive world economy. These functions, however, are not totally complementary. Indeed, as the cases of immigration control (security) and Mexican migrant labor (opportunity for both U.S. capital and Mexican laborers) demonstrate, these functions are sometimes conflicting. And as such, they help illustrate why U.S. efforts to pacify the U.S.-Mexico border region through the deployment of infrastructural power have fallen far short of their stated goal of establishing full control over the movement of peoples and goods across the international divide.

Immigration Control and Boundary Enforcement: Pacification through Territorial Security

Intensifying migratory links between the United States and Mexico—within a larger context of growing migration to the United States from a variety of countries around the world—led to increasing, albeit irregular and inconsistent, efforts to control the movement of people into the country in the late nineteenth century. Given the suppression of rebellious populations in the borderlands during the nineteenth century and the absence of serious challenges to its national boundaries, U.S. efforts increasingly relied on infrastructural or institutionalized state power in the form of the law and law enforcement agencies to secure those boundaries. Yet these efforts occasionally drew upon despotic forms of power as well, a manifestation of the relatively poorly developed state apparatus, especially within the border area, and of the marginalized position of unauthorized migrants and the population of Mexican origin more generally within the United States.

The construction of the boundary between the United States and Mexico was important for giving the two countries territorial definition, as well as for allowing the building of an effective level of territorial control in the border region. This process necessarily entailed an attempt to regulate the movement of people across the boundary. While the boundary has always represented a line of control, one that contains the national body politic and regulates the flow of goods and peoples, there has long been a huge gap between this territorial state-centric ideal and the reality of a transnational world. As discussed above, U.S. efforts along its boundary with Mexico in the mid- to late 1800s concentrated on pacifying the subject populations in the borderlands. By trying to construct "order" the United States laid the basis for a regime of law in the region, albeit one based on the dictates of a conquering power.

The principal concerns of U.S. law enforcement authorities (largely the U.S. Army) during this period were smuggling and cattle rustling, Indian raiding, and all sorts of transboundary criminal activity by assorted gangs, vigilantes, and filibusters. Cooperation between the United States and Mexico was often lacking as officials from the two countries engaged in frequent accusations against one another of complicity in transboundary criminality.[40] While the efforts of U.S. officials along the boundary with Mexico in the late 1800s and early 1900s concentrated on containing violence and large-scale challenges to the state, it was during this period that controls over the transboundary flow of immigrants coming from Mexico began to emerge.

U.S. efforts to control the boundary in a more systematic manner began with the placing of customs officials on both the northern and southern boundaries soon after the signing of the Treaty of Guadalupe Hidalgo. Customs officials concentrated their efforts on "nonsmuggling customs frauds and on the smuggling of both licit and illicit goods: diamonds, watches, textiles, opium, booze, Chinese 'coolies,' garlic, and just about anything that could be transported."[41] Many of these activities were merely a continuation of commercial relationships that predated the imposition of the international boundaries with Canada and Mexico. Most, however, undoubtedly grew out of the desire to earn the lucrative profits entailed by illicit economic activities.[42]

While controls over movement have existed within Europe for centuries (with some polities limiting, for example, the movement of beggars or the unauthorized departure of soldiers and merchants),[43] national immigration controls are more recent creations—not only along the U.S.-Mexico boundary, but throughout the world. To the extent that control of movement existed, it was largely limited to movement within a defined political territory. Institutionalized restrictions on the movement of peoples from one area of the world to another are relatively recent phenomena in human history. Throughout the nineteenth century, for example, border controls and passports were largely unknown in Europe. With the rise to dominance of the nation-state system and capitalism in nineteenth-century Europe, however, national governments began significant efforts to exercise control of movement into and out of their territories.[44]

In the case of the United States, boundary controls between the United States and Mexico were basically nonexistent through the early twentieth century. As Leo Grebler explains, "Controls were so minimal that no records whatsoever were kept from 1886 to 1893."[45] The U.S. government focused its resources on immigration from Europe and on the land border with Canada rather than that with Mexico. The relatively limited points (and methods) of entry into the United States, as well as insufficient infrastructure and resources of the U.S. state apparatus, meant that the United States relied relatively little on a boundary strategy to control unauthorized immigration. The nation focused its efforts to control immigration largely at official ports of entry such as Ellis Island, near New York City. To the extent that the Mexican border was monitored, "controls and statistical reporting concentrated on the illegal entry of Chinese . . . and of other people who were not of Mexican origin."[46]

With the exception of the Alien Act of 1798, there was no federal legislation restricting immigration into the country until 1875.[47] From that time until the early twentieth century, the U.S. Congress passed a whole host of laws barring the entry of non–U.S. citizens on the basis of qualitative characteristics such as race, national origin, physical and mental health, and political beliefs.[48] As legislative prohibitions against certain types of immigrants increased, so did the efforts of would-be immigrants to enter the United States without authorization, thus the origins of the "illegal" immigrant. The rise of these unauthorized immigrants led to the emergence of immigration enforcement and, concomitantly, boundary policing.

Prior to the Immigration Act of February 14, 1904, the "apprehension of aliens" was the responsibility of the U.S. Customs Service's "line riders"—men who rode horseback among the various ports of entry. According to Clifford Alan Perkins, these men "were charged with preventing the smuggling of anything into the United States, but their principal duty was to prevent the illegal entry of cattle, since there was a heavy protective tariff to keep them out."[49] In 1904, the Commissioner-General of Immigration assigned a small number of immigration inspectors on horseback ("mounted watchmen") along the Canadian and Mexican borders to prevent smuggling and unauthorized entry.[50] At the time, the Mexican boundary was of far greater concern to U.S. authorities than the Canadian boundary. According to the commissioner-general, U.S. authorities had the Canadian boundary under sufficient control and unauthorized immigrants were thus finding it quite difficult to enter the United States from Canada. One of the feared consequences was that unauthorized entrants would now turn to the Mexican boundary, which the commissioner-general described as "a point of weakness in our defense from undesirable immigration that has already been discovered and utilized by the most resourceful of alien peoples—the Chinese." For this reason, the commissioner-general explained, the Immigration Service was strengthening its policing of the U.S. southern boundary.[51]

Unauthorized entry of Mexicans, however, was of little concern to U.S. authorities until well after 1910. Historian Linda Gordon describes the Arizona-Mexico boundary of 1900, for example, as one in which "[t]here was no need for *coyotes*, guides to sneak illegals through the border; there were no border markings (save a few stone pillars here and there), no immigration control, and thus no illegals."[52] Similarly, oral histories from U.S. authorities and Mexican crossers in the area of El Paso, Texas, attest that Mexicans could walk freely across the boundary into the United States. As George Sánchez explains,

> The laxity with which American authorities patrolled the border crossing in 1910 was not due to an absence of immigration statutes on the books.... [T]here were restrictions against border crossings by those deemed morally suspect, diseased, engaged in contract labor, and "likely to become a public charge." Any of these categories, particularly the "LPC" provision, could have barred most entrants from Mexico in this period. But the presence of a strong

border culture in which passage had been largely unregulated—this area, after all, had been known as "the northern pass"—mitigated against stringent enforcement of these regulations. Instead, civil servants working at the border concentrated their efforts on the surreptitious entry of the Chinese and patrolled against criminal activity. Thus the economic function of the border passage took firm root relatively unencumbered.[53]

Overall, the force of U.S. boundary authorities was clearly insufficient. For every one hundred migrants apprehended by U.S. immigration authorities, an estimated one thousand eluded them and once they did so there was little worry of apprehension in the interior as there were no authorities charged with searching out and deporting unauthorized immigrants.[54]

The disorder brought about by the Mexican Revolution played an important role in turning the boundary into an obstacle for Mexican migrants. U.S. officials often warned Americans not to cross into Mexico, as border towns were often the sites of intense revolutionary conflict, often resulting in the disrupting of transboundary traffic.[55] Even more important, the passage of the Immigration Act of 1917, while exempting Mexicans (until a new law in 1921), led to a formalization of immigration control procedures as well as to an increase in the number of U.S. authorities and immigration inspection sites along the U.S.-Mexico boundary. The new practices applied to Mexican migrants attempting to cross the boundary included (depending on the assessment and dictates of the U.S. immigrant inspectors at official ports of entry) vaccination, bathing, and delousing. Medical experts hired by the Immigration Service designated the migrants as either "desirable" or "undesirable" based on their health, thus excluding many migrants.[56]

The implementation of a literacy test, mandated by the 1917 legislation, further complicated the process of crossing the boundary from Mexico, as did the imposition of an eight-dollar-a-head-tax for all immigrants. U.S. authorities denied entrance to 5,745 Mexican migrants during the first full year of the implementation of the 1917 law for inability or refusal to pay the head tax. The addition in 1924 of an obligatory visa (for a ten-dollar fee) for all immigrants only added to the financial burden of crossing the boundary, thus leading to an increase in unauthorized immigration.[57] Furthermore, the growing difficulty and costs associated with entering the United States led to a decline in the circular migration that characterized Mexico-U.S. migration before 1917. This made it more likely that Mexicans would settle in the United States rather than risk the possibility of not being able to reenter the country. Nevertheless, most unauthorized Mexican migrants still managed to enter successfully. In the El Paso area, for example, many migrants would simply board freight trains outside the city heading for employment destinations in the interior—particularly in California, where immigration enforcement was practically nonexistent during this time. As the Chief Immigration Inspector in El Paso remarked around 1920, "practically any alien desirous of entering the United States and possessed of ordinary intelligence and persistence could readily find the means to do so without fear of detection."[58]

Rising numbers entries by unauthorized migrants led the Bureau of Immigration to create a larger force of boundary inspectors in March 1914, a group whose equipment now included automobiles and boats. It quickly became clear, however, that this new force was not sufficient to address the organized smuggling of contraband and unauthorized immigrants as the patrolmen were also responsible for inspecting legal immigrants. U.S. authorities thus came to the conclusion that only the establishment of a unit whose exclusive purpose was to patrol the border area could prevent the smuggling of contraband and illicit entry into the United States.[59] As of 1919, there were only 151 immigrant inspectors; they were responsible for more than 2,000 miles of boundary, and most were obligated to remain at one of the twenty official ports of entry. At times, the Immigration Service had a total force of mobile guards that numbered no more than 60.[60]

The outbreak of World War I led the U.S. government to implement travel restrictions and to deploy troops along the boundary. These developments led to a decrease in unauthorized immigration and in illegal activity in the border region during the World War I years of 1917–1918.[61] This occurred despite the passage of additional restrictionist immigration legislation in 1917 that, under normal circumstances, would have led to an increase in unauthorized immigration as immigrants who would have previously gained legal access to the United States would have had to have resorted to clandestine methods to enter. Yet the increased demands on boundary enforcement officials brought about by the war (including the inspection of all peoples crossing from the United States into Mexico) overwhelmed the authorities. It was during this time that discussions to establish a permanent patrol force along the U.S.-Mexico boundary began. Thus, the roots of the U.S. Border Patrol are to be found not only in concerns about unauthorized immigration, but also (and perhaps more so) in a preoccupation with matters of national security as related to the boundary.[62]

Unauthorized entries picked up quickly following the end of the war and intensified as Congress placed additional restrictions on immigration. As a result, pressures for the Bureau of Immigration to increase its efforts to fight illegal boundary activity grew. The bureau's commissioner-general stressed in 1919 that such efforts were needed in the face of large numbers of apprehensions (seeming to suggest that many more were entering successfully) of unauthorized European and Chinese immigrants smuggled in from Canada, Mexico, and Cuba. In the case of Cuba, reports in 1922 stated that there were more than 30,000 unemployed Chinese immigrants on the island who soon intended to attempt to enter the United States. In the aftermath of the destruction of World War I, there was also widespread fear that huge numbers of immigrants from Europe might try to enter the United States extralegally. Indeed, the number of entries into the United States in 1920 was 300 percent that of the previous year. Such factors led to the passage of the temporary Quota Act of 1921, limiting the number of admissions of any one particular nationality to three percent of the group's population already in the United States as reflected by the 1910 census. This marked the first quantitative immigration restriction in U.S. history. The Immigration Act of 1924 made these quotas permanent, but used the census of 1890 as its base. The act also required immigrants for the first time to obtain visas from U.S. consular officials abroad before traveling to the United States. These restrictions had unintended consequences, leading to a rapid rise in the number of unauthorized European immigrants who would enter from Canada or Mexico, countries not subject to quantitative immigration restrictions.[63]

Two days after the May 26, 1924 passage of the Immigration Act, the U.S. Department of Labor appropriations legislation granted one million dollars for "additional land-border patrol," thus creating the U.S. Border Patrol out of the previous boundary policing unit. One year later, Congress, through the Immigration Act of 1925, expanded the Border Patrol's duties to the policing of the seacoasts in the face of large-scale immigrant smuggling from Cuba to Florida and the Gulf Coast. As Border Patrol officers lacked any specific authority to act, Congress also empowered all employees of the Bureau of Immigration (of which the Border Patrol was part) to execute any legal warrant concerning the admission, exclusion, or deportation of immigrants. In addition, the 1925 law permitted bureau employees to arrest without warrant "any alien who, in his presence of view, is entering or attempting to enter the United States in violation of any law or regulation made in pursuance of law regulating the admission of aliens." The 1925 act further authorized bureau agents to board and search sea vessels within U.S. territorial waters or any vehicle within the United States that an agent might suspect is transporting unauthorized immigrants into the country.[64]

The Border Patrol had an initial force of 450 officers assigned to the Mexican and Canadian borders as well as to the Florida and Gulf of Mexico coasts. Through the 1920s and 1930s, the Border Patrol grew slowly. By the 1930s, the Border Patrol utilized cars, trucks, motorboats, and radios, in addition to horses, to patrol the country's boundaries.[65] During this time, roughly an equal number of agents worked in the Canadian and Mexican border regions. The Border Patrol added autogiros and airplanes to their equipment in the 1940s. Until the repeal of Prohibition in 1933, the Border Patrol concentrated a significant amount of its resources to preventing the smuggling of alcohol into the United States. Following the repeal, the Border Patrol concentrated its efforts on preventing the entry of unauthorized immigrants from Mexico.[66]

The year 1940 marked a turning point for the Border Patrol. In the aftermath of a massive deportation and repatriation campaign of people of Mexican origin from the United States in the 1930s,[67] the Border Patrol grew considerably. The outbreak of World War II caused great consternation within the administration of Franklin Delano Roosevelt, which feared that foreign agents with anti-American intentions would attempt to enter the United States clandestinely. The administration played an important role in constructing immigration and border enforcement as issues of national security. As a result, the administration transferred the Immigration and Naturalization Service from the Department of Labor to the Department of Justice. (President Hoover had consolidated the Bureau of Immigration and the Bureau of Naturalization into the INS in 1933.) Two weeks later, Congress appropriated two million dollars to add 712 Border Patrol officers (almost doubling the size of the force), 57 auxiliary personnel, and the needed equipment.[68] The Border Patrol carried out many functions during the war, including guarding "enemy alien" detention camps and diplomats as well as helping the U.S. military guard the country's east coast against the potential entry of agents from the Axis powers.[69]

While the Border Patrol, and concomitantly the boundary, grew as an institution, larger realities undermined its stated mission. First and foremost, the length of the boundaries for which the Border Patrol was responsible limited its effectiveness, especially in the face of the agency's relatively small size, the sophistication of smugglers, and the large numbers and sheer determination of migrants. As early as 1927, for example, reports stated that smugglers were operating at least fifteen airplanes in the Los Angeles district alone.[70] Furthermore, the Border Patrol had to contend with the intense transboundary social networks of the border region, many of which long preceded the establishment of the international boundary. As the Immigration and Naturalization Service (INS) observed in 1934, "Most of the towns in the southwest have a large population of Mexican descent, aliens and citizens, and many of these people make frequent trips to border towns, hoping to cross the international line. Many persons living some distance below the line in Mexico frequently visit border towns in the United States, and illiterates in Mexico have long sought the privilege of making purchases and visiting friends and relatives in the United States."[71]

For such reasons, the INS issued identification cards to non–U.S. citizens who lived in the border region (on either side of the boundary) to permit them to cross the boundary and, in 1934, extended the issuance of crossing cards to frequent crossers from the Mexican interior. It is probable, however, for the reasons mentioned above, that many Mexican citizens were able to cross the boundary and remain within the border region, despite not having a crossing card. In addition, farmers along the U.S. side of the boundary actively encouraged Mexican workers to step across the line and work on their farms.

According to the INS report in 1934, this was a practice difficult to stop given the Border Patrol's insufficient numbers, and difficult to prosecute successfully because of the sympathy of juries to the needs of growers.[72]

Such developments were a function of two interrelated developments: intensifying migratory links between the United States and Mexico, and growing dependence of U.S. capital—largely agricultural—on Mexican migrant workers. While the building up of the boundary—in a physical and legal sense—was a manifestation of the security aspect of the state, state encouragement and facilitation of immigration and transboundary economic activity were manifestations of the opportunity aspect, one pursued by social actors within and outside U.S. territory.

Undermining Pacification: Territory as Opportunity

Migration between what became the United States and Mexico long preceded the imposition of the modern-day boundary. One of the earliest mass migrations from Mexico took place in 1848, just as the United States was annexing what had been northern Mexico. Large numbers of Sonorans as well as others migrated to California upon learning of the discovery of gold.[73] But such an event was exceptional. Although it was not until the twentieth century that Mexican migration became significant in scale or in geographical extent,[74] there was a continuous flow of migrants to the United States from Mexico's densely populated central plateau (states such as Jalisco, Michoacán, and Zacatecas) beginning in the 1880s.[75]

Agricultural policies during the reign of Porfirio Díaz (1876–1910) discouraged small-scale agriculture, thereby further stimulating out-migration from central Mexico, the area of historic concentration of the country's population "as the arid north and the tropical south provided less opportunity for successful farming."[76] Transportation improvements within Mexico played a significant role in facilitating the migratory outflow. Regular railroad passenger service between Mexico City and El Paso, Texas, began in 1884.[77] American railroad companies—in violation of the Alien Contract Labor Law of 1885—recruited Mexican contract laborers and thereby "set the mass migration of the early twentieth century in motion"; once started, the migration "took on a life of its own."[78] Between 1900 and 1930, about 685,000 Mexicans migrated legally to the United States, approximately 3.6 percent of total legal immigration.[79] Sixty percent of these migrants went to Texas, reflecting the state's much larger population and economy than those of the other border states. Much of the migration was circular in nature, with migrants frequently moving back and forth between the United States and Mexico.[80]

Mexican migration began to pick up at the turn of the century, especially in the Southwest. The Mexican consul observed in 1900 that "[t]he large number of Mexicans . . . arriving daily in Los Angeles is truly notable." Most

Mexican migrants were still concentrated in the Southwest, but as a 1908 report for the U.S. Department of Labor noted, Mexican immigrants were increasingly living outside of the Southwest. Indeed, "[b]y the 1920s Mexicans could be found harvesting sugar beets in Minnesota, laying railroad tracks in Kansas, packing meat in Chicago, mining coal in Oklahoma, assembling cars in Detroit, canning fish in Alaska, and sharecropping in Louisiana."[81] Immigration from Mexico in the period of 1900–1909 was still modest, however. While the U.S. Southwest was growing economically and demanding an increasing number of foreign laborers, most of the laborers during this time came from earlier waves of immigration from Asia. Conditions within Mexico also played a factor in undermining immigration as "[t]he vast majority of the Mexican population was immobile geographically as well as socially. Nearly nine-tenths of the total lived in rural areas, and large numbers of agricultural workers were held in peonage."[82]

Beginning in 1910, the Mexican Revolution radically changed this situation of relative social and geographical immobility, marking a significant upsurge in migration to the United States. Many rural Mexicans migrated to urban areas in search of greater physical safety and social stability. Similar reasons informed decisions to migrate across the boundary into the United States. The U.S. government admitted tens of thousands of Mexicans as economic refugees between 1911 and 1915. This upsurge accompanied a great increase in labor demand for and recruitment of Mexican labor. Key to the situation was a shortage of low-wage labor in the U.S. Southwest. The out-migration of poor white and black laborers to the cities of the northern United States, the so-called Gentlemen's Agreement between the United States and Japan by which Tokyo agreed to restrict the issuance of passports to those intending to emigrate to the United States, the U.S. entry into World War I, and the passage of restrictive legislation in the form of the Immigration Act of 1917 (which exempted Mexicans) all contributed to the regional labor shortage.[83]

The 1920s saw Mexican migration reach a new high. A long-simmering conflict between the Mexican government and the Catholic Church erupted into an armed insurrection, the so-called Cristero rebellion, causing thousands of workers to head to "el Norte." The completion of a railroad between Guadalajara, Mexico, and Nogales, Arizona, in 1927 further facilitated new migration. Almost 500,000 Mexicans entered the United States on visas during the decade.[84] Some estimate that by 1930, more than 10 percent of Mexico's entire population was living in the United States.[85]

The United States did not always welcome Mexican migrants with open arms, an outgrowth of the belief that immigrants undermined general social security. An economic recession in the aftermath of World War I, for example, facilitated hysterical nativist attacks against immigrants, especially Mexicans. As Wayne Cornelius notes, "Urged on by labor leaders and politicians, mobs of native-born Americans in Texas, Oklahoma, and other states launched attacks on Mexicans in their work places; vigilante groups terrorized them in their homes and destroyed their property." Between 1920 and 1921, almost 100,000 Mexicans left the United States "under varying degrees of coercion." Many were U.S.-born Mexican Americans.[86] This anti-Mexican restrictionist campaign was a prelude to something far greater in scale at the end of the decade.

The 1920s were a time of rising restrictionist sentiment against all immigrants. The Immigration Act of 1924 led to a sharp reduction in immigration from southern and eastern Europe as well as from Asia; Western Hemisphere immigrants were exempt. Restrictionists, however, demanded a quota on Mexican immigration and stronger administrative controls at the U.S.-Mexico boundary. Such pressures led the federal government in August 1928 to order consular officials to deny entry visas to most Mexican applicants and to enforce for the first time against Mexicans the provisions of the 1917 Immigration Act denying entrance to the illiterate. The authorities also began demanding the eight-dollar head tax called for in the 1917 legislation and the ten-dollar visa fee imposed by the 1924 law.[87] Such increasing restrictionism led to great fears among U.S. growers and ranchers that Congress would seriously limit Mexican immigration. As a result, they engaged in a variety of political lobbying activities—especially in 1928, when Congress considered applying immigration quotas to Mexico.[88]

The onset of the Great Depression of 1929 greatly changed the parameters of the debate as restrictionist sentiment further intensified, with organizations ranging from the American Federation of Labor to the American Legion and the Veterans of Foreign Wars leading the charge. Mass deportations of people of Mexican origin ensued, often using methods that even a 1932 U.S. government commission characterized as "unconstitutional, tyrannic and oppressive."[89] According to one study, U.S. authorities forcibly expelled an estimated 415,000 Mexicans between 1929 and 1935, with another 85,000 leaving "voluntarily," usually under intense pressure from local authorities. Some estimates of the deportations run as high as one million, including tens of thousands of U.S. citizens of Mexican descent. A significant effect of the mass deportations was to slow Mexican immigration to a negligible level. Not until 1942 did it pick up again—in response to labor shortages brought about by the Second World War. That year also marked the beginning of a contract labor program, the so-called Bracero Program.[90]

Many expected the Bracero Program to reduce unauthorized immigration from Mexico, but the opposite seems to have happened. While INS expulsion figures are problematic as a measure of unauthorized immigration,[91] they can serve as a crude proxy. While the first half of the 1940s saw a little more than 57,000 expulsions of "illegals," there were almost 856,000 in the second half of the decade.[92] Many growers continued to prefer hiring "illegal" immigrants as it was less cumbersome and less expensive than hiring braceros, so grower practices significantly facilitated the rise in extralegal immigration. Through its actions, moreover, the INS actually encouraged unauthorized immigration.[93] The legalization of unauthorized migrants by U.S. authorities (popularly known as "drying out the wetbacks") served to increase extralegal immigration from Mexico as the news spread that the easiest manner to obtain a bracero contract was to enter the United States extralegally.[94]

As unauthorized immigration grew, a number of state officials began to argue that such levels of uncontrolled immigration could potentially present a threat to the stability of the agricultural economy and, more generally, to the larger society. The 1951 report of the President's Commission on Migratory Labor was the first to sound the alarm, blaming "illegal" immigration for depressing wage rates in the Southwest and warning of its implications for public health and substandard housing. Although growers and their congressional allies attacked the report, it led to rapidly growing critical attention on "illegal" immigration, linking the phenomenon to all sorts of social ills, including crime. Organized labor also fanned the flames. Such critiques resonated with large segments of the public, especially given the severe recession of the early 1950s. Furthermore, the Cold War and prevailing anticommunism played a role in facilitating the rise of anti-"wetback" sentiment.[95] Some, while stressing the national security dimensions of the perceived crisis, also emphasized the law and order aspect. One INS official, for example, proclaimed the increasing number of extralegal entrants from Mexico to be "the greatest peacetime invasion ever complacently suffered by another country under open, flagrant, contemptuous violations of its laws."[96]

The Eisenhower administration, however, was ambivalent in its response. While President Dwight D. Eisenhower's attorney general Herbert Brownell helped to incite public opposition to "illegal" immigration, his actions demonstrated the administration's uncertainty. Thus, after having reported to Congress that the "wetback problem" had never been so bad, Brownell recommended that there be no increase in the Border Patrol's budget, and that there be a reduction in the INS's overall budget, suggesting that it was premature to deport "illegal" workers. Nevertheless, in the face of growing pressure, the Eisenhower administration demonstrated some commitment to fighting unregulated immigration by announcing the start of its infamous Operation Wetback on June 9, 1954.

Led by INS Commissioner General Joseph Swing, the operation involved the massive roundup of suspected "wetbacks" in border states. According to the INS, the agency apprehended over one million migrants during fiscal year 1954, most of the apprehensions taking place during the operation. By means of high-visibility shows of force in restricted locales and highly sensationalized media coverage, the INS was able to give the impression of being far more powerful than it was, thus causing, according to the INS, "uncounted thousands" of unauthorized migrants to leave the United States on their own accord. Although Operation Wetback resulted in a record number of deportations, the U.S. government compensated agricultural interests by greatly increasing the number of braceros admitted into the United States. In this regard, the operation's most important outcome was to increase state and grower control over migrant labor.[97]

At the same time, opposition to the Bracero Program quickly began to rise, especially from religious groups and organized labor. In response, the Department of Labor issued increasingly restrictive regulations regarding bracero contracts. Combined with the rapid mechanization of cotton harvesting (no agricultural sector employed more braceros), these restrictions led to a decline in bracero contracts in the period from 1959 to 1964, resulting in a rapid rise in unauthorized immigration from Mexico. This process intensified and continued in the aftermath of the termination of the Bracero Program in 1964.[98]

An important contributing factor to the continuation and rise in unauthorized immigration was the immunity enjoyed by employers of undocumented migrants. Although Congress had passed a law in 1952 that made it illegal to "harbor, transport, or conceal" extralegal entrants, the law's so-called Texas Proviso considered employment of unauthorized migrants *not* to be a form of harboring.[99] Congress later even rejected an amendment to the law that would have penalized employers who *knowingly* employed undocumented workers.[100]

Such economic factors were the basis for what some analysts referred to as the "revolving door" function of U.S. immigration enforcement whereby the INS would effectively "open" and "shut" the boundary depending on the needs of domestic economic interests.[101] The emergence of the Bracero Program in 1942 and the INS's assistance in recruiting contract labor and "drying out wetbacks" for U.S. growers on the one hand,[102] and the agency's Operation Wetback in 1954 on the other, are the most obvious examples of the historically contradictory practices of the Border Patrol. Despite the fact that the Border Patrol is charged (among other things) to apprehend and exclude undocumented non-U.S. nationals, "it seems that in practice the Border Patrol functioned primarily to regulate the numbers that were already in the country."[103]

Powerful agricultural interests played a significant role in producing and maintaining a yawning gap between state rhetoric championing strong boundary policing, and actual state practice. This gap characterized U.S. immigration enforcement efforts through most of the twentieth century.[104] Thus, it not surprising that there appears to have long been little serious political will among national political leaders, especially those from border states, to fund the policing of the border adequately. In fact, in 1952 and 1954, at the height of "illegal" migration from Mexico, many members of Congress from border states voted to cut monies appropriated to the Border Patrol. As Ernesto Galarza later observed, "With the purse half shut the gate could remain half open."[105] In fact, in 1952 and 1954, at the height of "illegal" migration from Mexico, many border-state members of Congress voted to cut monies appropriated to the Border Patrol. By 1954, the Border Patrol was only able to employ two hundred guards at any one particular time.[106]

The inadequate provision of state resources for boundary enforcement continued into the 1960s and 1970s. Although the number of apprehensions of unauthorized entrants rose from about 71,000 in 1960 to 345,000 in 1969, for example, the number of permanent INS positions remained constant. The Border Patrol's 1980 budget was only $77 million, less than that of Baltimore's police department and far less than half that of Philadelphia's police department.[107] Thus, while attempts by the federal government to control the entry and residence of immigrants grew significantly over the first several decades of the twentieth century, these efforts were inconsistent and riddled with internal contradictions, especially in regards to unauthorized migrants from Mexico. The lack of effective state control over unauthorized immigration demonstrates that the United States-Mexico border region was not pacified in large part due to the influence of economic actors whose goals in terms of immigration control often contradicted those of the federal government.

This is not to suggest, however, that boundary and immigrant policing have merely served the interests of capital, nor that such policing has been a mere show. Rather, it is to argue that the nature of boundary policing is the outgrowth of the complex interplay of competing social actors and that, to understand the relative "success" or "failure" of boundary policing, we need to understand this interrelationship better. Along a similar vein, the condition of the boundary speaks to the somewhat contradictory nature of two of the most important functions of the modern territorial state—namely, the provision of opportunity and the provision of security. At the same time, we need to appreciate the sheer magnitude of the task of regulating the movement of large numbers of unauthorized migrants across almost two thousand miles of boundary.

Nonetheless, the Border Patrol and the U.S.-Mexico boundary became more "real," and the Border Patrol slowly grew from the time of its establishment through the early 1970s.[108] As such, the Border Patrol's de facto and de jure powers grew over space and time. The "border" became not only the physical line separating Mexico from the United States, but a social and legal division that empowered U.S. authorities to carry out all sorts of acts under the rubric of the law. As such, the boundary increasingly helped to define and separate the United States and Mexico.[109] In this regard, the pacification of the U.S.-Mexico border region was a success despite its relative failure to achieve significant control over the transboundary movement of goods and people. Apart from eliminating geographically extensive and large-scale challenges to U.S. domination of the region, it succeeded in establishing U.S. ideological hegemony vis-à-vis the boundary. U.S. efforts to control the boundary with Mexico became increasingly "normal," an acceptable function of a modern territorial state, both within the United States and, at least in terms of official opinion, within Mexico.

In a little more than one hundred years, the governments of the United States and Mexico eliminated the frontier and constructed an international boundary. During this period, the dividing line between the two countries became increasingly real in the sense of having a physical presence characterized by entry and exit points, fences and other physical demarcations, and patrols and inspections by a variety of law enforcement bodies. In other ways, however, the division between Mexico and the United States became increasingly blurry—more a border than a boundary—as transboundary links intensified, a process greatly facilitated by the high levels of population growth in the border region. By 1970, for example, U.S. border states had a combined population of almost 34 million, while Mexican border states had almost 8 million residents. The combined population of San Diego and Tijuana was at the time over one million.[110]

While the U.S. Border Patrol—given myriad factors (most notably its inadequate institutional resources)—was largely unable to realize its mission of preventing unauthorized immigration during the period discussed in this chapter, the creation and development of the Border Patrol was, nevertheless, very significant. The establishment of a legal regime and a government bureaucracy relating to immigration, as well as the construction of the boundary and boundary policing organizations, marked a shift from almost total reliance upon despotic power to growing reliance upon infrastructural power. This shift helped lay the basis for the institutionalization and normalization of the U.S.-Mexico boundary. It also furthered the construction of social boundaries distinguishing between desirable and undesirable immigrants and, more important, citizens and "aliens" and their concomitant social relations. These developments represented an increasing pacification of the U.S.-Mexico border region and the increasing boundedness of U.S. state power. At the same time, the construction of the boundary in all its aspects, while a function of numerous national phenomena, was also an outgrowth and constructor of local social geographies. For this reason, as well as for establishing the local historical geographical roots of Operation Gatekeeper, I next examine the emergence of Tijuana and San Diego, as well as the construction of the boundary and the rise of boundary and immigration policing in the region.

Local Context and the Creation
of Difference in the Border Region

Appeals to the past are among the commonest of strategies in interpretations of the present. What animates such appeals is not only
disagreement about what happened in the past and what the past was,
but uncertainty about whether the past really is past, over and
concluded, or whether it continues, albeit in different forms, perhaps.
This problem animates all sorts of discussions—about influence,
about blame and judgement, about present actualities and future
priorities.

—Edward Said[1]

The national- and binational-level processes of competition, conquest, and
pacification discussed previously manifested themselves locally, as well as
nationally. Factors specific to particular cities, towns, and regions along the
U.S.-Mexico boundary mediated these national- and international-scale
processes that as a result played themselves out in different ways throughout
the border region. These local contexts, in turn, helped to shape the larger
processes of competition, conquest, and pacification, and to influence how
they affected border life. For such reasons, I now examine local contexts in the
border region with a focus on the San Diego–Tijuana area to ascertain how
the dynamic interrelationship between the local and the national/binational
scales manifested itself in the border region. The argument I advance is a paradoxical one: the establishment and construction of the international boundary
and its associated practices facilitated increasing sameness (in the sense of
sharing and interacting) between Mexico and the United States while simultaneously heightening the sense of difference between the "Americans" and
the "Mexicans" on either side of the international divide.

Difference and social distance as they display themselves in the region of
present-day San Diego–Tijuana were far from predestined. A number of
factors came together to bring about the region's social divisions that reveal
themselves most overtly in the form of national difference. The making of the
modern territorial states of Mexico and the United States have inevitably
involved the production of national difference as nation-state–building and
the production of boundaries—in both the physical and social senses—are
inextricably intertwined.[2] Had the international boundary between Tijuana

and San Diego been located north or south of the two cities, or had the political geographical organization of what are today the United States and Mexico been different, the nature of the social distinctions and the breadth of the social distance that manifest themselves in San Diego–Tijuana would be something other than they are today. This is not to say that social divisions based on race, class, and gender are not also present; rather, it is merely to suggest that nationalism—at least in the context of the U.S.-Mexico boundary—is the most salient form of difference and, as such, embodies and helps to mask other forms of difference that underlie conflicts surrounding the boundary.

A variety of individuals, social agents, and institutions created the long-term historical geography of the San Diego–Tijuana region, a process that involved the construction of social differences—especially between citizens and "aliens"—across the boundary, and that ultimately facilitated the emergence of Operation Gatekeeper in 1994. The account of this process is necessarily somewhat cursory given the poverty of the historical record regarding the making of the local boundary. Nevertheless, the available pieces of the much larger puzzle illustrate the significant role the imposition of the U.S.-Mexico boundary had in advancing the growth of San Diego and Tijuana, their increasing integration, and, simultaneously, the heightened sense of difference that characterizes the attitudes and practices of the local population toward those from the other side of the international divide.

SAN DIEGO AND TIJUANA: GROWING UP AND COMING TOGETHER

Spanish missionaries established their first mission in the Mexican province of Alta California (present-day California, U.S.A.) in San Diego in 1769. Until the early nineteenth century, San Diego remained a small mission town. It began to change following Mexico's independence from Spain in 1821 as an emerging class of wealthy Mexican landowners began to make their mark on the town's landscape by constructing relatively large buildings. Nevertheless, San Diego remained a relatively insignificant place through the mid-nineteenth century. At the time of the outbreak of the U.S-Mexico War in 1846, for example, the town's population numbered only 350 people. The drawing of the boundary in 1848 by the Treaty of Guadalupe Hidalgo made San Diego part of the United States, along with the rest of Alta California. The gradual severing of San Diego's links with Baja California and Mexico coincided with the beginning of the settlement's transformation from a rural village to a regional urban center whose political economy and culture became increasingly linked with the United States.[3]

The period between 1850 and 1880 saw San Diego evolve from a mission and Mexican cattle-ranching settlement to a growing town integrated into southern California's economy, one of the most important regions of economic expansion in the United States. The arrival of settlers and capital from other parts of the United States during the first two post–Guadalupe Hidalgo decades led to a rapid decline in Mexican influence in the area in terms of culture and large-scale property loss. Anglo encroachment gradually pushed local Mexicans (also known as *Californios*) out of their positions of prominence in San Diego, a process that was basically complete by the 1880s.[4]

As the city continued to grow, the local elites campaigned intensively to attract railroad interests to make San Diego the western terminus of the transcontinental railroad coming from Yuma, Arizona. The railroad capitalists decided, however, to make Los Angeles the endpoint, a process completed in 1887. It was not until 1919 that railroad interests constructed a direct link between Yuma and San Diego. During this time period, Los Angeles rapidly grew to a size of over 500,000 while San Diego grew much more slowly to a population of 74,361. But other developments boded well for the future, at least as envisioned by city elites. San Diego celebrated the establishment of a deep-water port and a U.S. naval base in the early twentieth century.[5] These developments helped lay the basis for San Diego's future growth as a city heavily dependent on military-related activities, as well as facilitating the city's rapid growth. Between 1930 and 1940, San Diego grew at a rate of 37.3 percent (from 148,000 to 203,300), a manifestation in many ways of California's general population growth (which was 21.6 percent during the decade while that of the United States as a whole was only 7.2 percent).[6]

Between 1950 and 1960, the population of the San Diego region almost doubled, rising from 556,808 to 1,033,011. High levels of investment in military-related industries help fuel the rapid growth as San Diego emerged as an important national center of aircraft and aerospace manufacturing. As time passed, manufacturing sectors emerged, including those of chemicals, apparel, and machinery.[7] But while San Diego's growth and development were very much linked to developments within California and the United States as a whole, its ties to Tijuana also informed the city's development. Nevertheless, the relationship between San Diego and Tijuana, while somewhat symbiotic, has never been an equal one, as the former has influenced the latter to a far greater degree than the reverse.

At the time of the drawing of the international political boundary between Mexico and the United States, Tijuana was the largest of a series of small cattle-ranching villages distributed across the Tijuana River Valley in Alta California. Catholic missionaries during the period of Spanish colonialism were the principal force behind the settlement and population patterns in the region until the mid-nineteenth century. The drawing of the international boundary in 1848 was a subject of controversy, as Mexico feared losing fertile lands along the California coast. The treaty, to Mexico's dismay, bisected the Valley of Tijuana, leaving Mexico the hilly lands south of the Tijuana River's flood plain while the United States gained the relatively flat lands.[8]

While the Treaty of Guadalupe Hidalgo formally cut off the ties of Tijuana and Baja California (the new name for all of California south of the new international boundary) to San Diego, it was the United States, far more than Mexico, that influenced the region's development during the second half of the nineteenth century. Like most border areas, Tijuana and Baja California were very isolated—politically, economically, and geographically—from the center of Mexico, where most of the country's resources, people, and political power were located. The arrival of large amounts of capital into southern California in the late 1800s had a spillover effect in Baja California, a process facilitated by the government of Porfirio Díaz, who championed an "open door policy" for U.S. capital in the border region. Díaz offered numerous concessions to foreign capital to encourage investment, offers that U.S. interests readily took up, especially in the mining and transportation sectors. It was primarily U.S capital, for example, that financed the construction of railroads from Mexico's interior to the northern border region, thus facilitating the rapid increase of the exporting of Mexican raw materials and labor and the importing of U.S. manufactured goods. U.S.-based capital quickly came to dominate the region's economy, engaging in projects ranging from cotton production in the Mexicali Valley and to the real estate development of Ensenada.[9] Indeed, "[a]t the peak of American control in Lower California, about 1885, little that was Mexican remained. Lands, minerals, resources, culture, population, orientation, and even the apparent destiny of the territory were American." But the failure of many mining and "colonization" ventures by American interests led to a significant decline in U.S. activity in Baja California by 1915.[10]

Nevertheless, such transnational economic activity had a long-term effect on Baja California, engendering a heavy dependency on the United States. Although border towns in Mexico supported themselves through agriculture, ranching, and regional trade prior to the imposition of the boundary, dependence on foreign products (largely American) increased steadily as the area's population grew in the aftermath of the Treaty of Guadalupe Hidalgo. The establishment of the boundary between Mexico and the United States in 1848 had significant effects on the commercial relations of what became the border region. Thereafter, the Mexican government implemented tariffs on goods imported from the United States, causing many Mexican families to migrate to the north side of the international boundary. But pressure from Mexican border residents led Mexico City to allow for the duty-free importation of foreign goods to the border region. For some Mexican border states, however, the concession was insufficient and they unilaterally implemented *zonas libres*, or free trade zones, along the boundary with the United States. The free trade zones were controversial within Mexico as they were seen as undermining national production and led to a loss of tariff revenues. While the zones were "on-again off-again" propositions for a number of decades as a result of changing governorships in Mexican states, U.S. goods continued to flow into the Mexican border region nonetheless. By the time the Mexican government formally abolished the free trade zones in 1905, the dependence of Mexican border consumers on U.S. products and on the American economy was firmly established.[11]

Tijuana was an archetype of this process. Indeed, the original layout and orientation of the city—its first city plan was developed in 1889—was a manifestation of its intense ties with southern California, the local tourist economy being the "driving force behind location decisions made by households and investors in the early periods of Tijuana's growth."[12] The rise of San Diego, especially as a seaport and a naval base, fueled Tijuana's growth in such a way that the latter served the needs of the former.[13] Tijuana thus grew at a rapid pace. Whereas the population of Tijuana in 1900 was only 242 people, it rose to 956 in 1910. By 1930, there were 11,000 people living in Tijuana; ten years later the figure was almost 22,000.[14]

Tijuana's development in the early decades of the twentieth century was a manifestation of its function as a center of recreation for southern Californians and the ability of U.S. capital to shape the area's growth. The construction by a U.S. capitalist in 1906 of a railroad linking Yuma, Arizona, with San Diego crossed the boundary, thus connecting Mexicali, Tecate, and Tijuana with San Diego and in the process furthering Tijuana's integration with the north.[15] The sanctioning by the Mexican government in 1908 of gambling in Baja California led to a significant influx of U.S. tourists into Tijuana. The efforts of the reformist movement in California to impose its puritanical notions of morality and religion on the state's population from 1900 to 1920 greatly intensified the flow. Horse races, casinos, thermal baths, alcohol, and prostitution were the city's principal tourist attractions, gaining the city the nickname of "sin city." The implementation of Prohibition in the United States in 1920 brought about the so-called golden age of tourism as Americans flocked to Tijuana to satisfy their vices.[16]

The U.S. Depression of 1929 and the repeal of Prohibition in 1933 brought an end to this "golden age," but continued visits by wealthy tourists from southern California enabled Tijuana to weather the economic storm. The economic downturn and the end of Prohibition nevertheless hit Tijuana hard as alcohol-related establishments were the town's primary source of income. Many establishments closed their doors, leading to a rapid rise in unemployment and out-migration from the border city. During the same period, however, President Rodríguez of Mexico created free trade zones in Tijuana and Ensenada in 1933, which provided great benefits to the local consumers, and served as a significant catalyst for local economic development. But as the free trade zones were limited to the urban areas, the rural population near Tijuana was at increasing disadvantage in relation to their urban compatriots. This situation resulted in an increase in rural to urban migration in the region. The Depression era was also the time when the United States expelled hundreds of thousands of Mexicans,[17] many of whom settled in Tijuana, thus further contributing to Tijuana's population boom.

By the time Mexican president Lázaro Cárdenas ordered the closing of all Tijuana's gambling establishments in 1935, Tijuana had undeniably intense economic and cultural ties to the United States. Many of the Tijuana residents who lost their jobs as a result simply looked for work in San Diego. At the same time, the resulting decline of the tourist industry also marked the end of strong U.S. influence in Tijuana's economy (U.S. business interests had owned many of the tourist establishments).[18] U.S. capital played a moderate role in Tijuana's boom during the 1940s, but by that time it was Mexico-based capital that was dominant as Cárdenas had nationalized almost all the holdings of foreign capital in the late 1930s. The 1940s also were a time of dramatic migration to Tijuana (largely from central Mexico) as the establishment of the U.S. Bracero Program in 1942 attracted thousands of migrants to the northern boundary. Tijuana's population more than tripled during the decade, reaching almost 70,000 by the year 1950.[19]

As Tijuana grew, so did the transboundary linkages with San Diego. These linkages were not merely economic, but also social, cultural, and political. Some were unconscious in terms of their origins and reproduction, while others were formal or intentional. In terms of the latter, the reality of a transborder region necessitated overt attempts by state and nonstate actors to establish cooperative endeavors between the peoples of San Diego and Tijuana in spite of the presence of the international boundary. This was a trend throughout the border region, one discussed in the next section, with a focus on San Diego and Tijuana.

TRANSBOUNDARY COOPERATION

As historian Oscar Martínez states, "Borders simultaneously divide and unite, repel and attract, separate and integrate."[20] This observation certainly applies to the U.S.-Mexico boundary, which has not only helped to divide the people of Mexico and the United States, but also brought them together, especially in the border region. This togetherness, of course, long preceded the imposition of the international boundary. Given the strength and profundity of the transboundary links within the border region, cooperation across the international divide has long been a hallmark of border life. As discussed previously, there were times of cooperation between the governments of Mexico and the United States during the nineteenth century involving, for instance, transboundary raiding by indigenous groups in the border region.

On a local level, numerous border communities on different sides of the international boundary long engaged in cooperative practices through the early twentieth century, not least due to the relative weakness of the boundary as a line of control and separation. In some areas of the border region, local transboundary culture was such that the boundary served not so much as a national divide as it did as one of economic class. In Ambos Nogales (a reference to Nogales, Arizona, and Nogales, Sonora) as of the early 1920s, for example, most Mexicans of relatively privileged means lived on the U.S. side of the boundary while most working-class Mexicans employed on the U.S. side lived in Nogales, Mexico. Such a situation made it difficult to distinguish between the two national territories in the area in a meaningful sense. As the U.S. consul in Nogales wrote in 1924, "The two towns are practically one, only a street separates them." It is thus understandable that intense transboundary cooperation marked the lives of many towns in the border region in the early part of this century. In the case of Calexico, California, and Mexicali, Sonora, for example, the towns had such strong economic and social ties in the 1920s that their respective fire departments responded to calls in either town.[21]

The post-Depression era coincided with a U.S. military buildup in the border region during the 1940s and 1950s. The increase in the size and quantity of U.S. military bases within easy driving distance of the international boundary helped to provide the clientele needed to reinvigorate the entertainment and tourist economies of Mexican border towns that had suffered from the combined effects of Prohibition and the Depression. Mexican migration from the southern interior to the border region (Mexican border towns were a staging area from where migrants left to work as agricultural laborers in the U.S. Southwest) during the 1950s further transformed Mexican border cities. As a result of these changes, the largest Mexican border cities (Ciudad Juárez, Mexicali, Tijuana, Nuevo Laredo, Reynosa, and Matamoros) grew between three and ten times their 1940 populations by 1960.[22]

The most recent phase of growth of the border region has its roots in the early 1960s when the Mexican government launched the Programa Nacional Fronterizo (PRONAF), or National Border Program, in 1961. The program was an initiative that aimed to beautify Mexican border towns and build up their tourist infrastructure to attract greater levels of tourism from the United States, as well as to create favorable conditions for industrialization in the border region. An outgrowth of the PRONAF was the highly successful Border Industrialization Program (BIP). Launched in 1965, the BIP established the border zone corridor of export processing industries known as *maquiladoras*. The stated intention of the program was to create location-specific magnets for economic growth and thus serve as a development engine for the entire northern border region and even for Mexico as a whole. In the same vein, the BIP sought to reduce high levels of unemployment in border cities—a situation significantly exacerbated by the ending of the Bracero Program and, more generally, the growing mechanization of U.S. agriculture in the Southwest that preceded the Bracero Program's demise. The PRONAF and the BIP also helped to fuel significant migration to border cities from other parts of Mexico, albeit at a scale (relative to the cities' total growth) less than that of the 1940s and 1950s.[23]

Similar to the Mexican side of the boundary, annual population growth rates for U.S. border cities have far surpassed the national average. During the 1970s, for example, the growth rate for U.S. border cities was three to four times that of the country as a whole. Most Mexican border cities grew at even faster rates and it is likely that the populations of these cities are underestimates given that a high proportion of their residents are seasonal migrants to the United States and that many new immigrants to these cities live on property not registered with the government.[24] With the exception of San Diego, cities on the U.S. side of the boundary are generally noticeably smaller in population than their Mexican counterparts. This is a manifestation of these Mexican border cities' significant dependence on the United States, which has thus historically transformed Mexican border cities into "reception areas" for Mexican migrants intending to travel to the United States for work. This function of Mexican border cities has seen a relative decline as their own local economies have grown and diversified, thus providing economic opportunities for many would-be international migrants.[25]

As the cities on either side of the boundary have grown, so have the cross-boundary linkages—what Herzog has described as "part of a transboundary economic system that involves growing volumes of intercity exchanges of goods, services, people, workers, technology, and capital." These linkages exist at the scale of the border region as a whole as well as at local scales between paired cities on either side of the U.S.-Mexico boundary. The size and complexity of these transboundary linkages have increased as the border region population has grown. As one might expect, most of the importing and exporting to and from Mexico and the United States takes place within the border region. Over the years, Mexico and the United States have become very important trading partners. By 1990, about 65 percent of Mexico's exports went to the United States, while 60 percent of all its imports came from there.[26]

Increasingly shared space has necessitated increasingly formal methods of transboundary cooperation. It is for such reasons that the United States and Mexico created the U.S.-Mexico Commission for Border Development and Friendship (CODAF) in 1966 to facilitate ties between the nine U.S. agencies and numerous Mexican agencies charged with managing border issues. Although the Nixon administration abolished CODAF upon its coming to power in 1969, transboundary cooperation became increasingly institutionalized over time. These cooperative endeavors ranged from joint efforts by the U.S. and Mexican governments to eradicate screw worm among cattle and rabies in dogs in the 1960s to the establishment of the binational Border Cities Conference, which meets on an annual basis. In addition, there were all sorts of informal transboundary cooperative efforts, including bicultural music programs, kinship ties, and transboundary community organizations. Thus, by the 1970s, an international symbiosis of sorts existed in the border region.[27] Such efforts have only increased in the last three decades.

Interdependence characterized social relations in the region of what is today known as San Diego–Tijuana long before the imposition of a U.S.-Mexico boundary in the area. Diegueño Indians north and south of the present-day boundary were dependent on each other economically, spiritually, and medically before the arrival of the Spaniards.[28] As the area grew demographically, transboundary interdependence increased. Through the 1920s, for example, Tijuana's ranchers marketed hides and agricultural products in San Diego, while San Diego ranchers drove their cattle south of the boundary in search of greener pastures in times of drought.[29]

Levels of cooperation between San Diego and Tijuana, however, were not as intense as in a number of other places in the border region. Prior to Prohibition, Tijuana was a very small town; its population numbered only about 1,000 in 1920. But it grew rapidly in the context of Prohibition, as the city's population increased eightfold between 1920 and 1930. While Ambos Nogales and El Paso-Ciudad Juárez were able to work out local agreements to deal with transboundary smuggling and thus minimize the effects of (U.S) federal intervention on local transboundary relations, such an arrangement proved untenable in the San Diego–Tijuana border region. San Diego was sixteen miles north of Tijuana at the time and was a bastion of prohibitionist activism, a factor that played a significant role in influencing local transboundary relations. (While the city's geographic center is unchanged, its overall expansion since the 1920s and '30s, has, in some ways, lessened both the geographic and social distance between San Diego and Tijuana.) Opposition to Tijuana as a center of vice emerged in the early part of the twentieth century, resulting in Southern California voting "dry" in 1915. The next year, the United States barred all uniformed military from entering Mexico. As Secretary of the Navy explained in 1920, Tijuana was "one of the most infamous vice resorts on the Western Continent."[30]

Efforts by the Prohibitionist lobby and southern California politicians led to a daily closing of the boundary ports of entry at 6 P.M. in 1926. The San Diego and Tijuana chambers of commerce worked to end or liberalize boundary crossing hours, but to no avail. In trying to counter the early closing of the boundary and the associated negative images of Mexicans, for example, the Tijuana Chamber of Commerce wrote to U.S. president Herbert Hoover, "[W]e do not consider ourselves an inferior race whose contact means danger at night nor as a body afflicted with an infectious plague and consequently request equal consideration and the same treatment accorded other peoples."[31] But the region's cross-boundary social networks exercised little influence on U.S. boundary policy and practice in the context of Prohibition. Rather, it was

U.S. domestic political forces that shaped local policy.[32] Indeed, "Prohibition marked a watershed in government-border community relations."[33] The inability of some border communities like San Diego to resolve conflicts between hard-line Prohibitionists and economic interests opposed to strong restrictions led to federal government intervention in a number of localities. These interventions took various forms, including mediation between the opposing factions and the imposition of certain policies and practices relating to the closing times of official ports of entry.[34]

Despite such transboundary conflicts, economic integration, transnational kinship ties, and cultural miscenegation have all helped to lessen the social distance between San Diego and Tijuana by engendering concrete cross-boundary links. Growing cross-boundary integration, for example, has necessitated a variety of state efforts to address binational concerns, most notably in the area of environmental issues.[35] San Diego and Tijuana began exploring cooperation on matters of air pollution in 1976, two years before the United States and Mexico agreed to the establishment of a binational air-quality task force. The two municipalities also share water, and have long cooperated in matters of flood prevention and control.[36]

As the case of Prohibition illustrates, however, the relationship between Tijuana and San Diego has not just been one of free transboundary exchange and cooperation. Actions by both U.S. and Mexican authorities over time helped to turn the boundary from a mere cartographic ideal into a real, albeit highly porous, division—materially and ideologically. It is imperative for us to understand this process of division as it has significantly informed the nature of the cross-boundary integration experienced by Tijuana and San Diego. It is to this process that I now turn.

THE MAKING OF THE SAN DIEGO–TIJUANA BOUNDARY

As geographer Wilbur Zelinsky points out, "In every sovereign country of the modern world, the workings of the state have set their mark upon the land."[37] Landscapes reflect nationalism in a variety of forms including monuments, government buildings, place names, theme parks, and historic sites. But probably the most obvious manner in which one sees the embodiment of nationalism as state practice is the construction and reproduction of national territorial boundaries. San Diego stands out in this respect, as it was there that U.S. authorities began surveying the boundary.

The Treaty of Guadalupe Hidalgo designated the boundary between the United States and Mexico to be "one marine league due south of the southernmost point of the Port of San Diego." It also mandated that both governments appoint a commissioner and a surveyor who, within one year of the exchange of ratifications of the treaty, would "meet at the Port of San Diego, and proceed to run and mark the said Boundary in its whole course."[38] The

American team was unable to arrive by the May 30, 1849 deadline set by the treaty, however. Though they had set out in March for Panama, the discovery of gold in California in January of that year made transportation to San Diego extremely difficult, and the team of thirty-seven waited for more than one month in Panama before finally securing transportation that brought them to the boundary area only one day late, on June 1, 1849. The Mexican team seemingly had just as difficult a time as their U.S. counterparts, not reaching San Diego until July 3, despite having departed from Mexico City on April 18.[39]

On October 10, 1849, the U.S. and Mexican commissions met and officially designated the initial point of the boundary on the Pacific. The treaty mandated that the boundary follow the division between Upper (Alta) and Lower (Baja) California until the point where the Gila River emptied into the Colorado River (a point along the present-day boundary between Arizona and California). There was some controversy over the location of this point, but both sides reached agreement on January 28, 1850. During this time, the U.S. team experienced major financial difficulties, resulting in the resignation of many members, as Congress was extremely slow to appropriate the necessary funding. But by April 2, 1850, the binational commission had constructed monuments at frequent intervals for the first thrity miles east of the Pacific along the boundary—"the settled portion of the country."[40] For reasons that are unclear, authorities resurveyed and remarked the entire U.S.-Mexico boundary during the years 1891 to 1896, with a total of fifty-three monuments reerected along the boundary west of the mouth of the Gila River.[41]

The designation of the international boundary in the area of San Diego had been a major point of contention between the United States and Mexico during the negotiations that resulted in the Treaty of Guadalupe Hidalgo in 1848. The Mexican negotiators were under instructions to try to establish the boundary two leagues north of San Diego so that Mexico would retain hold of the valuable port of San Diego, but the United States was under strict instructions from President James Buchanan to include San Diego in the lands ceded by Mexico. As Buchanan explained, San Diego was "for every commercial purpose of nearly equal importance to us with that of San Francisco."[42] While the Mexican delegation tried to argue that San Diego had always been part of Baja California, the U.S. delegation was able to convincingly document that San Diego had always been part of Alta California and had once, in fact, briefly been the capital of the province.[43]

When the United States took over Alta California, U.S. authorities took over from Mexican authorities the collection of customs duties. The U.S. government first appointed two customs inspectors to patrol the California border region on horseback in 1871 to guard against the smuggling of tobacco, sugar, and cattle into the area of San Diego.[44] A few years later, customs officials established a presence at the boundary itself, operating out of a general store just north of the line and, later, out of the home of a customs official.[45] On the other side of the international divide, the Mexican government established a customs station in Tijuana in 1874 to collect revenue on goods headed for Ensenada, a site of American "colonization."[46]

The passage of the Chinese Exclusion Act in 1882 presented the first significant challenge to the U.S. Customs Service, as many Chinese used the overland route from Mexico to enter the United States clandestinely. Until 1882, the Bureau of Immigration, established during the Civil War, functioned merely as a gatherer of statistics. The passage of the Chinese Exclusion Act, however, resulted in the bureau receiving field operatives who worked from ports of entry along the international boundary under the jurisdiction of the Collectors of Customs. The so-called Chinese Inspectors in San Diego were responsible for patrolling 180 miles of boundary.[47] However, the fact that the smuggling of Chinese migrants into the United States was a highly lucrative and well-organized business, combined with the porosity of the boundary, ensured that most Chinese migrants who wanted to enter the United States from Mexico without authorization surely did so.[48] By 1910, the smuggling of opium concerned U.S Customs officials in San Ysidro as much as the smuggling of the Chinese—phenomena that were often related.[49]

The construction of the boundary as a physical line of surveillance and control was a slow process. As a U.S. Customs official described in an undated report probably from 1902 or 1903, there were only three U.S. authorities on the entire California boundary: two at "Tia Juana" (today known as San Ysidro) and one at Campo (thirty miles east of San Ysidro).[50] The writer went on to complain that "[e]xcept in the vicinity of Tia Juana and Campo . . . the entire boundary line is unguarded and open, presenting no barrier to free and unrestricted trade between the two countries. . . . Along the whole line between the coast and Jacumba [about sixty miles], stock of all kinds roam at will on either side of the line, a constant source of irritation and damage to the United States citizens along the line, most of whom are engaged in farming."[51] The number of Customs and Immigration officials increased thereafter, but boundary policing remained quite lax for the next few decades. Even though the Immigration Service began requiring passports in 1917, "standards of eligibility were low and the requirements were not strictly enforced." According to people who lived in the border region at the time, one could cross from Tijuana into San Ysidro before 1930 "as if a border did not exist."[52] In June 1907 there were only eight immigrant inspectors for the entire California boundary (whereas in 1904 there had been eleven plus a Chinese interpreter). This led the immigration inspector in charge to decry the impossibility of enforcing the Chinese Exclusion laws, especially in light of the new duties brought about by the Immigration Act of February 20, 1907, which required that all boundary crossers enter the United States through an official port of entry.[53]

The outbreak of World War I had a serious impact on San Diego and on the border region more generally, as the U.S. government established a number of military bases in the area during this period. In late 1917 the Immigration Service began requiring passports of all who wanted to cross from the United States into Mexico to limit the ability of individuals who were in the service of enemy governments to communicate with those governments. Such war-related hysteria, combined with the campaigning of the growing reformist movement against the "vices" of Tijuana and the instability brought about by the Mexican Revolution, led to an official closing of the boundary by U.S. authorities in December 1917, a closing that remained in effect for two years. That said, even during the war, the ability of U.S. authorities to patrol the boundary was very limited. As of February 1918, for example, there were five immigration inspectors stationed in Calexico, one in Campo, and four in Tia Juana. As the Supervising Inspector of the Mexican Border District wrote at the time, the inspectors, given the myriad demands on their time, "are able to give but little attention to patrol duty." And despite the nominal stationing of U.S. troops along the boundary at the time, it appears that their numbers were very much insufficient.[54] As the supervising inspector wrote about enforcement measures along the U.S.-Mexico boundary in general, "so long as the border is not adequately guarded, the restrictive measures employed at ports of entry simply tend to divert the illegal traffic to unguarded points, of which there are literally thousands."[55]

The 1930s marked a time of significantly increased boundary enforcement in the San Diego–Tijuana area, presumably because of the Depression. But, as of February 1934, the two Border Patrol subdistricts in southern California each only had a total of forty "Patrol Inspectors" or Border Patrol agents.[56] As of 1940, the number of Border Patrol agents in southern California remained unchanged.[57] Thus, it is not surprising that there were still gaping holes in boundary policing. A report by a U.S. naval intelligence officer argued that the section of the boundary in the vicinity of Tecate, for example, was "absolutely unguarded." As the officer surmised, "the border patrol agents ... are absolutely indifferent and apparently too lazy to take any action which would interfere with anyone desiring to cross the border in this area."[58]

Despite World War II, the U.S. port of entry in San Ysidro remained open (unlike during World War I), but there were boundary-related restrictions specific to the war. Immigration authorities, for example, inspected all individuals leaving the United States in order to detect German nationals, a process begun even before the Japanese bombing of Pearl Harbor, which led to the United States entering World War II on the side of the Allies. Immigration laws also prohibited the taking out of the country any written materials, thus resulting in the confiscation of books, letters, and the like at the boundary.[59]

Just as the Border Patrol on the national scale saw significant growth induced by the war in the early 1940s, so did the Border Patrol in southern California, with the San Diego area (the Chula Vista subdistrict) receiving the lion's share of the increase. Between June 1940 and December 1943, the number of Patrol Inspectors increased by 50 percent in the Chula Vista subdistrict (subdistricts later became known as sectors), reaching a total of sixty.[60] Given the unavailability at this time of official documentation on the size of the Border Patrol in the San Diego area during the 1950s and 1960s, it is not possible to know to what extent the agency's staffing increased (assuming it did) over the next two decades.[61] But it is likely that, whatever its size, the Border Patrol was unable to meet the growing challenge represented by the flow of unauthorized immigrants through the San Diego portion of the international boundary.

U.S. boundary enforcement efforts were not limited to the deployment of Border Patrol agents. Such efforts also included observation towers along the boundary and physical barriers in the form of fences. As early as 1936, Civilian Conservation Corps members began building a "high, barbed-wire fence strung on metal poles set close together" going west from Tecate, the intention of which was to join an apparently similar and already existing fence that began at the Pacific Ocean and went all the way to the Marone Valley, about eight miles west of Tecate.[62] It is unclear as to whether or not this fence was ever completed, but even if it had been, such physical obstacles seem to have had a very limited effect; it is probable that unauthorized immigrants and smugglers easily circumvented these barriers or cut holes in them after their construction. At a U.S. Senate hearing in San Ysidro in 1948, for example, a local Immigration and Naturalization Service (INS) official explained, "At present time, with no fence worthy the name [sic], it is very easy for any alien who is turned back at the port . . . to cross within a short distance of the port."[63]

According to a 1956 letter from INS Commissioner General Joseph Swing, fences (of an unspecified length) existed along the boundary in San Ysidro and Calexico in California and in Nogales and San Luis in Arizona to prevent smuggling, unauthorized entry, and the uncontrolled passage of animals. The location of such fences, according to Swing, was a reflection of "the density of population in adjacent areas and . . . the volume of illegal crossings." Officially, the Mexican government fully approved of such fences, at least as indicated by the 1955 report of the Joint Mexican-American Migratory Labor Commission, in order "to assist the Mexican and United States border authorities in deterring the illegal crossing of the border into the United States and Mexico."[64]

As the 1970s approached, the boundary enforcement capacity of U.S. authorities in the area of San Diego was formidable, at least in relation to what had existed in the early part of the twentieth century. But it is also clear that the enforcement capacity was very much inadequate given the geographical expanse for which U.S. boundary authorities were responsible. The rapidly intensifying links between Tijuana and San Diego and, more generally, the United States and Mexico only served to undermine further the enforcement capacity of the INS. As a result of these links, and the strength of the one-way migratory highway from Mexico to the United States, San Diego became an increasingly important destination and transit point for unauthorized migrants from Mexico. This became especially true following the termination of the Bracero Program in 1964, which led to the (previously legal) flow of migratory labor simply going "underground."[65] We can thus assume that the scale of unauthorized immigration across the boundary in the San Diego area increased at a far greater rate than did the capacity of U.S. authorities (in the form, for example, of the number of Border Patrol agents) to police the boundary. In this regard, the *relative* strength of U.S. boundary policing efforts in the San Diego area declined significantly over time vis-à-vis the amount of illegal boundary-related activity, leading to a further blurring of the distinction between Mexico and the United States in southern California.

At the same time, however, the ability of state efforts to control immigration certainly grew as such efforts became institutionalized legally and practically. These efforts also had the effect of rendering the boundary and its associated practices less problematic as they became increasingly "normal" in the eyes of the domestic population. In this sense, the state played a key role in constructing social boundaries between those who belonged and those who did not. It is the construction of these nationally based social distinctions that the next section examines.

CREATING DIFFERENCE ACROSS THE BOUNDARY

Modern territorial states implement a variety of practices to distinguish between citizens and "aliens."[66] State practices relating to immigration and boundary policing subject people to the law, distinguishing between those who belong (and under what conditions) and those who do not, thus constructing subjects and identities. Such "dividing practices" along the U.S.-Mexico boundary have been crucial in constructing U.S. and Mexican identity.[67] According to historian George Sánchez, writing about the situation in El Paso, Texas, in the late 1920s, the creation of the U.S. Border Patrol was "crucial in defining the Mexican as 'the other,' the 'alien,' in the region. . . . [U.S. immigration officials] would consistently denigrate those who crossed at the bridge, even if their papers were perfectly legal. Eventually crossing the border became a painful and abrupt event permeated by an atmosphere of racism and control—an event that clearly demarcated one society from another."[68] Even well before that—as early as 1903—U.S. immigration officials in El Paso would occasionally fumigate people arriving from Mexico.[69] In this regard, the establishment of a boundary and immigration enforcement apparatus not only helped to define Mexico and its citizens, but also helped to define the United States, the boundary, and the citizenry within. The changes in immigration and boundary policing during the first three decades of the twentieth century were manifestations of a process that gave much greater significance to the boundary line between Mexico and the United States, making it "a much more rigid line of demarcation." U.S. boundary policing and inspection of immigrants "made it clear that passage across this barrier in the desert was a momentous occasion, a break from the past."[70]

It was during this period (1900–1930) that U.S. authorities first began to use the label "alien" to describe Mexicans in the Southwest; it was an outgrowth of the imposition of a new, legal-geographical context in the border region. The creators of the new laws were generally people outside of the social networks that encompassed the border region, while the subjects of these laws were largely those whose had deep, prenational roots in this transnational region known as "the border." The construction of the boundary made Mexicans outsiders in their own society (if conceived of in nonterritorial terms). As Sánchez observes, "Though Mexicans knew that they would have to come to terms with the new reality, the irony of history was surely not lost on them. They were now interlopers on familiar land, even as their labor became increasingly crucial to its economic development and they had begun to settle their families in the United States. Mexican immigrants learned to live with the contradiction, partly because they continued to feel wholly Mexican, but mostly because they could do little to change their lot."[71] As the Border Patrol and boundary enforcement grew over time and space, Mexico and the United States and their respective national citizenries became increasingly defined (at least in part) by U.S. state practice along the international divide.

Until 1924, one could clandestinely cross the southern U.S. border "in either direction, at almost any point from Brownsville to San Diego, with the greatest of ease."[72] And, once in the country, the unauthorized immigrant faced little risk of apprehension. As Jorge Bustamante explains, "Previous to the creation of the Border Patrol, it was only necessary for the Mexican worker [without visa] not to implicate himself in any action involving the intervention of the police or the judicial authorities in order to consider himself completely safe on the U.S. streets and roads and fairly free to choose the most convenient work. Only a judge could decree his deportation."[73] The creation of the U.S. Border Patrol, however, raised the costs for unauthorized Mexican migrants, effectively making the "wetback" a lawbreaker and altering his patterns of behavior, most significantly because of the subsequent change in the relationship between the immigrant worker and the employer. U.S. immigration officials could now apprehend the "illegal" and send him back to Mexico.[74] Of course, the process of "illegalizing" the unauthorized immigrant was gradual as the necessary state apparatus required time and resources to grow. The Act of March 4, 1929, for example, made the entry of non-citizens at locations other than those designated by the U.S. government or by means of "a willfully false or misleading representation" a misdemeanor, and made reentry of a previously deported "alien" a felony. Both "crimes," according to the act, were punishable by fine and/or imprisonment.[75]

Such legal developments were significant elements of a process of establishing and hardening the juridical distinctions between "citizens" and "aliens," and "legals" and "illegals." Similarly, the mass deportations of Mexicans and Mexican Americans that took place beginning in 1929 helped to differentiate those with full (U.S.) citizenship rights from those who were temporary and often extralegal workers. Arguably, this outcome was most significant within the Mexican-origin population in the border region. As Josiah Heyman argues in the case of the zone shared by Arizona and Northern Sonora, "The result was that kin networks spread on both sides of the border before 1929 became differentiated into distinct branches, Mexican and Mexican American. This does not mean that they no longer see each other, or do not send money across the border, or forget their kinship, or cease to immigrate from Mexico to the United States. But as state control of immigration and citizenship rights grew, the international boundary increasingly defined two different populations—'Sonora' and 'Arizona'—in a form that had not existed before."[76]

That said, it is important to make the obvious point that the construction of insiders and outsiders was and is not a process unilaterally undertaken by the United States. Mexico has certainly played a significant role in helping to define the "other" as perceived by U.S. society. For a variety of reasons, Mexico City generally viewed Tijuana with suspicion, as it was geographically and, to a significant extent, socioeconomically and culturally cut off from the Mexican heartland. Indeed, as late as the 1940s, there was neither a paved road nor a railroad from Tijuana to the interior, and the U.S. dollar was the dominant currency in the city until the 1970s.[77]

Mexicans from the interior have long criticized their compatriots living in the border region for their adoption of *norteamericano* ways and susceptibility to criminal enterprises. Accusations of "de-Mexicanization" have been especially persistent. Concerns of such have led to efforts by Mexico City to increase awareness of Mexican history and culture in border cities. As part of PRONAF in the 1960s, for example, the Mexican government constructed a variety of cultural and educational centers in the border region, which the country's secretary of public education targeted for increased dissemination of books on Mexico and for the development of school programs aimed at strengthening national identity. The Mexican government's establishment of the National Commission of the Defense of the Spanish Language was probably the most obvious manifestation of its concerns around "de-Mexicanization." The Commission focused its efforts to protect Spanish from the encroachment of English in three "disaster" zones: (1) Mexico City, Guadalajara, and Monterrey; (2) centers of tourism; and (3) northern border cities.[78]

Such efforts of the Mexican state to "Mexicanize" the border region undoubtedly helped to strengthen the U.S.-Mexico boundary as a binational social divide. In a more obvious sense, the very fact that Mexico has established ports of entry and customs inspections along its boundary with the

United States has helped to fortify the U.S.-Mexico boundary as well as to define Mexico and the United States. At times, moreover, the Mexican government has even cooperated directly with the United States in policing the boundary. One of the most famous examples followed the assassination of U.S. president John F. Kennedy in 1963 when Mexican authorities completely sealed off ports of entry into Mexico for nineteen hours to prevent a possible escape by the assassin.[79]

Mexico has also used the boundary to control the entry of "undesirable" persons from the United States. In the late 1960s and early 1970s, for example, Mexican officials prevented U.S. "hippies" and men with long hair from entering Tijuana at various times for fear that they were influencing Mexican nationals in terms of dress and antiwork attitudes.[80] In this manner, albeit to a far lesser degree than the U.S. government, the Mexican government helped to lay the basis for the heightened sense of difference that was to inform the rise of concerns surrounding the border and unauthorized immigration in the 1970s.

In terms of San Diego, there certainly was a strong sense among the local population by the early twentieth century that (Anglo) San Diegans were different from their Mexican neighbors. One striking manifestation of this perception was San Diego's participation in the mass deportation of Mexicans and Mexican Americans that took place in the context of the Great Depression beginning in 1929.[81] This sense of difference was one based on, among other factors, nationality, and thus was inherently territorial in nature. As the boundary became more real, so did the sense of difference.[82]

Yet if newspaper coverage is any indication, border issues were of little concern to San Diegans in the first few decades of the twentieth century. *The San Diego Union,* for example, carried only a handful of border-related reports during the 1920s, '30s, and '40s. The 1950s saw a dramatic increase in the newspaper's reporting on matters related to unauthorized immigration and the border region in southern California—a result, to a significant extent, of the INS's Operation Wetback.[83] In the late 1950s, however, the major border-related concern of San Diego, at least as reported in the *Union,* was the perceived threat that Tijuana represented to San Diego youths attracted to the vice-ridden Mexican border city.[84] As the *Union* reported in paraphrasing the remarks of a San Diego sheriff stated, "youths could get into trouble with narcotics, liquor, and women across the border." Such concerns led to the establishment in 1953 of a checkpoint at the entry gate into Tijuana in San Ysidro.[85] San Diego County sheriffs maintained the checkpoint for a number of years on a nightly basis and annually turned back thousands of young people unescorted by, or without a note of permission from, a parent or guardian.[86]

Unauthorized immigration seemed to be of such little concern at the time that the primary reason given by James Utt, a San Diego congressman, to build a boundary fence from the Pacific Ocean to a point ten miles inland was to prevent diseased Mexican cattle from crossing the boundary and potentially contaminating dairy cattle on the U.S. side of the line.[87] Part of the reason for such low concern might have been the fact that there was very little labor demand for unauthorized immigrants in the San Diego area; such demand was "being met very satisfactorily by Braceros," according to a 1956 Border Patrol intelligence report. Thus, the intended destination of most unauthorized migrants crossing the boundary in the San Diego region was the Los Angeles area.[88] In this regard, unauthorized migrants did not have a relatively high level of visibility in the San Diego area, at least through the early 1960s.

Probably the greatest perceived threats from Tijuana and, by extension, Mexico were those relating to vices. Given Tijuana's origins as a site for U.S. pleasure seekers to satisfy their needs for sex and illicit substances, "the international boundary between Mexico and the United States has long been imagined as a border that separates a pure from an impure body, a virtuous body from a sinful one."[89] For this reason, many in southern California have long seen the need to protect themselves from Mexico, especially in terms of drugs, through enhanced boundary policing.

The smuggling of illegal substances has been of concern to U.S. boundary authorities since the linking of unauthorized Chinese immigration and the trafficking of opium into the United States around 1910. The passage of Prohibition only added to such concern as many southern Californians attempted to smuggle alcohol into the United States from Tijuana.[90] Opium remained a popular form of contraband for many decades, but during the 1940s and '50s, other drugs came to surpass opium in importance—especially marijuana. Heroin, morphine, and cocaine also began to rise as drugs of choice. Efforts to thwart the flow of such substances into the United States led to American efforts to enlist Mexican cooperation from time to time. As early as 1920, U.S. authorities solicited Mexico's help in stymieing the flow of alcohol into the United States, an effort that met with little success given the lucrative and sophisticated nature of the smuggling business.[91]

Similar to the movement of people across the U.S.-Mexico boundary before the rise in immigration restrictions in the early 1900s, the illegal drug trade between the United States and Mexico has its roots in legal cross-boundary commerce in marijuana in the 1800s. During that time, marijuana from Mexico, along with a variety of opiates and coca-based products, was welcome in the United States as a cure for various medical ailments. Even after marijuana became illegal in the early twentieth century, U.S. authorities showed little concern about small-scale shipments of marijuana from Mexico through the 1950s, possibly due to the fact that consumption was largely limited to populations of Mexican origin in the United States.[92] As demand for marijuana within the United States grew and a conservative-led war on crime and drugs emerged in the 1960s,[93] however, the attitudes of U.S. authorities hardened.

Mexico began its own drug production eradication campaign in 1948 when the country's soldiers began destroying marijuana stalks and opium poppies by beating the plants with sticks. The manual labor eradication campaigns were not able to keep pace with growing production, so the United States sent the Mexican government aircraft and other military equipment from the Korean War as well as U.S. advisers in 1961.[94] Official and popular opinion began to increasingly associate "dope" with Mexico and the boundary. As early as 1957, the head of California Bureau of Narcotic Enforcement advocated closing the boundary to stop the flow of illicit substances into the United States.[95] Such official advocacy probably influenced groups like the California chapter of the Veterans of Foreign Wars to also call for a closing of the boundary at its 1960 convention for identical reasons.[96] Drug production, however, still continued to climb for identical reasons, fueled by growing demand in the United States. In the context of the growing 1960s war on crime and drugs, the trans-boundary drug trade and increasing drug consumption by young people in the United States became one of the primary domestic political causes of the law-and-order administration of President Richard Nixon.

The Nixon administration thus launched Operation Intercept in September 1969.[97] The program included "the use of pursuit planes to force down suspected smuggler aircraft; expanded radar watches along the Mexican border; reinforced Navy and Coast Guard patrols; possibly employing PT boats; extension of border fences and the use of dogs to help spot narcotics caches."[98] The operation, the most controversial aspect of which was the searching of every person and vehicle entering the United States, greatly interrupted cross-boundary traffic and border commerce. The purpose of Intercept was to compel Mexico to "cooperate" at greater levels with U.S. antidrug efforts. U.S. pressure soon compelled Mexico to agree to step up measures to eradicate drug production and trafficking. Three weeks after launching Intercept, U.S. authorities ended the operation, announcing a new U.S.-Mexico program to combat illicit drugs entitled Operation Cooperation. Although Intercept had no immediate measurable effect on illegal drugs entering the U.S. from Mexico, it succeeded in raising the profile of the border–illegal drug nexus and in forcing Mexican cooperation with U.S. state objectives.[99] In doing so, the Nixon administration significantly contributed to the linking of "law and order" issues, including unauthorized immigration, with the U.S.-Mexico boundary.[100]

The making of the boundary in the area of San Diego and Tijuana was not merely a process of building up the boundary in a physical sense. Just as on the national scale, it was necessary to construct social boundaries between those who belonged and those who did not. The "legitimacy" (as perceived in terms of public opinion) of U.S. state efforts to control immigration grew as boundary policing efforts became institutionalized legally and practically. In this sense, the state effectively helped to produce social boundaries between "Americans" and "Mexicans," "citizens" and "aliens," thus setting the stage for the "war on illegals" in the United States that has emerged over the last couple of decades. Such a situation would soon help to engender a rising sentiment in favor of "beefing up the border" and would provide cannon fodder to those in favor of immigration restriction more generally, locally and nationally.

As unauthorized immigration into the area of San Diego increased over the course of the twentieth century and distinctions between Mexico and the United States seemed to be increasingly breaking down in southern California, the roots of an anti-immigrant backlash, with a focus on unauthorized migrants from Mexico, were developing. Increasing sameness or regional and binational integration, thus, led to a perceived need to heighten difference, a sentiment that would peak in southern California in the early 1990s and facilitate the emergence of Operation Gatekeeper in 1994. Gatekeeper, of course, was not simply an outgrowth of objective factors, but also a manifestation of a complex set of cultural and ideological factors on the scale of the United States, California, and San Diego as well. Thus, it remains to explore the changing national and local political climates that intersected and led to the emergence of Gatekeeper, a task undertaken in chapter 4. Furthermore, these shifts need situating within a larger ideological context, one in which the cultural construction of the undesirable immigrant and its relationship to contemporary anti-"illegal" (as well as antiauthorized) immigrant sentiment have taken place, a topic I explore in chapter 5.

The Bounding of the United States
and the Emergence of Operation Gatekeeper

When I asked one Customs agent about it [boundary enforcement], he simply said: "It's control out of control. There's just no other way to put it."[1]

—Douglas Kent Hall, *The Border*

By flooding the state with 2 million illegal aliens to date, and increasing that figure each of the following 10 years, Mexicans in California would number 15 million to 20 million by 2004. During those 10 years about 5 million to 8 million Californians would have emigrated to other states. If these trends continued, a Mexico-controlled California could vote to establish Spanish as the sole language of California, 10 million more English-speaking Californians could flee, and there could be a state-wide vote to leave the Union and annex California to Mexico.

—Linda R. Hayes, Southern California
media director for California Proposition 187, 1994[2]

Beginning in the early 1970s, the United States experienced a sharp rise in official and public sentiment in favor of boundary enforcement and immigration restriction in the United States. Southern California, and San Diego in particular, were among the hotbeds of these feelings. These political and ideological developments took place on the national and local scales and were the medium-term roots of Operation Gatekeeper. These changes dovetailed with a heightening of enforcement activities along the southwest boundary with Mexico and, more specifically, in the San Diego area from the mid-1970s until the early 1990s.

The birth of Gatekeeper is also tied to numerous short-term factors. In California in the 1990s, these included various local political initiatives undertaken, most notably by then governor Pete Wilson, to link worsening socioeconomic conditions to unauthorized immigration. These local initiatives intersected with a number of national-scale events and developments, as well as with actions taken by the Clinton administration and members of California's congressional delegation within what became an increasingly polemical debate over unauthorized migrants. Taken together, they facilitated a greatly heightened sentiment in favor of increased boundary and immigration enforcement. In a context of a perceived "crisis" of "illegal" immigration, the emergence of the Border Patrol's Operation Blockade/Hold-the-Line in El Paso in 1993 served to provide the intellectual and political inspiration of sorts for Gatekeeper's creation and implementation.

The emergence of Operation Gatekeeper—or, more specifically, the emergence of the context that led to the Immigration and Naturalization Service (INS) strategy's implementation—demonstrates the power of the boundary and its related sociogeographical practices in forming an almost reflexive consciousness in favor of boundary and immigration enforcement.[3] The social construction of the territory of the United States and, by necessity, the boundary with Mexico, have taken place both in a physical and sociopsychological sense. In this regard, the period covered herein illustrates the growing material and ideological reality of the U.S.-Mexico boundary and the increasing social acceptability of the boundary's accompanying practices and institutions. Gatekeeper not only represents an expansion of the U.S. state in terms of its power and functions, but also its ongoing attempt to pacify the border region. Finally, the crystallization of long-, medium-, and short-term trends emanating from multiple scales that resulted in the establishment of Operation Gatekeeper illustrates the dialectical relationship between the national state and the local. The national state did not simply impose the "nation" and its associated social and territorial boundaries on southern California. Californians were also very much agents in constructing the social and territorial boundaries between Mexico and the United States in the area of San Diego and Tijuana. In this sense, local agents and institutions have played a significant role in constructing the United States.[4]

THE RISE OF THE "ILLEGAL" AND THE STATE CREATION OF THE "CRISIS" OF UNAUTHORIZED IMMIGRATION

While the 1950s and '60s were times of relatively liberal sentiment toward immigration, the 1970s marked the beginning of the rise of neo-restrictionism.[5] Prior to that time, the U.S.-Mexico boundary rarely received significant national attention,[6] but beginning in the late 1960s, there was growing public perception of the international boundary with Mexico as "out of control," as a dangerously porous line of defense against unprecedented numbers of "illegal" immigrants entering the United States from Mexico.

A number of factors dovetailed to precipitate the perception of a crisis of "illegal" immigration, one associated mostly with immigrants from Mexico. The advent of a Chicano civil rights movement in the late 1960s, whose most notable accomplishments took place in the border region, led many American elites to fear the rise of an "American Quebec" in the U.S. Southwest.[7] At the same time, the early and mid-1970s saw the emergence of the energy crisis and an economic downturn in the United States. As in the past, economic recession proved to be an important factor facilitating the rise of immigration restrictionist sentiment.[8] Simultaneously, apprehensions of unauthorized immigrants by the U.S. Border Patrol were rising rapidly, approaching the levels that preceded the implementation of Operation Wetback in 1954. In this context "illegal immigration" and "border control" emerged as topics of intense media interest around 1973. Indeed, all the major media, beginning in the 1970s, featured stories highlighting the putative problems associated with unauthorized immigration, and largely that from Mexico.[9]

A variety of federal government officials and national politicians, along with a compliant media, helped to construct the perception of a crisis and to stoke public fears. This is not to suggest that the "problem" of unauthorized immigration was a mere mirage. There were certainly a number of real events and developments that prorestrictionist forces were able to draw upon to substantiate their arguments in favor of enhanced boundary and immigration enforcement. But what a society deems as a "problem" or a "crisis" and how it understands that problem is far from inevitable. Why one particular issue becomes especially salient—as opposed to a whole host of other potential "problems"—is a matter that requires an explanation that not only contextualizes the putative problem, but also establishes the social actors that construct its popular image. Here, the role of state actors in producing the "illegal alien" as a threat to the sociopolitical fabric of the United States is particularly important.

As with Operation Wetback, the person heading the INS during the Ford administration (1974–76) was from the military—in this case, ex-marine general Leonard Chapman. INS Commissioner Chapman greatly contributed to the perception of a crisis through his outspokenness about unauthorized immigration and the problems allegedly associated with it (such as poverty and unemployment), and his effective use of the media platform afforded by his position.[10] Even President Gerald Ford tried to blame the country's economic problems on unauthorized immigrants, stating in 1976, "The main problem is how to get rid of those 6 to 8 million aliens who are interfering with our economic prosperity."[11] Not surprisingly, both nonstate and state actors began agitating for increased resources for the INS and, especially, boundary policing in the 1970s.

Increasingly politicians and public officials began putting forth dire warnings of the security "threat" to the United States represented by unauthorized immigration, often employing metaphors suggesting an invasion. William Saxbe, the U.S. attorney general under Ford, for example, called the presence of unauthorized immigrants "a severe national crisis." Citing jobs, crime, and welfare costs, Saxbe called for the deportation of one million "illegal aliens" whom he described as mostly Mexicans.[12] Former Central Intelligence Agency director William Colby sounded the alarm about a future emergence of a "Spanish-speaking Quebec in the U.S. Southwest" and stated that unauthorized Mexican immigration was a greater future threat to the United States than the Soviet Union.[13] "The most obvious threat," Colby warned, "is the fact that ... there are going to be 120 million Mexicans by the end of the century.... [The Border Patrol] will not have enough bullets to stop them."[14]

The problem of unauthorized immigration from Mexico even appeared in television "entertainment" programs.[15] The press played a key role in legitimating the perception of a "Mexican invasion" by uncritically reporting INS reports alleging that unauthorized migrants were producers of poverty, crime, and joblessness (among U.S. citizens).[16] INS Commissioner Chapman fanned the flames by frequently putting forth wildly exaggerated and inconsistent estimates of the number of unauthorized immigrants in the United States. As he reported to the House Subcommittee on Immigration, Citizenship and International Law, "We now estimate ... that the number of illegal aliens in this country may be between 4 and 12 million."[17] Chapman also effectively linked, in the minds of the U.S. public, unauthorized immigration to a whole host of social ills. In arguing for increased resources for the INS and employer sanctions before a congressional subcommittee in 1974, for instance, the commissioner claimed that he could open up one million jobs "virtually overnight" for unemployed Americans.[18] As he wrote in *The Reader's Digest*, "[I]f we could locate and deport three to four million illegals who currently hold jobs in the United States, replacing them with citizens and legal residents, we could reduce our own unemployment dramatically—*as much as 50 percent*."[19] In addition, Chapman played a major role in making unauthorized immigration and Mexican immigration synonymous by grossly overstating the percentage of total extralegal migrants from Mexico. One report cited Chapman as claiming that 90 percent of "illegals" were of Mexican origin.[20]

This media activism arguably facilitated an increasingly anti-immigrant public sentiment as evidenced by opinion polls. While public opinion was rather positively inclined toward immigrants in the 1960s, with less than 30 percent of sampled adults responding negatively to legal immigration, 42 percent thought that immigration was excessive by 1977. A 1980 Gallup poll discovered that 66 percent of respondents desired an immigration moratorium until the U.S. unemployment rate improved. And by 1984, a Roper survey showed that 72 percent of the public considered immigration levels excessive.[21] This trend continued through the 1980s, reaching its apex in the early 1990s. According to a 1986 New York Times/CBS poll, 49 percent favored a decrease in immigration rates; the figure rose to 61 percent in June of 1993.[22]

The roots of growing congressional activism around, and media attention toward extralegal immigration go back to 1971, when Representative Peter Rodino (Democrat, New Jersey) began a series of hearings that took place throughout the country on unauthorized immigration. Out of these hearings (1971–1972) emerged a five-volume congressional document on the putative dangers of unauthorized immigration and the negative effects of "illegal" immigrants on employment and wage rates.[23] In early 1972, a House immigration subcommittee drew up recommendations that the House Judiciary Committee, led by Rodino, endorsed. The resulting legislation became identified with Rodino and served as the basis for much of the congressional debates on issues relating to unauthorized immigration and boundary enforcement during the 1970s and 1980s. At the center of Rodino's proposals was an employer sanctions bill similar to one successfully passed in the California assembly in 1971 that established fines against employers hiring unauthorized workers.[24]

Members of the U.S. House of Representatives introduced a number of employer sanctions bills over the next few years that passed by wide margins.[25] But these died in the Senate because of the opposition of Senator James Eastland (Democrat, Mississippi), the chair of the Senate Judiciary Committee and a cotton grower with strong ties to southern agribusiness. Eastland refused to allow hearings to go forth on the Senate's versions of the bills, despite strong support for the legislation from the Nixon and Ford administrations. Ford established a cabinet-level Domestic Council of Illegal Migration in 1975, chaired by his attorney general, that recommended an employer sanctions law and a legalization program.[26]

The Carter administration (1977–1980) continued the trend. At the very beginning of his administration, President Jimmy Carter established, in the words of *The Washington Post*, "a special Cabinet-level panel to deal with the rapidly increasing problem of illegal aliens."[27] A number of months later—in the summer of 1977—Carter announced his immigration plan, which included a call to double the size of the Border Patrol and closely resembled that of Representative Rodino.[28] In launching the proposal, Carter argued that unauthorized immigrants "had breached [the] Nation's immigration laws, displaced many American citizens from jobs, and placed an increased financial burden on many state and local governments."[29] His bill included employer sanctions, a legalization program, and enhanced boundary enforcement, but it was ultimately unsuccessful. It was in the aftermath of this temporary defeat that Carter established his U.S. Select Commission on Immigration and Refugee Policy in October 1978 (also known as the Hesburgh Commission after its chair, Father Theodore Hesburgh).[30]

This "blue ribbon" commission to examine immigration issues helped to reframe official debate around immigration. Its charge was "to study and evaluate ... existing laws, policies, and procedures governing the admission of immigrants and refugees to the United States and to make such administrative and legislative recommendations to the President and to the Congress as are appropriate."[31] In its final report,[32] the commission identified "the problem of undocumented/illegal migration" as "most pressing": "The message is clear—most U.S. citizens believe that the half-open door of undocumented/illegal migration should be closed."[33] In his personal views attached to the report, Hesburgh argued that the United States had to "get illegal immigration under control and continue a legal immigration policy,"[34] thus implicitly linking the continuance of state-sanctioned immigration to the successful implementation of practices to deter unauthorized immigration.[35]

The Select Commission's final report called for a substantial increase in resources for boundary policing and interior enforcement, the passage of legislation making it illegal for employers to hire unauthorized immigrants, and the establishment of a program to legalize unauthorized immigrants already in the United States. In championing both increased boundary and interior enforcement, however, the commission acknowledged that existing enforcement efforts against unauthorized immigrants were selective given the disproportionate amount of resources focused on the border region as opposed to interior enforcement, thus serving to create a disproportionate emphasis on unauthorized immigrants from Mexico and, to a lesser extent, Central America. The commission argued that such an emphasis was necessary and should continue given the difficulty of implementing effective employer sanctions and that it was "both more humane and cost effective to deter people from entering the United States than it is to locate and remove people from the interior."[36] More generally, enhanced enforcement efforts against unauthorized immigration were a necessary precondition for the implementation of a legalization program; otherwise such a program "could serve as an inducement for further illegal immigration."[37] Although the commission only had the power to make recommendations, its recommendations, and the assumptions that informed them, served as the basis for subsequent debate and legislation regarding immigration control. Its final report proved more powerful than it might have given its publication at a time of a rising tide of immigration restrictionist sentiment and a growing perception of an immigration crisis.

If any single event contributed to the crisis mentality that was increasingly informing much of the public debate on issues of boundary policing and immigration, it was the Mariel boatlift from Cuba, which saw about 125,000 Cuban refugees arriving along the Miami coast in 1980.[38] Advocates of enhanced boundary policing and stricter immigration laws quickly seized upon the influx of Cuban refugees to support their positions.[39] As Norman and Naomi Flink Zucker have noted, "Domestically, the watchword was control. Immigrants, refugees, asylum seekers, illegal entrants, all were lumped together in the public mind as opportunists trying to defraud a system that was 'out of control.' Election campaigns from the local to the presidential level would sound the alarm that Americans had lost control, were losing their country—to crime, to welfare, and to immigration. And the Mariel boatlift had come to symbolize all three."[40] Immigration control issues increasingly resonated with the public in Mariel's aftermath. A growing number of Americans now perceived their country as under siege from without. Such fears culminated (at least for the time being) in the passage of the 1986 Immigration Reform and Control Act (IRCA).[41] Not coincidentally, the IRCA incorporated, albeit in an altered form, the main recommendations of the U.S. Select Commission on Immigration and Refugee Policy.

One year after the Select Commission had published its recommendations, the first versions of what would become the IRCA emerged out of the Senate and House judiciary committees, both closely mirroring the commission's proposals. While the bill (known as Simpson-Mazzoli after its Senate and House sponsors, respectively) easily passed the Senate, concerns of civil rights advocates, the U.S. Chamber of Commerce, and agribusiness effectively defeated it in the House. A number of changes over the years, most notably a clause that released employers from the responsibility of having to verify the authenticity of their employees' documents and a provision that provided temporary residency and eventual eligibility for citizenship to anyone who had worked in agriculture for at least ninety days, led to the bill's passage in October 1986.[42]

The growing concerns of public officials and the public at large, as well as increased legislative activism surrounding unauthorized immigration, had real effects on the U.S.-Mexico boundary, leading to an unprecedented growth in federal resources dedicated to boundary policing beginning in the late 1970s. Combined with a "war on drugs" begun during the Reagan administration, efforts to fight unauthorized immigration in the border region had a transformational effect on the nature and scale of boundary policing. It is to this process that I now turn.

MAKING WAR ON "ILLEGALS" AND DRUGS IN THE BORDER REGION

The increase in federal resources dedicated to boundary enforcement commenced in the latter half of the administration of President Jimmy Carter. Growth in INS enforcement efforts during the last years of the Carter administration laid the basis for a boundary buildup process that was to accelerate significantly in the succeeding administrations. Yet, in terms of personnel and funding (to a lesser extent), the Border Patrol only grew slightly during the 1978–80 period. Although there was strong sentiment in Congress for significantly increasing the size of the Border Patrol, the Carter administration argued for postponing any such potential increase until the Select Commission had completed its report. Nevertheless, the INS underwent significant qualitative changes during the Carter years. There was a significant upgrading of equipment, for example, ranging from increased construction of fences to the deployment of helicopters and improved ground sensors.[43]

After Ronald Reagan assumed the U.S. presidency in 1981, the INS expanded to unprecedented levels. His administration used the issue of unauthorized immigration to galvanize political sentiment for "regaining control of our borders." At times, the administration presented unauthorized immigration as a national security matter.[44] As Reagan warned in 1984, "The simple truth is that we've lost control of our borders and no nation can do that and survive"[45]; he also justified his administration's controversial interventionist policies in Central America on the basis of stemming the influx of refugees into the United States. He contended that if Congress did not approve aid to right wing forces in the region there would be "a tidal wave of refugees—and this time they'll be 'feet people' and not boat people—swarming into our country seeking safe haven from communist repression to our south."[46]

Congressional funding appropriations increased 130 percent and staff positions grew 41 percent for the INS during Reagan's eight years (1981–1988). The majority of these funds (60 percent) and new staff positions (82 percent) went to the INS Enforcement Division. Increasing the amount and quality of immigration enforcement-related infrastructure and equipment was one of the INS's primary foci during Reagan's time in office. U.S. officials justified much of the increase on the grounds of fighting drug trafficking during Reagan's second term, although much of the increase helped immigration enforcement as well. The INS planned, funded, and/or constructed a number of new Border Patrol stations and checkpoints and expanded its detention centers. Much of this new construction took place in the Southwest, an obvious indication of the agency's geographical focus.[47]

In the context of the Reagan administration's growing drug war, the Border Patrol became increasingly preoccupied with drug enforcement following the 1986 passage of the IRCA. This contrasted with its earlier, almost exclusive focus on unauthorized immigration. Consequently, the INS "cross-designated" (deputized) Border Patrol agents as Drug Enforcement Administration (DEA) and Customs agents to fight drug and contraband smuggling, respectively. This shift is a manifestation of what Timothy Dunn refers to as the "militarization" of boundary and immigration enforcement, a development with its roots in the Carter administration, but which increased significantly during Reagan's tenure. In the mid-1980s, for example, the INS participated in a multiagency effort in the Department of Justice known as the Alien Border Control Committee (ABCC). The ABCC's charge of creating contingency plans for so-called immigration emergencies and the roundup of "alien terrorists and undesirables" was probably the most obvious instance of boundary militarization. An ABCC subcommittee was responsible for undertaking "a review of contingency plans for removal of selected aliens from the U.S. and sealing off the borders." Other instances of boundary enforcement militarization included the Border Patrol's joining the multiagency Southwest Border Drug Task Force, and the establishment of joint Border Patrol/local police foot patrols in certain border locales. The Reagan administration directly linked extralegal immigration to the political and social instability that was pervasive in Central America in the 1980s. It feared parallel (and worse) scenarios if similar unrest were to develop in Mexico.[48]

Reagan's fearful scenario became a self-fulfilling prophecy of sorts when his militarisitic foreign policy in Central America led to a significant refugee exodus northward from the region into the United States. An influx of Central American refugees—largely from El Salvador, Guatemala, and Nicaragua—into the Rio Grande Valley in the area of Brownsville, Texas, in late 1988 led to a major INS operation in the region. It was the most massive immigration enforcement effort since the INS's Operation Wetback in 1954. INS efforts to stem this influx of refugees included the use of U.S. intelligence assets, the deployment of a large, mobile Border Patrol task force, the detention of thousands of political-asylum applicants, strong public relations outreach, and "intimate cooperation between the INS and U.S. government intelligence agencies"[49] The bulk of the operation took place in the first half of 1989 and again, although on a smaller scale, during the winter of 1990. The main thrust of the operation was the introduction of an additional 250 Border Patrol agents to the region, augmenting the normal contingent of about 375 agents.[50]

INS activities in the Rio Grande Valley during this time marked the beginning of the Bush administration's reign, one characterized by two general trends. First, immigration enforcement became increasingly severe, as best demonstrated by the aforementioned INS operation in the Rio Grande Valley. Second, the emphasis on drug enforcement expanded, involving an increasing blurring of the distinction between the INS's immigration and drug enforcement efforts. Although the number of congressionally funded INS staff positions shrunk by 23 percent during Bush's term of office (1989–1992), overall funding appropriations grew by 19 percent, with the Enforcement Division receiving the majority of the increase.[51]

The so-called war on drugs waged by the two Republican administrations was certainly one of the most significant factors prompting the "border build-up." [52] While the U.S.-Mexico boundary had long seen efforts by U.S. authorities to stem the flow of illegal drugs into the United States, it was the "sustained sense of urgency" characterizing this interdiction effort that made the Ronald Reagan–George Bush "war" unique.[53] In this regard, the Reagan and Bush administrations also significantly helped to associate boundary enforcement with criminal activity.[54]

Although intensified policing along the U.S-Mexico boundary to interdict both drugs and unauthorized immigrants had taken place on numerous occasions in the past, what marked the buildup beginning in the second half of the Carter administration was its sustained nature. Rather than being a merely temporary phenomenon, the boundary militarization that began in the late 1970s,[55] and the thinking that informed it, marked the beginning of a trajectory, one that significantly intensified another process begun in the mid-1800s—namely, the pacification of the border region and the making of the U.S.-Mexico boundary. While this process had long been largely a national one, in terms of its ideological and practical origins, localities in the border region were increasingly important players in this process. In some ways, localities became "the tail that wagged the dog" in that they pressured the national state to fulfill its duty of making the boundary "real." Nowhere was this more true than in southern California.

NATIONAL STATECRAFT FROM BELOW:
SAN DIEGO AS A NATIONAL TERRITORIAL AGENT

Rising concerns about unauthorized immigration and a border region "out of control" beginning in the early 1970s certainly affected the political climate and the collective political-geographical imagination of the San Diego populace. Yet San Diego seemed to lag noticeably behind Washington, D.C., in terms of the beginning of efforts in favor of increasing boundary enforcement. This is not to suggest that southern California merely reacted to national-scale political developments. As discussed earlier, the California State Assembly passed legislation in 1971 that established fines against employers with unauthorized workers.[56] This legislation was the forerunner of the federal employer sanctions legislation that Congress passed in 1986. However, concerns about unauthorized immigration and boundary enforcement-related issues were limited to a small number of local politicians and Mexican-American and Chicano groups and not deeply rooted in mainstream, popular political culture.[57] Overall, it seems that at the time San Diego was reactive to national-scale events. San Diego newspapers, for example, did not noticeably increase their coverage of boundary-enforcement-related issues. To the extent that coverage occurred, it was usually in response to national-scale initiatives, or initiatives by local federal authorities (such as Border Patrol officials).[58] Disinterest in boundary enforcement issues is reflected in a 1975 report on efforts to repair the boundary fence, which attributed the source of the effort to the San Diego Cattlemen's Association as it was worried about its members' cattle wandering into Mexico.[59] In that same year, however, the San Diego County Board of Supervisors commissioned a study on "the impact of undocumented workers" on the county, publishing it in January 1977.[60] As such efforts grew over time, San Diego increasingly became a producer of national concerns toward unauthorized immigration and the U.S.-Mexico boundary, and thus very much a territorial agent—nationally as well as locally.

The Carter administration's arrival in office coincided with a noticeable increase in San Diego newspaper coverage of boundary-enforcement-related issues and with a growth in activism around these matters. While much of the initiative for these activities came from Washington, D.C., local officials played a significant role in raising the boundary's profile as it related to a whole host of issues. By this time, the relationship between the local and national scales was much more a dialectical or recursive one in which there was a dynamic interaction between the local and the national in producing heightened consciousness of the boundary and its putative relationship to issues of law and order.

Very early on in the Carter administration (February 14–15, 1977), Mexican president José López Portillo visited the White House. Anticipation of his visit was cause for the formation of the congressional "border caucus," the members of which met with President Carter a few days prior to López Portillo's visit to request that the U.S. president raise a number of issues with his Mexican counterpart, including those of unauthorized immigration, the revival of the Bracero Program, drug trafficking from Mexico, and sewage flowing across the boundary from Mexico.[61] Around the same time, San Diego mayor Pete Wilson wrote an appeal to Carter asking for "federal help in dealing with the economic and crime problems caused by the flood of illegal aliens," explained *The San Diego Union*. Wilson also requested a meeting in San Diego between local law enforcement and federal officials to examine boundary-related crime.[62] Local liberals also helped fan the flames of anti–unauthorized immigrant sentiment. San Diego congressman Lionel Van Deerlin, for example, partially blamed "illegal aliens" for San Diego's high unemployment rate and overburdened social safety net.[63]

Rising violent crimes (including robbery, rape, and murder) committed by so-called border bandits became a subject of increasing concern in San Diego in the late 1970s and helped to strengthen the perception of the boundary as a line of defense in need of fortification.[64] The increase in attacks led to the establishment of a special task force by the San Diego Police Department to patrol "hot spots" along the eight miles of boundary within the city limits.[65] *The San Diego Union* compared the perils of the task to "guerrilla warfare in Vietnam." Among other things, the newspaper called for an increase in Border Patrol agents, more boundary fencing and lighting, and access roads to make the police efforts "less of an exercise in jungle warfare."[66] Los Angeles police chief Ed Davis, a potential Republican candidate for governor at the time, joined the growing chorus in favor of enhanced boundary control, calling for a strong boundary fence and an increase in the Border Patrol.[67] George Deukmejian, the California Senate minority leader, went even further, proposing the establishment of a fourteen-mile-long "military reservation" along the westernmost section of the boundary to make it easier to prevent unauthorized entries into the United States.[68] As *The San Diego Union* reported in an article entitled "Illegal Alien Tide Continues to Rise," 1977 marked a record year for apprehensions in the Chula Vista Sector, with Border Patrol officials predicting even more apprehensions for 1978.[69]

It was during this time that the federal government announced that it was considering the installation of a ten-foot high chain-link security fence along the seven westernmost miles of the boundary, backed by floodlights and increased helicopter patrols. Although unauthorized immigration was an important factor informing the announcement, drug smuggling was paramount.[70] Soon thereafter, the U.S. government began building a dirt road along the boundary from the Pacific to the Otay Mountains, about fourteen miles inland, to improve the Border Patrol's ability to police the boundary.[71] A few months later, the federal government added one hundred Border Patrol agents to the Chula Vista Sector's contingent, bringing the total force to around 450.[72]

The proposed new fence proved to be highly controversial, especially as the Carter administration proposal evolved to include two six-mile steel fences (essentially walls) between San Ysidro and Tijuana, and El Paso and Ciudad Juárez. Critics of the proposal quickly dubbed the barrier the "Tortilla Curtain" or the "Carter Curtain." The proposal and surrounding controversy inadvertently helped raise the profile of the boundary in the minds of San Diegans. From the perspective of U.S. authorities, there was little question of the need for a new fence. Indeed, in many areas, the boundary was hardly demarcated.[73] But many in San Diego, including members of its U.S. Congressional delegation and the San Diego City Council, opposed the new fence on the grounds that it was unnecessary, would prove to be ineffective, and would hurt U.S.-Mexico relations.[74] And within the Mexican-American community, the opposition was very strong; in February 1979, for example, thirteen hundred Chicanos marched along the boundary in San Ysidro to protest the Carter plan.[75]

Despite such opposition, the Carter proposal seemed to enjoy widespread support with the general San Diego populace. Participants in a 1977 poll conducted by Congressman Van Deerlin highlighted "the illegal alien problem" as their greatest concern (more than 15,000 of his constituents responded). Almost 89 percent of respondents favored federal penalties for employers who knowingly hired unauthorized immigrants and more than 77 percent supported a national identification card for all job applicants. A survey conducted by the congressman almost two years later demonstrated 82.3 percent support for employer sanctions and 64 percent support for enhanced fencing along the boundary.[76] But support for the fence was apparently not well organized nor mobilized. And thus it was the opposition to an enhanced boundary fence that eventually won out.[77] Indeed, Van Deerlin states that he received basically no pressure from his constituents to ensure the construction of a boundary fence during his term in office (1963–1981).[78] When a new fence was eventually built, it was neither sturdier nor any more difficult to scale or cut than the one it replaced.[79] Within one year, there were at least twenty large holes—some large enough for a truck to pass through—in the four miles of already-completed new fencing.[80]

The fence controversy, however, was a manifestation of a much larger problem: namely, the inability of U.S. authorities to control the boundary in a manner sufficiently effective to reduce unauthorized crossings from Mexico into the United States. Despite increased activism in Washington, D.C., in favor of enhanced boundary enforcement, the necessary resources to realize this sentiment were slow in coming due to insufficient state and public interest in, and continuing opposition to, enhanced boundary enforcement. During the period from 1972 to 1986, for example, increased legislative activity aimed at stemming the flow of illegal immigration coincided with a *reduction* in the amount of growth of the INS budget (in real dollars).[81] Thus, as the scale of unauthorized immigration continued unabated in the San Diego area, many local elites became increasingly critical of the federal government's seeming impotence. As *The San Diego Union* warned in a May 25, 1979 editorial, "The inability of the administration to deal with massive illegal immigration is fast leading to chaos on our border with Mexico." The *Union* pronounced U.S. border policy "at a dead end" in a situation where the country was being "[i]nundated by [a] torrent of humanity." In a context of escalating violence in the San Diego border region, such sentiments led to the emergence of a crisis mentality among many policymakers. Michael Walsh, the U.S. attorney for Southern California, for one, described the situation in the border region as "potentially explosive" and warned that "as the number of apprehensions increases, the potential for violence or misunderstanding goes up."[82]

San Diego media coverage of boundary-related issues increased considerably, resulting in heightened concerns about unauthorized immigration and border region crime. In January 1980, for example, *The San Diego Union* published a five-part series entitled "The Border Country." Four of the five installments emphasized the lawlessness and out-of-control nature of the region, thus presenting the boundary and its concomitant phenomena as potential threats to San Diego, with one exploring the possibility of "Hispanic secession" by the year 2000.[83]

Such coverage reflected increasing popular and official concern over extralegal immigration and its effects on San Diego County. In July 1979, the San Diego County Board of Supervisors voted to hire a research firm to update and expand its 1977 study on the impact of the undocumented on the county. Then, in January 1980, the board appointed a Border Task Force to formulate and present public policy recommendations. The task force's recommendations included amnesty for unauthorized immigrants in the United States since January 1975; the implementation of a guest worker program; reimbursement by the federal government to the California state and local governments for the costs of health care and social service benefits provided to unauthorized immigrants; and the liberalization of trade between the United States and Mexico.[84]

The influx of unauthorized migrants from Mexico into the United States grew significantly in the mid-1980s in the context of a serious downturn in Mexico's economy. In an article ominously entitled "Cross-Border Flow of Aliens Becomes Flood," *The San Diego Union* reported that the first four months of fiscal year 1986 saw a 43 percent increase in Border Patrol apprehensions over the same period the previous year.[85] Such factors facilitated increasingly severe proposals regarding boundary policing. Republican U.S.

Senate candidate Mike Antonovich, Senator (and former San Diego mayor) Pete Wilson, and San Diego congressman Duncan Hunter all called for the deployment of troops along the boundary at various times in 1986 to stymie drug smuggling, unauthorized immigration, and potential terrorist attacks.[86] Pete Wilson went so far as to voice support for a physical closure of the boundary if Mexican officials refused to cooperate with American efforts to stem the influx of unauthorized immigrants.[87]

Such advocacy for building up the boundary intensified over the next few years. The U.S. attorney for southern California, Peter Nunez, for example, voiced his support for the deployment of the military along the boundary.[88] And, as in the 1970s, there were increasing calls to improve upon the boundary fence. Some even called for concrete barriers and a fourteen-foot wide trench along the boundary to prevent "drive-throughs" by smugglers. National groups, most notably the Federation for American Immigration Reform (FAIR) helped fan the flames in San Diego by issuing highly publicized calls for a variety of types of barriers along the boundary. But, as before, such proposals generated a great deal of controversy, and local officials were far from unanimous in their support.[89]

Nevertheless, San Diego was notable among U.S. border cities for the level and intensity of pro-boundary-enforcement activism, a trend that greatly intensified in the late 1980s and early 1990s. The rise in such activism was an outgrowth of the increasingly dialectical relationship between the local and the national scales in constructing and reproducing "the American nation." It was also a manifestation of the increasing political and ideological integration of San Diego into the national core as well as the growing normalization of the boundary. Rather than merely reacting to and being the product of processes initiated at the national scale, San Diego–based agents increasingly became constructors of the national state. This trend manifested the growing socially and territorially constructed distinctions between those on opposing sides of the U.S.-Mexico boundary within the San Diego–Tijuana region. As Peter Sahlins explains, "National identity is a ... continuous process of defining 'friend' and 'enemy,' a logical extension of the process of maintaining boundaries between 'us' and 'them' within more local communities. National identities constructed on the basis of such an oppositional structure do not depend on the existence of any objective linguistic or cultural difference but on the subjective experience of difference. In this sense, national identity, like ethnic or communal identity, is contingent or relational: it is defined by the social or territorial boundaries drawn to distinguish the collective self and its implicit negation, the other."[90]

We now need to analyze the larger socioeconomic factors that informed this growing sentiment in favor of increasing the social distance between "Americans" and "aliens" in the area of San Diego in the late 1980s, and the state response of increased enforcement of the U.S.-Mexico boundary.

SHRINKING DISTANCE AND INCREASING VISIBILITY:
THE BLURRING OF THE SOCIAL BOUNDARY BETWEEN MEXICO
AND THE UNITED STATES IN SOUTHERN CALIFORNIA

What makes San Diego unique—in comparison to other American locales in the U.S.-Mexico borderlands—is its racial/ethnic composition. San Diego stands out in stark contrast to Tijuana as a predominantly "Anglo" city whereas other major U.S. border cities are predominantly composed of people of Mexican origin. As Sahlins argues, we should not assume that such "objective" differences produce social and territorial boundaries. However, given the historical development of Mexico and the United States and the social relations between "Mexicans" and "Americans" in the aftermath of the Treaty of Guadalupe Hidalgo (a topic explored in chapter 5), such differences matter. In this regard, San Diego was less equipped culturally and politically to deal with Mexico, especially as Mexico (broadly construed) failed to confine itself to south of the international boundary.[91]

Census figures for 1980 show that in California, San Diego, and Chula Vista were 70 percent and 68 percent Anglo, respectively, while in Texas, El Paso had an Anglo population of only 33 percent and Brownsville a mere 16 percent. By 1990, these figures were 59 percent, 50 percent, 26 percent, and 9 percent, respectively.[92] What is curious is that southern California cities such as San Diego and Chula Vista saw actual increases in the number of white residents between 1980 and 1990, while most U.S. border cities saw an absolute decrease in their white populations. This speaks to the high number of non-Anglo (largely Latino) immigrants to the area.

The racial and ethnic disparity in northern San Diego County (often referred to as North County), with the exception of isolated pockets, is even more pronounced and is heavily intertwined with economic class distinctions. Anthropologist Leo Chavez characterizes the region as having two distinct socioeconomic group: affluent whites, and the working-class Mexican immigrants who service them.[93] As a 1988 report in the San Diego edition of the *Los Angeles Times* described the local human geography, "Northern San Diego County is today a land unlike any other along the U.S.-Mexico border. . . . A place where squalid, plywood-and-cardboard shacks sit in the shadow of $1-million mansions, where the BMW and Volvo set rubs elbows at the supermarket with the dusty migrants fresh from the fields, where the haves run routinely head-on into the have-nots."[94] It is thus not surprising that a number of the more notable clashes between "natives" and immigrants that were symptomatic of a growing preoccupation with the U.S-Mexico boundary and unauthorized immigration took place in North County.[95]

Local officials helped to bolster the increasing association of unauthorized immigrants with crime. While unauthorized immigrants were guilty of a number of crimes during this period, they were mostly " 'public disorder misdemeanors' such as urinating in public, and nonviolent 'survival crimes,' such as thefts of bedding, food, and cash."[96] So-called border bandits and the rob-and-return bunch were guilty of almost all violent crimes committed by Mexicans without authorization to be in the United States. Such individuals were not immigrants, at least as one normally understands the term *immigrant,* but instead residents of Tijuana who would cross into the San Diego area simply to commit crimes and then return to Mexico.[97] Yet such distinctions were largely invisible in the public debate on border-related crime. Local officials often implicitly conflated unauthorized migrant workers with such individuals from Mexico who took advantage of the international boundary to commit crimes. For example, Susan Golding, a member of the San Diego County Board of Supervisors (and until recently, the mayor of San Diego), blamed unauthorized immigrants for the county's fiscal problems due to court, jail, and health care costs and called for the county to sue the federal government for the related expenses.[98]

Images of the migrant as a criminal dovetailed with the reality of increased drug trafficking from Mexico through the San Diego area in the mid-1980s. The success of U.S. and Mexican authorities in reducing drug production in and trafficking from Mexico in the early 1970s provided opportunities for traffickers in Colombia, who began shipping through south Florida. But U.S. anti-drug-trafficking efforts curtailed the success of the Colombia-based cartels. Thus, beginning in the early and mid-1980s, the cartels began cooperating with associates in Mexico and shifted their trafficking routes to San Diego.[99] As a result, U.S. drug seizures in the San Diego area skyrocketed. Media efforts to highlight the trend only added to the image of a border "out of control" and to anti-immigrant sentiment as migrant workers from Mexico became increasingly associated with drug trafficking. As the headline of the September 16, 1986 issue of *The Tribune,* at the time one of San Diego's two major daily newspapers, exclaimed, "Border emerges as a war zone." Such hyperbole led to increased calls for an enhancement of boundary policing.[100]

At the same time, local officials often blamed a perceived decline in the local quality of life on unauthorized immigrants. In proposing the stationing of U.S. Marines every fifteen or twenty feet along the U.S.-Mexico boundary, for example, the sheriff of San Diego County stated, "Illegal aliens are gradually affecting the quality of life as we know it. For example, now we have to admit illegal aliens into our colleges, which means my grandchildren may not be granted entry because of an illegal alien and they'll probably require her [sic] to be bilingual."[101] Such statements undoubtedly helped to aggravate tensions between "native" San Diegans and the area's growing community of unauthorized immigrants.

One of the more extreme cases was that of the nearby city of Carlsbad,[102] where some local residents accused (apparently without grounds) unauthorized immigrants of extorting money from children going to school. In

conjunction with opportunistic posturing by local politicians, polemical statements by INS officials, and an intense media spotlight, the alleged events
helped to create a hysteria against the community of unauthorized immigrants in the area. Clyde Romney, a candidate for the San Diego County
Board of Supervisors, for instance, called upon the Border Patrol to establish
an office in North County to address increased concerns surrounding unauthorized immigrants. In doing so, he wrote, "Nowhere else in San Diego
County do you find the huge gangs of illegal aliens that line our streets, shake
down our schoolchildren, spread diseases like malaria and roam our neigh-
borhoods looking for work or homes to rob. We are under siege in North
County, and we have been deserted by those whose job is to protect us from
this flood of aliens."[103] In October 1986, the Border Patrol responded to such
sentiments by conducting a roundup of unauthorized immigrants in the area,
resulting in the arrest and deportation to Mexico of three thousand migrant
workers.[104] A similar clash erupted in the nearby city of Encinitas in the late
1980s in response to the growing presence of migrants soliciting work on the
city's street corners and migrant encampments on the outskirts of the
community.[105]

The events in Carlsbad and Encinitas were in part a manifestation of the
changing social and economic geography of much of northern San Diego
County. In a few short years, Carlsbad went from a largely undeveloped area
to one characterized as "typically suburban, with several shopping centers,
some light commercial and business areas, and many new middle-class
housing developments, all sprinkled among fields, farmlands, and green-
houses."[106] The nature, scale, and speed of the area's economic transformation led to a rapid rise in the influx of Mexican migrant laborers. And given
the reduction in the amount of space for migrant squatter settlements, the
visibility of the migrant workers greatly increased. As a San Diego County
assistant sheriff and area resident explained, the Mexican migrant worker
population "went from largely invisible to the general population to, in less
than two years, a point that certainly elevated concerns."[107]

The increasing visibility of Mexican migrants in the San Diego area was not
simply a figment of the imagination. In the 1980s and early 1990s, the Border
Patrol's San Diego Sector was responsible for a significantly increasing number
of apprehensions of unauthorized immigrants, especially following Mexico's
severe recession in the mid-1980s. Fiscal year 1986, for example, saw a 47
percent increase over the previous year's total of Border Patrol apprehensions
in the San Diego Sector, reaching a figure of 630,000. This led Howard Ezell,
the outspoken western regional commissioner for the INS to label the influx
of unauthorized immigrants in the San Diego area "an invasion." As Ezell saw
it, "Our borders are, indeed, out of control."[108]

Although most unauthorized immigrants who crossed the boundary in the
San Diego area had no intention of staying in the region, an apparently

increasing number were opting to do so in the 1980s, especially given the region's very strong economic and demographic growth. Between 1980 and 1990, Carlsbad's population grew by 79 percent, that of Oceanside by 64 percent, and that of nearby Vista by 89 percent.[109] During the same period, the city of San Diego grew 28 percent (to a population of 1,118,282) and San Diego County by 35 percent (to a figure of more than 2.5 million).[110]

From a context of rapid economic growth, growing Mexican migration, and a changing racial and ethnic landscape emerged a number of violent incidents. The grassroots response to these changes took a turn toward heightened vigilantism—a form of "statecraft from below."[111] A variety of violent incidents took place from the mid-1980s to the early 1990s. These included a series of nighttime attacks by off-duty Marines against Mexican migrant workers (so-called beaner raids, *beaner* being a derogatory term for Mexicans), and an attack with guns by three teenagers in Encinitas against migrant workers. At the same time, several groups began protesting in the area of the boundary to pressure U.S. authorities to construct a strong infrastructure of control along the boundary. Some of the groups, like the white supremacist American Spring and the White Aryan Resistance, were openly racist; others, such as Light Up the Border, cast their arguments more strictly in anti-immigration and/or national sovereignty terms. In practice, however, the line between these two types of pro-boundary-control groups was often rather blurry. U.S. authorities were at times involved in some of the anti-immigrant groups. Howard Ezell, for example, was the founder of Americans for Border Control, which he set up while INS western regional commissioner, to help further anti-unauthorized immigrant sentiment.[112]

Such local groups did not exist in a national sociopolitical vacuum, but rather in a sea of sympathy (at least in terms of anti-immigration sentiment). A 1990 Roper poll found 77 percent opposition among Americans to expanding the numbers of legal immigrants (among Latinos, the figure was 74 percent), 80 percent support for the deployment of troops along the U.S.-Mexico boundary to stymie the entrance of unauthorized immigrants, and 71 percent in favor of sanctions against employers who knowingly hire unauthorized immigrants.[113]

As a result of hardening political positions locally and nationally, and of increasing congressional support, boundary enforcement began intensifying noticeably in the San Diego Sector starting in the late 1980s. Beginning in September 1989, the Border Patrol began experimenting with high-intensity floodlights along the Tijuana River portion of the boundary in San Ysidro.[114] By May 1990, there were sixteen permanent lights in the same location.[115] Gradually the number of these forty-foot high lights grew, as did the Sector's contingent of Border Patrol agents. In 1990, the number of agents grew from 740 to 830. Road construction in the boundary area also increased significantly. Most newsworthy, however, was the construction by U.S. military personnel of a steel wall, made from Vietnam War–era corrugated steel landing mats, along the westernmost portion of the boundary in San Diego. Gustavo De La Viña, the new Border Patrol chief for the San Diego Sector as of June 1990, helped bring about many of the changes.

Prior to his arrival, the area along the boundary in San Diego was often one of lawlessness and violence. Border bandits from Tijuana killed seven unauthorized immigrants on the U.S. side of the boundary in the first six months of 1990, and there were numerous assaults, rapes, and robberies of migrant workers attempting to cross into the United States. De La Viña took a hardline approach to the problem of border crime; as he explained in an interview with *The San Diego Union*, "I couldn't believe that a bunch of punks working on the Mexican side could have that much control. I just could not tolerate that."[116] Fiscal year 1990 also saw an increase in the number of Border Patrol apprehensions in the sector, a 29 percent increase over the previous year's total after three successive years of declining apprehensions in the aftermath of the legalization program associated with the 1986 Immigration Reform and Control Act. In this regard, the San Diego Sector clearly had insufficient resources.

While the sector had approximately nine hundred Border Patrol agents, when one takes into consideration days off, vacation, and other duties, the sector would sometimes only have twenty agents for an eight-hour shift in its Imperial Beach station area—the sector's station responsible for approximately the six westernmost miles of the boundary. The next two line stations (stations responsible for an area adjacent to the boundary) would sometimes only have eight agents per shift. This was a time when the sector would sometimes apprehend 2,000 people on busy nights—the vast majority in Imperial Beach, by far the busiest station in the United States. (Migrants liked crossing in the Imperial Beach area because it was the closest point to an urbanized area— San Ysidro.) Most afternoons, large numbers of migrants would gather along the boundary and cross once night fell. According to De La Viña, the first time he toured the boundary in the San Diego Sector he saw groups of three to four hundred unauthorized migrants at different hills—on the U.S. side of the boundary—in the Imperial Beach area, all waiting to travel northward. Given such numbers, it was impossible for the Border Patrol to control them. And, in certain areas along the boundary, only the remnants of a chainlink fence existed. In many ways, the boundary as a physical, visible line barely existed. This led De La Viña to conclude that what he had to do was "delineate the border ... to show the migrants and us where the U.S. began and where Mexico ended." Building the new steel wall (or "fence," in INS parlance), was the way to do so.[117]

The wall caused great controversy—especially in Mexico, which regarded the construction as an insult and an unfriendly act. Many dubbed it "the new Berlin Wall."[118] Although most of the San Diego establishment seemed to accept the wall, many only did so begrudgingly. The *San Diego Tribune*, for example, in a September 5, 1991 editorial referred to it as an "ugly border band-aid" that "rightly offends many" but "is the best we can do for now." While smugglers succeeded on a number of occasions in cutting holes in the wall (some large enough for cars), there is no question that the wall had a significant effect on unauthorized activities along the boundary—one far greater than anticipated by the Border Patrol itself. The wall had the effect of significantly reducing attacks on migrants on the U.S. side of the boundary, noticeably shifting the migrant traffic eastward, and lowering the number of "drive-throughs" by cars and trucks coming from Mexico.[119]

An important part of this gradual process of creating "order" along the boundary in San Diego was enlisting the cooperation of Mexican authorities. Early on in his command of the Border Patrol's San Diego Sector, De la Viña approached the local Mexican consulate to try to establish links with a police force on the Mexican side of the border "to create a sandwich around the bandits." Eventually the Mexican federal government sent eleven agents to the border region to fight crime against migrants. This was the beginning of the so-called Grupo Beta whose stated mission is to protect migrants crossing from Mexico into the United States.[120] The establishment of Grupo Beta was also a manifestation of increasing cooperation between U.S. and Mexican authorities in fighting criminal activity in the border region.[121] Perhaps the most important aspect of the increasing cooperation, however, was Mexico's heightened role—albeit a somewhat indirect one—in helping to limit unauthorized crossings into the United States, a subject explored in greater depth later.

SAN DIEGO AND TIJUANA: A DISAPPEARING BOUNDARY?

In one sense, increasing transboundary cooperation in policing is an example of San Diego and Tijuana growing closer together. One would expect intensifying ties between the two border cities as both San Diego and Tijuana have experienced rapid demographic and economic growth as well as intensifying transboundary integration. Between 1950 and 1980, Tijuana's population grew by 1,000 percent, having experienced a significant diversification of its industrial base and the growth of a large service sector during the period. The city's population was over one million by 1985.[122] By 1995, one study calculated the combined population of San Diego County and the Municipio of Tijuana to be more than 3.2 million,[123] more than twice the size of the second largest cross-boundary pair of counties. And the San Diego–Tijuana corridor—in terms of per capita income—was the wealthiest in the entire U.S.-Mexico border region.[124]

The rapid growth of U.S. and Mexican border cities and the accompanying transboundary links facilitated by this growth has meant increasing economic and political importance for the border region. By 1990, the population of the U.S.–Mexico border region had reached more than nine million.[125] This regional development translated into significantly heightened attention from national elites and the media. Interestingly, a good deal of the media coverage emphasized the unique nature of the area, often explicitly suggesting the increasing irrelevance of the international boundary and the rise of a new country—namely, the *transnational* border region.[126] Paradoxically, however, the regions abutting the boundary were arguably more similar to their respective countries than they had ever been due to the increasing nationalization of border regions in the United States and Mexico that had taken place throughout the nineteenth and twentieth centuries. If the border region had ever been "almost a country unto itself, neither Mexican nor American,"[127] it had become decreasingly so over time. The U.S. border region was more "American" and the Mexican border region was more "Mexican" than they had ever been due to intensifying ties between the two countries' national cores and territorial peripheries. Thus, in the case of the United States, enhanced media attention to the relatively distinctive nature of the border region was less a statement of the border region's uniqueness than it was about the region's growing national importance. It also manifested the region's increasing integration into national political economic life, as well as the relative inattention it had hitherto received from national media and policy makers.

In the case of the San Diego–Tijuana region, by the onset of the 1990s the scale of the transboundary ties was indeed impressive: a host of links existed between local state government agencies, higher education institutions, business groups, civic organizations, and nongovernmental organizations.[128] The value of exports to Mexico processed through official San Diego checkpoints in 1990 was $3.3 billion, while the value of goods coming from Mexico to San Diego were worth $3.8 billion. At the same time, an estimated 50,000 Tijuana residents held full- or part-time jobs in San Diego. Such factors most likely informed the decisions of the second annual Border Mayors Conference in Tijuana in June 1991 to adopt a resolution calling for the establishment of a twenty-five-mile transboundary zone that would allow free movement of all people, regardless of country of origin.[129]

Increased transboundary links manifested themselves on the landscape through significant demographic and economic growth in the southern region of San Diego. The late 1960s and early 1970s saw the establishment of two interstate highways linking the San Ysidro port of entry with points to the north.[130] In 1981, a trolley line joining San Ysidro and downtown San Diego opened; by 1991 an average of 17,200 persons per day boarded and disembarked at the station at the San Ysidro port of entry.[131] At the same time, the population density and the geographical expanse of San Diego's southern region grew noticeably. During the 1970s, for example, San Ysidro's population doubled.[132] Chula Vista and National City (situated between the core of the City of San Diego and the San Ysidro section of the city) grew 11 percent and 61 percent, respectively, between 1980 and 1990.[133] In the 1970s, San Diego-based interests began developing the Otay Mesa area east of the San Ysidro port of entry; as a result of similar developments on the Mexican side of the boundary, a second boundary crossing between Mexico and the United States opened at Otay Mesa in the early 1980s.[134] All these developments had the effect of tying Tijuana and San Diego closer together—albeit in a highly unequal fashion.[135]

Understandably, the demographic growth and increasing density of the humanized landscape presented heightened challenges to U.S. boundary authorities. In addition to increasing numbers of unauthorized immigrants, improvements in various forms of transportation and their accessibility, and hyperurbanization along both sides of the boundary all served to lessen the social distance between the United States and Mexico and to undermine the ability of U.S. authorities to control the border region. While U.S. officials sometimes did try to prevent development near the boundary to facilitate enhanced policing and undermine the ability of migrants and smugglers to engage in transboundary activities,[136] such efforts appear to be the exception rather than the norm.[137]

Despite (or perhaps because of) the growing intensity of transboundary ties in the area, only 40 percent of San Diego County residents responding to a 1991 *San Diego Union*/KNSD Poll believed that the two cities were "gradually becoming part of a single interdependent region with a shared economy and culture." And a majority of respondents opposed closer cross-boundary ties and less restrictive boundary checks. An astonishing 54 percent stated that they never visit Tijuana, with another 19 percent saying that they visit their Mexican neighbor only once a year.[138] It is for such reasons that historian Ramón Eduardo Ruiz argues that it is a mistake to label San Diego and Tijuana as twin cities. Those who do are "forgetting that San Diegans never think of themselves living in a border town." Ruiz writes,

> From day one, San Diegans have prided themselves on being Anglos and Protestants, though they delight in bestowing Spanish names on their streets. To dwell for a moment on the irony of this, until a few years ago, the covenant that governed the plush community of Rancho Santa Fe in San Diego County barred all but Anglos from residing there, in a place where all the street names are in Spanish, including some that are grossly misspelled. The vast majority of San Diegans never venture south of the border and have no contact with Mexicans who live in Tijuana. San Diego's mayors refer glowingly to Mexican trade ties, but they speak no Spanish and know almost nothing of their southern neighbors. Tijuana ranks low in the esteem of San

Diegans, and the fling with Spanish names is nothing but nostalgia for a romantic myth concocted by real estate speculators who wanted to sell lots to Midwesterners.[139]

Undoubtedly there are significant differences between the San Diego–Tijuana area and other U.S.-Mexico transboundary urban regions, but there are also a lot of similarities due to the presence of the international boundary and its associated practices and ideologies. Thus, although the results of the San Diego poll might have been somewhat extreme relative to what one might have found had one conducted a similar poll in other U.S. border cities, it is doubtful that the results as they pertained to boundary and immigration enforcement would have varied in a fundamental way. As the case of the Border Patrol's Operation Blockade/Hold-the-Line in El Paso (an overwhelmingly Latino city) demonstrated, strong support for enhancing boundary enforcement is not unique to predominantly white border cities like San Diego.[140] This speaks to the complexity and nonessential nature of social identity—especially among Mexican Americans in the border region. We should not assume Mexican Americans as a whole to be any less "American" than other ethnic group in the United States simply because the United States shares a boundary with Mexico. Indeed, Mexican Americans, while opposing specific immigration and boundary-related initiatives in greater numbers than the general population (due to their discriminatory focus on people of Mexican descent), have historically supported immigration and boundary enforcement at levels similar to those of the white population.[141] In this regard, Mexican Americans are just as "American" as any other national origin group in the United States[142] That said, identity is a highly multifaceted and often contradictory phenomenon, an observation that applies no less so to Mexican Americans who live in the border region.[143] Like all people, Mexican Americans have multiple identities; in their particular case, while many often strongly distinguish themselves from non–Mexican Americans and embrace their Mexican heritage, they also often harbor strong anti-Mexican sentiment.[144]

That Mexican Americans generally support boundary and immigration enforcement is a manifestation of historically rooted processes that inform the worldview of Latinos and of the general U.S. population: namely, the growing nationalization of territory and the social construction of the U.S.-Mexico boundary landscape and of associated spatial imagery as it relates to national territory within the American mind-set.[145] Furthermore, the growing sense of difference felt by "Americans" in the U.S. border region toward their Mexican neighbors in the context of increasing regional integration perhaps also speaks to a frequent tendency for the sense of difference to be strongest where the intergroup and/or transboundary relationships are most potent—an outgrowth of what Freud referred to as the "narcissism of minor differences."[146] This growing sense of difference and the resulting shift in practice and thinking helped lay the basis for the emergence of Operation Gatekeeper in 1994, the short-term roots to which I now turn.

THE EMERGENCE OF OPERATION GATEKEEPER

Even though there is a good deal of documentation that analyzes the medium-term roots of the ongoing intensification of boundary enforcement and the "war on illegals" of which Operation Gatekeeper is a part, uncovering the short term-roots of Gatekeeper has proven more difficult. There is very little documentation on the operation and the events surrounding it given that Gatekeeper is recent or current history. Furthermore, government agencies and officials have a tendency to be less than forthcoming in providing information about the motives and goals behind particular policy decisions and practices—especially as regards an operation as highly politicized as Gatekeeper. To get around these obstacles, one must be able to draw upon a wide array of resources, such as interviews, transcripts, and other primary—as well as secondary—sources.[147] It is this prescription that I follow in order to get beneath the official rhetoric that surrounds Gatekeeper and to uncover its short-term political roots.[148]

Although the 1986 Immigration Reform and Control Act led to a rapid decline in Border Patrol apprehensions (largely due to a program that legalized upward of three million "illegals"—the vast majority of whom were Mexican—living and working in the United States), apprehensions along the southern U.S. boundary quickly began to rise again in 1989.[149] The perceived failure of the IRCA to address the issue of unauthorized boundary crossing from Mexico helped to fuel a resurgence of anti-immigration sentiment (again, with a focus on "illegal" immigration). This was especially true in California, to where an estimated 400,000 people a year migrated (legally and extralegally) in the late 1980s and early 1990s.[150]

By the early 1990s, California was experiencing a serious recession (one that hit *southern* California especially hard), the breakdown of local government, a widening gap between rich and poor, and a massive racial recomposition.[151] It was one of the whitest states in the United States in 1960 but today it is "the most polyglot."[152] (In August 2000, the U.S. Census Bureau released figures showing the ethnic and racial "minorities" had recently become the majority in California.) All of these developments dovetailed neatly with California's long and sordid history of anti-immigrant sentiment (a topic explored in chapter 5), and provided ample fuel for demagogic politicians and a host of anti-immigrant groups. It is thus not surprising that California was the national leader in the 1990s in raising the anti-immigration banner and in fighting "bad" immigrants. And probably no figure played a more important role in creating this image on a state-wide scale than Governor Pete Wilson.

In early 1991, Governor Wilson blamed both legal and extralegal immigration for significantly contributing to California's budget crisis, with a $12.6 billion deficit.[153] Wilson soon went national with his anti-immigration campaign. In a November 18, 1991 interview with *Time* magazine, Wilson contended that the state's generous welfare benefits and social services served as magnet for unauthorized immigrants, as well as the domestic poor.[154] Less than two weeks later, Wilson went to Washington, D.C., to lobby for federal funds to help pay for costs created by California's immigrant population.[155] He blamed the federal government for failing to compensate state and local governments adequately for costs related to immigration and for its failure to control unauthorized immigration across the U.S.-Mexico boundary.[156]

Whatever his intentions, Wilson undoubtedly set the stage for immigrant bashing. Many Republican politicians in California soon jumped on board an immigration restrictionist and boundary-buildup bandwagon that focused primarily on unauthorized immigration from Mexico. About the same time that Wilson went to Washington, Alan Nelson, a consultant to the Federation for American Immigration Reform and former INS commissioner from the Reagan administration, called for California to cut off jobs, social services, driving privileges, college education, and tax refunds to unauthorized immigrants, claiming that they "seriously hurt all areas of California society: Employment, welfare, health, crime, housing and our basic values."[157] Also in 1991, Republican Assemblyman Richard Mountjoy tried to amend the California state budget to cut off state-funded education and health care benefits for unauthorized immigrants.[158]

These California-based efforts soon infected the national body politic. In October 1991, Republican Congressman Elton Gallegly (from Simi Valley, near Los Angeles) introduced a bill in Congress that would deny citizenship to children born in the United States if neither parent was a U.S. citizen and the mother was not at least a legal resident. In a speech in support of the bill on the floor of the House, Gallegly stated, "Today, in many parts of this country our cities and towns are being overrun with immigrants, both legal and undocumented, who pose major economic and law enforcement problems for local governments and place an added burden on their already strained budgets."[159] While Gallegly's bill focused on unauthorized immigrants, his statements made clear that his efforts were part of a larger project of reducing immigration, regardless of its legality.[160]

That 1992 was a federal election year only aggravated the rising tide of anti-immigration efforts on the part of national-scale politicians. Republican presidential candidate Pat Buchanan, for example, called for the construction of a solid barrier along the entire length of the U.S.-Mexico boundary. Two San Diego–area Republican congressmen, Randy "Duke" Cunningham and Duncan Hunter, introduced a bill to strengthen the federal government's ability to prevent owners of property along the boundary from blocking the government from building access roads and boundary "security fences." The bill also called for the establishment of a five-hundred-foot-wide "demilitarized zone" along the boundary within which development would be restricted—a position endorsed by the *San Diego Tribune*.[161]

Despite these moves, the issue of unauthorized immigration still seemed relatively low among the priorities of San Diegans. When asked what problems government should address the next five years, 40.9 percent of San Diego County residents polled identified the economic recession as one of the most pressing and 32.1 percent cited unemployment. Only 3.7 percent identified unauthorized immigration as among the most important, while 13.5 percent picked homelessness.[162] It is probably for such local reasons that immigration received relatively little attention in Washington, D.C., whether from Congress, the White House, or think tanks early in the 1990s. The 1990 Immigration Act, which led to a considerable *increase* in the number of immigrants admitted annually, for example, passed Congress despite the opposition of FAIR, which was not able to find sufficiently powerful allies in Congress to block its passage.[163]

Thus, despite Pete Wilson's efforts, boundary control and unauthorized immigration were not important topics in the 1992 elections for national office. While Pat Buchanan and his "America First" platform tried to push the Republicans to a more restrictionist stance, his efforts ultimately failed.[164] In terms of the Democrats, their national platform maintained its historical silence by not even mentioning extralegal immigration and boundary enforcement. That said, Bill Clinton did speak about the matter in his presidential campaign book, but only in very vague terms. Under the heading "Enforce and Improve Border Controls," Clinton articulated the following three goals[165]:

> Enhance the enforcement of the laws controlling our borders, and ensure that the human rights of all immigrants are respected.
>
> Improve the border patrol and ensure that it is held accountable for its actions.
>
> Provide new technology and training in the latest enforcement techniques.

Yet despite these words, it soon became clear that boundary enforcement issues were a very low priority for the Clinton administration. President Clinton's first budget proposal (released in early 1993) actually called for a *reduction* of ninety-three agents in the Border Patrol,[166] and the federal Office of Management and Budget told the Border Patrol that in the future the agency would have to "do more with less" in terms of resources.[167] But as the national environment quickly changed, so did the position of the Clinton administration.

Although the national political climate at the beginning of the decade did not seem favorable to the Wilsons and Buchanans of the world, sentiment was hardening in Congress and the White House "to get tougher on undocumented immigrants." A persistent economic recession significantly drove such sentiment.[168] Among both liberal and conservative elites, the earlier pro-immigration consensus was breaking down. Most important, efforts by conservatives and the Republican Party over the years had provided fertile ideological ground for the issues of unauthorized immigration and boundary enforcement by the early 1990s.[169]

After the Democrats won the White House in 1992, prorestrictionist forces greatly intensified their offensive. During the presidency of fellow Republican George Bush, Pete Wilson's complaints about the fiscal costs borne by California due to unauthorized immigration were "perfunctory and polite"; but Wilson greatly escalated his anti-Washington rhetoric when Bill Clinton assumed power in 1993 by castigating the federal government for failing to control the U.S.-Mexico boundary and to appropriate billions of dollars promised (by the Reagan administration) for health, education, and welfare services to immigrants—both legal and unauthorized.[170] In the summer of 1993, Wilson bought full page advertisements in a number of newspapers with an "open letter" to Clinton "on behalf of the People of California." As the one that appeared in the *New York Times* stated, "MASSIVE ILLEGAL IMMIGRATION WILL CONTINUE AS LONG AS THE FEDERAL GOVERNMENT CONTINUES TO REWARD IT. WHY EVEN HAVE A BORDER PATROL AND I.N.S. IF WE ARE GOING TO CONTINUE THE INSANITY OF PROVIDING INCENTIVES TO ILLEGAL IMMIGRANTS TO VIOLATE U.S. IMMIGRATION LAWS?"[171] Wilson alleged that unauthorized immigration was costing the state about $3 billion annually and was bankrupting California.[172] What was curious about Wilson's position is that he had played a key role, while in the U.S. Senate, in undermining boundary and immigration enforcement. In 1983, for example, then Senator Wilson coauthored legislation that disallowed the INS to raid farm fields without a judge's warrant. The provision became law in 1986 with the passage of the IRCA and basically put a halt to INS farm checks.[173] On a number of other occasions, Wilson pressured INS officials to stop workplace raids on California companies. And in the late 1970s, he and his wife had employed an unauthorized immigrant as their maid.[174]

While Pete Wilson's immigration politics showed a certain inconsistency, his efforts to highlight the putative fiscal and social costs of unauthorized immigration had a significant effect on national politics. Wilson undoubtedly played an important role in pushing Clinton toward a more activist stance on boundary enforcement. Wilson's hardline position on immigration and the U.S.-Mexico boundary clearly resonated with an increasingly restrictionist California electorate. Given the electoral importance of California, it was not possible for the Clinton administration to ignore the vote-rich state.[175] The waging of an "immigration war" by congressional Republicans was also putting the Clinton administration and the Democrats at a disadvantage in the face of upcoming elections in 1994.[176] But Wilson and anti-immigrant politics in California, as well as Republican efforts in Congress, were not the only factors explaining why unauthorized immigration became an issue of such national importance, arguably to a degree never seen before. A number of other contextual factors and high-profile events helped to bring the issue to the fore, and rather quickly.

A significant point of contention between then President George Bush and candidate Bill Clinton during the 1993 presidential campaign had been the exodus of refugees from Haiti fleeing that country's repressive military junta. Clinton strongly criticized the Bush administration's practice of intercepting the refugees at sea and repatriating them to Haiti and promised to end the practice. But in the weeks prior to Clinton's arrival in office, Bush administration officials put forth exaggerated estimates of 200,000 to 500,000 Haitian refugees that would attempt to flee to the United States upon Clinton's assuming the presidency, and FAIR ran frequent radio announcements in Florida and Georgia warning of an impending huge influx of Haitians. Fearing the potential political fallout, Clinton reversed his policy and announced a continuation of the Bush practice of interception and repatriation.[177]

In early 1993, a persistent economic recession, the bombing of New York's World Trade Center by suspected unauthorized immigrants,[178] and the assassination of two Central Intelligence Agency employees in Virginia by an unauthorized immigrant from Pakistan helped to fuel anti-immigration sentiment further.[179] If any single issue helped create the popular image of the United States under invasion from foreign hordes, however, it was the discovery offshore of ships carrying unauthorized Chinese immigrants.[180] The discovery of the *Golden Venture* and its cargo of 286 smuggled Chinese immigrants off the coast of New York City on June 6, 1993 brought the issue of unauthorized immigration to the forefront of national attention. National magazines such as *Time, Newsweek*, and *U.S. News and World Report* all featured high-profile stories.[181] As Peter Kwong contends, "the story of the *Golden Venture* became a national obsession" as "every television station and newspaper around the country carried its own investigation into what seemed to be an invasion of illegal aliens."[182] While such events had nothing to do with unauthorized immigration from Mexico, they significantly contributed to a growing perception of a country under siege from without.[183]

The Clinton administration was greatly worried about the political fallout from these events and claimed that it needed to increase efforts to decrease unauthorized immigration in order to protect state-sanctioned immigration. As one Clinton advisor explained, "There is a fear that unless the administration gets out in front, you'll see what you did in Germany: a violent reaction against immigration."[184] Thus, at a July 27, 1993 press conference, President Clinton announced initiatives to enhance boundary enforcement. In doing so, he employed rhetoric that was a marked departure from his relatively innocuous statements on the matter in the past:

> The simple fact is that we must not, and we will not, surrender our borders to those who wish to exploit our history of compassion and justice. We cannot tolerate those who traffic in human cargo, nor can we allow our people to be endangered by those who would enter our country to terrorize Americans. . . .
>
> Today we send a strong and clear message. We will make it tougher for illegal aliens to get into our country.[185]

At the media gathering, Clinton also voiced his support for an amendment introduced by Congressman Duncan Hunter that proposed adding six hundred agents to the Border Patrol (the amendment had already easily passed the Republican-dominated House of Representatives). In fact, Clinton acted as if the proposal was his idea.[186]

Around the same time, politicians began tripping over one another to take a tough stance on boundary enforcement and unauthorized immigration. This was especially true in California. In 1993, for example, members of the California Senate and Assembly introduced almost forty separate measures aimed at addressing both legal and extralegal immigration.[187] Such efforts were not limited to Republicans, as California's Democrats scampered to curry favor with an increasingly prorestriction electorate. Democratic gubernatorial candidate Kathleen Brown, for example, called for the deportation of unauthorized immigrants convicted of crimes in the United States; Democratic Senator Dianne Feinstein proposed a $1 toll on all boundary crossings from Mexico to pay for an expansion of the Border Patrol; and two days after the Clinton press conference, California Senator Barbara Boxer (Democrat) called for the deployment of the National Guard to augment the Border Patrol. Administration officials (most notably Attorney General Janet Reno) and numerous politicians visited the border region in San Diego to provide the appearance of substance to their heightened concerns.[188]

Such moves were undoubtedly popular in California. An August 1993 Field Poll showed that 74 percent of Californians believed that unauthorized immigration hurt the state. Among non-Hispanic whites in California, 81 percent believed extralegal immigration to be a very serious problem.[189] While opinion was most intense in California, anti-immigration sentiment reached historic highs on the national level. An August 1993 *Newsweek* poll reported that 60 percent of Americans thought that current levels of immigration were bad, with 62 percent of poll respondents worried that immigrants might take jobs from native-born workers.[190] Although opinion polls have consistently shown that since 1945 Americans have wanted lower levels of immigration,[191] the 1993 results reflected the highest level of hostility toward immigrants "since the heyday of nativism in the 1920s."[192] Indeed, a September 1993 Gallup Poll found three out of ten Americans listing "illegal immigration" as the country's most important problem.[193]

While the Clinton administration began laying the groundwork for enhanced boundary policing, Silvestre Reyes, the Border Patrol chief of the El Paso Sector, unilaterally launched Operation Blockade (later renamed "Hold-the-Line" as the former proved to be quite offensive to the Mexican government) in the El Paso border region. On September 19, 1993, Reyes deployed four hundred agents and their vehicles in a highly visible "show of force" along a twenty-mile section of the boundary dividing El Paso from Ciudad Juárez. Inspections at official ports of entry also intensified. The strategy represented a radical departure from the prior Border Patrol strategy of pursuing and apprehending unauthorized immigrants after they had crossed the boundary into the El Paso area. Almost immediately, Blockade had a significant effect in deterring unauthorized crossings into El Paso; Border Patrol apprehensions fell dramatically.[194] Within one week, in what had been the Border Patrol's second-busiest sector (after San Diego), apprehensions fell from a daily average of about 800 per day to about 150 per day.[195]

Operation Blockade received a good deal of favorable national publicity. And locally, many San Diego politicians, especially Republicans, reacted positively to the new strategy. Shortly after its implementation in El Paso, San Diego Republican Congressmen Cunningham and Hunter met with Attorney General Reno to ask her to implement a similar strategy along the boundary with Tijuana.[196] (The attorney general heads the Department of Justice, within which is the INS.) A few days later the San Diego County Board of Supervisors turned up the heat on the Clinton administration by voting in favor of sending a monthly bill to the federal government for reimbursement of costs related to unauthorized immigration.[197] The next week, local INS border chief Gustavo De La Viña and the heads of the San Diego county and city police departments called for a significant increase in federal resources for boundary enforcement to stem the flow of unauthorized immigrants and to fight the associated drug smuggling, crime, and poverty.[198] Soon thereafter, Governor Pete Wilson called for expanding the El Paso strategy along the U.S.-Mexico boundary and implementing a similar operation in San Diego. He suggested that the federal government pay for the additional resources needed through cuts in public assistance programs.[199]

While the Clinton administration publicly lauded the El Paso strategy, privately its reaction was lukewarm at best, and occasionally openly hostile.[200] Privately, many INS officials were irritated with what they saw as Chief Reyes's irresponsible, unilateral action in El Paso. Many feared that the operation, which led to serious short-term tensions along the Mexican side of the boundary,[201] would hurt relations with Mexico and possibly undermine ongoing negotiations surrounding the North American Free Trade Agreement

(NAFTA). There were also feelings that Reyes was threatening an emerging consensus within the INS for a national boundary-enforcement strategy that favored concentrating enforcement efforts in the geographical areas with the highest volume of unauthorized immigrant traffic, such as San Diego.[202] Like a number of San Diego elites,[203] the Clinton administration felt that the blockade sent the wrong kind of message to Mexico. At the same time, some argued that the El Paso–style operation was inappropriate for San Diego given the local physical geography and the nature of unauthorized crossings (more long-term, long-distance crossers, with the majority of crossings taking place at night rather than during the day). Proponents of this view often contended that the best way to deal with the problem of unauthorized immigration was through cooperative measures aimed at boosting Mexico's level of development, most notably through NAFTA.[204]

Despite opposition to Operation Hold-the-Line, a slow but significant buildup along the boundary was taking place,[205] most notably in the San Diego Sector. The Clinton administration announced high-profile plans to enhance control of the boundary.[206] The passage of the so-called Crime Bill in August 1994 further helped by providing significant funding for most of the administration's immigration enforcement initiatives. It insured that boundary enforcement would continue to increase over the next six years.[207] Many Democratic supporters and politicians, as well as administration appointees, had urged the administration to get out in front of efforts to restrict unauthorized immigration in order to prevent the passage of more drastic Republican proposals. In addition, electoral concerns—both in terms of the 1994 congressional elections and Clinton's reelection bid in 1996—did not allow the White House to avoid a proactive stance on the issue.[208] For its part, the Clinton administration represented its efforts to fight unauthorized immigration as being part of a larger project protecting state-sanctioned immigration.[209] As President Clinton stated in July 1993, "The solution [to the problem of illegal immigration] is to welcome legal immigrants and legal legitimate refugees and to turn away those who do not obey the laws. We must say no to illegal immigration so we can continue to say yes to legal immigration."[210] Father Theodore Hesburgh had made almost the exact same argument as head of the U.S. Select Commission on Immigration and Refugee Policy in 1981.[211]

Despite Clinton's efforts, however, Republicans kept attacking his policies as inadequate. These attacks intensified as the November 1994 elections approached, especially in California in the midst of a gubernatorial race and intense debate over Proposition 187, the so-called Save Our State (SOS) ballot initiative. The proposition proposed denying public education (from elementary to postsecondary levels), social services, and health care services (with the exception of emergencies) to unauthorized immigrants. The product of local immigration control groups in California, in conjunction with FAIR, Proposition 187 received little attention until Pete Wilson adopted it as his own in mid-1994 in an attempt to turn around his flagging gubernatorial campaign.[212] Most Democratic politicians opposed Proposition 187, but appreciated that Wilson had his hand on the pulse of an issue that resonated with a majority of an increasingly restrictionist California electorate.[213]

We can thus interpret Operation Gatekeeper as a response to Proposition 187, and perhaps even an attempt to try to defeat it. By giving the impression that the Clinton administration was taking care of the perceived problem of boundary enforcement in southern California, it was the hope that the California electorate would feel less of a need to approve and implement Proposition 187. More broadly, it was an attempt by the Democrats to seize the lead in the battle against unauthorized immigration in time for the November 1994 elections.[214] Thus, on September 13, 1994, Democratic gubernatorial candidate Kathleen Brown—trailing in polls to Wilson by nine percentage points at the time—called upon the Clinton administration to implement an El Paso–style operation in San Diego.[215] Surely she was aware of the pending announcement of a high-profile boundary enforcement strategy in San Diego by Attorney General Reno four days later in Los Angeles. This strategy, launched on October 1, 1994, was Operation Gatekeeper.

CONCLUSION

Operation Gatekeeper is many things, one of which was a political sideshow designed for public consumption to demonstrate the Clinton administration's seriousness about cracking down on unauthorized immigration. Efforts by the White House and the INS to maximize coverage of the implementation of the operation demonstrate that Washington, D.C., was acutely aware of the importance of the operation for purposes of public consumption. In this regard, the U.S.-Mexico boundary became a stage with a national audience. But it is not my intention to reduce Gatekeeper to a media event, as it is undoubtedly a serious attempt to enhance state control over a stretch of the U.S.-Mexico boundary. At the same time, it is too simple to argue that Operation Gatekeeper was merely the Clinton White House's answer to Pete Wilson, Proposition 187, and growing restrictionist sentiment in the United States. Although short-term political pressures were decisive factors informing the emergence of Gatekeeper, something somewhat similar probably would have eventually emerged along the U.S.-Mexico boundary even without those exact same pressures, albeit without all the political and media fanfare that surrounded Gatekeeper.[216] A whole host of long-, medium-, and short-term factors at the international, national, and local scales came together to create the operation. As this chapter and chapters 2 and 3 have demonstrated, there has been an intensification of boundary enforcement and a reification—both in the physical and ideological senses—of the U.S.-Mexico boundary over time. These processes intensified greatly, beginning in the mid-1970s. In this sense, Gatekeeper was not only a boundary-enforcement strategy, but more importantly a crystallization of a variety of temporal, social, and spatial trends.

These developments represent, among other things, a significant change in U.S. perception of the U.S.-Mexico boundary, at least in terms of immigration, and in governmental actions/practices in regards to the international division. These developments are a manifestation of a shift from the divide being a border, or a zone of transition within which there is a common culture, to a boundary that represents a stark, linear demarcation between "us" and "them"—both territorially and socially. As Congressman Duncan Hunter, one of the principal instigators of increased border policing, stated in 1994 in voicing his support for a plan initiated by Attorney General Janet Reno to enhance control of the boundary, the initiative was "necessary to establish a border for the first time."[217]

Jeannette Money contends that local conditions informed by competition between "natives" and immigrants trigger anti-immigrant sentiment. She identifies three dimensions of this competition: (1) labor market competition in the context of an economic recession; (2) competition over state resources in the midst of an economic recession, the rate of growth of the immigrant community, and the access of that community to state resources; and (3) competition over societal identity informed by the size of the immigrant community and its rate of assimilation.[218] While such an analytical framework certainly helps to shed light on rising restrictionist sentiment in California and, more generally, in the United States in the early 1990s, it seems to assume that anti-immigrant sentiment is an almost automatic response to the aforementioned dimensions of competition, rather than one created by concrete choices and subsequent actions of individuals and institutions, as well as one conditioned by a host of historical, geographical, and ideological elements. Local politicians, both Republican and Democratic, in New York City and the state of New York (long important destinations for both legal and unauthorized immigrants), for example, did not employ the type of prorestrictionist posturing so common in California to the influx of immigrants.[219] Similarly, the state of Texas, like California a major recipient of extralegal immigrants from Mexico, adopted a less divisive stance toward the putative problems associated with unauthorized immigration.[220] Undoubtedly, there are numerous reasons for these interstate differences. In the case of Texas, for example, the fact that the state is more economically integrated (and thus more dependent) on Mexico than is California helps, perhaps, to explain the different response to the various common factors that facilitated the surge in favor of a crackdown on unauthorized immigration in California.[221] Nevertheless, while prominent Texas politicians did not champion Proposition

187–type "solutions" to the putative problem of unauthorized immigration, prorestrictionist sentiment within the state—as throughout the United States—was still strong. And, as throughout the country, this sentiment focused largely on the boundary with Mexico and Mexican immigrants. For such reasons, we need to turn to the matter of ideology and to analyze the role that the sociocultural construction of the undesirable immigrant—specifically coming from Mexico—has played historically in fueling heightened sentiment in favor of intensified immigration restriction. This is the subject that follows.

The Ideological Roots of the "Illegal": The "Other" as Threat and the Rise of The Boundary as the Symbol of Protection

In the West there was panic when the migrants multiplied on the highways. Men of property were terrified for their property. Men who had never been hungry saw the eyes of the hungry. Men who had never wanted anything very much saw the flare of want in the eyes of the migrants. And the men of the towns and of the soft suburban country gathered to defend themselves; and they reassured themselves that they were good and the invaders bad, as a man must do before he fights. They said, Those goddamned Okies are dirty and ignorant. They're degenerate, sexual maniacs. Those goddamned Okies are thieves. They'll steal anything. They've got no sense of property rights.

—John Steinbeck, *The Grapes of Wrath*[1]

The hostility that Mexicans encountered as they moved onto the land that that was once Mexico is simultaneously ironic, offensive, and indicative of much about the Anglo-American society that they were confronting. The legacy of the Mexican-American War awaited Mexican immigrants as they arrived in the north. The inheritance of history denoted them as a defeated and inferior people for whom unskilled labor was their only fitting role.

—Douglas Monroy, *Rebirth: Mexican Los Angeles from the Great Migration to the Great Depression.*[2]

It is . . . not only the discursive practices manifested in legal statutes that create identities, but also the way that these practices are infused with societal norms and values. In examining the discursive production of national identity, one needs to examine not only laws per se, but the debates, interpretations, and professed needs and interests that surround legal statutes and the social practices to which these are linked.

—Roxanne Doty, "The Double-Writing of Statecraft: Exploring State Responses to Illegal Immigration."[3]

The manner in which American society talks and writes about unauthorized immigration has changed significantly over the last several decades, entailing a growing emphasis on the legality of migrants. Through the 1930s, the categories employed to describe unauthorized immigrants were such that they differentiated largely between "legitimate" and "illegitimate" or "ineligible" immigrants.[4] The contemporary emphasis on "illegals" (as opposed to "wetbacks" or "undesirables") is of relatively recent origin. A database search of judicial decisions, for example, found no reference to the term *illegal* in regards to immigrants prior to 1950.[5] Over the last few decades, however, public discourse has increasingly employed the term to describe unauthorized immigrants to the point where, today, it is almost exclusively the term of choice.

This development is not a mere point of narrow academic interest. Language has a power of its own; As Hugh Mehan points out, "The language we use in public discourse and the way we talk about events and people in everyday life makes [sic] a difference in the way we think and the way we act about them."[6] And language, of course, also reflects our ways of thinking and living; it is for such reasons that I interrogate the rise of the "illegal" as a discursive category. The central argument that I make is that we cannot divorce growing emphasis on "illegal aliens" from the long history in the United States of largely race-based anti-immigrant sentiment rooted in fear and/or rejection of the those deemed as outsiders, a history that is inextricably tied to a context of exploitation and political and economic marginalization of certain immigrant populations. Operation Gatekeeper, as a state strategy to enhance control over unauthorized passage over the boundary in southern California, is, in no small part, a manifestation and outgrowth of such sentiment.

To appreciate why the "illegal" as a threat to national society and the image of a U.S.-Mexico boundary "out of control" resonate so deeply with the American public, we must examine the dialectical relationship between political and economic factors (most notably the state) and culture (or the motivating passions represented by the nation).[7] Such a project is necessarily historical in that, while Gatekeeper and the multiplicity of factors behind it are unique, they are also part and parcel of numerous elements built up over time and space—many of which are ideological.[8] Thus, I begin with a brief overview of the history of exclusionist practice in the United States. I then turn to the case of California to compare and contrast the historical development of exclusionism on the national level with that in the state, especially in southern California. In doing so I establish the roots of American fears about immigration-related "illegality" in historical debates over who belongs, or should belong, to the "American nation." Finally, I look at how public discourse vis-à-vis unauthorized immigrants shifted in the period from 1924—the year of the founding of the Border Patrol—and 1994, the year that Operation Gatekeeper began.

NATIVISM: AS AMERICAN AS APPLE PIE?

Certainly there is much truth to Jeannette Money's account of the conditions under which anti-immigrant sentiment arises.[9] The peaks of anti-immigrant fervor in the United States have all taken place during times of economic uncertainty and decreasing job security, when the social, ethnic, and cultural disparities between the dominant culture and new immigrants have loomed large, and when "large and sustained" inflows of immigrants have occurred.[10] But under these conditions, a variety of responses are possible, anti-immigrant sentiment being just one of the possibilities.

To comprehend anti-immigrant sentiment in the United States, it is important to realize that such thinking is but one of a number of contending positions historically. Although anti-immigrant sentiment has dominated political discourse and practice at particular points in time and space, the history of American thought toward immigration is far more complex. Indeed, as sociologist Joe Feagin argues, there is much merit to the view that the United States is a "nation of immigrants."[11] But rather than counterposing tolerance or pro-immigrant sentiment with anti-immigrant sentiment, we should see the seemingly dichotomous ideologies as part and parcel of a complex culture as well as an outgrowth of competing interests—namely those of labor and capital. While labor has at times favored strong immigration restriction, capital has largely championed an "open door." These conflicting positions partially explain why, as Feagin contends, a certain schizophrenia has long marked U.S. thought on immigration.[12] U.S. immigration policies have generally reflected "the desires, interests, and purposes of Americans of European descent," thus resulting in the United States having a very high percentage of peoples of European ancestry.[13] We need to examine the dynamic interrelationships among ideas, social conditions, and state policies and practices to understand how and why this has come to be.

There has clearly long been fertile ground for nativist sentiment in the United States. Nativism is not simply anti-immigrant sentiment, but is opposition to sociocultural difference, and thus involves rejection of internal "minorities" as well as "foreigners."[14] Although the bases for such thinking have been multiple, including political beliefs, poverty, and health, the most important factor over time has been that of race.[15] At the same time, while nativism, in the form of anti-immigrant thought, has a long history in the United States, it is hardly a homogeneous one. Indeed, the content and central themes of anti-immigrant sentiment have varied over time, "corresponding to shifting ideological and political needs and their structural underpinnings."[16] Material factors always dovetail with political symbolism to produce nativism[17] and, for that reason, we must investigate the dialectical relationship between the "real" and the "ideal" to ascertain the specific dimensions of various periods of anti-immigrant sentiment.

Nativist thought and movements in the United States date back to at least the late 1700s. Most early settlers from Europe, while coming from different parts of the British Isles, shared a commitment to Anglo-Protestant culture,[18] central to which were variations of the English language. And it was a "fierce commitment to the English norms, values, and ways of operating" that laid the basis for modern nativism.[19] The Puritans helped construct a foundation for the American nation based on, among other things, ethnocentrism and parochialism of which genocide against Native Americans and the enslavement of Africans were constituent elements. European settlers contrasted themselves with "savages," the indigenous inhabitants of the territory. To be civilized was to be "Christian, rational, sexually controlled, and white." By the eighteenth and nineteenth century, theories arguing for the racial and cultural inferiority of "uncivilized savages" were common in England and what became the United States.[20]

Negative images of outsiders were not limited to Native Americans and Africans. In the 1700s, Euro-Americans began to view certain types of European immigrants, especially non-Protestants, as savages as well. Prior to the American Revolution, nativistic sentiment was based chiefly on the religious and supposedly moral characteristics of newcomers, often resulting in barriers to immigration to the colonies for members of certain religious groups (especially Catholics), the very poor, and convicts.[21] The primary focus of anti-immigrant sentiment at the time was upon non-English-speaking groups. Following the Revolution, George Washington's Federalist Party was very concerned about the support of non-British immigrants for Jeffersonian ideas. It was in this context that the first federal immigration restrictions, the 1798 Alien and Sedition Acts, became a reality.[22] The part known as the Alien Act empowered the president to arrest and deport any foreigner regarded as "dangerous." The intent of the law was to prevent the spread of supposedly radical ideas emanating from the French Revolution. Another part of the law (the Naturalization Act of 1798) required the registration of all aliens and greatly increased the residency requirement for citizenship.[23]

In any case, European immigration to the United States did not reach significant levels until after 1820. While "push" factors in Europe played an important role in prompting rising emigration from Europe, U.S. policies and private sector recruitment of immigrants also played an important role.[24] Despite widespread nativistic sentiment, national elites very much championed an open door policy for European immigration in the early days of the republic. The so-called open door of immigration came about as a result of the rise of industrialization and the accompanying need for an industrial labor force.[25] Given that the United States did not have to cover the costs of social reproduction of immigrant adults, U.S. elites were happy to receive the "gift" of free labor. As the December 13, 1892 issue of the *New York Journal of Commerce* gushed, "Men, like cows, are expensive to raise and gift of either should be gladly received. And a man can be put to more valuable use than a cow."[26]

Undoubtedly, the influx of immigrant laborers—a disproportionate number of whom were "unskilled"—facilitated the interests of domestic capitalists, who often used the new immigrants to break strikes and to ratchet down wages. Given the scale of immigration (the U.S. population tripled between 1820 and 1860, from 9,600,000 to 31,500,000), the supply of low-wage labor was plentiful and concentrated in the country's largest urban areas. That so many of these new immigrants were Catholic served to exacerbate further the divide between "new" and "old" immigrants. All these factors came together in the mid-nineteenth century to produce "the most violent and vehement anti-immigration protest in U.S. history."[27] Armed conflict between native and immigrant workers was taking place in almost every state by the 1850s.[28]

Despite such anti-immigrant violence and rising nativist sentiment within the general populace, the U.S. Congress did not vote on any bills to restrict immigration in the first few decades of the nineteenth century. Sociologist Kitty Calavita argues that this congressional inaction was most likely due to the power of capital and its need for the very immigrants protested by a fragmented nativist movement.[29] Indeed, to the extent that the federal government did take action, it was usually to facilitate immigration. During the Civil War, for example, the federal government implemented the Act to Encourage Immigration (1864), the first comprehensive federal immigration law. The legislation established the first U.S. Immigration Bureau, the primary function of which was to increase immigration so that U.S. industries would have a sufficient labor supply during the Civil War. Despite the legislation's repeal in 1868, it laid the foundation for the proliferation of private labor recruitment agencies that were vital in encouraging European emigration in the late nineteenth century.[30]

After the war, during the 1870s and 1880s, industrialists picked up after the federal government and actively recruited immigrant labor. As the immigrant influx began to take on a life of its own, immigration again became a serious handicap for organized labor as employers took advantage of the enlarged labor pool to lower wages and break strikes.[31] This was a time of extraordinary industrial expansion, mechanization of production being an important component of the growth. Mechanization allowed industrialists to replace skilled, unionized labor with "the thousands of unskilled, nonunionized immigrants that entered the country each month."[32]

In spite of employer efforts to undermine labor organizing and because of rapid industrialization (and thus significant growth of the workforce), organized labor was still able to grow to unprecedented levels during the post–Civil War era. Its growing power as a national force reached an apex in 1885 and enabled organized labor to engage in highly effective strikes. Industry's primary weapon against the increasing power of organized labor was, as before, the importation and employment of recent immigrant workers. Despite this strategy of pitting worker against worker, the "ideal of fraternity toward European immigrants" among unions was stronger than the restrictionist tendency for much of the nineteenth century.[33] In the 1860s, for example, the National Labor Union, although perturbed by the trouble caused by high levels of European immigration, did not call for restriction, but instead called upon European unions to urge their members not to migrate to the United States during periods of high unemployment. In the 1880s, again rather than advocating restrictions, the Knights of Labor fought against contract labor importation, ultimately succeeding in having Congress outlaw the practice.[34]

Although organized labor often had a somewhat benign attitude toward European immigrants in the nineteenth century, it did not extend such levels of relative solidarity to non-European immigrants. While many post–Civil War labor organizations had progressive attitudes toward race relations, there was a gap between rhetoric and practice. In the late 1860s, for instance, black workers "found the National Labor Union reluctant to organize them" despite the union's "declaring that it recognized 'neither color nor sex on the question of the rights of labor.' "[35] At the same time, there was most definitely an overtly nativist and racist component of a significant sector of the labor movement. New waves of immigration and disruptive economic changes brought about by accelerated industrialization during the Civil War provided a fertile context for organized labor's nativism. The rapidity and the extent of the new immigration exacerbated divisions within the U.S. working class between settled workers trying to organize and the new immigrant underclass seeking jobs.[36] Organized labor, for example, was "a major force" in obtaining the passage of the Chinese Exclusion Act of 1882.[37] Most analysts would seem to agree with historian David Reimers's assessment that "[t]he late nineteenth century, with its ugly racism toward blacks and American Indians, offered fertile ground for racist attitudes toward Chinese immigrants" and other undesirable racial and ethnic groups—including immigrants from southern and eastern Europe.[38]

Passage of the Chinese Exclusion Act was one in a series of laws passed by Congress, beginning in 1875, to regulate immigration through qualitative controls (immigration controls based on social, political, economic, and racial/ethnic criteria).[39] But as legal scholar Gerald Neuman argues, we should not make the mistake of thinking that the boundaries of the United States were legally open until the enactment of federal immigration legislation in the 1870s and 1880s.[40] Although neither Congress nor the states established quantitative limits on immigration, a wide variety of qualitative regulations, primarily at the level of the states, applied to the transboundary movement of persons in the nineteenth century.[41] State legislation on immigration policy focused on five major categories of movement restriction of citizens and noncitizens: criminals; public health risks; the poor and disabled; slaves; and people of marginalized racial and/or ethnic groups.[42]

The Chinese Exclusion Act of 1882 marked the beginning of a process by which the federal government "codified in immigration law the elision of racist and nationalist discourse."[43] A combination of rising racialist ideologies, growing domestic unemployment, and general economic uncertainty worked together to restrict immigration and put an end to the so-called open door. Congress excluded a number of other groups on the basis of "race" over the next few decades, culminating in the passage of the Immigration Act of 1917. As Ronald Wyse notes, by the act's terms "most classes of persons who were feeble minded, destitute, seriously ill or morally undesirable were barred from admittance."[44] It also restated all past qualitative exclusions and established the "Asiatic Barred Zone," a geographic area that included most of Asia and the Pacific Islands, further restricting the entry of Asian immigrants. Included in the legislation was the Burnett or Literacy Act in 1917, which required a literacy test for entry.[45] Immigration restrictionists believed that the literacy law would distinguish between "unfit" immigrants from southern and eastern Europe and "desirable" ones from northern Europe. As Representative William Richardson of Alabama argued, "The latter are people who helped us lay the foundation principles of our Republic and an unsurpassed civilization [while] the former are represented chiefly in the bum, the pauper and criminal aliens."[46] While a number of factors—including white supremacy, social Darwinism, and political opportunism—informed the efforts of immigration restrictionists, all "shared the beliefs that the increase in immigration that took place from 1890 onwards, especially from Southern and Eastern Europe, threatened to overwhelm the nation's ability to absorb and 'Americanize' newcomers."[47] Congressional efforts to enhance immigration restriction at the time overlapped with the extension by Congress of Jim Crow segregationist laws into the District of Columbia. Indeed, many southern senators and congressman who led the fight for Jim Crow in Washington played leading roles in formulating restrictionist immigration policies, a number of them urging their legislative colleagues to apply "southern methods" of racial segregation and control to the country's immigration regime.[48]

An unprecedented attack led by nativists against organized labor, the left, and immigrants emerged in the aftermath of the Russian Revolution of 1917 and the end of the First World War.[49] This development, along with rising nativism in the labor movement (especially in the context of a severe postwar recession in 1920–21), helped restrictionists to facilitate the passage of the temporary Quota Act of 1921. Restrictionists put forth a theory known as "alien indigestion": "In substance, this meant that because of the great numbers of persons who had immigrated in previous years, the melting pot needed time to melt."[50] The 1921 act limited the number of admissions of any one particular nationality to three percent of the group's population already in the United States according to the 1910 census; this marked the first quantitative immigration restriction in U.S. history.

The Immigration Act of 1924 made the quotas permanent, but lowered the permitted percentage of immigrants to 2 percent and used the census of 1890 as its base. The legislation also included the Oriental Exclusion Act, which banned all Asian immigration except that from the Philippines.[51] As opposed to the temporary Quota Act of 1921, economic arguments were secondary to ones of racial purity in 1924 ("alien indigestion" became "racial indigestion").[52]

The 1921 and 1924 acts effectively created fixed concepts of "race," which the legislation effectively conflated with the concept of the "nation." As has been noted by Bob Carter, Marci Green, and Rick Halpern, the acts had two important effects: First, they "firmly tied immigrants to national levels which in many cases bore no connection to their cultural self-identities or even their geographic origin: terms like 'Bohemian' and 'Jew' referred, quite literally, to imagined communities, while labels such as 'African' were so broad as to be meaningless. Secondly, on the level of popular consciousness, the quota machinery legitimated ideas about assimilability, identified certain kinds of immigrants as being incapable of 'fitting in' . . . and validated the belief that 'race' classification was the most accurate way of making sense of the world's peoples."[53] The 1924 law resulted in 85 percent of the new immigrant quota (of a total of 150,000 immigrants permitted annually) allocated to northwestern Europe.[54] Along with the mass deportation of Mexican immigrants in a context of Depression-induced anti-Mexican hysteria during the 1930s, the 1924 legislation had the effect of severely restricting immigration from what would come to be known as the third world.[55]

Efforts to alter the racist nature of U.S. immigration policies began in the 1940s. In 1943, Congress repealed the Chinese exclusion laws, granting China an annual immigration quota of 105 persons. Although the repeal occurred largely as a result of the U.S. entry into World War II as an ally of China against Japan, race- and ethnic-based bigotry began to subside slowly after 1940. Rising prosperity also facilitated the lowering of racial barriers. In 1946, Congress passed legislation allowing annual immigration quotas of one hundred to both India and the Philippines (which gained its independence from the United States that year).[56]

Then, in 1949, the House of Representatives passed a bill establishing similar quotas for most other Asian countries, including Japan, but the Senate took no action on the bill.[57] Eventually the bill became law as part of the McCarran-Walter Act of 1952. The act included a restatement of the race-based, national-origins quotas as well as harsh national security restrictions that barred suspected "subversives" from entering the United States. But the law also made persons from all "races" eligible for immigration and citizenship—for the first time since Congress originally restricted citizenship to "free white persons" in 1790.[58] While significant, the law had little effect in changing the geographic origin and racial/ethnic composition aspects of immigration. Indeed, due to the continuing effect of the national origins quotas, the vast majority of immigrants from the Eastern Hemisphere from 1945 to 1965 were Europeans.[59]

Meanwhile, the immigration system established in the 1920s and reinforced by McCarran-Walters gradually eroded as presidential action and special congressional laws created all sorts of exceptions. Thus, by the early 1960s, two-thirds of those immigrating to the United States were nonquota, half of whom were from outside the Western Hemisphere.[60] This reality, combined with growing racial and ethnic tolerance, the rise of the civil rights movement, general economic prosperity, and the landslide election in 1964 of Lyndon Johnson and congressional Democrats greatly facilitated the passage of the Immigration Act of 1965. The act eliminated national origins quotas (over a three-year period) and provided 170,000 visas annually to persons from the Eastern Hemisphere and 120,000 to those from the Western Hemisphere. Perhaps most significantly, the act exempted from the quotas "immediate" family members of people already in the United States with authorization.[61]

Arguably, the changes that culminated with the passage of the Immigration Act of 1965 made race an unacceptable criteria in U.S. immigration discourse and policy. And, in one sense it certainly did. On the other hand, however, the effects of the pre-1965 immigration policies, and the associated ideologies, were profound in shaping American culture and notions (both then and now) of "we" and "they."[62] Race continues to animate U.S. immigration debates and to inform ideas as to who and what should constitute the American "nation." But race is not a static concept, nor is it simply a manner to categorize supposedly biologically based groups. It is far more complex and nuanced. In the contemporary world, race is often inextricably tied to notions of nation.[63] But before further developing this line of argument, I want to examine how the processes of racialization of non-"American" groups played itself out vis-à-vis people of Mexican origin, especially in the context of California.

NATIVISM TOWARD THOSE FROM "SOUTH OF THE BORDER"

As discussed earlier, in addition to conflict, cooperation often characterized social relations in the U.S.-Mexico border region in the early part of the twentieth century. It was in part a reflection of the highly porous nature of the international boundary, as well as the border region's physical and social isolation from the "centers" of Mexico and the United States. Similarly, racial, ethnic, and national boundaries were also relatively porous in most areas of the border. As Linda Gordon writes of the Mexican origin population along the international boundary in the early 1900s, "They lived in a border culture (and many of them in twin towns that straddled the border, like Douglas and Agua Prieta, Bisbee and Naco, El Paso and Ciudad Juárez); they were not so much binational as they were border people, as if border itself were their nationality."[64] Relatively quickly, however, border Anglos came to see the Mexican-origin population less in the diversity that it embodied, and more as an undifferentiated body. *Mexican* came to mean "poor, ignorant, degraded."[65]

This shift in thinking and practice reflected a complex web of politicoeconomic, geographical, cultural, and ideological forces.[66] These forces came together to "alienize" the population of Mexican descent on the U.S. side of the international divide, to create and essentialize differences on the basis of race, gender, ethnicity, class, and/or nationality. In its most benign appearance, the goal of this process was to "Americanize" the Mexican population. In reality, however, the effect was to relegate a population that had been "insiders" to a position of sociocultural, political, and economic inferiority. This process of marginalization and racialization had many different components. Commodification of Mexicans as low-wage labor through the creation of an apartheid-like dual wage system, for example, paid Mexicans—regardless of skills and experience—less than Anglos for comparable work. Culturally, the education system "taught Mexican children from the 1870s on that the way to be a good American was to reject Mexican culture." In this manner, cultural marginalization and economic exploitation were very much intertwined.[67]

Persons of Mexican origin were targets of nativist and racist sentiment from the beginning of the process of "Americanization" of the territories that would become the United States. Stephen Austin, an American colonizer and the leader of the erstwhile Republic of Texas, for example, described the war with Mexico as one of "barbarism and of despotic principles, waged by the mongrel Spanish-Indian and Negro race, against civilization and the Anglo-American race."[68] While anti-Mexican sentiment shared much with the general xenophobic practices aimed at "undesirables," there were important differences in how Americans perceived and treated Mexicans in comparison to other "foreign" groups. And given the geographical concentration of the Mexican population in what would become the U.S. Southwest, the unique nature of anti-Mexican nativism was highly localized.

Mexican immigration was a very small proportion of total immigration into the United States through the beginning of the twentieth century. But as American elites began to call into question the costs and benefits of immigration from Europe, and to form the opinion of European immigrants as sources of potential political radicalism who had no intention of returning to their country of origin, these same elites began to perceive some benefit in increasing immigration from Mexico. The federal government's Dillingham Commission on Immigration expressed such a view in 1911, saying "Because of their strong attachment to their native land . . . and the possibility of their residence being discontinued, few [Mexicans] become citizens of the United States. The Mexican immigrants are providing a fairly adequate supply of labor. . . . While they are not easily assimilated, this is of no very great importance as long as most of them return to their native land. In the case of the Mexican, he is less desirable as a citizen than as a laborer."[69] Such thinking informed the decision of U.S. authorities to exempt Mexican immigrants temporarily from the literacy test required under the 1917 legislation, from the head tax and from the contract labor clause. Important to these exemptions was pressure from labor-hungry growers in the Southwest. Similarly, Congress exempted Mexicans from the 1921 and 1924 race-based quota system partly because of lobbying by agribusiness interests.[70]

So, while nineteenth- and early-twentieth-century national-scale anti-immigrant sentiment largely focused on peoples from southern and eastern Europe as well as Asia, Mexican immigrants remained largely invisible until the early twentieth century. Indeed, "most Americans remained unaware of this new immigrant invasion since Mexicans were confined to predominantly to the Southwest and hidden from sight in the boxcars, tents, and shacks of railroad and migrant farm labor camps."[71] But as Mexican migration grew and moved farther north and increasingly into the cities, it became more visible and increasingly subject to restrictionists' concerns. While *The Reader's Guide to Periodical Literature* listed nineteen articles on the subject of the "Mexican Problem" from 1910 to 1920, it recorded fifty-one such articles from 1920 to 1930. Reportedly, the articles focused largely on statistics regarding Mexican delinquency, the poor state of housing, low wages, low rates of literacy, and disease.[72]

Debate over the implementation of a quota for Mexican immigrants erupted between 1926 and 1930, with a number of restrictionists arguing that Mexican immigration was rapidly increasing, absolutely and relatively as a percentage of total immigration. Proponents of a quota for Mexican immigration employed three principal arguments, that "Mexican labor displaced Anglo native workers and kept wages low; the economic benefits derived from a cheap labor force was a short-term gain and a long-term cost; and the Mexican nationality posed a social threat to the 'white race' because Mexicans were *mestizos*, i.e., miscegenated, thus inferior. These views were, in turn, supported by allegedly 'objective scientific studies,' which rationalized the racist beliefs common to many whites."[73] The racist arguments often focused on the potential for a cultural and political swamping of the United States by Mexicans given their growing rates of immigration and the supposed hyper-fertility of Mexican women. Harry H. Laughlin, an advisor on eugenics to the House Immigration and Naturalization Committee, presented the alleged threat from Mexico in almost military terms, arguing that the Mexican influx was so immense "as to almost reverse the essential consequences of the Mexican War."[74] The Mexican was, according to many, inassimilable. As *The New York Times* opined in 1930, "It is folly to pretend that the more recently arrived Mexicans, who are largely of Indian blood, can be absorbed and incorporated into the American race."[75]

Quota opponents countered these arguments in a variety of ways, often using race-based reasoning as well to make their case. As a prominent doctor from Pasadena, California, stated while speaking before Congress, "The Mexican is a quiet, inoffensive necessity in that he performs the big majority of our rough work, agriculture, building, and street labor. They [sic] have no effect on the American standard of living because they are not much more than a group of fairly intelligent collie dogs."[76] Similarly, W. H. Knox of the Arizona Cotton Growers' Association, while testifying to Congress in 1926, dismissed fears of Mexicans threatening American society, saying, "Have you ever heard, in the history of the United States, or in the history of the human race, of the white race being overrun by a class of people of the mentality of the Mexicans? I never have. We took this country from Mexico. Mexico did not take it from us. To assume that there is any danger of any likelihood of the Mexican coming in here and colonizing this country and taking it away from us, to my mind, is absurd."[77] And for those who feared the "mongrelization" of the "white race" from miscegenation with Mexican immigrants, supporters of Mexican immigration advised that there was little reason for concern. As Harry Chandler (publisher of the *Los Angeles Times* and a large California landowner) informed Congress, Mexicans "do not intermarry like the negro with white people. They do not mingle. They keep to themselves. That is the safety of it."[78] Opponents of quotas also argued that Mexican migrant workers would be subject to restrictions such as the head tax and a host of others that denied entrance to "undesirable" immigrants, which would thus serve to filter out the worst of potential Mexican immigrants.[79] In addition, the anti-restrictionists held one last "trump card." They argued that if Mexican immigrants did cause serious racial or social problems, they "unlike blacks, Puerto Ricans, and Filipinos who were not legally aliens could easily be deported" given the proximity of Mexico to the United States.[80]

This debate took particular forms in California, a state with a long history of white supremacist thought and practice.[81] California played a key role in constructing immigration restrictionism more generally—especially in producing the "yellow peril" supposedly represented by Chinese and Japanese immigrants. The California chapter of the Knights of Labor (often touted as a progressive force despite the organization's formal exclusion of Chinese workers), for instance, was a leading force of the campaign to expel the Chinese from the West Coast. At the Knights-sponsored San Francisco Labor Conference in 1885 the delegates passed a resolution condemning Asian immigrants for "their bad moral habits, their low grades of development, their filth, their vices, their race differences from the Caucasians and their willing status as slaves."[82]

California developed a highly stratified racial hierarchy, in part a legacy of both Spanish and Mexican control of the territory.[83] Indians or Native Americans were at the bottom of the ladder, a product of a strict racial hierarchy that informed the structure of "American" California from the time of its establishment. White Californians saw Indians as their "complete antithesis" and as "the lowest level of humankind imaginable."[84] As Tomás Almaguer notes, "The California Indians wore little clothing, were perceived as horrendously ugly and dirty, ate foods 'Americans' deemed unpalatable, and practiced tribal rituals and ceremonies that were anathema to European Christian practices. In short, they were cast as the extreme incarnation of all that was both uncivilized and heathen."[85] Anglo California, on the other hand, deemed Mexicans as "half-civilized" and much closer to Euro-American notions of civilization than Indians. This was due to the mixed European ancestry and the resulting linguistic and religious practices of Mexicans. And the lingering political influence of the pre-U.S.-conquest Mexican or *Californio* elite had a moderating effect on the most extreme forms of Anglo anti-Mexican sentiment.[86]

The position of blacks and Asian immigrants was located somewhere in between the "half-civilized" Mexicans and "uncivilized" Indians. Despite widespread antiblack sentiment, blacks were Christian and English speaking and, because of the experience of slavery, had taken on a number of European cultural traits—factors reluctantly acknowledged by most whites in California.[87] Asians, however, given their highly different cultural practices, were deemed as relatively uncivilized and closer to Native Americans in the racial hierarchy.[88]

These racial boundaries were the subject of contentious debate at California's State Constitutional Convention in 1849. The result was the designation of Mexicans as "white" and thus eligible for citizenship, while California Indians—like other Indians throughout the United States—received the status of "nonwhite."[89]

Probably more so than most states, especially those in the East, California's white population was relatively unified, avoiding the often tense intra-European, ethnic antagonisms that plagued social relations in other parts of the country during the nineteenth and early twentieth centuries. Sociologist Tomás Almaguer argues that this state of affairs was an outgrowth of the migration to California of a diverse European-American population, which served to produce an overall racial identity of "white" that proved stronger than ethnic differences.[90] As noted in chapter 2, white supremacy—more specifically, the alleged superiority of the Anglo-Saxon "race"—very much informed the ideology and practice of Manifest Destiny that underlay the U.S. conquest of California.[91] As in other parts of the country, race—not class—became "the key organizing principle of hierarchical relations of inequality,"[92] although, in practice, race and class very much overlapped and were mutually constitutive.

The influx of European Americans into California quickly worked to marginalize the territory's pre-1848 population. As of 1848, the non-Indian population of California was approximately 15,000, the majority of whom were Mexican Californians who lived alongside a few thousand European Americans. The estimated size of the Indian population as of 1850 was 100,000 persons. But the discovery of gold in California in 1848 changed matters rapidly. Indeed, by 1849, the European-American population was approximately 100,000 while that of Mexican origin was only 13,000. By 1870, the state's population had risen to over 500,000. While people from China, Germany, England, Ireland, and France were the most important countries of origin for immigrants to California, native-born Americans were the largest segment of California's new population.[93]

California Indians were the most adversely affected by the Americanization of California. A combination of diseases (the most significant factor), malnutrition and starvation, and military and (European-American) vigilante assaults quickly led to an almost total decimation of the indigenous population. By 1870, the state's Indian population had declined to 30,000. As of 1880, it had plummeted to 16,000.[94] By the early 1870s California Indians no longer represented any sort of threat to Euro-American hegemony in California: "In later years they eked out a meager existence on segregated federal reservations where many languished through the rest of the century."[95]

However, the white population did not ruthlessly marginalize Mexicans, but rather tried to integrate them into American society—albeit in a very much subordinated position. Unlike Indians, Mexicans had the right of suffrage and initially greatly outnumbered the Anglo population. But the rapid influx of white settlers enabled the new Anglo elite to legislate the subordination of the Mexican population, passing a number of laws in the state legislature that were aimed at Mexicans. The legislature, for example, passed an antivagrancy law—the so-called Greaser Act—that defined as vagrants "all persons who [were] commonly known as 'Greasers' or the issue of Spanish or Indian blood . . . and who [went] armed and [were] not peaceable and quiet persons."[96] Economically, a combination of capitalist market forces combined with a new system of taxation that imposed taxes on land, rather than on the products of the land, created great hardship for much of the Mexican landed class, contributing to widespread dispossession.[97] As a result, the Mexican population became increasingly "alienized" and proletarianized, serving to intensify the apartheid-like relationship between whites—who usually occupied positions of management, and white-collar and relatively skilled positions—and Mexicans working in the poorly paid, blue-collar, manual labor and service positions.[98]

Mexican immigration to the Southwest was largely limited to Texas until the early part of the twentieth century. California was de facto off limits as Asian immigrants, particularly Chinese, dominated the low-wage labor market, leaving little room for Mexican immigrants. As of 1900, Mexicans were only 1 or 2 percent of the state's population and were largely concentrated in southern California. This population of Mexican origin was about the same size as that of blacks and Japanese immigrants and smaller than the Chinese and Native American populations. And, given the intense ties Mexican labor had to the agricultural economy—a sector most European-American workers at the time had little interest in entering—as well as the slow integration of Mexicans into the white-controlled labor market, labor competition between Mexicans and whites was very limited through the beginning of the twentieth century. It was for this reason that Mexicans experienced a "surprisingly low level of racial conflict with European-American workers."[99]

This began to change, however, as Congress passed increasingly restrictive immigration legislation aimed at Asians and Europeans in the late nineteenth and early twentieth centuries. Mexican immigration to California grew rapidly after that time as farmers increasingly turned to Mexican labor.[100] The number of Mexican immigrants to California tripled between 1920 and 1930. At first, California growers were quite effusive in their praise of Mexican laborers.[101] As Dr. George Clements of the Los Angeles Chamber of Commerce stated, "No labor that has ever come to the United States is more satisfactory under righteous treatment. The Mexican as the result of years of servitude, has always looked upon his employer as his patron and upon himself as part of the establishment."[102] A lobbyist for California growers explained to a congressional committee that "the Mexican likes the sunshine against an adobe wall with a few tortillas and in the off time he drifts across the border where he may have these things."[103] As the flow of Mexican migrant workers continued, "agricultural labor became virtually synonymous with Mexican labor, and Mexican wages with 'cheap' wages in the U.S. Southwest."[104]

While employers might have appreciated Mexican workers, California nativists did not. Local nativists made immigrants their primary economic scapegoat during the 1913–1914 depression, leading to an anti-Mexican crusade of sorts that linked Mexicans in Los Angeles to Communist and radical causes. Significant growth in Mexican migration to the area caused by the Mexican Revolution and by World War I-induced labor shortages (in the U.S.) exacerbated the anti-Mexican hysteria. Los Angeles County supervisors in March 1916, for example, called upon the federal government to deport "cholos likely to become public charges."[105]

Even the love of the growers for Mexican migrant laborers quickly disappeared as these workers became involved in militant unions and often participated in strikes, which local authorities—in conjunction with the growers—frequently repressed with great violence.[106] By 1930, few California elites still believed in the docility of Mexican workers. As George Clements wrote, "The Mexican on relief is being unionized and is being used to foment strikes among the few still loyal Mexican workers. The Mexican casual labor is lost to the California farmer unless immediate action is taken to get him off relief."[107] Combined with the context of the Mexican revolution, American elites in general increasingly came to see Mexican workers as a threat—often a communist-inspired one. As one prorestrictionist congressman (John C. Box, from east Texas) described, "Mexico is by far the most Bolshevistic country in the Western Hemisphere."[108] These same elites generally perceived Mexicans as being of inferior intelligence and naturally docile, characteristics that made them easy pawns for nefarious leftist forces such as the International Workers of the World, or "Wobblies."[109]

In the context of the Great Depression, Mexicans became a convenient scapegoat, blamed for a variety of social ills. As one Los Angeles County supervisor stated, "If we were rid of the aliens who have entered this country illegally since 1931 our present unemployment problem would shrink to the proportions of a relatively unimportant flat spot in business."[110] It was in such a climate that the forced repatriation of tens of thousands of Mexicans took place in the 1930s (see chapters 2 and 3). While members of Los Angeles's business class supported the deportations, they were also confident that they could lure the Mexicans back to the area were the need to arise. As historian Ronald Takaki observes, "the border existed only when Mexican labor was not needed."[111] But the social boundary between people of Mexican origin and European Americans did not simply come and go. The "war propaganda" employed during the mass deportation of hundreds of thousands of Mexican immigrants—including tens of thousands of U.S. citizens of Mexican descent—during the 1930s, in fact, merely "reinforced in the minds of many Euroamericans the idea of Mexicans as 'aliens' and 'the other.'"[112]

People of Mexican ancestry in California remained second-class citizens throughout the World War II years. Mexicans generally occupied the worst housing stock, with blatant discrimination leading to a form of residential apartheid in places such as Los Angeles.[113] Segregation was common, with many recreational facilities formally excluding Mexican Americans. And in the aftermath of the mass internment of Japanese Americans, Mexicans became the target of nativist sentiment in California. Institutionalized subordination facilitated the criminalization of Mexican youths and arguably led to a number of ugly incidents of violence directed against them. The most infamous case was the so-called Zoot Suit Riots in June 1943, when thousands of U.S. military personnel, along with many civilians, attacked Mexican Americans—mostly youths—in East Los Angeles over a period of several days, supposedly as part of a battle against "hoodlums." Local police aided and abetted the anti-Mexican rioters, doing little to nothing to stop the violence. All the while the *Los Angeles Times* and other local media fanned the flames of vigilante violence.[114]

While such events were indicative of continuing nativist sentiment against people of Mexican descent in the United States (and California in particular), they also occurred at a time when racist sentiment was changing. Biologically based theories of racial inferiority were falling out of favor. Local Los Angeles officials, for example, were very defensive in responding to charges of racism from critics of the riots.[115] Of course, dominant groups continued marginalizing Mexican Americans and recent Mexican immigrants. This was apparent in the early 1950s, as Mexicans became the focal point once again of nativist sentiment in the wake of an economic recession and, to a lesser extent, an anti-communist hysteria. The climax came with Operation Wetback in 1954 (see chapter 2).[116]

But in the wake of the civil rights and Chicano movements of the 1960s, combined with the growing demographic and political power of Mexican Americans, there was a significant decline in the expression of overtly racist sentiment by elites. At the same time, harsh, large-scale state measures against people of Mexican descent became far less common. That said, we cannot ignore the weight and power of the historic practices of racism and exclusionism as applied to Mexican immigrants and Mexican Americans in trying to understand contemporary social relations in the United States. While American society of today is, in many ways, far more inclusive of these groups previously excluded and marginalized, American society—like any other society—still exercises exclusionism, and history certainly informs the content of this practice.

All social entities require social boundaries and thus inherently define "insiders" and "outsiders." The question is, what are the criteria by which the society defines those who belong and those who do not? More specifically, how does contemporary American society talk about unwanted immigrants and how has past discourse informed the present? The next section attempts to answer these questions through an analysis of media content.

THE RISE OF THE "ILLEGAL"

A preoccupation with "illegal" immigrants and boundary enforcement—at least in a sustained manner with widespread popular support—is of relatively recent origin. The national platform of the Republican Party, for example, did not mention immigration enforcement for the first time until 1980. It was not until four years later that the party affirmed the right of the United States to control its boundaries and voiced concern about illegal immigration. In similar fashion, the Democratic Party's national platform did not even mention illegal immigration until 1996 when it took a stand akin to that of the Republicans.[117] This is not to say that unauthorized immigration had not hitherto been of any concern. As demonstrated previously, there were a number of points in twentieth-century U.S. history prior to the 1970s when unauthorized immigration and boundary enforcement did raise state and public concern, such as during World War II and in 1954 with Operation Wetback. But what is striking—at least as indicated by media coverage—is how shallow that concern has been on a popular level until relatively recently. Not surprisingly, as official and popular concerns have grown, so have the levels of institutionalization of the U.S.-Mexico boundary and associated enforcement practices. At the same time, the labeling of unauthorized immigrants—again, as manifested by media coverage—has changed.

At the time of the creation of the Border Patrol in 1924, major media outlets generally referred to unauthorized immigrants (to the extent that the media talked about them at all) as simply "aliens." By 1954—the time of Operation Wetback—however, the term "wetback" was most popular, with the term "illegal" (such as in "illegal alien") being the second most common label. As media interest in the boundary and unauthorized immigration increased significantly beginning in the 1970s, a considerable shift was evident in the language employed to describe unauthorized immigrants as demonstrated by media coverage around the time of Mexican president José López Portillo's visit to Washington, D.C., in February 1977. On the basis of an analysis of major media outlets, "illegal" was the term most commonly ascribed to unauthorized immigrants (in 76 percent of the cases). The term "wetback" was only present in three percent of the cases, whereas it was the label of choice in 39 percent of the cases identified in the media items examined from 1954.[118] This shift is not surprising given a growing perception beginning in the 1960s that labels such as "wetback" were disrespectful (at best) or racist. The Immigration and Naturalization Service (INS) began to prohibit the use of such terms in the early 1960s.[119] The growth in the use of the term "illegal" continued into the 1990s. Although the Carter administration in the late 1970s forbade the use of the term "illegal alien," instead using terms such as "undocumented worker" or "undocumented alien,"[120] this linguistic sensitivity quickly disappeared in official circles. State authorities now almost exclusively use the term "illegal" in public and official discussions to describe unauthorized immigrants—a development replicated in public discourse as a whole.

The rise in emphasis on the legality of migrants coincided with a substantial increase in national media coverage of issues relating to unauthorized immigration and boundary control. A review of the annual indices of *The New York Times* from the 1970s, for example, found a considerable change in the number of articles that discussed extralegal immigration over the course of the decade. From 1970 to 1972, the *Times* published an average of slightly more than 8.5 articles per year on the subject. During the next eight years (1973–1980), a time of economic recession and increasing activism by politicians and state actors toward unauthorized immigration and boundary enforcement (see chapter 4), it produced an average of more than fifty-seven articles annually, an increase of more than 650 percent. Only about 15 percent of the articles during the 1970–1972 period discussed unauthorized immigration specifically from Mexico, while the figure reached 36 percent between 1973 and 1980. On an absolute scale, the average number of articles (on an annual basis) that linked unauthorized immigration to Mexico increased from 1.3 in the 1970–1972 period to 20.6 from 1973 to 1980.[121] Of course, most of the articles dealing with extralegal immigration from Mexico (and many of those dealing with "illegal" immigration more generally) explicitly or implicitly discussed the U.S.-Mexico boundary and its enforcement. In this sense, the articles contributed to a growing awareness of the boundary, thus making it (and alleged problems associated with the international divide) more "real" in the minds of the U.S. public.

As the labels applied to unauthorized immigrants changed and the amount of media coverage increased, the actual content of the coverage changed in terms of the representation of unauthorized immigrants. The media coverage surrounding the Carter–López Portillo summit in 1977, for example, manifested an increasing tendency to associate unauthorized immigrants with criminal activity and a declining standard of living for U.S. citizens.[122] Another study revealed a significant increase from the period 1959–1972 to that of 1973–1986 in the number of articles suggesting that "illegals" were overwhelming the United States in terms of sheer numbers, that illegal immigration was a Mexican problem, that unauthorized immigrants were a financial burden to U.S. taxpayers and were taking jobs away from U.S. workers, and that immigration was purely a (U.S.) domestic issue that could be solved through unilateral action.[123] The cover of the December 1974 issue of *The American Legion Magazine*, for example, contained a cartoon image of U.S. territory being overrun by an influx of immigrants for an article entitled "Our Illegal Alien Problem." The cover depicted the vast majority of the immigrants by means of a throng of cartoon-like Mexicans with sombreros smashing through U.S. boundary blockades, overrunning boundary inspectors, and flooding into buildings with descriptive signs such as "schools," "welfare department," "medical aid," and "jobs."[124]

Media coverage of unauthorized immigration reached such a level in the 1970s that the Gallup Organization found in a 1976 poll conducted for the INS that over half of those polled had recently read or heard something about "the problem of illegal aliens." The figure was particularly high—over two-thirds—in the West and in states that bordered Mexico.[125] *U.S. News and World Report* was especially aggressive in highlighting the alleged threat "illegals" presented to U.S. society. The January 17, 1972 issue, for example, contained a report entitled "Surge of Illegal Immigrants across American Borders" in which it stated that the number of unauthorized immigrants in the United States could be high as ten million and reported that "illegals" pay no taxes (a patently false claim), contribute to the flow of U.S. dollars out of the country, and take jobs from U.S. citizens. A July 23, 1973 report from the same magazine carried the provocative title "'Invasion' by Illegal Aliens and the Problems They Create." The magazine also indirectly suggested that unauthorized Mexican immigrants were less desirable than the European immigrants who arrived in the United States in the late-nineteenth and early twentieth centuries.[126]

The mass media clearly helped to construct the image of an immigration and boundary enforcement crisis.[127] As a 1977 *Time* magazine report ominously described, "The U.S. is being invaded so silently and surreptitiously that most Americans are not even aware of it. The invaders come by land, sea and air. They fly commercial and private aircraft; they jump ship or sail their own boats; they scale mountains and swim rivers. Some have crawled through a mile-long tunnel; others have squeezed through the San Antonio sewerage system. No commandos or assault troops have shown more ingenuity and determination in storming a country that tries to keep them out."[128] The "invasion," according to *Time*, was largely Mexican in nature. The report stated that "[s]ome 80% of the illegal aliens now living in America come from Mexico." (At that time, about 66 percent of the unauthorized immigrant population was of Mexican origin.[129]) The article quoted INS commissioner Chapman warning that "We have become the haven for the unemployed of the world. I think it's going to be catastrophic."[130] Such thinking continued to inform public and official perceptions and representations of unauthorized immigration and boundary through the 1970s, 1980s, and into the 1990s when the notion of an "illegal" immigration "crisis" reemerged with a vengeance.

The power of the "illegal" as a perceived threat to the American social fabric emerged most strongly in California during the debate surrounding Proposition 187. Somewhat surprisingly, however, a linking of crime with unauthorized immigrants was not a major theme in the media around the time of the proposition. The most common pro-187 theme emphasized the illegal nature of unauthorized immigration, often arguing that the United States should not "reward" those who break the law with social benefits, and that the survival of the U.S. immigration regime required a strong distinction between "legal" and "illegal" forms of immigration. It was local and federal government officials who most frequently put forth this argument.

The second most popular argument in favor of the measure was one that argued that "illegals" were taking scarce social services and undermining the American socioeconomic fabric in the process.[131] Kitty Calavita refers to this position as "balanced-budget conservatism,"[132] a stance that blames immigrants as well as government spending (but almost exclusively social spending) and budget deficits, rather than deindustrialization and the dismantling of the social safety net, for prevailing economic and social problems.

A minority of media items voicing support for Proposition 187 argued for the need of the United States to protect itself from threats from without, often contending that "illegal" immigration was leading to the creation of a "Third World" country "balkanizing" American society, and/or undermining the cohesiveness of the country's culture (implicitly a Euro-American one). It is important here to point out that the various themes are not equal in terms of their effectiveness, as certain of them "have a natural advantage because their ideas and language resonate with larger cultural themes."[133] And it is probably the fear of "third worldization" that dovetails best with the long history of nativism in the United States, demonstrating that negative perceptions about the "other" are still very much present in public discourse about unwanted immigrants—especially "illegals"—in the 1990s. As historian David Gutiérrez contends,

[M]uch of the rhetoric about immigrants presently being heard in government and in the media is virtually identical to the anti-immigrant pronouncements that were commonly heard in the 1890s, the 1920s, the 1950s, and again
in the 1970s. In a litany that can be found daily in virtually every newspaper
in the country, a new, vocal group of restrictionists argues that immigrants—
particularly undocumented immigrants—are stealing jobs from Americans,
undermining wage rates and working conditions, committing crimes, overwhelming the public education and health systems, and abusing welfare and
other social programs. Insisting that the current rate of immigration threatens
the very fabric of American life, these critics demand that strong action be
taken to regain control of the nation's borders by increasing enforcement
efforts and by sharply limiting the number of immigrants allowed into the
United States.[134]

While Gutiérrez may overstate the frequency with which such sentiments
appeared in newspapers in the early to mid-1990s, they were undoubtedly
common. Justifications for cracking down on unauthorized immigration, for
instance, often took the form of proenvironment and neo-Malthusian population analyses, blaming a supposed glut of immigrants for traffic congestion,
air pollution, and overburdened schools.[135] In this manner, the environment
provided a host of unflattering metaphors (such as "pollution" and "contam-
ination") to attach to immigrants.[136] Similarly, racialized fears of immigrant
criminality, hyperfertility among women of Mexican origin,[137] and potential
cultural and even political conquest by immigrants disrespectful of (implicitly white) "American" territorial hegemony were also important elements of
the discourse.[138] As quoted in one *Los Angeles Times* article, Ruth Coffey, the
head of a Long Beach–based group called Stop Immigration Now, wrote, "I
have no intention of being the object of 'conquest,' peaceful or otherwise, by
Latinos, Asians, blacks, Arabs, or any other group of individuals who have
claimed my country."[139]

Such views dominated much of the pro-187 literature emanating from
grassroots, pro-restrictionist groups, and they also were very prominent in a
number of right-wing periodicals.[140] These views echo those of a variety of
right-wing groups and publishing houses that began promoting the issue of
illegal immigration at the beginning of the 1980s. Two of the most prominent
organizations were the Federation for American Immigration Reform (FAIR)
and the American Immigration Control Foundation (AICF). Before immigration became a hot issue, self-identified "paleoconservatives" were waging
the anti-immigrant war, while most of the Right was preoccupied with its anti-
communist crusade.[141] Paleoconservatives rejected economic questions
around immigration, instead focusing on the putative threat the influx of non-
white immigrant groups was creating for U.S. cultural homogeneity. This focus
on cultural homogeneity was central to early anti-immigrant activity, such as

that of the group U.S. English, which believed in the establishment of English as the "official" language of the United States. In 1986, for example, California's Proposition 63, an official English amendment, passed with 73 percent voting in favor. Dr. John Tanton headed U.S. English and had been the founder of FAIR in 1979.[142]

It is important to point out, however, that a number of the themes raised by the so-called paleoconservatives were at home with a large sector of the U.S. population. An August 1993 Gallup Poll, for example, reported that more than six out of ten Americans felt that there were too many immigrants from Latin American, Asia, and Arab countries. And almost the same number stated the presence of immigrants from Mexico, Haiti, Iran, and Cuba created problems for the United States.[143]

Negative stereotypes about Mexicans, and Latin Americans more generally, have a long history in the United States.[144] It is impossible to separate these deeply rooted stereotypes from support for measures favoring more restrictive measures against immigrants—legal or "illegal." As historian Robin D. G. Kelley argues, "Anti-immigrant sentiment . . . is not just about class anger, because there really is no mobilization against Canadians or European immigrants taking what are essentially skilled jobs. It is about dark people, whether wetbacks or some invisible Pacific Rim empire run by sneaky Chinese. The history of conquest, repatriation in the Southwest, stereotypes of 'Latin' hypersexuality, even racialized and gendered myths of the welfare mother, are fundamental to understanding anti-immigrant sentiment, the English-only movement, and pro-Proposition 187."[145] Indeed, how else can we understand the significant differentials among racial/ethnic groups in terms of support for certain types of immigration restrictionist measures, such as Proposition 187? While about 67 percent of white voters in California supported the measure, only about half of African-American and Asian-American voters did so. And only 23 percent of Latino voters approved of the proposition,[146] despite the fact that Latinos opine to a degree similar to whites that rates of immigration should be lower and that enhanced boundary enforcement is desirable.[147] Clearly, the historical weight of white supremacy and anti-Mexican sentiment outlined earlier informed voting patterns, most notably among whites.

A racialized notion of "the nation" was a central component to debates surrounding "illegal" immigration in the early 1990s. As former Republican presidential candidate Pat Buchanan wrote, "Proposition 187 [is about] . . . the deepest, most divisive issues of our time: ethnicity, nation, culture." Buchanan called for "a timeout on immigration" to have the time to assimilate those who are already here (thus resurrecting the idea of "racial indigestion"), lest Quebec-like secession result in the U.S. Southwest, and interethnic conflict intensify.[148] Such sentiments are very common among anti-immigrant, pro-restrictionist activists and groups that organized in favor of Proposition 187 and continue to agitate in favor of enhanced boundary policing. The Voice of Citizens Together

(VCT), a Sherman Oaks, California–based group, for example, had an ad in the November 4, 1996 issue of the *Los Angeles Times* warning that "A VOTE FOR BILL CLINTON AND THE DEMOCRATS MAY BE A VOTE TO RETURN CALIFORNIA TO MEXICO." When Cruz Bustamente became speaker and Antonio Villaraigosa majority leader of the California Assembly, the VCT's newsletter (November/December 1996) proclaimed that "Mexicans Take Over State Assembly."[149] A widely circulated 1995 book, *Alien Nation* by Peter Brimelow, a senior editor of *Forbes* and the *National Review*, openly called upon the United States to revert back to its pre-1965 immigration policies when racial and ethnic factors were primary to ensure the survival of the United States as a white, English-speaking country where European values reign.[150]

The proponents of these views almost always vehemently deny that such views are racist in nature,[151] but such disavowals do not mean that racism is not present; "on the contrary, that is the way racism usually works," notes George Lipsitz.[152] Although few people in contemporary American society subscribe to biology- or religion-based theories of racial inferiority or superiority—indeed, the vast majority of whites surely reject such views and espouse universalistic views of human equality—that does not mean that racism is not still very much present. A 1990 National Opinion Research report, for example, disclosed that 50 percent of U.S. whites viewed blacks as innately lazy as well as less intelligent and less patriotic than whites, while 56.3 percent felt that blacks preferred welfare to employment.[153]

What has changed are the forms that racism takes and the social purposes that it serves.[154] A cultural argument has come to dominate racist discourse since roughly the 1950s, one that denounces the notion that a given people might not have a capacity equal to that of other people. Instead, the argument here is that "inferior" groups have proven unable (or unwilling) to realize their capacity because of their "inferior" culture and/or because they have not learned or they do not practice what it takes to be "successful."[155]

Earlier I advanced the argument that a number of contextual factors facilitated the rise of political concerns about unauthorized immigration in the early 1990s, and a U.S.-Mexico boundary "out of control." In California, these included a serious recession, the breakdown of local government, a widening gap between rich and poor, and a massive racial recomposition.[156] Similar factors—albeit with less intensity—played themselves out on the national level. Certainly the arrival of large amounts of unauthorized immigrants had some negative effects—especially on the social safety net of specific locales (given that the federal authorities do not adequately refund to local governments the tax revenues garnered from extralegal immigrants) and on particular segments (largely minority) of the low-wage labor market. But, as the foregoing discussion illustrates, it is far too simple to suggest that "illegal immigration" has been the primary factor motivating the most recent outbreak of nativism.[157]

The focus on unauthorized immigration is part and parcel of a more general restrictionist sentiment, one rooted historically in notions of undesirable "others" who have typically been non-white, non-English-speaking people from relatively poor countries. Fear and/or rejection of "illegals" is often fear and rejection of Mexicans or, more generally, non-white, non-English-speaking persons. Analysis of the term "illegal alien" in context makes clear that it most often refers specifically to unauthorized Mexican immigrants and draws upon stereotypes of Mexicans as criminals, at least in the southwestern United States.[158] Like any other discursive device, a term such as "illegal" can serve to obfuscate: "the discourse of legal status permits coded discussions in which listeners will understand that reference is being made, not to aliens in the abstract, but to the particular foreign group that is the principal focus of current hostility."[159] Thus, while many unauthorized immigrants come from Canada, Ireland, and Poland, the dominant image of the "illegal" (and almost exclusively so) is the former "wetback"—an unauthorized entrant coming from Mexico.[160]

Such a line of analysis leads some to conclude that the emphasis on the legality of immigrants is merely a cover for race-based arguments that are no longer publicly acceptable.[161] From this perspective, the emphasis on legality undoubtedly serves as a cover for a larger set of concerns: namely, a preoccupation with the putative threat that the new wave of (predominantly non-white) immigrants represents to the American "nation." And, indeed, as numerous scholars have pointed out,[162] the issue of "illegal immigration" in the early 1990s quickly led to an attack on immigrants and immigration more generally. At the same time, however, the conflation of concerns about "illegal" immigration with those concerned with the race/ethnicity of immigrants ignores the role that issues of class and gender also play in fueling anti-immigrant sentiment (an omission for which I must also plead largely guilty). Immigration restrictionists focus almost exclusively on poor immigrants, rarely discussing the many relatively wealthy and high-skilled immigrants that come to the United States. These attacks on poor immigrants dovetail with efforts to highlight the putative burden poor immigrant women create for U.S. society because of their mythical hyperfertility and high use of welfare services.[163] In this respect, the war on unauthorized immigrants overlaps considerably with the conservative-led onslaught against the poor (rather than against *poverty*), a political program significantly informed by traditional patriarchal values.[164]

Finally, we need to appreciate the power of the law to shape our worldview or culture. To argue that anti-"illegal"-immigrant sentiment is a mere cover for racialized ideas of undesirable outsiders, ideas that intersect with ideologies of classism and sexism, implicitly suggests that the relationship between law (the state) and culture (our ways of thinking) is one-sided, rather than dialectical in nature. The "illegal" is both a cultural and national territorial identity. As such, the unauthorized migrant represents a putative threat to sociocultural stability as well as to national territorial integrity. It is for this reason that fear and rejection of the "illegal" are as strong as they are in contemporary American society. Why the image of the "illegal" became so prominent in media presentations over the last few decades, with coverage climaxing in the early 1990s, is a question I will now address.

THE NOT-SO-HIDDEN HAND OF THE STATE

The implicit or explicit sociopolitical views contained in the media are not a mirror image of general public opinion. The media are important because they are a highly significant source of information about society and politics for the general population and because of their ability to set the agenda of public debate. Sociologist Katherine Beckett, for example, demonstrates that public concern about crime and illegal drug use has very little to do with the actual levels of crime and illicit drug consumption. Statistical analysis clearly demonstrates that the extent to which political elites highlight crime and drug "problems" through the media is by far the most significant factor in generating public concern about these matters.[165] Indeed, studies show that the public is most likely to identify as important those social issues and problems that receive a high degree of attention from the news media. So, it is thus very likely that increased state activism toward the U.S.-Mexico boundary and unauthorized entries is the most significant reason for the substantial rise in public concern about "illegal" immigration over the last twenty-five years.

Media coverage can influence policy in two important ways: one, it can influence policy makers, regardless of its effect on public opinion; and two, while it is too simple to state that media discourse *causes* changes in public opinion, it is nonetheless a very important part of the context in which people form their political opinions.[166] In this regard, the media imagery and rhetoric discussed above undoubtedly helped to lay the basis for the perceived "crisis" of immigration and boundary control that emerged in the 1990s.

The media—in terms of their sources—tend to represent a very narrow spectrum of opinion. A study of the media from 1982 to 1984 found that, among sources for network television news, officials from government and elite institutions—especially the two major political parties and business—predominate.[167] But this does not mean that the state almost always shapes media representations. Conflicts among elites and efforts by groups representing nonstate interests can and often do result in alternative media representations. In this regard, the media are a contested terrain, but one that clearly favors elite interests.[168]

In terms of the "illegal" immigrant, the state has been the primary shaper of the category through its practices establishing the geographical and social boundaries discussed in previous chapters. Similarly, in terms of the representation of unauthorized immigration in the media, it has been the state that has been most responsible in constructing the "illegal" as a category of social identity and as a threat to the social fabric of the United States.[169]

At times, however, state actors are sometimes very divided in terms of specific measures aimed at redressing the putative problems associated with unauthorized immigration. A significant number of state actors, for example, opposed California's Proposition 187. Apart from suggesting the pitfalls of treating "the state" as a monolithic entity, the diverse nature of state discourse on the proposition is illustrative of the increasing number of sectors of the state involved in debates over immigration.[170]

That voters approved Proposition 187 by a wide margin despite strong opposition to the measure by many prominent state actors and establishment figures might seem to suggest that it is the entity of "the people" and not the state that primarily shapes immigration discourse (and thus, practice). Sociologist Hugh Mehan, for example, argues that the passage of Proposition 187 undercuts "[t]he power and prestige of traditional authority figures." But as even Mehan admits, the elite opponents of the proposition all agreed that "illegal" immigration was a serious problem.[171] Although a significant number of state officials and politicians opposed the measure, the overall message of political elites was unequivocal: "illegal" immigration is wrong and we must stop it. Many state actors opposed to 187, for example, argued that the federal government needed to take serious measures to combat unauthorized immigration, but that the so-called Save Our State initiative was not the correct way to do so. In this regard, they made strong arguments urging an intensification of efforts to fight extralegal immigration. Combined with the almost universal characterization of the unauthorized immigrant as "illegal," it is little wonder that voters ignored the anti-187 advice of numerous establishment figures (many of whom asked the same voting public to join them in other efforts to fight "illegal" immigration). Indeed, voter approval of Proposition 187 was the logical outgrowth of a largely state-produced discourse (one constructed over many decades) that increasingly associated unauthorized immigrants with "illegal" activity and the destruction of the country's sociocultural fabric.[172]

It is obvious that negative criteria relating to race and geographic origins significantly inform the externally imposed identity of the undesirable immigrant. In addition, the undesirable immigrant also embodies stereotypical "un-American" characteristics of class (such as poverty) and family life (the extended family with many children, which thus stigmatizes immigrant women). In this sense, the racialized "other" in anti-immigrant thinking represents a variety of geographical, social, and economic characteristics.

At the same time, there has undoubtedly been progress in reducing overt racism in the United States. Indeed, one could argue that the growing use of legal criteria (such as the successful completion of the bureaucratic procedures necessary to gain legal entrance) to distinguish between those who have state sanction to enter and stay in the United States and those who do not is a significant advance over race-based criteria that reigned prior to the 1965 immigration reforms. It was striking to note how many seemingly well-meaning defenders of Operation Gatekeeper within the federal bureaucracy and Congress told me in interviews that they sympathized with the plight of unauthorized immigrants and that they only wanted them to go through the proper legal channels to gain entrance. In almost all cases, however, numerical limits and the lack of qualifications (in terms of factors such as wealth and skills) make it nearly impossible for such individuals to gain admission sanctioned by the state. Thus, they can only enter through extralegal means.

It is no mere coincidence that many of today's "undesirables" are from groups previously excluded or marginalized for overtly racist criteria. While yesterday's undesirables were distinguished by racial factors, today's unwanted immigrants are marked by their legal status—or lack thereof. And given the power of "the law" as an ideological construct dividing good from evil in the contemporary United States, this very fact—in addition to their "otherness"—serves to marginalize these immigrants in the eyes of much of the public. Indeed, a striking feature of contemporary California is "the reassignment of Mexicans—especially the undocumented, non-English-speaking population—to the bottom of the new racial and ethnic hierarchy."[173]

But again, the "illegal" is not a mere discursive cover for racism. The putative problem of "illegal immigration" resonates so profoundly with the public at large not simply because of the ideological baggage in terms of race, ethnicity, class, and national identity that the term conveys about outsiders (although undoubtedly highly significant), but also because of the power of the state in molding the collective mind-set of its citizenry to distinguish between "right" and "wrong" and to appreciate the almost-sacred nature of its national boundaries. The supposed illegality of the unauthorized immigrant is not based (at least overtly) on social, economic, political, or racial/ethnic characteristics of the immigrant; rather, it is based on what the immigrant has done through entering the territory without authorization and exceeding the limits established by her visa. In this regard, the "illegal" is guilty of a geographical transgression for the putative crime of being in a particular space without state authorization.

Rather than simply responding to the supposed crisis of "illegal" immigration, the state has helped to construct the "illegal" through the expansion of the INS's enforcement capacity as the very existence of a policed boundary, and the accompanying social agents and institutions of immigration control create immigration that is "illegal." The state has also played a significant role in creating the "crisis" posed by "illegals" through the various discursive devices employed to justify its efforts to bring order to the U.S.-Mexico boundary and to rid U.S. territory of those without state sanction to be within its boundaries.[174] Indeed, government officials often group unauthorized immigration with what we normally think of as criminal activity, such as transboundary drug smuggling.[175]

The power of state discourse vis-à-vis the national citizenry illustrates the ability of the state to construct not only political and juridical categories, but also cultural forms. As Philip Corrigan and Derek Sayer note, "[these cultural forms] define, in great detail, acceptable forms and images of social activity and individual and collective identity."[176] In doing so, the state normalizes what might otherwise be very contentious. Through routines and rituals the state constructs particular sociopolitical practices and identities, an outgrowth of the dynamic interaction between the state and culture.[177] These social boundaries, combined with nationalism, have led to, among other phenomena, the establishment of territorial boundaries as barriers to unauthorized immigrants. Operation Gatekeeper is a manifestation of this process. The construction of the "illegal" and the associated criminalization of unauthorized immigrants is one of the most obvious and most pernicious outgrowths of the dialectic between culture and state in the context of the ongoing boundary buildup and the war on "illegals"—a development analyzed in more detail in the next chapter, which interrogates the effects of Gatekeeper and the effects of the (social and territorial) boundary buildup more generally.

The Effects and Significance of the Bounding
of the United States

An old truth about California is disintegrating. . . . The old truth goes
like this: The border with Mexico will never, ever, be controlled. . . .
[T]he entire border along San Diego is now eerily quiet and peaceful.
It's the quiet that comes from control.
   —Robert A. Jones, *Los Angeles Times*, "It's Quiet—Too Quiet"[1]

[W]hat has Gatekeeper accomplished other than getting illegal border
crossers out of the public eye?
   —Claudia Smith, "Operation Gatekeepers' Darker Side"[2]

The effects of Operation Gatekeeper, and the great increase in boundary and
immigration enforcement more generally, have been undoubtedly significant—especially on the unauthorized migrants caught in the growing net of
state surveillance. At the same time, logistical, geographical, and political
economic realities—combined with human ingenuity and persistence—limit
in a very real way the ability of any social organization such as the state to
achieve absolute control over a subject population. A couple of my own
personal experiences illustrate the efficacy of enhanced Immigration and
Naturalization Service (INS) efforts along the U.S.-Mexico boundary, as well
as their profound limitations.

  Around 5 A.M. on April 6, 1996, I was accompanying a Border Patrol agent
in the western area of the El Paso Sector as part of a "ride along." In response
to a "click" of an underground sensor, an infrared camera unit on top of a
nearby mesa sighted an individual crossing in a very sparsely populated area.
Communicating via radio, the agent working the camera directed the vehicle
in which I was traveling and one other Border Patrol unit to the general area.
With searchlights flashing back and forth, the two units followed the pinpoint
directions of the infrared unit until told to stop. After we got out of the vehicle,
the infrared unit had to tell the agent that the "alien" was lying in brush behind
(and to the right of) the right, rear wheel—literally within ten feet of the
vehicle. (It turned out that the unit I was in had almost hit the migrant.) When
the agent illuminated his flashlight on the migrant—a modestly dressed man
who appeared to be approximately forty years of age and of Mexican origin—
he stood right up and went with the other unit without a peep of protest.

  More than four years later, in August 2000, I had to move to a new house in Los Angeles. The new landlord had hired a women's cleaning cooperative to tidy up the place after the old tenants. While dropping off some stuff, I met the two women sent from the cooperative. Both were immigrants—one from Germany, the other from southern Mexico. After exchanging small talk, I learned that the woman from Mexico—I'll call her Rosa—had only been in the United States for a little more than six months. During the course of our conversation, Rosa informed me that she did not have any papers, and that she had relied on the services of a professional smuggler to take her from Tijuana to Los Angeles via San Diego. But rather than hiking through the tough terrain to the east of San Diego, Rosa—along with a few other migrants—had come right through the port of entry at San Ysidro in a car driven by the smuggler in the early hours of the morning. Rosa was under instructions to say that she was a Mexican citizen who lived in Tijuana and had forgotten her border crossing card. In this manner, if questioned by an INS inspector, the would-be immigrants would be able to turn around and go back to Tijuana without any delay. According to Rosa, however, the INS inspector just waved her vehicle through—potentially a sign that the smuggler had paid him off,[3] or perhaps a manifestation of an inspector too tired or overwhelmed to perform his job adequately.[4]

Taken together, these two anecdotes embody the potential and limits of enhanced boundary enforcement. On the one hand, the infusion of many Border Patrol agents, modern technology, and a whole host of other enforcement-related "tools" have certainly increased the INS's policing capacity along the boundary and, in this regard, significantly augmented the challenges faced by unauthorized immigrants. On the other hand, human resourcefulness and ingenuity, combined with human fallibility—among many other factors—significantly undermine the ability of the INS to create a pervasive web of control.

In terms of bringing "law and order" to the border region, Gatekeeper has had a very significant impact in limiting unauthorized crossings of the boundary in the most urbanized sections of the San Diego Sector. But overall, it has merely pushed the great bulk of extralegal crossers to more rural areas along the U.S.-Mexico boundary. (This is hardly a controversial or novel argument.) In this regard, one of Gatekeeper's more noteworthy accomplishments has been to render the "illegal" less visible. But while unauthorized immigrants are still crossing the U.S.-Mexico boundary (overall, probably with rates of success similar to those they had at the beginning of the 1990s) they must pay a much higher price to do so—literally and metaphorically.

If we limit our analysis of Gatekeeper's importance to measurements of its success and/or failure in meeting the official goals of curtailing unauthorized immigration and achieving control of the U.S.-Mexico boundary, however, we will miss much. First, Gatekeeper has had many important effects that go beyond narrow measures of "success" or "failure"—most notably the dramatic jump in the number of deaths of unauthorized immigrants crossing into California. Second, and perhaps most important, we must recall that Gatekeeper—while significant in and of itself—is the culmination of a much larger process of increasing boundedness of the United States vis-à-vis the U.S.-Mexico divide (at least in terms of unwanted immigration). In this regard, we cannot confine our evaluation to a single, highly localized operation. As part of a more general and extensive set of developments, Gatekeeper is part and parcel (somewhat paradoxically) of a growing openness of the boundary as illustrated by the increasing transnational flow of goods and capital. At the same time, to the extent that Gatekeeper embodies a growing attempt to regulate migrants, it has contributed to an increasing marginalization of unauthorized immigrants, largely through a process of criminalization of "illegals." Such developments are representative of radical changes—over the long term—in official and public perception and practice of unauthorized immigrants and of the U.S.-Mexico boundary.

OPERATION GATEKEEPER: RESTORING THE RULE OF LAW?

In line with the strategy of Operation Gatekeeper, the Border Patrol has channeled the flow of unauthorized immigrants away from the heavily populated areas of San Ysidro/San Diego to more sparsely populated areas, where it is more difficult to cross, "to force alien traffic eastward to deter and delay aliens' attempts to reach urban areas."[5] The first phase of Gatekeeper concentrated on the five westernmost miles of the sector, the area covered by the Border Patrol's Imperial Beach station,[6] which commences at the Pacific Ocean and continues eastward to the international port of entry at San Ysidro.[7] The operation quickly resulted in a marked shift eastward of the unauthorized migrant flow to more difficult terrain and to lesser-known routes. The migrants responded in part by increased use of professional smugglers, also know as *coyotes* or *polleros*. In response, the Border Patrol launched Operation Disruption in May 1995. Disruption targeted the smugglers and, through the establishment of a number of new highway checkpoints in the interior, enhanced the likelihood of apprehending those unauthorized migrants who made it past the front line of Border Patrol agents.[8]

The Clinton administration strengthened its boundary enforcement strategy on October 1995 by launching phase 2 of Gatekeeper. Among its measures was the appointment of Alan Bersin, the U.S. Attorney for the Southern District of California, as the Attorney General's Special Representative on Southwest Border Issues (popularly known as the "border czar"). The Department of Justice also established the first Immigration Court at the boundary itself (at the San Ysidro Port of Entry). This "port court" has expedited administrative hearings for, and subsequent deportations of, those apprehended for attempting to enter at official ports of entry with false documents or through oral misrepresentation (by falsely claiming, for example, to be a U.S. citizen).[9] And as more and more unauthorized migrants attempted to gain entrance into the United States by fraudulent means, the INS strengthened the ports of entry with more INS inspectors. Phase II also introduced a computerized identification system called IDENT, which has enabled the INS to identify better repeat (unauthorized) crossers as well as so-called criminal aliens—that is, non–U.S. citizens who have criminal records or pending arrest warrants. In addition, beginning in January 1996 Gatekeeper saw the acceleration of the deployment of personnel and resources to the Border Patrol's San Diego Sector and the expansion of partnerships with local law enforcement. These efforts focused on expanding control east of the Otay Mountains (about fourteen miles from the Pacific Ocean) to where unauthorized migrant traffic had significantly shifted. The INS formalized this part of Gatekeeper in May 1996 by significantly adding personnel and resources to the sixteen-mile stretch from the Otay Mountains to the Tecate port of entry in "East County" (the eastern part of San Diego County).[10]

Such efforts continued and intensified during 1997. October of that year saw the implementation of phase 3 of Gatekeeper, with the expansion of the operation into the neighboring El Centro Sector (which extends from the eastern boundary of the San Diego Sector/San Diego County to the California/Arizona border), to where much of the unauthorized migrant traffic has shifted as Operation Gatekeeper has extended its control eastward from the Pacific Ocean.[11]

Developments such as these have led the INS to pronounce the operation "an outstanding success." As the agency noted in 1997, "Only a few years ago, nearly half of all illegal border crossers were apprehended in this sector [the San Diego Sector], crime rates in border communities were up, and drugs moved freely across the border, severely impacting the quality of life in ... border towns and communities. Today, crime rates have dropped nearly 30 percent, drug smugglers have been forced to move narcotics through the more controlled ports of entry, and apprehensions in the San Diego Sector are at their lowest point in 17 years."[12] Whereas in fiscal year (FY) 1994 the San Diego Sector had been responsible for 46 percent of the apprehensions of unauthorized migrants in the United States, the sector's apprehensions were only 16 percent of the national total in FY 1998. The Tucson Sector, on the other hand, was responsible for 26 percent, and the El Centro Sector was responsible for 15 percent of the apprehensions in FY 1998.[13] The INS has presented the apparent shift in migrant traffic as further proof of Gatekeeper's success in thwarting would-be "illegal" crossers in the San Diego area.[14]

Many long-time observers of boundary enforcement efforts in the San Diego region seem to agree with the INS's assessment. As *The San Diego Union-Tribune* editorialized in July 1998,

Think back less than 10 years ago. The Tijuana River Valley was like a war zone, with ill-equipped, outnumbered Border Patrol agents chasing wave after wave of illegal immigrants.

Otay Mesa was also overwhelmed. And the San Ysidro crossing was even worse. Illegal immigrants would simply run through the checkpoints in packs.

Today, all that chaos is history. And Operation Gatekeeper is the reason for the success.[15]

There is certainly much truth in this description, but it is not merely Gate-keeper that has led to these changes. Rather, a whole series of developments have increased the human and material resources dedicated to boundary enforcement. Of course, many of these developments preceded the implementation of Operation Gatekeeper.

Undoubtedly, Gatekeeper (and associated developments) is a considerable success in bringing a certain order to the most urbanized sections of the border region in San Diego. Indeed, an explicit tactic of the enhanced national-scale boundary enforcement strategy—of which Gatekeeper is one manifestation—was a concentration of resources in urban areas. As the national strategy of the Border Patrol stated in 1994, "The current enforcement posture in [San Diego and El Paso] is to first control the entry of illegal entrants into and through the large urban areas. When urban areas are uncontrolled, they provide illegal entrants an opportunity to assimilate with the population, making it difficult for the Border Patrol to quickly identify and arrest individual illegal entrants. When the Border Patrol controls the urban areas, the illegal traffic is forced to use the rural roads which offer less anonymity and accessibility to public transportation."[16] Yet, it is not at all clear that Gatekeeper has had a significant effect in reducing the overall number of unauthorized crossings of the boundary. It is probable that, as in the case of Operation Hold-the-Line in El Paso,[17] Gatekeeper has succeeded in curtailing local migrants—especially day workers or street vendors and so-called juvenile crossers—but has not seriously diminished the crossings by long-distance or long-term migrants.[18]

Interviews of immigrants in 1996 found that Operation Gatekeeper had not noticeably limited the number of extralegal immigrants arriving in the San Diego area. The study conducted by researchers from the University of California, San Diego (UCSD) found no shortage of workers present at the street-corner labor markets used by unauthorized immigrants from January 1996 through July 1997. Furthermore, while the study acknowledged that the boundary is more difficult to cross in certain locations, unauthorized immigrants were still having a good deal of success in crossing at other points. The researchers found that unauthorized immigrant workers who entered the San Diego labor market prior to January 1995 averaged 1.42 boundary crossing attempts before successfully gaining entry, those who arrived in 1995 averaged 1.18 attempts, and migrants arriving between January and June 1996 required 1.63 attempts on average. In terms of successfully crossing on the first attempt, 78 percent did so before January 1995, 87 percent during 1995, and 81 percent in the first half of 1996. As the study's author surmises, "prospective illegal immigrants have learned quickly to avoid the most heavily fortified segments of the border altogether and cross elsewhere."[19]

Not surprisingly, part of the risk-avoiding response of prospective migrants to the boundary buildup has been a predictable increased reliance on professional smugglers, or *coyotes*. Indeed, the Border Patrol uses increased fees charged by coyotes (presumably a result of increased demand as well as hardship) as one of their indices of success of the operation.[20] The UCSD research team found a steady increase in the proportion of people employing the services of smugglers as the implementation of Operation Gatekeeper progressed (42 percent before January 1995, 44 percent during 1995, and 52 percent in the first six months of 1996). Similarly, the prices of coyotes increased significantly.[21]

A different study involved extensive interviews in thirty-nine Mexican communities with long migrant-sending histories. The researchers found that increased INS boundary enforcement efforts had little effect on the likelihood of apprehension by Border Patrol agents. Apprehension rates, in fact, declined over time due somewhat to an increase in the average level of maturity and crossing experience of the migrants surveyed. To a more significant degree, the dramatic increase in Border Patrol resources (and thus time) dedicated to drug interdiction lowered the probability of apprehension during the time period studied.[22] A potentially significant limitation of the study is the fact that the vast majority of the community surveys took place prior to 1994, at which time U.S. boundary enforcement efforts increased dramatically. Furthermore, the study says nothing about communities that have little migrant-sending experience. It is probably safe to assume that enhanced boundary enforcement raises the likelihood of apprehension of migrants from these communities.

An unintended consequence of Operation Gatekeeper and the increased resources dedicated to boundary enforcement more generally may well be that unauthorized migrants are staying in the country longer. A recent investigation of extralegal migrants from Mexico found that 73 percent stay in the United States less than ten years before returning to Mexico to reestablish their residence.[23] Traditionally, many of these migrants—especially those in agriculture—have been seasonal workers, migrating back to Mexico in the off season. Yet, "by raising the costs and risks of reentering the United States, heightened border surveillance may be transforming what has been a sojourner farm worker stream into settlers."[24] Indeed, the UCSD study found that unauthorized immigrants in the San Diego area have been staying longer in the United States than they had intended in the face of increasing boundary enforcement.[25] Similarly, a 1995 staff report by the U.S. Commission on Immigration Reform discovered that some unauthorized migrants were responding to Gatekeeper by staying in the United States longer.

The ultimate goal of the INS boundary enhancement strategy is to make it so difficult and costly to enter the United States extralegally that fewer unauthorized migrants try to do so. For this reason, the INS points to lower apprehension figures in the San Diego Sector as a sign of Gatekeeper's success. But the use of apprehension data to measure the number of unauthorized immigrants successfully crossing the boundary is very problematic.[26] That said, even the INS's own apprehension data—in terms of the entire southwest boundary—indicate that apprehensions have actually increased over the last few years. What this means is another question, but a May 1999 report by the U.S. General Accounting Office declared itself unable to conclude whether or not the new southwest boundary strategy—of which Gatekeeper is the most important component—is successful, stating that "available data do not yet answer the fundamental question of how effective the strategy has been in preventing and deterring illegal entry."[27]

Gatekeeper has a number of pro-boundary-enforcement critics. During the Clinton administration, for example, some prominent detractors argued that the INS and the Clinton administration were not really interested in controlling the boundary, that Gatekeeper—and similar INS operations in other locales in the border region—were a mere show. These critics pointed to accusations by the union of Border Patrol agents that Border Patrol supervisors in various stations in the San Diego Sector were underreporting apprehension numbers in an effort to make the operation look more successful than it was in reality.[28] Such critics also pointed out the limitations of a strategy that is largely focused on the boundary rather than on the "magnet" of employers for whom unauthorized immigrants work.[29] As Wade Graham, in an article for *Harper's* contended, "The truth about illegal immigration is that until such time as U.S. law barring the employment of illegal aliens is enforced . . . poor foreigners will continue to come here. Our elected representatives have neither the political security nor the will to alter this fact. . . . [T]here will no doubt be more dramatic demands that the border be properly policed. These demands our government will oblige with grand operations and congressional bills designed to pacify the populace until after the next election. We should, however, expect little by way of substantive change—just more empty gestures."[30] There is much truth to such an analysis. The length of the U.S. boundaries and the strength of the various factors that push, pull, and facilitate unauthorized immigration to the United States make boundary enforcement a daunting project under the best of political circumstances. These factors, combined with the multiple political constraints that limit the level of boundary enforcement that would be needed to impact significantly migrants' ability to enter the country extralegally, suggest that enforcement of immigration laws as they relate to employment is really the only way to make a serious dent in unauthorized immigration (assuming this is a desirable goal). Employment of unauthorized immigrants is rife throughout the United States in the low-wage manufacturing and service sectors (obviously, in addition to agriculture) and is usually concentrated in specific industries, often as a result of capital's effort to "restructure" by having a lower-wage, more pliable workforce. But there is insufficient political will in Washington, D.C., to enforce already existing employer sanctions or to strengthen them.[31]

That said, critics such as Graham overstate the case when they argue that Gatekeeper is largely a show that has little real effect and/or that the federal government is not serious about trying to achieve control of the boundary. While the creation of an image of control is arguably the most important effect of the Clinton administration's boundary buildup,[32] we cannot reduce enforcement efforts to such symbolic outcomes (or intentions, for that matter). As argued above and as will be demonstrated below, Gatekeeper has had some important material outcomes.

THE ONGOING PACIFICATION OF THE BORDER REGION AND GROWING MEXICAN GOVERNMENT COLLABORATION

A trip today to the U.S.-Mexico boundary in the area around San Diego reveals a very different scene than one would have found a decade ago. The boundary fence with gaping holes is gone, replaced by a steel wall increasingly coupled with a second tier of fencing, along with sophisticated technology that makes it easier for the Border Patrol to detect unauthorized crossers.[33] No longer do large crowds of migrants and smugglers gather along the boundary waiting to cross at nightfall. Similarly, the days of "banzai runs"—when groups of unauthorized immigrants run through the ports of entry—are gone. And the frequent attacks against unauthorized migrants and crimes (mostly against property) by "border bandits" are largely phenomena of the past. Thus, a semblance of order has replaced the image of chaos that once seemed to reign in the urbanized border region of the San Diego Sector. Partially as a result, the high-volume debate surrounding unauthorized immigration and boundary enforcement has died down considerably.[34]

Appearance is key. Indeed, many of the media images employed by California Governor Pete Wilson and by prorestriction politicians and groups, and even at times by the INS, to justify Proposition 187 and/or an increase in state resources to combat unauthorized immigration misrepresented the state of the boundary vis-à-vis immigration enforcement. As discussed earlier, efforts to enhance state control over the most urbanized portions of the boundary in the San Diego area increased considerably beginning in 1990—a process that continued through 1994. Yet many of the boundary images employed by social actors arguing in favor of Proposition 187 or for a Gatekeeper-type strategy in San Diego were from the 1980s. Even Graham's widely read article in *Harper's* employed such images, but did not inform the reader that the images did not correspond at all to the situation along the boundary pertaining to immigration control at the time of the publication.[35] In this regard, Gate-keeper was the solution to a "problem" that did not exist, or at least did not exist to the extent that it *appeared* to exist in the public eye. And to the extent that representations of the "problem" exaggerated its extent, it became all the easier for state actors to garner the desired resources to boost the state's enforcement capacity, and subsequently to construct an image of success and reap considerable political gain in the process. As political scientist Peter Andreas explains,

> [F]or those in charge of border enforcement, how Congress and the broader public *feel* about the integrity of the border is arguably as important as impor-tant as the actual deterrent effect on the border. The deterrence function of borders has always been as much about image as reality, a political fiction providing an appearance of control that helps reproduce and reinforce state legitimacy. Indeed, the very premise of the current push to "regain control of the border" reinforces the myth that the border was actually controlled in the first place. It also perpetuates the myth that the problem and the solution are located at the border rather than having to confront the problems of formally managing a transnational labor market. In other words, statecraft in this case is not merely about curbing illegal immigration but about propping up state claims to territorial authority.[36]

In other words, Operation Gatekeeper and boundary policing are as much about performance as they are about fulfilling a particular task. This is not to suggest that state elites are engaging in manipulative practices merely to fool the public and serve their own ends. Rather, what we are seeing is "social role taking,"[37] boundary construction and maintenance being one of the state's most important functions. And, arguably, in no matter is the modern territo-rial state more sovereign than in matters of immigration control and boundary enforcement.[38]

To the extent that the image of a boundary under control corresponds to reality, a number of factors have led to this state of affairs. These include new fences and walls along the boundary; a dramatic increase in the number of Border Patrol agents; and a significant change in the Border Patrol's strategy from chasing and apprehending migrants *after* they have crossed the boundary to deterring the unauthorized from entering in the first place. These changes have received a good amount of media attention, but one of the most signif-icant and less acknowledged changes has been the increase in the Mexican government's support of U.S. efforts to bring order to the border region.

As illustrated in previous chapters, there have been a number of instances of cooperation between the United States and Mexico—sometimes caused by U.S. pressure—regarding boundary policing. But such developments—until relatively recently—have been rare occurrences due to the unwillingness of Mexican authorities to participate in such efforts. Mexico has long refused to deny exit to its citizens trying to emigrate to the United States. Indeed, there is an article in Mexico's constitution prohibiting the government from doing so. Furthermore, migration to the United States has long served as a "safety valve" for relieving potential political tensions within Mexico while simultaneously serving as a major source of hard currency for the country.[39] At the same time, Mexico's relative lack of cooperation is a manifestation of the country's historic ambivalence toward the imposition of the U.S.-Mexico boundary by the Treaty of Guadalupe Hidalgo in 1848 and the concomitant seizure of a vast amount of what had hitherto been Mexican territory. As recently as 1943, for example, maps were still in use in Mexico's schools that described the lands lost through the treaty as "territory temporarily in the hands of the United States."[40] While Mexico has long abandoned such claims, it still officially refuses to prevent the passage of unauthorized migrants from Mexico to the United States. Subtle practices now seem to be slowly and effectively eroding this refusal, however.

The lack of cooperation from Mexico officials emerged as a serious issue in the 1970s in the context of a significant rise in unauthorized entries from Mexico and growing official U.S. concern about such matters. American authorities were especially concerned about migrant smugglers. Joint governmental efforts in fighting smuggling seems to have begun in 1977 in the aftermath of Mexican President José López Portillo's visit to the White House during the Carter administration. At that time, Mexican authorities became increasingly concerned about unauthorized immigration from Central America into their own country. In response to an American initiative, López Portillo appointed a special representative to study boundary issues and to draw up recommendations. This special representative headed a pilot program coordinating relations between Mexican police authorities and INS officials. The National Anti-Smuggling Program, a new special unit of the INS established during the Carter administration, significantly increased the number of arrests and prosecutions of suspected extralegal immigrant smugglers. Mexican authorities cooperated in a number of ways, arresting hundreds of smugglers during the late 1970s.[41] Nevertheless, such anti-smuggling efforts seem not to have seriously diminished the number of unauthorized entries into the United States. Proliferation of such smuggling networks, the intense cross-boundary social ties between communities in Mexico and the United States (which have long facilitated extralegal immigration), and the sheer volume of unauthorized crossers continued to frustrate state efforts to control the international boundary.

U.S.-Mexico collaboration in immigration enforcement further intensified during the 1980s. These efforts largely focused on preventing the passage of Central Americans through Mexico and on apprehending suspected criminals in the border region. Given its political sensitivity in Mexico, unauthorized immigration by Mexicans received relatively little attention in these collaborative efforts. During the INS crackdown in the Rio Grande Valley in the late 1980s (see chapter 4), for example, the INS sent intelligence agents to Mexico to analyze migratory patterns of Central Americans into Mexico. At the same time, the INS began training their Mexican counterparts and intensified their relationships (in terms of information exchange, for example) with a host of Mexican law enforcement agencies. Such collaboration certainly facilitated Mexico's crackdown on third-country nationals migrating to the United States, resulting in a huge increase in Mexico's apprehension and deportation of unauthorized (in terms of Mexico) immigrants who were overwhelmingly from Central America. While Mexico concentrated these efforts on the country's southern boundary with Guatemala and the southern part of the country more generally, its northern boundary also received increased scrutiny.[42]

The establishment of Grupo Beta in December 1990 (see chapter 4) is the most direct attempt by the Mexican government to regulate its northern boundary with the United States. While U.S. pressure might very well have informed Mexico City's decision to establish the group, Mexican authorities had their own reasons for wanting an institutionalized police presence in the border region. It appears that Mexican officials were concerned about border violence because it hurt the image of Baja California.[43] And the Mexican government wanted to reduce the appearance of disorder and instability along its boundary with the United States as it sought to strengthen economic ties with its neighbor to the north.[44]

The founding of Grupo Beta marked an important shift in relations between Mexican and U.S. law enforcement authorities. The U.S. Border Patrol donated radios and other surplus equipment to help Beta get started. Despite occasionally tense relations between the two agencies, the Border Patrol and Grupo Beta often cooperate in apprehending suspected criminals in the border region. Similarly, the San Diego Police practices shooting with Beta agents at a firing range in San Diego, and shares its radio frequencies with the group.[45] Grupo Beta's goal is to reduce violence against prospective unauthorized crossers on the Mexican side of the boundary, and by this criteria it has largely been a success. But Beta also inhibits extralegal migration to the extent that the police unit tries to curtail the activities of smugglers. The Mexican government has now established Beta-type groups in other locales in the border region, notably in Tecate (Grupo Alfa) in 1995, in Mexicali (Grupo Beta-Mexicali) in 1997,[46] and in Matamoros (across from Brownsville, Texas) and Nogales (across from Nogales, Arizona). In this regard, collaboration by Mexican authorities with INS objectives is a growth industry.

There is also increasing collaboration between the INS and local police officials in Mexico aimed at limiting the opportunities for unauthorized crossings into the United States. In Matamoros, for example, local police appear to
be working together with the Border Patrol, on occasion, to apprehend
extralegal immigrants deemed troublesome. Matamoros officials have also
built walls and fencing at a popular boundary crossing point along the Rio
Grande.[47] Similarly, local police in Tijuana now prevent people from gathering on the Mexican side of the U.S. port of entry in San Ysidro to limit the
potential for "banzai runs" through the port.

Such efforts at collaboration increased dramatically during the Clinton
administration, significantly due to the efforts of the U.S. Attorney for
Southern California and the U.S. Attorney General's Special Representative
for Southwest Border Issues.[48] Taking all these developments together, the
growing collaboration between the United States and Mexico is undoubtedly
important and has helped to create the semblance of a more orderly border
region, at least in its most urbanized sections. In this regard, U.S.-Mexico
cooperation is one piece of a larger strategy of pacifying the border. But given
the large numbers of unauthorized immigrants who still manage to enter the
United States from Mexico, such collaboration is far from the level needed for
U.S. authorities to control the boundary to the extent they would like. Furthermore, Mexico still refuses to accept the U.S. position that unauthorized immigrants are "illegal." Thus, direct interdiction of Mexican migrants by Mexican
authorities is not possible. As former "border czar" Alan Bersin states, "Further
progress . . . requires a binational engagement of enforcement authorities. The
present state of the bilateral border, however, is not conducive to such cooperation."[49] From an American perspective, full pacification of the boundary
requires the pacification of the Mexican government in relation to extralegal
migration to the United States. Although the U.S. goal is far from realized,
Mexico has become increasingly placated in terms of resisting American pressures to "cooperate" with boundary enforcement.

REINVENTING THE U.S.-MEXICO BORDER: THE "NAFTA-IZATION" OF THE BOUNDARY

The buildup of the U.S.-Mexico boundary, as I have already established, is
occurring at a time when the boundary is also increasingly porous. Economic
goods and services, as well as finance and cultural phenomena, flow massively
through it. U.S. elites have employed a variety of strategies and tactics—
consciously and unconsciously—to denationalize and/or internationalize the
space of the U.S.-Mexico border to facilitate this process. The implementation
of the North American Free Trade Agreement (NAFTA) on January 1, 1994 is
only the most obvious of ongoing attempts to establish a barrier-free border
zone for the flow of goods and capital. Such developments have led some to

proclaim the boundary as virtually nonexistent. As Jack McGrory, San Diego City Manager, explained in 1993, "Frankly, we're starting to operate as if the border didn't even exist, and it's paying off—in both directions."[50]

Despite such proclamations, I have already demonstrated that countercurrents are also at play—namely, the increasing implementation of structures and practices, especially along the international boundary itself, intended to control and limit the levels of immigration from Mexico to the United States. U.S. authorities justify such developments on the basis of defending national sovereignty and as a means of maintaining a long tradition of warranted, "legal" immigration to the United States. As President Clinton stated in 1995, "It is a fundamental right and duty for a nation to protect the integrity of its borders and its laws. This Administration shall stand firm against illegal immigration and the continued abuse of our immigration laws. By closing the back door to illegal immigration, we will continue to open the front door to legal immigration."[51] Thus, the modern boundary is conceived as one of law and order.

For the champions of what might seem to be two conflicting processes—one of "opening" the boundary to the flow of (non-illicit) goods and capital and "closing" the boundary to "illegal" activities such as unauthorized entries—these processes are part and parcel of a unified project of creating a border region where law and order as well as economic prosperity reign. As Alan Bersin explains, "[W]e are moving decisively toward a border that functions effectively; one that is a lawful and orderly gateway; one that manages significantly better the problems of illegal immigration and smuggling; and one that promises and routinely delivers handsome dividends from an investment in regional integration."[52] In fact, these two processes, argue Clinton administration officials, are actually inextricably linked.

According to Robert Bach, the executive associate commissioner for policy and planning for the INS, the policy of the Clinton administration perceived the U.S-Mexico border region as an opportunity, a place, and an anchor.[53] The border is an opportunity in that its proper organization allows regional integration and NAFTA to occur and allows for economic progress on both sides. The border is a place in the sense that its sociocultural patterns are geographically unique—an important factor that the administration takes into consideration so that federal policy works for families, workers, and employers on both sides of the international divide. And although border policy is only one piece of a much larger strategy of immigration enforcement, the border is an anchor, primarily for the purposes of law enforcement. To realize its vision, the Clinton administration sought to build an institutional framework within and upon which "the market" can flourish. As a set of institutional relationships based on the law, this market is taken to be one in which everyone can participate, and from which people on both sides of the boundary can and will benefit.[54]

The administration's "comprehensive border control strategy," then, is part and parcel of this effort to construct these law-based institutional relationships. The official strategy is one that puts workplace enforcement (inspection and monitoring of worksites for the employment of unauthorized immigrants) at the center, along with enhanced boundary enforcement, the deportation of "criminal aliens" (immigrants convicted of criminal offenses), and the provision of more assistance to states most "burdened" by unauthorized immigration.[55] But it is clear that the actual strategy puts much greater emphasis on high-profile policing measures along the boundary than on workplace enforcement. As of late 1997, for example, the INS had only twenty-three workplace inspectors in the San Diego area, thirteen of whom the INS added during Gatekeeper. In the Los Angeles District of the INS (an area comprising a population of more than twenty million people), the INS issued only eighteen "intent to fine" notices to employers for hiring extralegal migrants in fiscal year 1996. Even though the INS issued thirty notices in FY 1997, such numbers are a proverbial "drop in the bucket" given the amount of unauthorized migrants working in the United States. The estimate for San Diego County alone stands at 200,000.[56] On a national scale, the number of fines levied against employers actually decreased from 2,000 in FY 1992 to 888 in FY 1997; the amount of fines levied decreased from $17 million to $8 million.[57] While INS arrests and deportations of noncriminal "illegal aliens" (apprehended through interior enforcement measures) increased in 1996 and 1997, they declined significantly in 1998 and 1999—arguably a manifestation of the strong U.S. economy, the very low unemployment rate, and the accompanying need of U.S. employers for workers (especially low-wage ones). As *The New York Times* reported in March 2000, "[workplace] raids have all but stopped around the country over the last year." While crossing the boundary is harder than ever, "once inside the country, illegal immigrants are now largely left alone."[58] In terms of interior enforcement, the INS concentrates on apprehending immigrants who have committed a crime. As Robert Bach explains, "It is just the market at work, drawing people to jobs, and the I.N.S. has chosen to concentrate its actions on aliens who are a danger to the community." As such, unauthorized immigrants face little risk these days once inside the United States, according to Bach, "unless the employer turns a worker in, and employers usually do that only to break a union or prevent a strike or that kind of stuff."[59]

Furthermore, as suggested above, it is far from clear that Gatekeeper is having a significant effect in actually decreasing unauthorized entries into the United States. Indeed, the UCSD study found that 69 percent of immigrant-dependent employers in the San Diego area had noticed no change during the preceding fifteen months in the supply of immigrant labor. Only 8 percent of employers detected a decrease, while 23 percent reported an increase.[60] Besides driving unauthorized boundary crossers into more challenging (and dangerous) terrain, Gatekeeper filters out older and weaker men, as well as many women and children, helping to create, in the words of scholar Michael Huspek, "the perfect workers."[61] As Huspek explains, "It is young, fit males who are most apt to make successful entry. . . . This shift in the type of worker gaining entry into the U.S. amounts to a strengthening of the labor pool available to U.S. employers while at the same time restricting access to those who in the past have been likeliest [among unauthorized immigrants and their U.S.-born (and thus citizen) children] to draw upon the state's social relief programs."[62] Thus, Operation Gatekeeper and the larger "crackdown" on unauthorized immigration appear to have had little effect on employers. But this outcome should not be surprising as the "marketization" or "NAFTA-ization" of the border region is one in which the rights and interests of capital and capitalists seem to be supreme.

As Ralph Nader and Lori Wallach contend, NAFTA seeks to eliminate restrictions that protect people while enhancing those that protect corporate interests.[63] It is thus not surprising that environmental and labor matters were only part of NAFTA's weak "side agreements," rather than central components of the treaty. But as illustrated above, the Clinton administration and many NAFTA backers assumed (or at least argued) that the simultaneous implementation of stronger immigrant enforcement measures and the development of a relatively barrier-free boundary to goods and capital would lead to greater levels of prosperity for people on both sides of the boundary. As an assistant to Alan Bersin explained to me in 1997, "[N]o one says that the immigration initiatives [of the Clinton administration] are the unilateral answer to economic problems [that exist in Mexico and drive unauthorized immigration]. But they are one way of responding to it and managing the problems so we can have this region that flourishes. That you decrease the amount of illegal activity and bring the benefits to the people that are law-abiding—the majority of the people. People want to come and see the Padres [San Diego's professional baseball team], they want to come and see the Chargers [San Diego's professional football team]. The types of joint programs that we could be doing are numerous, but we need a little bit more certainty."[64] It is through the creation of a regime of law in the border region that this vision will supposedly come to be.

Of course, the cost of buying a ticket for a Padres or Chargers game is far beyond the means of the vast majority of people in Tijuana, where the average daily wage is well below the price of such tickets. Furthermore, it is not possible for a significant proportion of the people in Tijuana—given their modest means and lack of participation in the formal economy (and thus possessing no proof of steady employment)—to gain permission to visit the United States. Nevertheless, government officials frequently mouth platitudes, proclaiming that their only desire is that people enter the United States *legally* by going through the proper channels. They ignore the fact that such efforts would be a complete waste of time for most people in Mexico given their inability to secure an immigrant visa or a so-called border crossing card through official channels. In this sense, their own rhetoric of law and order has blinded them to the reality experienced by many desiring to enter the United States from Mexico.

The buildup of the boundary and its NAFTA-ization are also linked in another, more nefarious, manner. Growing liberalization of the Mexican economy has facilitated a significant exodus from Mexico's countryside; from 1980 to 1990, for example, the amount of the country's population living in rural areas declined from 36 percent to 28 percent.[65] Numerous studies suggested that the implementation of NAFTA and the related liberalization of the Mexican economy would only intensify this process. Combined with the resulting intensifying links between the two countries, the research suggested that the rural exodus would lead to a significant increase in migration from Mexico to the United States[66]—a development of which the Clinton administration was very much aware.[67]

As INS commissioner Doris Meissner admitted during testimony to Congress in November 1993, she foresaw that NAFTA would most likely to lead to an *increase* in unauthorized immigration from Mexico to the United States in the short and medium terms. For this reason she stated that "[r]esponding to the likely short- to medium term impacts of NAFTA will require strengthening our enforcement efforts along the border, both at and between ports of entry."[68] In other words, NAFTA requires enhanced boundary enforcement not simply to create a border region of law and order to facilitate capital accumulation, but also to stymie the anticipated increase in unauthorized immigration caused by the liberalization of the Mexican economy. Thus, the "problem of illegal immigration" is, to a certain degree, of the U.S. government's own making, and is an extricable part of NAFTA-type processes that are supposedly making national boundaries redundant.[69] By increasing the porosity of the U.S.-Mexico boundary through trade liberalization, the state must strengthen the boundary in other ways. This seeming paradox is consistent with the observation that globalization does not necessarily lead to a decline in nationalism. In fact, globalization can actually serve to enhance differences between citizens and "aliens."[70] In this way, rising boundary-related "illegal" activity (such as unauthorized immigration) is an integral part of the NAFTA-ization of the U.S.-Mexico border region. From the perspective of U.S. government officials like Meissner, such a development is unavoidable and requires the state to respond with efforts to create order. And the immediate source of the disorder is the unauthorized immigrant, the transgressor of the law of the boundary and thus a criminal.

THE CRIMINALIZATION OF "ILLEGAL" IMMIGRANTS

There are a variety of reasons why one might support enhanced boundary enforcement measures as epitomized by Operation Gatekeeper. It is too simple to argue that it is xenophobia and hypernationalism that animate such sentiments, although they are certainly present and arguably dominant. But for those not primarily motivated by such feelings, it is often a desire to create order that underlies their support. The order they seek would protect people in the United States *as well as* unauthorized immigrants from the absence of regulation that has long permeated the U.S.-Mexico border region.

It is a basic tenet of liberal political theory that the establishment of the rule of law is a necessary (but not, in and of itself, sufficient) condition for the realization of justice. This view leads some to see the boundary buildup as a progressive development that actually helps migrants.[71] From such a perspective, the law can facilitate the creation of an order from which everyone benefits. In the case of unauthorized immigrants, for example, a greater boundary policing presence can lead to lower levels of violence against migrants by so-called border bandits along the U.S.-Mexico boundary.[72]

At the same time, many argue that the maintenance of the rule of law requires immigration to be orderly and legal since implicit acceptance of any lawlessness has the potential to undermine the larger culture of respect for the rule of law. Seen from this perspective, unauthorized immigration is a potential threat to the larger body politic. As the U.S. Select Commission on Immigration and Refugee Policy contended in its final report, "[T]here is evidence that shows that the toleration of large scale undocumented/illegal immigration can have pernicious effects on U.S. society. . . . Most serious is that illegality breeds illegality. The presence of a substantial number of undocumented/illegal aliens in the United States has resulted not only in a disregard for immigration law but in the breaking of minimum wage and occupational safety laws, and statutes against smuggling as well. As long as undocumented migration flouts U.S. immigration law, its most devastating impact may be the disregard it breeds for other U.S. laws."[73]

As shown previously, contemporary debate surrounding unauthorized immigration to the United States puts an increasing emphasis on legality. Such emphasis on the legality (or lack thereof) of the immigrant draws upon and reinforces a powerful ideological force or position in American society. The dominant view of the law sees it as rational, benign, and necessary, as well as independent of any specific social and/or geographical context as it supposedly rests on immutable principles. The effect of such a worldview is to put the law beyond question, and thus to normalize sociospatial relations. Of course, as a social creation, the law embodies (in terms of its origin and effects) particular power relations.[74]

The dialectical relationship between the law and the modern, national territorial state serves to reinforce the tendency to analyze and/or to perceive social phenomena only within the limits of national boundaries,[75] a tendency that very much informs thinking and practice on the question of unauthorized immigration. Thus, in the case of the United States, although the unauthorized immigrant is very much part of a transnational society of which the country is a part—that is, of a network of social relations that go and emanate from beyond U.S. territory, that impact upon Americans, and that Americans help to produce and reproduce—the dominant view is to regard the "illegal alien" as someone whose supposed criminal activity (in violating immigration laws) is independent of the actions of people and institutions in the United States. Thus, the "illegal" is someone for whom U.S. society need not accept any responsibility.[76] This is a view that seems to have grown in strength in the last couple of decades.

Legal scholar Alexander Aleinikoff argues that Supreme Court decisions from the 1980s are a manifestation of an increasingly "good alien/bad alien" distinction: legal entrants and residents are *good* and "illegals" are *bad*.[77] The Court thus views unauthorized immigrants as "uninvited guests, intruders, trespassers, law breakers. The Court sees illegal entry and residence as primarily problems in law enforcement."[78] As argued earlier, this division between "legal" and "illegal" immigrants is one that has become stronger over time—a manifestation of what Aleinikoff calls a "tightening circle of membership" regarding insiders and outsiders of the U.S. polity.[79] Some members of the U.S. Select Commission for example, argued in 1981 in favor of legalization of unauthorized immigrants in order to "acknowledge that the United States has at least some responsibility for the presence of undocumented/ illegal aliens in this country since U.S. law has explicitly exempted employers from any penalty for hiring them."[80] While employment of unauthorized immigrants is still pervasive in the United States,[81] sentiment in favor of recognizing our collective responsibility for the presence of unauthorized immigrants in the United States is far less common today than it was in the early 1980s due to the "tightening circle" and the greater levels of acceptance of the social boundary between "legal" and "illegal" immigrants.[82]

The strengthening of the sociolegal boundary advances the equation of the unauthorized immigrant with a criminal. As such, the "illegal" becomes subject to a whole host of practices legitimated by the full weight of the law. As legal scholar Gerald Neuman explains, "[The term 'illegal alien'] may be interpreted as implying that the alien's presence can give rise to no legal duties toward him because he should not be here in the first place. Like an illegal contract that creates no obligation, duties toward the alien are void or voidable. This notion reduces the alien to a non-person, an outlaw outside the protection of the legal system."[83] It follows then that the "illegal" deserves nothing from the United States, regardless of what her contributions to the society might be and of what her rights are as outlined in the U.S. Constitution, the wide body of American law, or in various international human rights covenants. The designation "illegal" and the concomitant ideology legitimate punitive legislation such as Proposition 187 and, for some, the employment of force and violence to expel those who are perceived to have no right to be in "our country."[84] Furthermore, because the law, for the vast majority, is seemingly neutral, unproblematic, and apolitical, it offers both a standard and a means by which to maintain order and to judge and treat human beings. The designation of the immigrant as "illegal" thus serves to stifle debate over border policing and the rights of unauthorized immigrants.[85]

The fusing of the law, territory, and social power makes the construction of the "illegal" immigrant a difficult one to counter. The contemporary emphasis on illegality has stacked the debate surrounding unauthorized immigration as it is very difficult to argue in favor of something "illegal." During the campaign surrounding California's Proposition 187 in 1994, for example, few if any of its opponents within the political mainstream spoke up for the rights of unauthorized immigrants.[86] (To the contrary, many opponents accepted the argument of 187 supporters that "illegal" immigration was a serious problem, but contended that enhanced boundary enforcement was the correct way to deal with the matter.[87] Many opponents went so far as to suggest that the passage of 187 would lead to an increase in crime activity by youths pushed out of school and to outbreaks of diseases because of untreated "illegals."[88] In this manner, many 187 opponents reinforced the perception of "illegals" as threats to the social fabric.) In addition to challenging the almost inviolable nature of "the law," to defend the rights of "illegals" is to call into question "the near sacred commitment in conventional political discourse to one of the cardinal norms of the system of state sovereignty—that countries have the rightful authority to control both the entry of foreigners into the national territory and (within certain limits) the terms of their membership once present."[89] Such "territorialization" of the law has created a mind-set that allows for implementation of harsh penalties for migrants who have committed the geographical "crime" of unauthorized entry. As then senator Alan Simpson (Republican, Wyoming) exclaimed in praising the U.S. Senate's passage of the Immigration and Financial Responsibility Act of 1996, "We have stuff in there that has everything but the rack and screws for people who are violating the laws of the United States."[90]

Paradoxically, Operation Gatekeeper and the general crackdown on unauthorized immigration has had the anticipated effect of increased criminal activity or what one analyst has called "a wider web of illegality."[91] Gatekeeper, for example, has led to a greater reliance of migrants on professional smuggling networks.[92] Indeed, the Border Patrol judges increased smuggling fees as a sign of "success" of its boundary deterrence strategy (ostensibly due to greater demand for smuggling services as well as to an increase in the obstacles faced by smugglers).[93] Despite the fact that the INS fully understands that increased smuggling is an inevitable outcome of the operation, it continues to argue that more enforcement resources can bring an end to migrant smuggling. In this regard, Gatekeeper-induced criminality serves to legitimate an even greater infusion of resources to boundary enforcement efforts.[94] Furthermore, the rise in smuggling justifies increasingly punitive sanctions against smugglers; U.S. authorities now increasingly treat immigrant smuggling as a form of organized crime.[95]

Similarly, Gatekeeper resulted in a predictable increase in efforts to enter the United States via official ports of entry through the use of false documents or oral misrepresentation (falsely claiming to be a U.S. citizen).[96] Those apprehended trying to enter the United States in such a manner—the vast majority of whom are women[97]—face formal deportation. If caught a second time trying to enter the United States without authorization, they face felony prosecution and prison time. Such prosecutions have increased manifold in southern California.[98] Curiously, the Border Patrol deems an increase in use of fraudulent documents and in "ports of entry activity" to be an indicator of success of its enhanced boundary policing strategy.[99]

All these developments, along with a number that precede the current immigration crackdown, have served to increase the criminalization of unauthorized immigrants and even, to a lesser extent, of authorized immigrants, leading to a significant rise in the number of people, including children,[100] held in detention by the INS. As of 2000, the INS was holding an average of 21,000 "aliens" in detention daily, at an annual cost of approximately $800 million.[101] Under the Illegal Immigration Reform and Immigrant Responsibility Act, noncitizen "aggravated felons" are subject to deportation, regardless of how long ago their crimes occurred. The 1996 law greatly expanded the list of crimes for which "resident aliens" can lose their residency. Prior to 1996, the list was limited to murder, rape, and other major felonies; the list now includes selling marijuana, domestic violence, some cases of drunk driving, and any conviction that carries a sentence of one year or more.[102] Noncitizens convicted of crimes, and who come from countries with which the United States does not have repatriation agreements, present problems. Because the INS is not able to deport them after they serve their sentences, they face INS detention indefinitely.[103]

Such developments have led to a significant rise in the number of deportations of so-called criminal aliens.[104] This phenomena is indicative of the slippery slope that results from a hardening of the distinction of "legal" and "illegal" immigrants. In a number of ways, the illegal/legal distinction has become one between citizens and "aliens" who now are held to a much tougher standard vis-à-vis law enforcement than citizens. Most deportees removed from the United States, for instance, are not, in fact, unauthorized immigrants. A majority are legal residents of the United States who have been stripped of their residency due to their legal transgressions.[105] Undoubtedly, many of the deportees have committed violent crimes. But assuming that the "criminal alien" population is similar to that which finds itself languishing in state and federal prisons in the United States, the largest group of the deportees are most probably nonviolent drug law offenders.[106]

Gerardo Antonio Mosquera Sr. was one such person. Convicted in 1989 for selling ten dollars' worth of marijuana, the INS stripped Mosquera of his permanent residency and sent the twenty-nine-year legal resident of the U.S. back to his native Columbia in December 1997. As a result, his seventeen-year-old son, Gerardo Jr., went into a deep depression; two months later, the high school junior committed suicide. The U.S. Embassy in Bogota would not even permit Gerardo Sr. to return to Los Angeles to attend his son's funeral.[107] In late August and early September 1998, the INS conducted Operation Last Call in Texas, rounding up over five hundred immigrants—mostly legal U.S. residents—for deportation. All had been convicted of drunk driving three or more times, although in some cases the convictions might have taken place years ago.[108]

Such examples illustrate the growing criminalization of all immigrants—especially the unauthorized—and increase the distinction between "us" and "them," between citizens and "aliens," placing "aliens" on the wrong side of the social boundary that distinguishes between law and order and criminality. This enhanced "alienization" of unauthorized immigrants surely contributes to a public mind-set that facilitates the numerous human rights abuses perpetrated by INS and Border Patrol officials.[109] It also serves to provide ideological legitimation to the very boundary buildup that has helped to criminalize the migrants. At the same time, it underlies the growing cooperation between the INS and a variety of police agencies, increasing the criminalization and political marginalization of immigrants—both documented and undocumented.[110]

By its very definition, "illegal" immigration is a problem.[111] And the personification of this problem are "illegal immigrants" who are "criminalized from the outset. . . . because they don't have the documents that grant them a modest place to stay and a lowly job to survive."[112] Thus, it should not be surprising that the so-called Crime Bill of 1994 contained the authorization for the budgetary increase that has resulted in unprecedented growth in the number of Border Patrol agents since fiscal year 1995.[113]

This criminalization of unauthorized immigrants and the growing emphasis on "law and order" in the border region have taken place since the 1960s in a larger national context of growing official and popular concern about fighting crime and a concomitant rise in resources for law enforcement—part of a conservative-led attack on the gains of the civil rights movement and the social welfare state.[114] The resulting shift in federal resources has led to the rise of what political scientist Peter Andreas calls "the American crimefare state."[115] In this regard, the rise of "illegal immigration" and the criminalization of the immigrant have intersected with efforts by conservative and neoliberal politicians and activists to redirect state resources away from redistributive endeavors and toward those of social control.[116]

CREATING A LANDSCAPE OF CONTROL AND FEAR

The criminalization of migrants and the boundary and immigration enforcement buildup have undoubtedly led to a climate of fear within immigrant communities as those guilty of even relatively minor infractions are now subject to deportation. This climate of fear is not limited to the interior of the United States. It also manifests itself in the border area, which has increasingly become a zone of state surveillance. As Josiah Heyman contends, the growing emphasis on boundary interdiction "has militarized border society, where more and more people either work for the watchers, or are watched by the state." In this regard, the U.S.-Mexico borderland has increasingly become "a society comprised substantially of 'police and thieves.'"[117]

Growing INS efforts to restrict the entry of unauthorized migrants has also created a "landscape of fear,"[118] and increasingly a landscape of death.[119] Over the years, the border landscape has become more ominous—not only in terms of fences, walls, spotlights, and Border Patrol vehicles and INS checkpoints (what Mike Davis refers to as the "second border"[120]), but also in terms of warning signs along the highway cautioning drivers to look out for migrants running across the road, and at a high-risk crossing points advising migrants not to risk a potentially life-threatening journey across an arduous landscape.

The boundary in southern California is now more difficult to cross. As a result, would-be unauthorized immigrants now must traverse more demanding terrain to cross successfully into the country's interior. The journey across mountainous and/or desert landscapes takes longer and often exposes the migrants to relatively high levels of risk. This situation has resulted in hundreds of deaths related to the crossing of the boundary.[121]

However, there is nothing new about risk and death being a part of extralegal boundary crossing. Entering the United States without authorization has long been dangerous. One writer described the situation in the years following World War II as follows:

> Near the international boundary, there was little to prevent Mexicans from crossing. . . . Yet the crossing was not devoid of dangers. As many unfortunate individuals discovered, the journey into the United States was fraught with natural and man-made hazards which at times turned the crossing into a nightmare, ending in severe injuries and death. Those who sought to enter illegally often faced torrid temperatures in the day and freezing weather at night. At times they could not carry sufficient food or water to make the

journey. There was the ever-present danger of snake bites or of falling victim to the vicious gangs that operated along the border. Unknown numbers of braceros and undocumented workers were robbed and even killed for their meager earnings or personal possessions. Undocumented workers were shot at or beaten by local ruffians as they attempted to cut across private lands. The Rio Grande claimed its share of victims through drownings. In 1953 its swollen flood waters claimed between 300 and 400 victims who attempted to cross it.[122]

Such tragedies were still common in the 1980s and the early 1990s, before the Gatekeeper boundary buildup.[123] In the context of increasing boundary enforcement since 1994, the number of migrant deaths has increased noticeably. (While the vast majority of them take place along the U.S.-Mexico boundary, they also occur in other "crossing" areas such as the Caribbean, where a high number of would-be immigrants from the Dominican Republic have drowned and/or been eaten by sharks while trying to enter Puerto Rico without authorization in order to board a flight to the United States free of immigration controls.[124] In addition to their numbers, what makes these deaths different are their causes and geography: far more people are dying due to exposure to extreme environmental conditions (heat or cold), and as a result of the effect of pushing extra-legal crossers away from population centers, the locations of their deaths are more geographically dispersed.[125]

In southern California, the number of crossing-related deaths has definitely increased in the context of Gatekeeper. In 1994, a total of 23 migrants died in the San Diego and El Centro sectors trying to cross. By 1995, the figure reached 61, staying about the same in 1996 (59). By 1997, the number of deaths had risen to 89, and then skyrocketed to 145 in 1998, dropping slightly to 110 in 1999.[126] Operation Gatekeeper's death toll reached the mark of 500 on March 22, 2000.[127]

By the Border Patrol's own criteria, as set out in its 1994 "Strategic Plan," such an outcome suggests that Gatekeeper is failing somewhat.[128] The Border Patrol and INS officials expected that Gatekeeper would discourage a significant number of migrants from crossing by pushing them out into mountain and desert areas where—after making a cost-benefit analysis—the migrants would rationally decide to forgo the risks and return to Mexico.[129] Given that this is not happening, the INS is arguably responsible (at least partially) for the deaths. By knowingly "forcing" people to cross risky terrain, the INS is contributing to the numerous deaths that have resulted.[130]

Yet the INS refuses to acknowledge any role in creating the undesirable consequences of its operations. Instead it blames smugglers for leading people into high-risk areas and then abandoning them. Interestingly, the INS explanation for the rise in extralegal crossing deaths often resonates in the larger society. For example, following the discovery in 1998 of eight partially decomposed corpses of unauthorized Mexican immigrants in the Imperial Valley desert (one of whom turned out to be the smuggler), the *Los Angeles Times* characterized smugglers as people who "too often do not care whether their clients live or die" and editorialized in favor of stiffer penalties for smugglers, including life imprisonment and the death penalty.[131] At the Los Angeles funeral of one of the dead migrants (Julio Cesar Gallegos, who was trying to rejoin his pregnant, U.S.-citizen wife and child), the Catholic priest officiating at the funeral—himself an immigrant from Mexico—and the victim's father denounced the smugglers as causing the man's death. No one—at least on the basis of the *Los Angeles Times* report—said anything that would suggest that the INS and its practice of boundary control had anything to do with the death.[132]

The INS actively promotes this view by trying to position itself as the defender of the unauthorized migrants. And, undoubtedly, U.S. Border Patrol agents have saved large numbers of at-risk unauthorized immigrants in the U.S.-Mexico borderlands over the last few years.[133] It instituted in 1998, for example, Operation Lifesaver—involving civil patrol flights to spot migrants in distress and increased search and rescue missions in hazardous areas. The agency has also posted warning signs at high-risk crossing points, handed out flyers in Mexican border towns, and placed advertisements on Mexican radio and television advising would-be migrants of the potential dangers they face.[134] Despite these efforts to create a landscape of safety (and one free of unauthorized migrants), the migrant toll over the last few years indicates that what was previously a relatively empty area east of San Diego in terms of extralegal crossers has become a landscape of death. As Claudia Smith of the California Rural Legal Assistance Foundation contends, "As long as the strategy is to maximize the dangers by moving the migrant foot traffic out of the urban areas and into the mountains and deserts east of San Diego, the deaths will keep multiplying."[135] Indeed. In November 2000, the Gatekeeper-related death toll in southern California reached six hundred.

THE INSTITUTIONALIZATION AND NORMALIZATION OF THE BOUNDARY

As implied in the previous section, perhaps one of the most noteworthy factors associated with Operation Gatekeeper is the lack of any significant public opposition to a strategy (and the assumptions and interests behind it) that has led to the growing criminalization of immigrants, as well as to the increasing exposure of "illegal" boundary crossers to mortal danger. And as suggested earlier, this lack of opposition is significantly related to the strengthening of the social boundary between "legal" and "illegal" immigrants. While ideas and practices around "illegal" immigration are undoubtedly rooted in a particular human geography constituted by racism, sexism, and economic scapegoating, the term "illegal" is at issue because it represents a new and problematic way of looking at non–U.S. nationals that justifies an increasingly punitive set of social practices.[136] This development represents a particular stage in the development of the United States as a nation-state, one in which, at least in terms of immigration, the division between Mexico and the United States is shifting from a border, a zone of gradual transition, to a boundary, a stark line of demarcation—one that divides law and order from chaos and lawlessness, and thus civilization from something less than fully civilized.

The designation of certain types of immigrants as "illegal" serves to stifle discussion. For many, there is no reason to debate policies that aim to stop "illegal" immigration, something that is simply wrong:

> [F]or a growing proportion of the American public, the issues involved in the immigration controversy are fairly straightforward. Adhering to a view in which the issue of an immigrant's standing in American society and ability to fit into the American way of life should be determined simply by ascertaining the individual's formal status before the law, many apparently believe that devising appropriate immigration policies should be a simple matter. For such individuals the question of who rightly should be considered a fully vested member of the American community is unambiguous: one is either legal or illegal, a citizen or an alien, an American or a foreigner.
>
> If one accepts this starkly bifurcated system of categorization, it follows that coming to basic decisions about who rightfully belongs to, and who must be excluded from, that community should be an easy matter.[137]

Such opinion is not limited to the unlearned masses. Many in what former Vice President Dan Quayle referred to as the "cultural elite" hold such views. As *The San Diego Union-Tribune* opined in an editorial, for example, "Americans are perfectly right to be angry about illegal immigration, and Congress and the president need to continue efforts to stop it. But the distinction must be made between illegal and legal immigrants. Legal immigrants have always been a boon to our society. They deserve our respect and welcome."[138] Implicitly, the *Union-Tribune* seems to be suggesting that unauthorized immigrants definitely do not deserve "our" welcome; they also do not deserve our respect.

This is because the "illegal" is someone who is officially out of place—in a space where he does not belong. Thus, the official relationship of the "illegal alien" to the particular national space in which he finds himself defines his status. The practice of territoriality—the effort to exert influence over people and/or other phenomena by asserting control over a defined geographic area—reinforces the designation of the "illegal." Territoriality helps to obfuscate social relations between controlled and controller by ascribing these relations to territory, and thus away from human agency. This phenomenon is manifest in our language "as when we say 'it is the law of the land' or 'you may not do this here.'"[139]

This obfuscation of social relations applies perhaps even more so to the U.S.-Mexico boundary, its associated immigration enforcement practices, and the "illegal" immigrant—especially the unauthorized entrant in the process of crossing into the United States (as opposed to one who has already settled within a community in the interior). Thus, for the vast majority of Americans—including Latinos[140]—the wrongness of "illegal" immigration is simply beyond question. As a spokeswoman for the National Council of La Raza (NCLR) stated, "We are all against illegal immigration."[141] Such a position is an outgrowth of what Aleinikoff calls the "tightening circle of membership," and has resulted in a situation in which immigrant and ethnic-advocacy groups now largely recognize that "enforcement of the border is a legitimate and significant public-policy goal."[142] In fact, groups like the NCLR have argued in favor of enhanced boundary enforcement as a substitute of sorts for employers' sanctions, which they see as failed policy and leading to discrimination against all Latinos—regardless of immigration status.[143] For most people in the United States (and in Mexico as well), the boundary has become decreasingly controversial—it has become *normal*. In this regard, we can understand Operation Gatekeeper as the latest stage of a process of normalization of the U.S.-Mexico boundary, one that has seen a growing institutionalization of the boundary in a physical sense as well as an ideological one. The result of this process has been to make the boundary and its associated practices and ideologies increasingly difficult to challenge. This, arguably, is the most significant effect of the buildup of the social and territorial boundaries of which Operation Gatekeeper represents a pinnacle of sorts.

I close this chapter as I opened it—in the El Paso Sector on April 6, 1996. Not long after apprehending the lone man hiding in the brush, our vehicle received radio communication from the infrared unit that there were sightings of people near the dump in Sunland Park, New Mexico—just to the west of El Paso. Sunland Park is across the boundary from a rapidly growing informal community in Mexico called Anapra.

The agent I was accompanying—Ed Reeves[144]—had already told me that people from Mexico regularly cross the boundary to go to the dump and scavenge to bring materials back to sell in Ciudad Juárez (El Paso's twin city). As we got close to the dump, we saw in the moonlight a couple of people on its rim. Apparently these two told the others of the Border Patrol unit's arrival as a group of seven soon descended down the slope of the dump toward the vehicle. I was shocked to see them come down in such a compliant and nonplussed manner.

There were two children (boys of roughly ten and seventeen years); two women (one seemed to be the mother in her mid-forties, the other in her early twenties); and three men (one seemingly the father in his mid-forties, and the other two at least ten years younger). There were also three small dogs. (Agent Reeves told me that the dogs would just run back to Anapra.)

The seven prisoners sat crouched on the side of the dump, holding their sacks (which did not appear to hold much) as a light but cold rain began falling. When the transport unit finally showed up, the migrants filed down the hill quietly and got into the unit. Ed Reeves told me that he had warned these same people before about coming across. (Had he let them go on a previous occasion?)

Despite the captors' cooperation, however, the arrest hit a temporary snag: two of the dogs would not leave the group behind without a fuss and insisted on running after the Border Patrol transport vehicle as it tried to pull out of the area. The driver was afraid of hitting the dogs, and had to keep on having to stop and try to shoo them away. Finally, Ed told the other agent just to drive faster at thirty miles per hour and the dogs would stop chasing the unit— which they did.

I tell this story because of the irony of a world in which dogs sometimes have more rights to freedom of movement than human beings. It pained me to witness the arrest of these seven human beings for the "crime" of trying to survive poverty. But of course their official sin was not that they were trying to seek their livelihoods; rather, it was that they had crossed a line without state sanction in the barren landscape of eastern New Mexico. The existence of such lines of control over the movement of people is a very recent development in human history. That we accept these boundaries and their associated prac- tices—largely without question—and have come to do so in a relatively short span of time is an amazing development. It also speaks to the extraordinary power of these lines of division and control in shaping the very ways in which we view the world and our fellow human beings.

It is for such a reason that the next chapter discusses the much larger histor- ical geographical context that is the foundation of this particular way of life by providing an overview of the origins and evolution of the nation, the modern territorial state, boundaries, and associated identities. In doing so, it illumi- nates the theoretical relationship between social and territorial boundary building and the rise of the "illegal" as a social, geographical, and juridical identity and as a putative threat to a social, geographical, and juridical order, a "threat" for which Operation Gatekeeper is a supposed solution.

Nationalism, the Territorial State, and the Construction of Boundary-Related Identities

[N]ations, like other forms of community, are not only symbolic constructions entailing a shared sense of membership. Nations and other communities gain their identities from a sense of distinction, from the boundaries drawn between themselves and outsiders.

—Peter Sahlins, *Boundaries: The Making of France and Spain in the Pyrenees*[1]

Generally speaking, every human-made boundary on the earth's surface—garden hedge, city wall, or radar "fence"—is an attempt to keep inimical forces at bay. Boundaries are everywhere because threats are ubiquitous: the neighbor's dog, children with muddy shoes, strangers, the insane, alien armies, disease, wolves, wind and rain.

—Yi-Fu Tuan, *Landscapes of Fear*[2]

Operation Gatekeeper and the increasing importance of the U.S.-Mexico boundary as a law enforcement barrier are manifestations of a series of much larger, interrelated processes involving the rise of the nation as a form of social organization, and its political geographical expression, the modern state. Associated with these developments are a host of practices and ideologies that have helped to create the "illegal" immigrant. The previous chapters developed an explicit explanation for Operation Gatekeeper and related matters. This chapter, on the other hand, puts forth a theoretical and historical framework to contextualize particular cases of boundary production and enforcement, as well as associated identities, most importantly that of the "illegal alien." By furnishing a generalized understanding of related phenomena and processes, this chapter provides an analytical framework for comprehending the specific issues that this book explores.

The production of territorial boundaries is a very contested process, one that inevitably draws upon social power and engenders resistance in doing so.[3] Territorial boundaries are inextricably related to the construction of social boundaries, the parameters that define specific social groups on both sides of the geographical divide. In this sense, territorial boundaries are lines of both inclusion and exclusion.[4] For the purposes of this book, such social boundaries are those that define (national) "citizens" and "aliens"—those inside and outside the geographically based community of the nation-state, respectively.

These boundaries, emanating from both ideal and material processes, are an outgrowth and, simultaneously, a producer of nationalism, state power, and the ability of the state and the nation to shape our collective consciousness, and thus, practices. In substantiating this claim, this chapter addresses the history of borders and boundaries, and the development of the modern territorial state, nationalism, and related identities. I then discuss the connection between the state and social power and their relationship to territorial construction and boundary policing. This last part ties together ideas about discourse and state power to illustrate the relationship between the modern territorial state and boundary building and the construction of the "illegal"— as a juridical-geographical-discursive category.

HISTORICAL ROOTS OF INTERNATIONAL BOUNDARIES

Territorial boundaries have long existed. The ancient Greeks and Romans, among others, employed techniques of boundary delimitation. But the ancient Greek and Roman notion of a boundary was certainly very different from the concept of boundary that helps define the modern territorial state and gives rise to state practices such as Operation Gatekeeper. "Natural" or physical boundaries such as mountains, marshes, and rivers often served as divisions between premodern states; such physical features remain important in informing the siting of modern territorial state boundaries. At the same time, traditional states sometimes established artificial boundaries when physical divisions were lacking. The walls built by the Romans and the Great Wall of China are two of the better known examples. Such boundaries of traditional states, however, were not the same as those of modern states. In traditional states, Anthony Giddens informs us, "walled boundaries remained frontiers, well outside the regularized control of the central authorities; the larger the state, the more this is the case. In neither Rome nor China did the walls correspond to the limits of 'national sovereignty' in the sense in which that term is applied today. Rather, they formed the outer extension of an 'in-depth' defensive system. Modern state borders may coincide with natural defensive boundaries, but while this may be important to the fortunes of a state in war, it is irrelevant to the character of borders."[5] The purpose of China's Great Wall, for example, was to keep out "foraging nomads" and "to limit the mobility of various peripheral groups inside."[6]

Due to the ever-changing nature of boundaries, we should study them only in relation to states in particular historicogeographical contexts, not in and of themselves.[7] The type of state relevant to this study is the modern territorial state or nation-state, a political geographical unit that is inextricably tied to and defined by a particular territory delimited by boundaries governed by a sovereign state of which all its citizens are theoretically equal in rights and duties. This particular type of political geographical formation has its roots in Europe.

In the eleventh and twelfth centuries, political boundaries between king-doms in Europe were very similar to the limits between feudal manors within a kingdom. It was in the latter part of the thirteenth century that a practical distinction between boundaries and frontiers became evident. As Peter Sahlins explains, "The word 'frontier' dates precisely from the moment when a new insistence on royal territory gave to the boundary a political, fiscal, and military significance different from its internal limits. The 'fron-tier' was that which 'stood face to' an enemy. The military frontier, connoting a defensive zone, stood opposed to the linear boundary or line of demarca-tion separating two jurisdictions or territories."[8] But the linear boundary that emerged in the sixteenth and seventeenth centuries was not the same as the one that began to materialize after the seventeenth century when the modern territorial state became the normative, dominant political model in Europe. During the former period, the French monarchy, for example, "continued to envision its sovereignty in terms of its jurisdiction over subjects, not over a delimited territory."[9]

There was no obvious distinction between the state and other forms of human society during the Middle Ages, such as a feudal lord's domain or an urban commune. The state at that time was "the product of the accumula-tion and agglomeration of lords' domains in varying numbers. And such lords' domains were less territories than collections of rights." The very concept of territorial sovereignty did not exist. It was thus not uncommon that the same territory had several sovereigns.[10]

The concept of a boundary in the modern sense began to emerge in the fifteenth and sixteenth centuries along with the concepts of territorial sover-eignty and the nation. These concepts became increasingly reified as state power, especially in the military sense, grew. Contrary to popular percep-tion, the 1648 Treaty of Westphalia was not the singular event out of which emerged the concept of sovereignty.[11] The preceding period was one in which the medieval was gradually giving way to the modern. The late Middle Ages saw the rise of increasingly autonomous cities in northern Italy and Flanders. Simultaneously, the era saw the gradual emergence of a chal-lenge to the feudal order as single rulers consolidated power and territory in the proto-English and French states. That said, the Catholic Church and feudal lords continued to exercise substantial power in the affairs of these new political entities, and numerous different political geographical entities also existed, including confederations, republics, principalities, duchies, imperial cities, and even free cities. But the trend toward the modern terri-torial state was unmistakable. By the seventeenth century, the territorial state was arguably the most important object of analysis of European political thinkers.[12]

The French Revolution of 1789 was a key event in this process as, for the first time, subjects and citizens within a bounded community became one and the same, at least in theory. With the revolution clear boundaries between France and its neighbors emerged for the first time. The French *frontière* as a zone of transition became synonymous with the *limite*, a line of strict demarcation.[13] But this new boundary was more of an ideal, a manifestation of the idea relating territory to the nation. It was not until the early nineteenth century that states began to politicize boundary lines "as the point where national territorial sovereignty found expression."[14] In other parts of the world, it took much longer for linear boundaries as a concept to emerge. Many of the precolonial kingdoms encompassed by modern-day Indonesia, for example, defined themselves by their centers, not their perimeters as the territorial extension of the state was always in flux. Thus, the amount of power at the center of the premodern state defined its geographic limits.[15]

The modern state, on the other hand, carries with it a very different notion of boundaries, as its boundaries mark the end of its powers: "Ten yards this side of the frontier, their power is sovereign; ten yards the other side, it does not exist."[16] Furthermore, the state's power and its citizens' rights and duties are theoretically homogeneous within the space bounded by the state's geographical limits, whereas the amount of power, for example, in traditional Southeast Asian kingdoms was a function of the geographic proximity to the center (i.e., the residence of the emperor or king). European imperialism changed all this in what is today known as the "developing world." European powers imposed the model of the modern territorial state on most of the rest of the world and, in doing so, created a political geographical norm for any group seeking self-determination. The modern-day linear boundary is one of the more obvious manifestations of this phenomenon.

Boundaries are normally not the result of consensual processes. Rather, they typically grow out of violence or the threat of force. Nevertheless, the history of violence and/or authoritarianism is rarely acknowledged in the political discourse of national elites. In not talking about the problematic origins of boundaries, state actors are effectively relegating important chapters of history to official oblivion.[17] As James Anderson and Liam O'Dowd contend, "[T]he legacy of undemocratic and often violent origins—whether in national conflict, political revolution or the slaughter of native populations—needs to be played down or concealed for territorial democracy to perform its legitimizing functions. The contemporary relevance has to be officially 'forgotten.'"[18] In this regard, the boundaries of modern territorial states are burial sites of history, despite their origins in historical struggles over territory between competing social entities.

The concept of territorial sovereignty that these boundaries embody is inextricably intertwined with the rise of capitalism. Interstate boundaries (in the material sense, as opposed to purely symbolic) are an outgrowth of the emergence of the capitalist world economy, with its origins in the sixteenth century. This emerging economic geographic order provided different opportunities for entrepreneurs throughout the world. In an increasingly competitive economic system, the state had to provide protection for domestic capital, resulting in a transfer of the commercial policies and practices of the trading city to the larger territorial state.[19] Territory-based trade restrictions thus became a major component of state making. At the same time, the rise of territorial states provided opportunities for profit-seeking entrepreneurs who could avoid customs duties by smuggling goods across state boundaries. States responded by establishing customs houses and the like and implementing boundary policing, in the process producing the modern territorial state.[20]

But the growth and spread of capitalism was part of a much larger set of processes that fundamentally challenged traditional notions of space and time and the relationship of people to their rulers. Nationalism, the ideological basis for the nation and the modern territorial state, was one element of these interacting processes. It is impossible to understand the production and the importance of national boundaries, and their almost sacred nature in many parts of the world, without understanding nationalism and changing conceptions of territory, an area to which I now turn.

NATIONS, NATIONALISM, AND THE RISE
OF TERRITORIAL SOVEREIGNTY

The proper context for studying boundaries is, arguably, through what Anssi Paasi sees as "the continual process of nation building, i.e., the process of creating viable degrees of unity, adaptation and a sense of national identity among the people."[21] Nations require and, indeed, nationalists demand boundaries, as their goal is to rule effectively a territorially bounded entity.

There is a wide variety of perspectives on the origins of nations and nationalism. Many, however, are of questionable utility—especially those that see the nation as simply a stage in the "natural" progressive evolution from social organizations such as the family and the tribe.[22] Such approaches do not address the manner in which nations and nationalisms are constructed, both materially and ideologically. Nor do they see the nation as a contested terrain. It is beyond the scope of this book to examine the myriad theories that discuss the origins and construction of nationalism. Suffice it to say that I accept the analysis of scholars who see nationalism as a social construct and a phenomenon associated with modernity[23]—now largely pervasive modes of social life and organization with roots in seventeenth-century Europe. Modernity is comprised of a set of social, political and economic features and institutions distinctly different from those of traditional societies; these include industrialization, international capitalism, and the nation-state. Furthermore, an unprecedented scope and pace of change characterize modernity.[24]

Changing perceptions of time and space during the Enlightenment helped to lay the foundations of thinking in favor of new relations between people and territory as well as rulers and the governed. The rise of the rational ordering of time in the form of schedules and precise clocks, and their wide diffusion, helped facilitate the rational management demanded by prototerritorial states. Innovations in mathematics, as well as the increasingly rational ordering of space in the form of cartographic innovations such as Renaissance maps, led to the definition, with increasing accuracy, of a variety of spatial entities such as property rights in land, territorial boundaries, and administrative areas.[25] These mapping innovations led to the depiction, for the first time, of the entire earth's surface within a single spatial frame, facilitating the rise of "otherness." It was then, David Harvey notes, that "[t]he diversity of people could be appreciated and analysed in the secure knowledge that their 'place' in the spatial order was unambiguously known. In exactly the same way that Enlightenment thinkers believed that translation from one language to another was always possible without destroying the integrity of either language, so the totalizing vision of the map allowed strong senses of national, local, and personal identities to be constructed in the midst of geographical differences."[26] Associated with the emergence of these phenomena was a changing conception of the individual "as the ultimate source and container of social power," but as part of a nation-state. Increasing economic competition between territorial states and other types of economic units served to further this revolution in the perception of space and time.[27]

While nationalism has its intellectual roots in the Enlightenment, it was not until the nineteenth century that Europe saw an explosion of nationalist thinking and activity. A number of developments contributed to this phenomenon, most notably the emergence of unification movements in the Italian and German states, the rise of pressures against the status quo within authoritarian states, and increasing attacks against European empires from within and without. These developments resulted in substantial changes in Europe's political map. Nationalism, as an ideology linking people with territory, was a key component of these changes. As such, sovereignty increasingly became vested with the nation rather than the ruler. The rise of nationalism was associated with the rise of positivist ideas about law (and thus a growing rejection of natural law and an embracing of human-inspired legal institutions) and social Darwinism (justifying an anarchic view of the world that legitimated nationalist territorial ambitions).[28] The relationship between nationalism and the aforementioned innovations in the organization of space and time was one of mutual reinforcement. Out of this complex web of rapidly evolving social relations emerged new social identities, most notably those of the national and the alien.

NATIONALISM AND THE CONSTRUCTION
OF TERRITORIALLY BASED IDENTITY

Nationalism is inherently geographical as it employs a geographic basis to argue for the unity of the nation and to distinguish the members of the nation from nonmembers.[29] As such, nationalism is fundamentally about identity and the relation of a particular "people" or "nation" to a defined territory. But the intensity of the relationship and the identity are clearly of a very different order from, say, those of a person who lives in and identifies as a citizen of a particular city. Membership in a "nation" is almost of a sacred quality. Thus, although nationalists might accept that people have many territorially based identities (as Angelenos, Californians, and Americans, for example), it is the nation that represents their primary form of political geographical membership.[30] And it is the nation that demands almost absolute loyalty of its members.

Like all processes involving the production of identity, nationalism simultaneously generates and draws upon social boundaries. As argued above, premodern identities were not necessarily tied to spaces. Niches within social systems defined identities. Thus, boundaries have shifted "from a more internal and all-encompassing level to a more external and territorial one. In contrast with the premodern world, the bases of modern nations are eminently geographical. Hence, nationalism is a struggle over the definition of spatial boundaries, that is, over the control of a particular land or soil."[31] Nationalism is also a struggle over territorial content. As such, nationalism simultaneously works to strengthen the nation's external boundaries while seeking to eliminate internal boundaries between members of the nation. These boundaries define those who do not belong, and thus, those who do.[32] But while social and territorial boundaries are very important in defining identity, we can and should not reduce identity to such boundaries. The content within said boundaries helps to legitimate and support the identity as well.[33]

The establishment of social boundaries is an inevitable part of the process of establishing and giving identity to a social phenomenon.[34] Social actors employ symbolism and boundary production to define membership. As suggested above, however, nationalism not only defines the members of the nation; it also defines those who do not belong, such as the foreigner or the alien. To the extent that nationalism creates an almost sacred bond between the members of the nation and "alienizes" those outside the nation, nationalism is a type of political religion that not only inevitably *creates* but also *needs* boundaries. One cannot have the national without the racialized alien. In this regard, the national and the alien are inextricably linked in nationalist thought and practice.[35]

The modern nation-state requires both nationalism and absolute boundaries; both facilitate the construction and maintenance of unity (among citizens) and difference—the essential prerequisite for the alien.[36] The "illegal" immigrant is just one form of the alien. In the case of the United States and Operation Gatekeeper, the growing emphasis on the legal status of immigrants is arguably a manifestation of a strengthening U.S. boundary with Mexico, at least in terms of immigration control. In addition to suggesting a material strengthening of the boundary, it also suggests an ideological shift, one that increasingly perceives the division between the United States and Mexico as a boundary rather than as a border. In this sense, the shift represents an increasing emphasis on difference. Gatekeeper, as nationalist practice, not only works to repel difference, but helps to construct and strengthen it.

Such a trend, a shift from a border to a boundary, would seem to be in direct opposition to the promises of the Enlightenment, of which the nation-state was an important component. Liberal ideology perceived the rise of the nation-state as significant progress on the ladder of teleological evolution, with primary citizenship advancing from the local to the scale of the nation and ultimately to that of the world. As Eric Hobsbawm describes this perspective, "the development of nations was unquestionably a phase in human evolution or progress from the small group to the larger, from family to tribe to region, to nation and, in the last instance, to the unified world of the future in which, to quote the superficial and therefore typical G. Lowes Dickinson, 'the barriers of nationality which belong to the infancy of the race will melt and dissolve in the sunshine of science and art.'"[37] "Progress" is clearly not the linear process that such thinking suggested. While "cultural flows" emanating outside of national territory weaken national sovereignty,[38] we should not assume that global culture, globalization, or transnational flows *necessarily* lead to greater levels of homogeneity and thus a weakening of nation-based cultural and political ideas and entities.[39] In fact, globalization, in that it simultaneously involves processes of partial homogenization *and* partial differentiation, might actually serve to enhance nationalism in its intensity and frequency.[40] And for nations aspiring to statehood, growing regional and/or global integration might actually serve to enhance the possibilities of their achieving their nationalist dreams.[41] That said, there is little question that forces from without present serious challenges to "nations" and modern territorial states. How states respond is significantly a function of their internal power as well as their power vis-à-vis other states. For this reason, I now turn to the question of "the state" and social power.

THE STATE, SOCIAL POWER, AND TERRITORIALITY

The state is the principal actor that employs the social power to repel the difference and challenge embodied by unauthorized immigration, and it is the state that makes Operation Gatekeeper a reality and strengthens the U.S. boundary with Mexico in the process. While many would have us believe that globalization is making the modern territorial state and its boundaries redundant, the U.S.-Mexico boundary enforcement apparatus is stronger than it has ever been, a manifestation—at least in this instance—of growing state power.

State is an extremely controversial term and a concept that is quite difficult to pin down.[42] With the exception of primitive societies, all societies have had states, but it would be foolhardy for us to attempt to construct a general (decontextualized) definition of the state. To do so would be to erase the highly varied state forms and functions that have existed over time and space.[43] Clearly, however, the modern territorial state is different from previous state formations and other social entities as it is has authoritative power over the entire expanse (at least in theory) of a bounded territory.[44]

In trying to define the modern territorial state, we need to interrogate the state's institutional (what it looks like) and functional aspects.[45] The dominant view, one first put forth by Max Weber, is a mixture of these two aspects, encompassing four main (largely institutional) elements, which comprise (1) a *differentiated* set of institutions and personnel embodying (2) *centrality* in the sense that political relations radiate outward from a center to cover (3) a *territorially demarcated area*, over which it exercises (4) a monopoly of *authoritative, binding rule making*, backed up by a monopoly of the means of physical violence. With the exception of the final element which seems to equate the state with institutional violence, this definition makes sense.[46] Nevertheless, it lacks a key element: a recognition of the fact that modern territorial states have a "monopoly of the legitimate means of movement"—that is, the modern state claims an absolute right to control whom (and what) enters and leaves its territory.[47] It is from this key state function that boundaries, passports, visas, and other aspects of the enforcement apparatus emerge.

There have long been major debates in the social sciences regarding the level of autonomy of the state vis-à-vis various interest groups.[48] It is beyond the scope of this book (and, perhaps, the patience of the reader) to review these debates. Suffice it to say that I reject views that see the practices of the state as the outcome of a highly democratic process in which various interest groups struggle over policy decisions on equal footing. In a country like the United States, for example, it is clear that economic elites have a level of influence highly disproportionate to their numbers; at the same time, capital places structural limitations on the state.[49] Yet we need to be careful not to assume a homogeneous capitalist class free of internal divisions, and to avoid downplaying the ability of non-capital-based social movements to affect the state. The case of immigration law and policy in the United States, for example, is a glaring counterexample to such a contention. Congress has passed restrictionist legislation on a number of occasions despite vociferous opposition from business interests.[50] Thus, an adequate theory of the state must explore empirically and theoretically the dynamic links between structural factors and human agency by demonstrating the ability of state actors, capital, and grassroots social movements alike to influence policy and pursue their own agendas.[51]

The discussion above begs the question of how we distinguish between a state actor and an agent from civil society—the "dense associational network" comprised of organizations above the family and below the state[52]—especially if the latter is involved in trying to effect state policy. While it is helpful to make an analytical distinction, there is, in reality, "a perpetual dialectic of movement between state and civil society."[53]

Despite the practical overlap between the state and civil society, the state and its practices often appear as external to society as a whole. As the state socializes individuals through institutions such as schools and militaries, the activities of the state—in terms of law enforcement, for example—increasingly take on an appearance of the normal, and, thus, the unproblematic. As a result, the social relations—and their underlying ideologies—that inform state practices are less obvious.[54] This world is one in which there appears to be individuals and their activities, on the one hand and, on the other hand, monolithic and unchanging structures that exist independently of human agency and contain and guide people's lives. The boundary of the modern state is an example, and, as Timothy Mitchell notes, "[B]y establishing a territorial boundary and exercising absolute control over movement across it, state practices define and help constitute a national entity. . . . This entity comes to seem something much more than the sum of the everyday activities that constitute it, appearing as a structure containing and giving order and meaning to people's lives."[55]

It would thus seem that a significant effect of the appearance of clear division between the state and society is the undermining of challenges to the state by making the state seem external to the actions of individuals and, thus, very difficult to influence. At the same time, the state-society divide has served to depoliticize certain phenomena, such as territorial boundaries, associated with the state. As such, certain phenomena seem beyond question, as if their existence were almost natural. In both these regards, the state-society divide facilitates the disempowering of the state's citizenry.

This territorial conflation of the state and society is highly problematic, especially in light of the forces of globalization and the various social factors from without impacting upon the territorial state; these forces range from the economic to the political to the cultural.[56] For this reason, the state must constantly reproduce boundaries (spatial, social, cultural, economic, and political) between "us" and "them," giving the boundaries the appearance of being natural and not in need of explanation[57]; indeed, it is one of the state's most important functions given the ambiguous nature of reality. Nation building, in this regard, is a continuous process, as the state constantly experiences external forces.[58]

State boundaries are an extremely powerful symbol of national identity and sovereignty. Discourse around illegal immigration reflects this. Calls for "regaining control of our borders" evoke a mythic and pure past of clear and unambiguous distinctions between the inside and the outside, a past that exalts "a compelling ideal according to which the nation deliberately chooses whom it wants, excludes those whom it does not want, and sanctions those who violate its rules."[59] Such discourse, however, only serves to mask the reality of a boundary that is *necessarily* porous to economic flows, particularly that of cheap labor. Indeed, the stability and prosperity of the "inside" depends upon such flows from the "outside." Thus, effective statecraft must maintain the image of autonomy, while implementing practices that expose the myth of national autonomy.[60]

There are a variety of practices the state implements to distinguish between citizens and aliens; some take place at the boundary, others within national space. These practices (which we can subsume under the term *statecraft*) permeate and emanate from all levels of society, ranging from official policy making to cultural activities to the everyday actions of individuals. In this regard, we can understand the numerous anti-immigrant and restrictionist movements around the world as "a kind of statecraft from below wherein 'authentic' citizens are motivated to engage in governmental practices that reproduce territorially bounded identities as natural and given."[61] Thus, the state is ever changing and contingent, produced by practices of statecraft that both draw upon and reproduce a worldview that assumes the territorial state to be a natural and inevitable order.[62]

All members of a society learn to think spatially (in terms of national territory, for example).[63] In the case of national space and its absolute boundaries, a "territorial trap"[64]—an assumption that the territorial state contains society—results and very much informs our collective thinking and actions on the question of unauthorized immigration. While the unauthorized immigrant is very much of "our" society—that is, of a non-bounded network of social relations that impact upon us and that we help to produce and reproduce—we regard the "illegal alien" as someone whose supposed criminal activity (in violating immigration laws) is independent of our own actions and thus is someone for whom we need not accept any responsibility. This is because the "illegal" is someone who is out of place—in a space where she does not belong. Thus, the relationship of the illegal alien to the particular national space in which she finds herself defines her status. Inevitably, the construction of such a bounded space—and concomitantly, the illegal alien—requires the employment of social power.[65]

In many ways, the state is the preeminent form of "power container" because it is a territorially bounded administrative unit.[66] Policing is an important maintainer of order vis-à-vis agents and forces that potentially undermine the authority of the territorial state and, more generally, civil society.[67] This is especially true in terms of the policing of international boundaries—arguably one of the most obvious manifestations of the geographical practice of territoriality, "the attempt by an individual or group to affect, influence, or control people, phenomena, and relationships, by delimiting and asserting control over a geographic area."[68]

The control of space is an integral part of power relations.[69] The state, as the preeminent power container, necessitates the control of space and the construction of territory, and therefore requires the construction of boundaries in both the physical (between national territories) and social senses (between citizens and "aliens"). Thus, the analysis of the U.S.-Mexico boundary contributes to our understanding of relations between various social groups within and outside the boundaries of the United States. But like any sociospatial process, the construction of the U.S.-Mexico boundary is a contested process. The San Diego border area and, for that matter, the entire borderlands are a contested terrain. It is a terrain challenged on many fronts, by a wide variety of social actors and institutions that try to define the space of the area in multiple ways.[70] One of the most significant ways in which we construct the borderlands, the boundary, and associated identities is through *discourse*—a term that embodies not only expression by words, but also their associated social practices.[71] This is the subject that I now explore.

DISCOURSE, SOCIAL POWER, AND BOUNDARY IDENTITIES

As suggested earlier, boundaries between different social groupings are arguably necessary for the protection of the integrity of the groups. Social boundaries are "the main definer of rights, separating members from strangers." For this reason, "it is essential to maintain the boundary, either by *expelling* polluting agencies . . . or by *excluding* threatening groups or individuals."[72] One of the most important ways in which social actors construct and reproduce social boundaries is through discourse.

In territorially defined social groupings such as the modern nation-state, the distinctions between citizens, residents, aliens, the "legal" and the "illegal" are the discursive manifestations of the perceived necessity to maintain territorial purity. Such a project results in attempts to homogenize space and erect boundaries and, concomitantly, practices of domination and control.[73] Of course, the notion of homogeneous space is an illusion.[74]

As Michel Foucault has argued, power emanates not only from formal organizations and institutions but is also present in the routine practices of social interaction, including discourse. Discourse always operates in the service of particular interests or power.[75] As such, discourse can help to construct territories and boundaries and those who belong within, the "we" as well as the "they" or "other."[76] By establishing binary oppositions between "us" and "them," discourse reinforces group identity.[77] But rather than thinking of "us" and "them" as opposites, we should think of them as mutually constitutive and potentially undermining one another, particularly in regard to large-scale immigration and the constitution of the inside of nation-states, "when elements from the 'outside' are constantly raising questions as to who should be considered on the 'inside,' that is, the people."[78] Official and hegemonic discourse, such as the law, is an integral part of the process by which the state creates a particular type of society and citizen. One of the most basic manners in which the state does this is by exercising control of entry into its territory, without which the whole idea of a territorially bounded nation-state would be highly dubious.[79]

By subjecting people to the law, the state produces subjects and identities. Gradually, the law and its juridical institutions become less obvious as state apparatuses develop to carry out the functions of the law. And as the relationship between the state and society is a dialectical one, the law emanates from, and produces, social values. As Roxanne Doty notes, "It is, therefore, not only the discursive practices manifested in legal statutes that create identities, but also the way that these practices are infused with societal norms and values. In examining the discursive production of national identity, one needs to examine not only laws per se, but the debates, interpretations, and professed needs and interests that surround legal statutes and the social practices to which these are linked."[80] In subjecting people to the law, the state categorizes and objectifies people. These categories become "discursive facts" that inform how people interact and perceive one another.[81] In terms of immigrant categories such as "illegal," they reflect the views of (and thus have been applied by) those in the receiving societies.[82] As such, these categories are tools of domination and social control.[83]

That the putative problem of "illegal" immigration resonates so profoundly within popular culture speaks to the power of the state to form and regulate "cultural forms" such as our social identities and our very values. States help to define "acceptable forms and images of social activity and individual and collective identity." By its very activities, the state privileges certain ways in which we do things and organize social life and marginalizes others. In doing so, the state normalizes highly politicized assumptions of the society, making the associated practices and ideologies seem natural and unproblematic.[84] Through routines and rituals the state gives enormous weight to particular social, political, and personal practices and identities. We can only understand the shape of the state and culture—and thus the perceived "crisis" of "illegal" immigration—as being an outgrowth of the recursive interaction between the two.[85]

Through the law, states claim to be all-powerful, a claim that has very real consequences—not least in terms of how we understand and act in the world. But states are not as strong as they claim and/or want to be—nor probably have they ever been, nor will they ever be. It is for this reason that immigration-related illegality persists, and will continue to do so.[86] It also persists because of the conflictive nature of the relationships among the various constituencies that the state serves. The relative strength and/or weakness of the boundaries that divide the "illegal" from the citizen are a manifestation of the outcome of this complex interplay.

Interstate boundaries are part and parcel of a variety of interrelated processes that have their roots in intellectual developments associated with the Enlightenment and associated political, economic, cultural, and technological changes that evolved as European feudalism deteriorated and capitalist social relations, largely through European imperialism, increasingly penetrated global space. The rise of nationalism and the modern territorial state were two of the most important political-geographical manifestations of these trends. As state power increased over space, national territories became increasingly reified and their boundaries became more sacrosanct. These changes have shaped our identities, consciousness, discourse, and social actions. As such, the nation, the territorial state, the citizen, and the "alien" are "normal" parts of our national and global cultural landscapes, reproduced by social actors through everyday practice. The next chapter continues to deal with these matters by exploring what Operation Gatekeeper tells us about the evolving nature of borders and boundaries, territory and national identity, and the nation-state and globalization—in terms of the United States and beyond.

Conclusion:
Searching for Security in an
Age of Intensifying Globalization

We called for workers, and there came human beings.
> —Max Frisch, Swiss playwright, referring to the "guest worker"
> system in Europe in the 1960s and 1970s[1]

People in California talk about the "illegals." But there was always an illegality to immigration. It was a rude act, the leaving of home. It was a violation of custom, an insult to the village. A youthful act of defiance. I know a man from El Salvador who has not talked to his father since the day he left his father's village. (It is a sin against family to leave home.) Immigrants must always be illegal. Immigrants are always criminals. They trespass borders and horrify their grandmothers.

But they are also our civilization's prophets. They, long before the rest of us, . . . they saw the hemisphere whole.
> —Richard Rodriguez, "Pocho Pioneer"[2]

It is time to face the facts: Anglos won't go back to Europe, and Mexicans and Latinos (legal or illegal) won't go back to Latin America. We are all here to stay. For better or for worse, our destinies and aspirations are in one another's hands. For me, the only solution lies in a paradigm shift: the recognition that we are all protagonists in the creation of a new cultural topography and a new social order, one in which we all are "others," and we need the "others" to exist. Hybridity is no longer up for discussion. It is a demographic, racial, social, and cultural fact.
> —Guillermo Gómez-Peña, *The New World Border*[3]

Even if we take [unjust social arrangements] as givens for purposes of immediate action in a particular context, we should not forget about our assessment of their fundamental character. Otherwise we wind up legitimating what should only be endured.
> —Joseph Carens, "Open Borders and Liberal Limits"[4]

Similar boundary-related controversies marked the beginnings of the George W. Bush and Bill Clinton presidential eras. Both concerned female nominees to cabinet positions and their relationships to "illegal" immigrant women. In the case of Bill Clinton, his first nominee for attorney general, Zoë Baird, became very controversial when it came to light that she employed two unauthorized immigrants from Peru as domestic servants—a common "crime" among two-career, professional couples.[5] Ultimately, the public and official pressure forced Baird to withdraw her nomination.[6]

A little less than eight years later, George W. Bush's original nominee for secretary of labor, conservative columnist Linda Chavez, felt compelled to withdraw her nomination after it became known that she had provided housing and money to Marta Mercado—at the time, an unauthorized immigrant from Guatemala—who, in return for what the nominee modestly characterized as acts of charity, performed a variety of tasks for Chavez.[7] Ironically, Chavez had been highly critical of Zoë Baird in 1993 for employing an "illegal."[8]

By examining the origins and significance of Operation Gatekeeper, I have sought to explain the rise of the territorial and social boundaries that have made the "illegal alien" such a focus of public and official concern. The controversies surrounding the aforementioned cabinet-level nominations of both Bill Clinton and George W. Bush are merely two of the more high-profile illustrations of the power of these boundaries. And Operation Gatekeeper, as the centerpiece of recent efforts by the federal government to increase the effectiveness of U.S.-Mexico boundary enforcement, is both a manifestation and producer of this power.

As this book has shown, Operation Gatekeeper is the outgrowth of the intersection of a variety of long- and medium-term social geographical trends emanating from the local (San Diego and Tijuana), regional ("the border"), national (for both the United States and Mexico), and international levels. These trends involved both the construction of the U.S.-Mexico boundary as a physical divide based on efforts of the state to regulate and to control trans-boundary movement, intermixed with the making of the associated (and necessary, in terms of the needs of the modern territorial state) social boundaries that help to define and make distinctions between "Americans" and "foreigners" (especially "Mexicans"). These social categories are not only those of "citizen" and "alien"; they are also heavily imbued with hierarchical concepts and practices vis-à-vis race, class, gender, nation, and geographical origins. Most important (in terms of this book) in the making of these identities has been the process of "illegalization," the process by which immigrants entering the United States without state sanction have become constructed and perceived as lawbreakers and alleged threats to the sociocultural and political fabric of the country. Taking these trends together, the state-sponsored enforcement strategy of Operation Gatekeeper is thus the latest phase of an ongoing project of territorial and social boundary construction between the United States and Mexico and, by extension, the rest of the world.

At the same time, such long- and medium-term developments—while absolutely necessary as contextual factors—are not sufficient to explain the outbreak of the significantly heightened public and official sentiment in favor of waging a war of sorts on "illegal" immigration in the early 1990s. The dramatic rise in public and official concerns came about at a time of a perceived immigration and boundary control "crisis," one that arose—most vociferously in southern California—in a context of economic recession, increasingly ineffective local government, and significant changes in the socio-cultural fabric of the society. In this environment, various state actors and nativist organizations created the perception of a crisis by effectively constructing the "illegal" immigrant not only as a lawbreaker, but more impor-tantly as a threat to national sovereignty and American society more gener-ally. Such imagery resonated in a society with a long history of largely race-based anti-immigrant sentiment—especially toward those from "south of the border." The resulting war against unauthorized immigrants led to a significant short-term shift in Immigration and Naturalization Service (INS) policing tactics along the U.S.-Mexico boundary and the massive infusion of enforcement-related resources into southern California in the form of Oper-ation Gatekeeper.

As the U.S.-Mexico border region has become more integrated into the American national body politic and gained significantly greater levels of demographic and economic importance, public awareness of "the border" has grown. As it has become more important, the U.S.-Mexico boundary has increasingly helped to shape and reflect the lives of people on both sides of the international divide. Operation Gatekeeper, as the pinnacle of a long historical geographical process that has reified the territorial and social bound-aries that embody the United States, is a manifestation of a radical change in how human beings live their lives, one necessarily tied to the rise and evolu-tion of the modern territorial state in a world of increasing globalization at the beginning of a new millennium.[9] As a result, the U.S.-Mexico boundary and its associated practices are relatively "normal," unproblematic, and uncon-tested components of the social landscape in terms of the vast majority of American society.

Of course, there are alternative interpretations. Although no other work has offered an extensive account of and explanation for the origins and signif-icance of Operation Gatekeeper, a number have explored the roots of the boundary buildup more generally. Christian Parenti, for example, perceives "La Migra's War" (of which Gatekeeper is an important component) as part of a much larger nationwide law-and-order crackdown that one sees in the boom in the U.S. prison population, the growth of militarized policing, and the federalization of the wars on crime and drugs.[10] He convincingly argues that these developments have their origins in the 1960s and early 1970s, when conservative politicians began waging a law-and-order campaign in response to the civil rights movement and growing political dissent more generally.[11] It was also a response by U.S. elites to a larger socioeconomic crisis that involved falling profit rates, increasing economic competition from abroad and—along with it—deindustrialization, as well as growing labor unrest as indicated by a rise in strikes by U.S. workers. This war on the poor, the dissident, the deviant, and the nonwhite greatly intensified with Ronald Reagan's coming to power in 1981.[12]

Parenti's analysis is certainly helpful in trying to understand the political-economic context that gave rise to the nationwide war on crime. It was undoubtedly an important component of the backdrop to growing perceptions of a southern boundary "out of control" and a country "under siege" by unauthorized immigrants beginning in the early 1970s, and, a bit later, the significant increase in boundary and immigration-enforcement-related resources that began in the latter half of the Carter administration. But as I have shown, the boundary and immigration war has deep roots in the creation of new ways of seeing a national territory, as well as to a process involving the construction of "outsiders" that did not exist prior to the imposition of the U.S.-Mexico boundary. Furthermore, in terms of understanding the medium- and short-term roots of the boundary and immigration war, one must take into account the fact that a very different set of political actors was involved in making it happen (although admittedly there is overlap with those involved with the war on crime—especially to the extent that the boundary buildup is tied to the "war on drugs"[13]). At the same time, local actors—especially in California in the 1990s—played a much more significant role in helping to realize the "border war" than in aiding in the rise of the national-level war on crime and drugs. In part, this difference is undoubtedly due to the highly concentrated nature of unauthorized immigrant populations and the very location of the U.S.-Mexico boundary.

As Grace Chang convincingly argues, a key component of the "border war" in the 1990s was the emergence of immigrant women—especially those from the "third world"—as a central focus of the public and media concerns about immigration control. Although Chang does not discuss the great increase in boundary enforcement specifically, she does address the policing of immigrants and the rise of anti-immigrant sentiment more generally, and tends to see these as derivative of an overarching economic logic and a resulting set of intentional, goal-oriented practices. Thus, for Chang, the "true function" of the INS (and, by extension, the increase in boundary and immigration enforcement) is "to regulate the movement, availability, and independence of migrant labor,"[14] and the purpose of California's Proposition 187 was "perhaps" to mold immigrant children into a "category entirely of super-exploitable workers—those with no access to language or other skills and, most of all, no access to a status even remotely resembling citizenship that might allow them the safety to organize."[15]

As this book has shown, such economically deterministic arguments imply a level of unity within the state, and coherency in thought among economic and political elites, that simply do not exist. In any case, as shown earlier, capitalists historically have been proimmigration. This is still true today. In the case of Proposition 187—as Chang herself reports—California employers, while collectively failing to take a public stand on the measure, generally opposed it for fear that they had much to lose if it passed. *The Wall Street Journal*, moreover, advocates the elimination of boundary controls for labor.[16] While this probably does not represent the view of most capitalists, the *Journal*'s position is significant nonetheless given the level of influence the paper has on the business "community" and power it embodies as probably the most important newspaper of American capital.

It is for such reasons that we need to appreciate the autonomous yet inter-related roles of race-, class-, gender-, and nation-based ideologies of exclusion and inclusion in informing much of the sentiment leading to widespread demands for "cracking down" on "illegal" immigrants—factors that do not always dovetail with the interests of capital. Indeed, they frequently contradict them. Yes, it is true that some anti-union employers have long tried to use the INS to undermine immigrant worker organizing (with a number of especially outrageous incidents taking place in the late 1990s[17]), and that anti-immi-grant backlashes do often facilitate the goals of employers by making immi-grants more marginal and exploitable. But just as the state is not a monolith, there are a variety of factors that explain these developments—the interests of capital just being one of them.

As Peter Andreas persuasively contends, political factors—those not simply derivative of economic matters—are central to the origins of Gatekeeper-like developments. Andreas criticizes arguments that suggest that the rise in boundary enforcement is a simply a response to a perceived "loss of control," that the state has merely reacted to a set of conditions beyond its control. Such a contention "understates the degree to which the state has actually structured, conditioned, and even enabled (often unintentionally) clandestine border crossings, and overstates the degree to which the state has been able to control its borders in the past. By characterizing state policing as largely reactive, it obscures the ways in which the state has helped to create the very conditions that generate calls for more policing."[18] For Andreas, specific developments such as Gatekeeper are often the "unintended feedback effects of past policy choices" as much as the result of particular bureaucratic incentives and rewards.[19] The 1986 Immigration Reform and Control Act (IRCA), for example, led to the legalization of large numbers of unauthorized immigrants as a way of ultimately reducing unsanctioned immigration. The IRCA's main effect, however, was "to reinforce and expand already well-established cross-border migration networks" and to create a booming business in fraudulent documents.[20] According to Andreas, such "perverse and unintended conse-quences" laid the foundation for the anti-immigrant backlash that emerged in the early 1990s.[21] In advancing this argument, Andreas cautions that his goal is "not to provide a general explanation of the anti-illegal immigration backlash." Rather, he seeks to show how political and bureaucratic entrepreneurs partially whipped up public sentiment and channeled it "to focus on the border as both the source of the problem and the most appropriate site of the policy solution."[22]

Although there is certainly much merit to such an approach, it is not sufficient. First, as many have argued, the backlash of the 1990s was not simply against "illegal" immigrants but, to a large degree, against immigrants in general—especially the nonwhite, non-English-speaking, and relatively poor immigrants. Moreover, as Andreas shows in comparing and contrasting similar developments along the Poland/Germany and Spain/Morocco boundaries, the seeming paradox of what he calls "a borderless economy and a barricaded border" is evidenced along boundaries that unite and divide rich and poor in other parts of the world.[23] Given the locales of these developments and their uneven impacts on different social groups, a fuller explanation must also incorporate matters of race, nation, socioeconomic class, and gender as they relate to inequality across global space.

DOWNGRADING THE "THREAT" OF "ILLEGAL" IMMIGRATION: FROM "CRISIS" TO "PROBLEM"

The fifth anniversary of Operation Gatekeeper on October 1, 1999 passed with very little media and official comment—as did the sixth, one year later.[24] The INS, which on its first three anniversaries had published and publicly released a glowing report of the operation's "progress," no longer does so. It is difficult to know why this is the case. Possibly it is the extremely high number of boundary-crossing-related deaths of unauthorized migrants in southern California that have occurred as a result of Gatekeeper, and the unflattering publicity these deaths have engendered. But a much more probable explanation is that Gatekeeper—like the numerous trends that it embodies—has become a "normal" part of the political and cultural landscapes in southern California. Gatekeeper is no longer as noteworthy as it was just a short time ago.

At the same time, immigration—specifically "illegal" immigration—is not the high profile issue it was in the early to mid-1990s. And, in general, public sentiment is more favorably disposed toward immigration than it was in the early 1990s.[25] Immigration was thus a non-issue in the 1998 and 2000 national elections. As a reporter for *The New York Times* explained in 1998, this was due to a growing recognition on the part of politicians and business people of the costs of restrictionist politics and immigration enforcement: "[T]here seems to be a growing consensus among lawmakers that too much control is not good—for politicians, who recognize that immigrants' votes could be pivotal in some races; for business and the economy, because valued employees have had to return home . . . or even for the Government itself, since control is

expensive and time consuming."[26] Similarly, in California the 1998 gubernatorial race was devoid of any discussion of immigration, except to the extent
that the candidates made favorable gestures toward immigrant communities.
Political analysts pointed to the growing clout of Latino voters in California,
as well as to a much improved state economy, as being the most significant
factors in limiting "immigrant bashing" in the 1998 elections.[27]

Nevertheless, the "problem" of "illegal" immigration is as present today as
it was in 1994, when public sentiment in favor of "getting tough" on the matter
reached record high levels. Such a development demonstrates the importance
of political economic context, as well as the role of individual politicians and
state actors, in helping to determine what issues become identified as societal
problems in need of radical redress. The current waning of public concern
about a U.S.-Mexico boundary "out of control" and a supposed "flood" of
"illegal" immigrants also illustrates the power of political elites to shape
popular consciousness. The "crisis" has waned as politicians and elements of
the state apparatus have decreased their anti-immigration activism.[28]

Despite these changes, however, a variety of state actors and influential
pundits continue to press for a reduction in immigration—especially of the
"illegal" variety. In one of its seemingly more benign forms, such advocacy
takes the form of championing reduced immigration through (in part)
enhanced immigration policing in the name of preventing social strife between native-born and immigrant workers. While such strife seems unlikely
in the context of a strong national economy, those championing this perspective argue that matters could quickly turn ugly if there were a pronounced
downturn in the economy. As James Goldsborough, the foreign affairs columnist for *The San Diego Union-Tribune*, warns, "[S]hort of a new [economic]
miracle, wages will fall, unemployment and welfare will rise, crime will
increase, social conflicts of the kind reflected six years ago in California's
Proposition 187 will break out. Americans will call for more and higher fences
along the Mexican border, more vigilante groups of the kind that now patrol
the border around Douglas, Arizona, will form, and hundreds of thousands
of immigrants seeking permanent residence in America will be on the
streets."[29] To prevent this seemingly automatic set of developments from
occurring, Goldsborough calls for the implementation of the 1995 recommendations of the U.S. Commission on Immigration Reform (popularly
known as the Jordan Commission) to cut authorized immigration by at least
one-third, and to eliminate "illegal" immigration through heightened workplace enforcement measures.[30]

Meanwhile, others beat the drums of cultural war. Prominent Harvard
University political scientist Samuel Huntington, for example, now seems to
be applying his "clash of civilizations" paradigm to questions of immigration
and assimilation within the United States.[31] Huntington warns that Mexican
immigration "looms as a unique and disturbing challenge to our cultural

integrity, our national identity, and potentially to our future as a country." This challenge is of a military, national security dimension, believes Huntington, who writes, "In almost every recent year the Border Patrol has stopped about 1 million people attempting to enter the U.S. illegally from Mexico. It is generally estimated that about 300,000 make it across illegally. If over 1 million Mexican soldiers crossed the border, Americans would treat it as a major threat to their national security and react accordingly. The invasion of over 1 million Mexican civilians is a comparable threat to American societal security, and Americans should react against it with comparable vigor."[32] Huntington's essay is in the December 2000 issue of *The American Enterprise*, whose cover story is entitled "Fixing Our Immigration Predicament." There are two photos on the cover. The first is of two Latino-looking young men flashing gang signs in front of a graffitti-covered wall; the caption for the photo reads "This is a problem." Underneath this first photo is a second one with the caption "This is the solution." The photo contains six, clean-cut, young people gathered around a bench while reading books preparing for the SAT college-preparatory exam. At least on the basis of stereotypical appearances, the group is composed of two whites, two blacks, and two Asian Americans. Thus, Latinos do not participate in the "solution." They are only (and *the* only) part of the "problem."

The editors of the publication call themselves "[d]efenders of healthy immigration," but they clearly have a very narrow notion of what is "healthy." They thus describe many of the schools in Los Angeles as "effectively Mexican rather than American schools" and criticize the Ford Foundation for funding "Mexican activist groups (like MALDEF)."[33] The persistence of such narrow, exclusivist, ethnic-based nationalist sentiment in an increasingly transnational world embodies many of the contradictions and paradoxes of our contemporary time—a topic to which I now turn.

THE GATEKEEPER STATE VERSUS THE GLOBALIZED STATE

As Operation Gatekeeper and the persistence of concerns about unwanted immigrants demonstrate, the modern territorial state is far from disappearing, despite the forces of globalization. Rather, the state is diversifying and developing.[34] This is not to suggest that globalization (conceived as a process rather than a state of affairs[35]) does not have any weakening effects on the state. Clearly, it does. Transnational processes such as migration have helped to transform the state, while making it increasingly difficult for the state to manage extraterritorial processes and, thus, what enters national territory.

Yet despite the evolution of this increasingly transnational world, modern states tend to cling to the concept of national sovereignty when it comes to immigration. In this regard, one important aspect of state policy, especially in the so-called developed world, is its concentration on immigration enforcement efforts through boundary policing. Meanwhile, international treaties such as the General Agreement on Tariffs and Trade (GATT) and the North American Free Trade Agreement (NAFTA) open these same national boundaries to flows of capital, finance, manufactured goods, and services.[36] It is in this sense that the state, in terms of its boundary functions, plays a "gatekeeper" role. Of course, there is nothing novel about the selective nature of immigration enforcement. What is new is the state's enhanced capacity to police its boundaries and to formalize its rules and practices governing boundary enforcement.

Apart from boundary enforcement, states also focus on individual migrants as the object of their policing efforts. Thus, while immigration is a highly complex phenomenon that involves processes on multiple geographical scales, and in which receiving states are *at least* partially involved in creating the conditions that engender international migration, migration is reduced to the actions of individual migrants.[37] The emphasis on individual migrants is one that has arguably increased in scope and intensity over the last few decades. Whereas the U.S. Select Commission on Immigration and Refugee Policy, for example, explicitly acknowledged that the United States had some responsibility for the level of extralegal immigration (and for this reason—among others—favored an amnesty program for unauthorized immigrants),[38] there is little such sentiment today among state elites.[39] Regarding extralegal immigration, a perspective emphasizing the supposedly free choices of individual rational actors in determining the decision to migrate increasingly predominates.[40] The enhanced criminalization of unauthorized immigrants would seem to be the logical outgrowth of immigration enforcement as viewed through this paradigm. As such, it is the individual migrant who must pay the consequences for being in a national space in which she does not belong—not those who create the conditions that fuel such migration. By framing individual actions as the problem, this perspective has the effect of exculpating the state of any responsibility for fostering the very immigration it claims to want to fight. This view corresponds to the dominant analysis of street crime in contemporary U.S. society, which sees the alleged criminal as almost totally responsible for his actions and largely rejects analyses that emphasize the social conditions and contexts that give rise to crime.[41]

The modern territorial state faces many limitations, however, on both "domestic" and international fronts, in trying to regulate immigration in a unilateral manner. Within the United States, court decisions and legislative enactments have led to greater civil rights protections for immigrants. At the same time, a network of immigrant rights groups, largely second-generation "immigrant politicians," immigrant associations, and the so-called ethnic lobby participate in the making of immigration policy to a far greater degree than ever before. Internationally, a rising regime of international law and human rights standards, and intensifying international linkages, have resulted (at least in certain times and places) in greater limits on state action toward immigrants.[42] In the case of the United States and Mexico, for example, there are an increasing number of binational mechanisms to address immigration questions.[43] Nevertheless, we should be careful about overstating the importance of such mechanisms. As argued earlier, such "cooperation" is largely on U.S. terms and has thus served to further U.S. enforcement efforts related to immigration and the U.S.-Mexico boundary. Such national and international factors have certainly circumscribed U.S. treatment of unauthorized migrants. For instance, it is difficult to imagine the U.S. engaging in a mass deportation or expulsion of foreign nationals such as those that took place in the 1930s or in 1954. Indeed, U.S. authorities have promised their Mexican and Central American counterparts that they will not do so.[44] The growing number of domestic and international actors and institutions that influence the state's immigration regime highlight the ever-elusive nature of the state-society boundary.[45]

The increasingly complex web of international socioeconomic relations has reduced state autonomy in the making of immigration policy.[46] Furthermore, the growing number of sectors within the state and civil society—a form of "statecraft from below"[47]—that participate in the formulation of immigration policy leads to an increase in conflict within the state apparatus. The growing capacity of different sectors of civil society to negotiate with the state over matters of immigration enforcement and civil rights perhaps helps to explain (at least partially) the emergence of an immigration enforcement regime that puts increasing emphasis on individual choice and action in trying to address unauthorized immigration. The current focus on individual immigrants and boundary enforcement has fewer domestic political costs as it threatens no powerful domestic constituency, although, for boundary enforcement, this only remains the case as long as it does not become overly effective in preventing extralegal entries.

Similar to the emphasis on the actions of individual migrants, growing emphasis on the legality of migrants and boundary enforcement helps to minimize international conflicts over immigration as such an approach bases its legitimacy on the principle of national sovereignty whereby (at least theoretically) no territorial state can deny the sovereign rights of another. Such an approach also helps to circumvent potentially sticky domestic political battles; in fact, the focus on the "illegal" and the boundary often has the effect of creating greater levels of unity within the nation. And to the extent that globalization—in the form of increasing transboundary migratory flows—involves greater numbers of unauthorized immigrants, it also helps to increase national unity.

Associated with growing national cohesion in the face of "illegals" and the perceived threat to territorial boundaries, globalization also facilitates an enhancement of state power—at least at the social and geographical margins—

toward international boundaries and unauthorized immigrants. Globalization often leads to increasing demands upon the state for an intensified "nationalization" of territory and society. Political attacks against immigration and immigrants in the United States—and in many parts of the world—are instances of such nationalization. The attacks have come about partly in reaction to economic globalization and a perception of rising levels of socioeconomic insecurity.[48]

We might consider this context of globalization and rising levels of perceived insecurity as part and parcel of "modernity," the consequences of which "are becoming more radicalised and universalised than before."[49] Modernity embodies a set of social, political, and economic features and institutions that are distinctly different from those of traditional societies and that experience change of an unprecedented scope and pace.[50] Such features and institutions include industrialization, international capitalism, the nation-state, international boundaries, and telecommunications. The result is contradictory: while creating vastly improved opportunities for standards of living superior to those of traditional societies, modernity also creates greater possibilities for unparalleled insecurity.[51]

If we accept that increasing globalization, one of the most basic consequences of the modern era,[52] is similarly a double-edged phenomenon, it makes sense that we see the simultaneous promotion—sometimes by the same actors—of the processes of internationalization and nationalization (as embodied respectively by NAFTA and the restrictive processes of Gatekeeper) in the border region in the United States.[53] If we further accept that increasing globalization and regional integration are decreasing the sense of security among a significant portion of the population in the U.S. borderlands with Mexico, we may then understand popular support for state efforts such as Operation Gatekeeper also as an attempt to reclaim a sense of security. Thus, popular support for the fight against the "illegal" is a fight for an ever-fleeting sense of individual and communal security,[54] a security undermined by some of the same forces—regional integration and modernization—that limit the potential and real success of Operation Gatekeeper.[55]

State actors and politicians often construct migrants—especially refugees or unauthorized immigrants—as a security problem. In doing so, they define not only national territory, but also membership in the nation. The construction of the center (in this case, the nation and/or national territory) depends on the construction of the periphery (from where the "threat" embodied by the unwanted migrant emanates). Just as the construction of center and periphery are inextricably intertwined, so, too, is the production of citizen and alien. In constructing the undesirable immigrant as a security threat, state actors give the immigrant the appearance of a destroyer of social harmony: the immigrant, we are told, takes "our" jobs, commits crimes, threatens the social safety net, and undermines cultural cohesion. Implicit in such an analysis is the assumption that there would be a great deal more social harmony if the migrant were not present.[56]

To the extent that such thinking essentializes difference on the basis of ethnicity and/or national origin, it is arguably racial and is often part and parcel of modern nationalism. As Kathryn Manzo notes, "[N]ationalism is racial when it treats permanent difference (especially difference found within the borders of state territory) as alien, threatening, and a problem to be solved. The famed tolerance of Western societies is no exception, because that which must be tolerated has already been constructed as unfamiliar, foreign, and less developed. Liberal humanism has been practiced as well, but only when prospects for assimilation or integration are not threatened by numbers. Only then do once racialized minorities ... cease to be represented through metaphors of dirt, disease, evil, and plague. National inclusion is contingent upon racial sameness."[57] But it is too simple to label immigration restrictionists who employ arguments emphasizing cultural difference as "racist." Perhaps more than anything, they are just "good" nationalists.[58]

The creation of boundaries between national and alien is one of the principal practices associated with nationalism. Maintaining and policing these social and territorial boundaries—especially those between rich and poor—can become all the more necessary in the face of the forces of globalization. Paradoxically, globalization, rather than destroying nationalism, actually serves to enhance it in many instances. Arguably, the construction of the alien would be much more difficult without the forces of globalization. In this respect, the dichotomy between foreign and domestic, similar to the theoretically stark boundary between citizen and "alien," is highly problematic as the foreign and domestic are mutually constitutive.[59]

As argued earlier, globalization often leads to an increase in demands upon the state to protect the nation. But as demonstrated previously, Operation Gatekeeper has largely failed to protect the national citizenry from the "threat" presented by "illegals." Where the state has been more successful has been in creating an image of security vis-à-vis "illegal" immigration. Today, the U.S.-Mexico boundary in high-visibility or highly urbanized areas appears far more orderly than it did several years ago. This appearance has helped to create, in turn, a much greater sense of order. It is for such reasons that current state efforts to combat unauthorized immigration enjoy high levels of public support and receive high praise from government officials. While these efforts have not succeeded in terms of their material goals (i.e. significantly reducing unauthorized immigration), they have succeeded politically and psychologically.[60] Gatekeeper, and boundary enforcement efforts more generally, thus have the effect of reinforcing the ideology of nationalism and the sense of security members of the nation derive from its material expressions.

Nationalism is not simply a state of mind; it is a manner of being and performance. National boundaries are part of the performance, one that is continuous. Boundaries "can be made to appear timeless and beyond question. But precisely because national boundaries are constructed and always contestable, the reproduction of the national and the alien requires constant practice. It occurs continuously in a range of social institutions, such as schools and media, and in daily routines associated with 'policing, suspicion, and crossing (or refusal of entry).' "[61] The principal actor in this performance of territorial boundary construction is the state. The goal of the actor is the maintenance and strengthening of the nation. Globalization's challenges to national boundaries lead to efforts to protect the uniqueness of the nation against alien forces. Gatekeeper is but one such effort. Therefore, the globalized state—apart from being a gatekeeper—is also a politicoterritorial entity, one of whose principle functions is to provide security, largely against real and imagined alien forces.

This task of security provision becomes all the more necessary in the face of the effects of a neoliberal-fueled form of globalization that intensifies competition between localities, weakens social safety nets, and generally increases socioeconomic instability.[62] A central component of the process of globalization in its contemporary form is the disciplining or restraining of the state "by money capital and finance" to an unprecedented degree.[63] As an ideological tool, globalization has become a useful weapon against those arguing for national-based alternatives such as socialism or a welfare state.[64] Rather than fighting the national-based sources of socioeconomic instability (largely corporate and financial interests) whose very interests the state disproportionately represents, the state in this increasingly neoliberal world casts its gaze beyond the nation's social and territorial boundaries, focusing on the alien as a principal source of its social problems. The alien takes the form of the criminal, the poor, and the foreigner who are often one and the same. It is thus not surprising that an important feature of the neoliberal state—especially in the contemporary United States—is the destruction of the social welfare functions of the state and an increasing emphasis on "crimefare"—whether in the form of more prisons to incarcerate individuals who reside within its territory or in the form of a significant increase in state resources dedicated to boundary and immigration enforcement.[65] In this respect, Gatekeeper is a manifestation of the weakness of the state (to the extent that it is autonomous) and civil society vis-à-vis capital.

While enhanced state efforts aimed at boundary and immigration policing are supposedly carried out in defense of "the nation" (and thus evoke populist visions), it is highly dubious that they will have any sort of significant effect in ameliorating socioeconomic insecurity—especially among society's most marginalized sectors.[66] Given the strength and persistence of the numerous national and international forces driving immigration to the United States from Mexico and Central America (which U.S. foreign policy and U.S.-based multinationals help to create and exacerbate), such efforts can only lead to the increased marginalization of poor immigrant communities and tragic results for migrants forced to take great risks to cross the boundary. State efforts to implement a high (non-poverty-level) minimum wage, a guaranteed minimum income, strong health and safety standards and labor rights—combined with vigorous workplace enforcement of these standards and rights—would go much further in minimizing any real or potentially detrimental effects of immigration on low-wage workers and communities in the United States. Of course, such alternatives are not on the current mainstream political agenda. Neoliberalism and globalization (in the form of NAFTA) go hand in hand with the buildup of national boundaries, at least those between countries with divergent levels of socioeconomic development. The "NAFTA-ization" of the boundary thus dovetails with the "gatekeeper" state, the task of which is to provide extraterritorial opportunities for national territory-based capital (thus intensifying the process of globalization) while, somewhat paradoxically, providing security against the perceived social costs unleashed by globalization—especially immigration.

THE FUTURE OF NATIONAL BOUNDARIES

Contrary to the opinion of some,[67] the forces of economic globalization are not making national boundaries redundant. Instead, globalization arguably seems to be having the opposite effect: it is making national boundaries—at least those between rich and poor—all the more "necessary," especially in the face of intensifying migratory pressures from without. In some ways, however, it is not very helpful to ask simply if boundaries—and, by extension, the modern territorial state—are (or are not) weakening. As political scientist Malcolm Anderson points out, the varied types of transnational "flows" have resulted in a situation in which boundaries have numerous, sometimes conflicting, functions.[68] Thus, in the case of the U.S.-Mexico boundary, the level of porosity of the boundary is a function of the type of transnational flow crossing the international divide. Various cultural flows, for example, are largely uninhibited, as are, increasingly, a number of economic flows. For transnational migrants, as demonstrated by Operation Gatekeeper, however, a very different outcome is often evident. These different boundary regulatory regimes relate to the security and opportunity components of the modern territorial state,[69] and the very complexity and often contradictory nature of its associated boundaries.[70] As border regions change, new opportunities emerge having to do with finance, education, culture, and leisure activities, or possibilities for new transboundary political alliances. These changes, however, can also alter power relations, undermine cultural patterns and identities, and lead to a general perception of growing insecurity.[71]

In the face of such challenges international boundaries will certainly not become redundant in the foreseeable future. Putative threats will most probably continue to challenge modern territorial states, especially across boundaries between highly "developed" and less developed countries (such as that between the United States and Mexico). These boundaries tend to be "the most difficult and sensitive" and will likely persist as state tools to maintain a world order marked by gross inequalities.[72] Assuming that the forces that facilitate "illegal" immigration across such boundaries remain, it is quite possible that efforts to fight "illegal" immigration and immigrants will intensify. As demonstrated earlier, increasing institutionalization of the boundary and related enforcement activities have a tendency to facilitate ever greater levels of boundary and immigration enforcement and to strengthen the nationalist ideology that legitimizes these developments.

While a significant decrease in unauthorized immigration might have a mitigating effect on such a development, there is little reason to think that the numbers of unauthorized immigrants attempting to enter the United States will decline anytime soon. Indeed, the destabilizing effects of the NAFTA-led liberalization of the Mexican economy will most likely continue to lead to significant migratory pressures on the United States for the foreseeable future. Measures often thought to reduce emigration from migrant-sending countries, such as foreign direct investment and export-oriented manufacturing, are also likely to produce higher levels of immigration from many other "developing" countries as past experience has shown. Market consolidation has long been a principal factor in facilitating migration.[73] Economic restructuring within relatively wealthy countries such as the United States has resulted in a transformation of the economy's occupational and income structure. Such restructuring works to promote further immigration from relatively low-wage countries. And social, political, and/or military ties between "developing" countries and "developed" territorial states such as the United States also serve to lessen the social distance between migrant sending and receiving areas, thus (unintentionally) encouraging immigration even more.[74]

It is for such reasons, among others, that the physical and the enforcement infrastructure of the U.S.-Mexico boundary—as well as the accompanying nationalist ideology—have grown to such unprecedented levels. It appears that these trends will continue. The INS budget for fiscal year (FY) 1994, for example, was $1.1 billion, whereas it was $3.8 billion in FY 1999.[75] And while the number of U.S. Border Patrol agents has not increased as quickly as Congress had intended, the number continues to grow.[76] Overall, there is an unmistakable trend toward ever higher levels of resources dedicated to boundary and immigration enforcement. To the extent that state officials acknowledge that such efforts keep falling short of the seemingly elusive goal of controlling unauthorized immigration, further increases in enforcement resources seem to be the almost automatic response of the state, rather than any fundamental reevaluation of policy.[77] Indeed, given the growing ideological significance of the boundary vis-à-vis unauthorized immigration and of boundary enforcement, it is difficult to foresee the possibilities of alternative responses by the state, barring a significant political shift within U.S. society. Continued development of the boundary and immigration enforcement regime appears only to strengthen our collective *inability* to imagine alternatives and to reinforce an already entrenched set of political interests in favor of maintaining and enhancing the status quo. The "territorial trap" further inhibits our ability to see alternatives,[78] especially those that challenge the logic of the modern territorial state system. Boundaries are not only a way of seeing (and thus a way of living), they are also a producer of our ways of seeing (or not seeing).

At the same time, however, the very extraterritorial "flows" that serve as catalysts for enhanced boundary enforcement will continue to challenge boundaries physically as well as politically. The most obvious example of boundary resistance is the unauthorized migrant who lives his life more as a citizen of a nonbounded society (one shaped by extraterritorial social, economic, and cultural forces) than as a citizen of a bounded territorial state. As such, the unauthorized immigrant directly challenges (although the typical individual migrant probably does not see her actions in this light) the legitimacy of national boundaries and the supposedly sovereign territorial state.

A presently weaker but potentially more potent challenge to national boundaries derives from the types of transboundary political alliances, hinted at above, that developing border zones can engender. At one level, these consist of largely elite, transboundary alliances or linkages, such as business associations, binational government agencies, and civic groups. But such entities tend to be geographically limited to border zones, "world cities," and national capitals. Given their focus on interregional problem solving they tend to be international rather than transnational (in other words, *outside* or *beyond* the realm of the modern territorial state[79]) in orientation. Of greater significance in terms of challenging national boundaries are transboundary movements that are implicitly or explicitly "internationalist" (suggesting an ethic of solidarity) or anti-capitalist and/or anti-nationalist in orientation. While these are small in number, such efforts are growing noticeably, especially in the context of economic globalization, which has in some ways forced previously nation-centric movements to engage in building links of solidarity with people in other countries.

During the debate over NAFTA in the United States, for instance, certain elements of the anti-NAFTA campaign preached and practiced a "globalism from below," an "internationalism" aimed at constructing political movements informed by a transnational notion of social justice.[80] The U.S.-based Teamsters Union and the United Electrical Workers are developing close links with Mexico's Authentic Workers Front.[81] And during a 1998 strike against the U.S.-based automaker General Motors (GM), the United Auto Workers organized with their fellow General Motors employees in Mexico, where GM is the largest private-sector employer. In this regard, NAFTA and the processes of economic liberalization and regional integration have great potential to further facilitate such efforts. Nevertheless, these efforts at transnational solidarity are relatively few and largely insignificant in the face of increasingly transnational forms of capitalism. Unfortunately for the global working class, most labor organizations remain highly nationalist in both vision and practice.[82] As Malcolm Anderson contends, "A world without frontiers in which solidarity with the whole human race dominates all intermediate solidarities remains a utopian dream."[83] For the time being, unfortunately, Anderson seems to be correct. The fusing of the law, territory, and social power make the present-day ideological construction of "the nation," "us," and "them" (and, by extension, the "illegal") extremely difficult to overcome in trying to forge a vision and practice consonant with the increasingly transnational world in which we live.[84] But as Eduardo Galeano states, "Reality is not destiny, it is a challenge."[85] And the enormity of the challenge should not deter us from confronting it. Rather, it should serve as a wake-up call, a reminder of the need for serious and far-reaching collective action to make progress toward the utopian visions that any vibrant society needs to survive and thrive.

The life of the nationalist (or the national citizen) is full of contradictions. In the American case, the nationalist may advocate stepped-up boundary enforcement to protect "us" from a potential "flood" of Mexican immigrants, while at the same time eating quesadillas and salsa (sales of the latter now exceeds ketchup sales in the United States), watching a television set manufactured in Tijuana (one of the world's leading producers of televisions), and consuming and enjoying goods and services that are relatively inexpensive thanks to "illegal" Mexican labor. In this regard, the nationalist unintentionally resists the bounding of the United States. In many ways, he does not live within boundaries, but rather in a border zone—that is, a zone of socioeconomic and political interaction between geographically distinct entities. His "resistance," however, is passive and does not challenge the assumptions underlying the production of the boundaries necessary for the maintenance of the nation, the modern territorial state, the citizen, or the alien—"legal" as well as "illegal." In fact, the cognitive dissonance as well as the perceived socioeconomic insecurity generated by these extraterritorial flows seem to lead him to strengthen his embrace of the apparent security offered by the nation, the territorially bounded entity of people with whom he theoretically shares a certain history, culture, and/or commitment to a set of principles. There are alternative possible responses, but the very organization of our world militates against them. As the political scientist E. Schattschneider once observed, all organizations reflect bias. In other words, organizations embody power, social relations, and worldviews. As such, they favor certain interests over others. In a world made up of nation-states, the nationalist response to insecurity is favored over the transnational one.

These nationalist responses take a variety of forms—Operation Gatekeeper and Proposition 187–type "solutions" being just two. One need not be a nativist to advocate a reduction in immigration—only a nationalist. And the rationales, assumptions, and visions underlying these positions are multiple. Almost all those advocating greater levels of immigration restriction (regardless of the form) in the United States, however, share a concern about what they see as an excessively high level of low-wage/low-skill immigration (involving largely non-white, non-English-speaking immigrants) to the United States.

Geographer William Clark, for example, argues that the growing percentage of poor, "low-skilled" immigrants to the United States necessitates the development of immigration admission criteria that are more focused on the skill levels of the immigrants rather than on uniting families. Of course, such a policy would inevitably end up favoring would-be immigrants from relatively wealthy countries (which are generally "white"), and lead to less authorized immigration from relatively poor (largely nonwhite, non-English-speaking) countries. At the same time, Clark recognizes that high levels of immigration by nonwealthy, non-English-speaking people is a fact of American life—one that will likely continue to be. For this reason, he worries that the ethnolinguistic composition of this migration is causing the United States to lose its identity as a single society with many ethnic backgrounds and identities. Instead, Clark fears, the United States is on the way of becoming separate ethnicity- and race-based societies sharing a common territory, but coexisting uneasily in a manner often beset with conflict. For this reason, he calls for a far greater public investment in education to assimilate or "Americanize" new immigrants as rapidly as possible.[86]

More toward the left end of the political spectrum is anthropologist David Stoll, who is concerned principally with the effects of immigration on the socioeconomic security of American workers. Stoll acknowledges that most economists agree that the net effect of immigration on the U.S. economy is beneficial—a position he seems to share. "But," he cautions, "net benefits for the economy can conceal serious losses for vulnerable sectors of the U.S. population." Immigration, according to Stoll, "clearly contributes to a downward pressure on wage levels and to decreased job availability in certain economic sectors" and, for this reason, he argues, the United States needs to restrict the numbers of immigrants. Stoll admits, however, that immigrant labor is "not the main reason for deteriorating wage levels, job opportunities, and labor conditions for U.S. workers." The profit-maximization behavior of capital, he suggests, is more important. Nevertheless, "if current immigration levels are indeed contributing to the transformation of the United States into a low-wage economy, then a new immigration policy is in order."[87] While in the past Stoll has advocated militarizing the boundary to achieve this end,[88] he now argues that such an approach is both ineffective and abusive in terms of the human rights of migrants. Instead, he calls upon labor advocates and policy makers to "give serious consideration" to a national worker identification card. If such documents were "[b]acked by rigorous enforcement of labor laws, [they] would deflate the political pressure for militarizing the Mexican border."

What is curious about Stoll's prescriptions is that, despite appearing in a publication called *Foreign Policy in Focus*, they have nothing to do with foreign policy. His putative solutions are purely domestic or national in nature. There is nothing in his analysis of what he identifies as immigration-induced problems that suggests transnational, or even binational solutions. Like William Clark, David Stoll limits his view to the vista offered by bounded national territory. In the process, he elevates the interests of national citizens over those of non-citizens and offers solutions—in terms of what's politically feasible within the political mainstream to whom he seems to direct his comments—that would, if implemented, probably do very little to help the most vulnerable sectors of the U.S. population while reinforcing the social boundaries that distinguish "citizen" from "alien," "legal" from "illegal." Such an outcome would potentially only serve to strengthen the long-term hand of the anti-immigrant nativism that Stoll, like Clark, undoubtedly despises.

The analyses and recommendations put forth by both Stoll and Clark also share a common approach in terms of assumptions. They both emphasize the allegedly negative effects of the relatively weak (low-income immigrants) as a means to help explain profound socioeconomic problems such as poor educational achievement in California's public schools (Clark) or the plight of low-income (native born) American workers (Stoll). They do this rather than focus on the activities of the rich and powerful, who are undoubtedly more responsible for these developments. In doing so, they serve the interests of the privileged by helping to reinforce the status quo rather than to challenge it, and divert attention from the structural inequalities that underlie American society's most pressing socioeconomic problems. As Joseph Carens contends, "One of the ways in which those in power maintain their privileges is by getting people to focus on potential tradeoffs between those who are badly off and those who are worse off, thereby treating their own privileges as a background given that cannot be challenged."[89] At the same time, approaches such as that of Clark and Stoll are informed by a tendency—one often unacknowledged—that reduces the immigration debate to one of costs versus benefits, which ultimately has the effect of reducing immigrants to commodities or investments. Instead, we should emphasize the human and worker rights of all immigrants. [90]

Of course, it is much easier to make sweeping statements advocating fundamental changes than it is to deal with the myriad practical complexities that surround the immigration debate. In many ways, however, debates as to what to do ultimately come down to philosophical and ideological differences, more than to the feasibility of specific prescriptions. These philosophical differences are serious and complex,[91] ranging from the positions of libertarians who champion freedom of movement on the basis of the principle of individual choice to political realists and nationalists who support the right of modern territorial states to restrict such movement in the name of national interests, but as a position of principle as well.

Needless to say, I reject the arguments of the realists and nationalists that implicitly see a world of modern territorial states and their associated powers as unproblematic and/or perceive the interests of the national community to be superior to those of all others. At the same time, while there is much to embrace in the libertarian position, its use of property rights and its employ-ment of "free market"-type arguments to justify their position is troubling as it elevates the rights of economic actors above all others and effectively reduces human beings to commodities. Indeed, many libertarians champion free movement, in part because they perceive it to be economically beneficial.[92]

A powerful philosophical argument (one based on liberalism) in favor of the right of relatively wealthy countries to regulate immigration is that which underlies the argument of David Stoll (and perhaps, to a certain degree, that of William Clark)—namely, that immigration controls help protect the most disadvantaged residents of those countries. Such a position openly assumes that a country is in the right to attempt to meet the needs of its own citizens before those of other countries—on the basis of the possible (there are limits to what we can do to help others), realism (there are limits to people's generosity), and intensity (connections within national boundaries are typi-cally more intense than those across them).[93] There are many problems with the assumptions behind this position, but perhaps most important, as Joseph Carens suggests, such an argument effectively pits those who are badly off against those who are in a worse state rather than challenge the powerful agents and institutions that are ultimately far more responsible for the plight of the less fortunate. Furthermore, it even denies people the right to work and try to build a community of justice that transcends hitherto unproblematized boundaries by restricting where they can go and live. Finally, it implicitly rejects the notion of universal justice by privileging one group over another by denying the latter a very important means to realizing a life of dignity.[94] All human beings have a right to work and to a life of dignity; migration is often a necessary component of the process to realize these rights. In this regard, freedom of movement and residence are basic human rights.

A nationalistic response to the putative problems caused by immigration conforms to a worldview that sees sovereign nation-states as a "natural," desir-able, and/or inevitable part of our world. It dovetails with the contention that justice is only possible within delimited communities, that a regime of rights is not possible unless there is a boundary separating those who have rights from those who do not.[95] The problem with such an analysis is that it seems to assume that a universal community is an impossibility. Undoubtedly, the making of such a community is and would be extremely difficult, but like the construction of any community, it would be the outcome of a social process. To begin doing so requires breaking out of the prison of our national imagination and constructing a "transnational integrationist vision," a vision that puts humanity above national citizenry, and an associated set of practices.[96] The increasingly transnational world in which we live compels us to reconceptualize narrow notions of citizenship that reduce membership and associated rights within a polity to "legal" status in a modern territorial state. We must recognize the reality that many people belong to more than one society and have multiple identities. In this regard, citizenship must become a category much more flexible than normally allowed by modern territorial states, a category in which membership is a function of participation within a social, cultural, and/or political economic entity that does not limit itself to national boundaries.[97]

EXPLORING GLOBAL APARTHEID

[Fear] tends to cause hatred of foreigners who offer their labor at desperate prices. It's the invasion of the invaded. They come from lands where conquering colonial troops and punishing military expeditions have disembarked 1,001 times. Now this voyage in reverse isn't made by soldiers obliged to sell themselves in Europe or North America at whatever price they get. They come from Africa, Asia, and Latin America, and, since the burial of bureaucratic power, from Eastern Europe as well.

In the years of the great European and North American economic expansion, growing prosperity required more and more labor, and it didn't matter that those hands were foreign, as long as they worked hard and charged little. In years of stagnation or weak growth, they become undesirable interlopers: they smell bad, they make a lot of noise, they take away jobs. Scapegoats of unemployment and every other misfortune, they are condemned to live with several swords hanging over their heads: the always imminent threat of deportation back to the grueling life they've fled and the always possible explosion of racism with its bloody warnings, its punishments: Turks set on fire, Arabs stabbed, Africans shot, Mexicans beaten. Poor immigrants do the hardest, poorest-paid work in the fields and on the streets. After work comes the danger. No magic ink can make them invisble.

—Eduardo Galeano[98]

Modern territorial states are not disappearing; they are merely changing. We can make the same observation about national boundaries. What this book demonstrates is that national boundaries are more than simply changing; they are also growing in strength, physically and ideologically—at least with respect to unauthorized immigrants. In this regard, the legality of the boundary—in terms of the degree to which law-based practices and assumptions penetrate it—has also grown. The enhancement of boundary policing and increased efforts to fight unauthorized immigration—along with scapegoating, criminalization of those deemed "foreign" and anti-immigrant sentiment in the broader society—are not unique to the United States. We see similar developments in a number of places throughout the world, from South Africa to Germany to Malaysia.[99] These tend to take place most in countries with high levels of socioeconomic development (relative to their neighbors or the countries of origin of the immigrant population).[100]

Such developments would seem to lend credence to the contention that boundary maintenance goes hand in hand with efforts to reproduce inequalities across space.[101] In a context of growing socioeconomic inequality internationally, some analysts speaks of a type of "global apartheid" characterized by "extreme hierarchy and unevenness of circumstances [and] acute deprivation and mass misery among the poor," socioeconomic divisions that most often correspond to race.[102] What such analyses fail to do, however, is demonstrate how control of residence and movement actually works to maintain and enhance the socioeconomic inequality embodied by the metaphor "global apartheid."[103]

For those of us interested in addressing such questions, it is necessary to move beyond the dominant paradigm of inquiry, beyond one that generally accepts as given (and largely unproblematic) the contemporary organization of the world as defined by state elites.[104] Given the intensifying "war on illegals" embodied by Operation Gatekeeper and the associated human suffering—from growing numbers of boundary-crossing-related deaths of migrants to the persistent criminalization of unauthorized immigrants—such an intellectual and political project is not only desirable, but also necessary.

EPILOGUE

On the occasion of a May 1999 visit to California by Mexican President Ernesto Zedillo, a statement by the Pacific Council on International Policy in the form of an opinion piece appeared in the *Los Angeles Times.* Entitled "Strengthen Ties between California and Mexico," the piece contained a list of high-profile signatories drawn from politics, business, academia, and the nonprofit sector and, as such, represented a consensus toward the border among a significant slice of California's establishment.[105]

The statement noted that "[i]ncreasingly intimate relations between Mexico and California are an irreversible reality, not an option" and advocated strengthening cooperation between the two political entities "in four key areas:

economic and social investment, immigration, border development and education." Its section on immigration called for California to "work actively with Mexico, directly and through federal channels, to develop mutually acceptable ways of managing migration flows so that labor needs are met and the rights both of migrants and of native-born citizens are protected." Subsequent sections championed improving transboundary transportation links, as well as border zone infrastructure and planning, and intensifying efforts aimed at harmonizing institutional cooperation across the boundary and at facilitating greater levels of investment in the border region.[106]

One of the most striking aspects of the piece was that at least two of the signatories to the statement, Alan Bersin and former California Democratic Party gubernatorial candidate Kathleen Brown, had actively championed the radical increase in boundary enforcement that resulted in Operation Gatekeeper. Bersin, in fact, was one of its chief architects in his former capacity as the United States Attorney General's Special Representative for Southwest Border Issues.

It is hardly a coincidence that we see such individuals working both to increase transboundary ties between California and Mexico as well as to enhance boundary enforcement. Transnational integration emanates from developments and produces outcomes that are simultaneously contradictory and complementary, especially between relatively rich and poor countries. As the Pacific Council on International Policy acknowledged in its *Los Angeles Times* piece, "as our two societies become more interdependent, frictions may well become more evident, frequent and bothersome."[107] In terms of the territorial boundary between the United States and Mexico, the processes of opening and closing are most pronounced in the San Diego border region, an area where the levels of economic integration between the two countries are highly pronounced, but where transboundary sociocultural differences remain significant. These seemingly contradictory developments are an outgrowth of the often clashing functions of the modern territorial state, functions that are intensified by increasing transboundary flows that embody an age of globalization.

José Luis Uriostegua was caught in between these two clashing functions. Border Patrol agents discovered his frigid body on Mount Laguna in eastern San Diego County, about twenty miles north of the U.S.-Mexico boundary, on March 22, 2000. From now on, he will be known as number 500—the 500th person to perish while trying to evade the U.S. Border Patrol in southern California since Gatekeeper's implementation.

Fleeing from Guerrero, one of Mexico's poorest states, where human rights abuses are rife, Uriostegua was struggling for a better life for himself and his family. Rather than seeing the world as divided, he saw it as whole. In this respect, the young man recognized what many of our political imaginations do not allow us to see: the U.S.-Mexico boundary, as a line of control and division, is, to a significant degree, an illusion. Mexico and the United States are increasingly one.

On a more practical level, moreover, a law enforcement approach to immigration is destined to fail. The ties between the United States and Mexico (and increasingly much of Latin America) are too strong, migrants are too resourceful and creative, and Americans are too resistant to the types of police-state measures that would prove necessary to reduce unauthorized immigration significantly.

Instead of trying to create new and improved methods to repel those who cross our borders (but whose hard work we welcome), we should be trying to embrace them. At the same time, we need to appreciate that immigration is often the result of the breakdown of political, economic, and social systems and/or institutionalized injustice—problems that are often induced to a significant extent by policies and practices of the relatively wealthy and powerful—and work at home and abroad with various sectors of developing countries to redress such phenomena. This would prove to be a far more humane and effective method for addressing the myriad factors that lead people to migrate than continue to build up the boundaries between "us" and "them."

Had José Luis Uriostegua made it to a place like Los Angeles, he might be mowing someone's lawn, bussing someone's table, or picking someone's tomatoes. He would be one of the hundreds of thousands of unauthorized immigrants—the so-called illegals—who form the backbone of California's huge economy.

Immigrants are first and foremost human beings who, regardless of their legal status, deserve our respect and solidarity rather than poverty wages or a potential death sentence in the form of Operation Gatekeeper. As such, we need to argue and struggle for practices and mechanisms that are consistent with the ethics demanded by a common humanity, one of the most important of which is solidarity—one that knows no boundaries.

Mexico's new president, Vicente Fox, has shown himself to be very open to rethinking the nature of the U.S.-Mexico boundary. This provides people on both sides of the international divide with an excellent opportunity to move beyond immoral, ineffective, and, ultimately, counterproductive approaches to the complexities of immigration that inextricably bind the United States to Mexico and to so many other countries. Such a historical moment requires unique visions and the political will to work to realize them.

Appendix A: The U.S.-Mexico Borderlands in Southern California

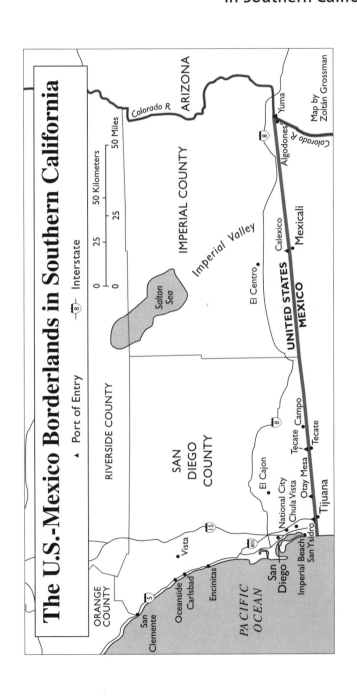

Appendix B: Mexico and the U.S.-Mexico Borderlands

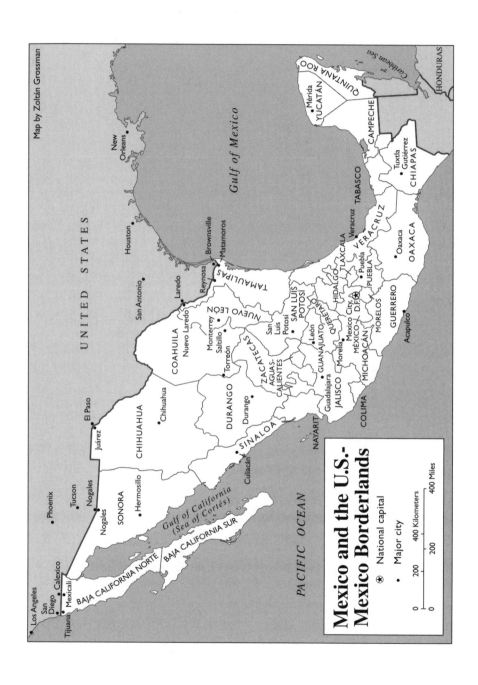

Map by Zoltán Grossman

Mexico and the U.S.-Mexico Borderlands

⊛ National capital
• Major city

0   200   400 Kilometers
0   200   400 Miles

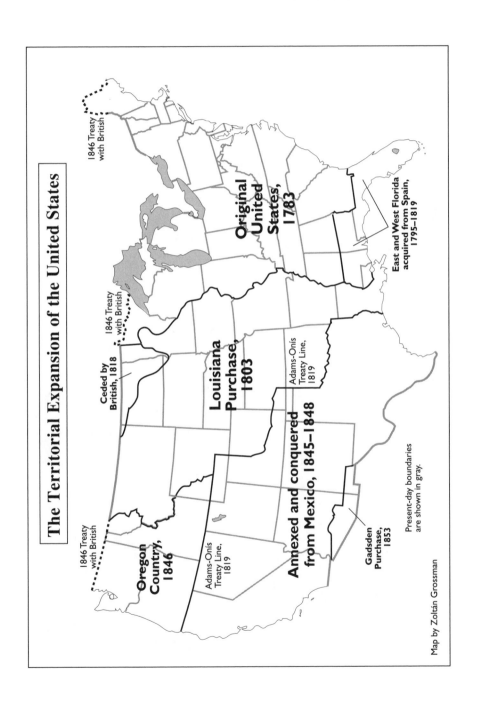

The Territorial Expansion of the United States

Original United States, 1783

East and West Florida acquired from Spain, 1795–1819

1846 Treaty with British

Ceded by British, 1818

Louisiana Purchase, 1803

Adams-Onis Treaty Line, 1819

Annexed and conquered from Mexico, 1845–1848

Oregon Country, 1846

Adams-Onis Treaty Line, 1819

Gadsden Purchase, 1853

Present-day boundaries are shown in gray.

Map by Zoltán Grossman

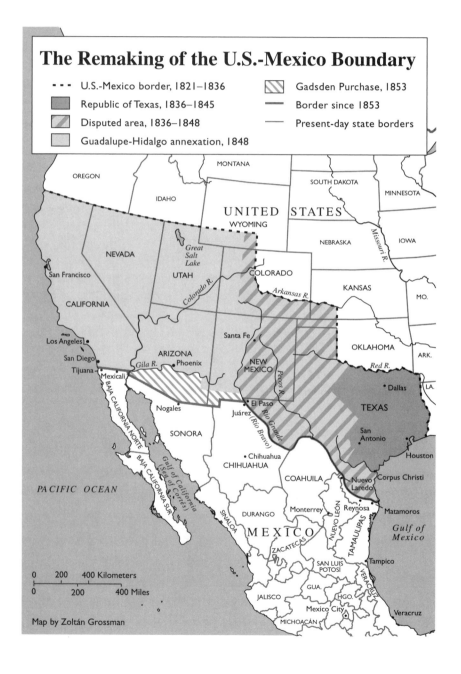

The Remaking of the U.S.-Mexico Boundary

- - - U.S.-Mexico border, 1821–1836

Republic of Texas, 1836–1845

Disputed area, 1836–1848

Guadalupe-Hidalgo annexation, 1848

Gadsden Purchase, 1853

Border since 1853

Present-day state borders

Map by Zoltán Grossman

Appendix E: Chronology of Selected U.S. Immigration- and Boundary-Related Legislation and Developments[1]

1798 Alien and Sedition Acts make it possible for the government to expel "aliens" judged to be "a danger to the peace and security" of the country. The various components of the acts expire within a two-to-four-year period due to their unpopularity.

1846 United States deliberately provokes Mexico by sending troops to the Rio Grande, soon resulting in a full-scale war between the two countries.

1848 Treaty of Guadalupe Hidalgo marks the end of the war. Under the terms of the treaty, the United States annexes 1,527,241 square kilometers of Mexican land, a territory equivalent in size to that of western Europe, and absorbed 100,000 Mexican citizens and 200,000 Native Americans living in the annexed territory. All or part of ten states result from the treaty: Texas, Arizona, New Mexico, Oklahoma, Wyoming, Colorado, Kansas, Utah, Nevada, and California.

1853 The Gadsden Treaty results in a redefinition of the United States-Mexico boundary. The United States gains additional land from Mexico, most notably the resource-rich areas of southern New Mexico.

1864 The first comprehensive federal immigration law, the Act to Encourage Immigration establishes the first U.S. Immigration Bureau to *increase* immigration so that U.S. industries will have a sufficient labor supply during the Civil War.

1875 The law bars the immigration of convicts and of women for the purpose of prostitution, marking the first federal legislation restricting immigration into the United States.

1876 Congress declares void all state laws regulating immigration.

1882 The Immigration Act of August 3, 1882 increases the restriction of immigrants, barring the entry of "idiots, lunatics, convicts, and persons likely to become public charges." The law also empowers the treasury secretary to administer immigration laws, thus formally giving the federal government the duty to regulate immigration for the first time. The act eliminates the ability of states to regulate immigration.

   The Chinese Exclusion Act bars the entry of Chinese laborers.

1885 Along with a law passed in 1887, legislation prohibits the admission of contract laborers. Laws are largely symbolic in nature, having almost no impact on the U.S. labor market.

1891 The Immigration Act of 1891 orders the deportation of those who enter the United States without authorization and creates the Office of Immigration within the Department of the Treasury. The law also prohibits the admission of "polygamists, persons convicted of *crimes involving moral turpitude,* and those suffering a loathsome or contagious disease."

1893   Legislation requires all vessels entering the United States to provide a list of passengers.

1903   The Immigration Law of 1903 adds to the list of barred immigrants the categories of epileptics, the insane, professional beggars, and anarchists. The law also transfers responsibilities for the administration of immigration laws from the Secretary of the Treasury to the new Department of Commerce and Labor.

1907   President Theodore Roosevelt signs a "Gentlemen's Agreement" with Japan by which Tokyo agrees to limit the exodus of Japanese migrants to the United States.

      Congress enacts a bill that authorizes the president to enter into international agreements to regulate immigration.

      The Act of February 20, 1907 requires that all boundary crossers enter the United States through an official port of entry.

1917   The Immigration Act of 1917 restates all past qualitative exclusions and also adds the categories of illiterates, requiring a literacy test and an eight-dollar head tax for entry. The legislation also establishes the "Asiatic Barred Zone," a geographic area that included most of Asia and the Pacific Islands, further restricting the entry of Asian immigrants.

1918   The Passport Act makes it a crime for any "alien" to enter the United States without a passport.

1921   The Temporary Quota Act of 1921 limits the number of admissions of any one particular nationality to three percent of the group's population already in the United States according to the 1910 census; this marks the first quantitative immigration restriction in U.S. history.

1924   The Immigration Act of 1924 (also known as the Johnson-Reed Act) makes the 1921 quotas permanent, but uses the census of 1890 as its base. The legislation includes the Oriental Exclusion Act, which bans all Asian immigration except that from the Philippines. The 1924 act also requires immigrants for the first time to obtain visas from U.S. consular officials abroad before traveling to the United States. As before, the restrictions have unintended consequences, leading to a rapid rise in the number of unauthorized European immigrants who would enter from Canada or Mexico, countries not subject to immigration quotas.

      The Department of Labor Appropriations Act grants one million dollars for "additional land-border patrol," thus creating the U.S. Border Patrol.

1929   The Act of March 4, 1929 makes the entry of noncitizens at locations other than those designated by the U.S. government or by means of "a willfully false or misleading representation" a misdemeanor. It also makes reentry of a previously deported "alien" a felony. Both "crimes," according to the act, are punishable by fine and/or imprisonment.

      The combination of the onset of the Depression and rising anti-Mexican immigrant sentiment results in the deportation of hundreds of thousands of Mexican immigrants between 1929 and 1935, including tens of thousands of U.S. citizens of Mexican descent.

1933   President Herbert Hoover merges the Bureau of Immigration and the Bureau of Naturalization to form the Immigration and Naturalization Service (INS).

1940   The INS moves from the Department of Labor and becomes part of the Department of Justice.

1942   The Bracero Program begins.

1943   Congress repeals the Chinese Exclusion Laws, largely as a result of the U.S. entry into World War II as an ally of China against Japan.

1954   The INS launches Operation Wetback.

1964   The Bracero Program ends.

1965   Immigration and Nationality Act implemented, ending national origin quotas for immigrants.

1981   The U.S. Select Commission on Immigration and Refugee Policy releases its final report.

1986   Congress passes the Immigration Reform and Control Act.

1993   On September 19, the El Paso Sector of the U.S. Border Patrol launches Operation Blockade (later renamed Operation Hold-the-Line).

1994   On October 1, the INS launches Operation Gatekeeper in San Diego.

On November 8, California voters overwhelmingly approve Proposition 187.

1995   The INS launches Operation Safeguard in Arizona.

1996   Congress passes the Illegal Immigration Reform and Immigrant Responsibility Act.

1997   The INS launches "Operation Rio Grande" in the Brownsville area of Texas.

1.   Sources: Calavita 1984 and 1994; Cockcroft 1986; Coppock 1968; Martínez 1995; McDonald 1997; Reimers 1992; U.S. INS 1953, 1991 and 1996; U.S. Select Commission on Immigration and Refugee Policy 1981; and Wang 1975.

Appendix F: Number of Border Patrol Agents Nationally, Fiscal Years 1925–2000

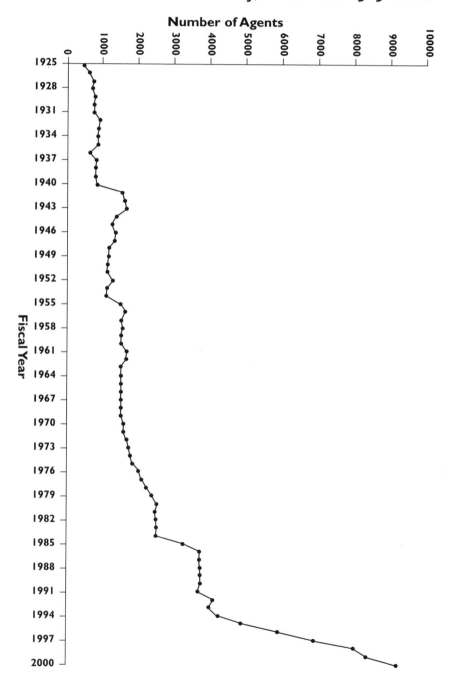

Appendix F: Change in Number of Border Agents Nationally, Fiscal Years 1925–2000

Fiscal Year	Number of Border Patrol Agents On-Duty Nationally	Fiscal Year	Number of Border Patrol Agents On-Duty Nationally
1925	450	1963	1493
1926	632	1964	1493
1927	742	1965	1491
1928	705	1966	1491
1929	767	1967	1494
1930	747	1968	1494
1931	742	1969	1494
1932	901	1970	1566
1933	855	1971	1554
1934	841	1972	1634
1935	841	1973	1704
1936	611	1974	1739
1937	800	1975	1803
1938	774	1976	1979
1939	773	1977	2057
1940	819	1978	2189
1941	1531	1979	2339
1942	1592	1980	2484
1943	1637	1981	2444
1944	1360	1982	2488
1945	1251	1983	2474
1946	1352	1984	2474
1947	1319	1985	3232
1948	1160	1986	3693
1949	1125	1987	3703
1950	1110	1988	3713
1951	1098	1989	3723
1952	1259	1990	3733
1953	1079	1991	3651
1954	1079	1992	4076
1955	1479	1993	3965
1956	1593	1994	4226
1957	1491	1995	4881
1958	1524	1996	5878
1959	1500	1997	6880
1960	1494	1998	7982
1961	1648	1999	8351
1962	1614	2000	9212

As I was not able to find realiable figures for 1987, 1988, and 1989, I simply assumed incremental growth between 1986 and 1990 and assigned figures on that basis.

Appendix G: Cover from December 1974
Issue of *The American Legion Magazine*

NOTES

CHAPTER 1

1. Quoted in Stern 1993.
2. U.S. Border Patrol 1994: 2.
3. Quote taken from *Weekly Compilation of Presidential Documents*, Vol. 32, No. 32, Monday, August 12, 1996: 1398.
4. The names used in this story are not real.
5. See the maps in appendices A and B.
6. According to the Border Patrol's national strategic vision,

   > The Border Patrol will achieve the goals of its strategy by bringing a decisive number of enforcement resources to bear in each major entry corridor [such as El Paso and San Diego]. The Border Patrol will increase the number of agents on the line [along the boundary] and make effective use of technology, raising the risk of apprehension high enough to be an effective deterrent. Because the deterrent effect of apprehensions does not become effective in stopping the flow until apprehensions approach 100 percent of those attempting entry, the strategic objective is to maximize the apprehension rate. Although a 100 percent apprehension rate is an unrealistic goal, we believe we can achieve a rate of apprehensions sufficiently high to raise the risk of apprehension to the point that many will consider it futile to continue to attempt illegal entry (U.S. Border Patrol 1994: 6).

7. So-called border bandits were usually from Mexico and would attack unauthorized immigrants on the U.S. side of the boundary and then flee back into Tijuana. For a more complete description of issues relating to law enforcement along the U.S.-Mexico boundary in the San Diego region at the beginning of the 1990s, see chapter 4.
8. Rotella 1998: 106.
9. See Portillo 1991b.
10. Jones 1998.
11. Ellingwood 1999a: A3.
12. The San Diego Sector of the U.S. Border Patrol is responsible for the sixty-six westernmost miles of the U.S.-Mexico boundary.
13. U.S. Border Patrol 1994: 5.
14. *Migration News*, November 1997.
15. *Migration News*, May 1999, September and December 2000; and Ellingwood 1999a: A35.
16. See, for example, Ellingwood 1999a.
17. The Border Patrol is only responsible for the boundary in between ports of entry. It is INS Inspectors who work the ports and decide who is eligible to enter the United States.
18. U.S. INS 1998.
19. See chapters 5 and 6 of this volume.
20. U.S. INS 1997: 1; Bersin 1996b: 1–2.
21. See, for example, *Los Angeles Times* 1994 and *The San Diego Union-Tribune* 1994.
22. U.S. INS 1997: 2–3.

23. *Migration News*, June 1999.
24. Herzog 1999: 5–6. The most significant factor informing the tremendous economic and demographic growth of Mexico's northern border region has been the rapid growth of *maquiladoras*, which increased in number from 170 in 1970 to 2,400 in 1995. According to Herzog, many experts predicted that the North American Free Trade Agreement would lead to a reduction in the concentration of the maquiladoras in the border region. Nevertheless, about 80 percent of Mexico's maquiladoras were still located along the boundary with the United States as of 1997.

    According to the *San Diego Union* (now defunct), as of 1991 upwards of $95 million was flowing annually into the San Diego economy from the Tijuana maquiladoras (Showley 1991). At the same time, the factories have provided a significant boost to the Tijuana economy. Tijuana maquiladoras employed 118,000 people in 1996, a 28 percent increase over the previous year (Smith and Malkin 1997: 67).
25. See Herzog 1990.
26. Smith and Malkin 1997: 64.
27. *Migration News*, March 2000.
28. Schneider 2000.
29. Ellingwood 1999b: A28. About 2.8 million trucks crossed from Mexico into the United States as a whole in 1994; the figure for the previous year was 1.9 million (Andreas 1996: 58).
30. Herzog 1992: 9.
31. *Migration News*, August 1999.
32. Weeks 1999: 18.
33. Bersin and Feigin 1998: 286.
34. *Migration News*, February 1997.
35. More generally, many observers have proclaimed that economic globalization and the concomitant growing liberalization of national economies have made national boundaries redundant. See, for example, Ohmae 1995.
36. Herzog 1992: 5–6.
37. U.S. INS 1997: 14.
38. *The San Diego Union* 1991b.
39. For an explanation of the term *militarization* as it applies to enforcement efforts along the U.S.-Mexico boundary, see Dunn 1996. See also Palafox 1996.
40. Anthony Giddens describes globalization as "the intensification of worldwide social relations which link distant localities in such a way that local happenings are shaped [implicitly, in part] by events occurring many miles away and vice versa" (Giddens 1990: 64).
41. See Appadurai 1990.
42. See Andreas 2000; Carr 1997; Drogin 1996; and King 1998. See also Andreas and Snyder 2000.
43. See, for example, Anderson and O'Dowd 1999; Kolossov and O'Loughlin 1998; Kristof 1959; Paasi 1996; Taylor 1993; and Waterman 1994.
44. See, for example, Friedmann 1994; Galtung 1994; Giddens 1987, Lattimore 1968; and Martinez 1994.
45. Peter Taylor argues that frontiers are a phenomenon of the past. Taylor contends that the globalization of capitalist social relations in the early twentieth century resulted in boundaries replacing frontiers throughout the world (Taylor 1993: 164). While this might be true in many, if not most parts of the word, such an argument overstates the case, largely because the level of penetration of capitalist social relations and/or of the modern nation-state is uneven across space. Thus, in many areas where there are nominal international boundaries, frontier-like divides still persist. See, for example, Rohter 2000. At the same time, "frontiers" at the very least continue to exist in people's minds

and thus inform social practices toward the people and the territories beyond "our" space.

46. These definitions are a synthesis of the work of Prescott 1987 and Taylor 1993.

47. Malcolm Anderson (1996: 10), among others, makes this argument.

48. On "ways of seeing" see Berger 1980.

49. See Sahlins 1989: 4.

50. In terms of the function of control over freedom of movement, see Torpey 2000.

51. I do not want to suggest that the practices of an individual or group associated with these institutions represent some sort of homogenous monolith called "the state." At the same time, the actions of prominent individuals or groups associated with the state apparatus take on a relatively high level of importance given the power of the institutions with which they work. In terms of public discourse, for example, the President of the United States is able to shape the parameters of debate to a far greater extent than almost anyone else in society. For instance, when the president makes a particular public statement, he might not be doing so based on a consensus within the institutions of governance, but rather on the basis of his own narrow political interests. Nevertheless, his words are much more powerful than they would be were he, say, a human rights activist. This is due to the advantage his position in the state apparatus affords. For this reason, I would categorize him, in all instances, as a state actor. Similarly, I also classify politicians from the two major parties running for elected office as state actors—again, because they have privileged access to the public bully pulpit and are thus able to shape social discourse to a disproportionate degree.

Of course, this agenda-setting ability is not limited only to individuals associated with the state apparatus (as defined above). Members of the socioeconomic and political elite classes can also do so. Examples might include business tycoons and religious leaders with strong organizational and institutional backing. For reasons of simplicity, however, I do not treat such individuals as state actors, but rather as nonstate actors.

52. The working definition of *nation* employed herein is a synthesis mainly of the work of Peter Taylor (1993) and Anthony Giddens (1987).

53. Michael Ignatieff (1994) calls this type of nationalism "civic nationalism."

54. Hobsbawm 1991: 5–6. In terms of contemporary parlance, the term *nation* is often synonymous with the modern territorial state. As Murphy (1996: 104) contends, by the 1950s most social scientists were employing the term *nation-state* to mean "any so-called sovereign state, no matter how ethnically or nationally heterogeneous that state might be."

55. Gutiérrez 1995: 254, note 64.

56. Huspek 1997; Neuman 1995; van Dijk 1996; and Willoughby 1997.

57. In analyzing the "illegal" immigrant, I focus on unauthorized boundary crossers and largely ignore visa overstayers, a very significant source of "illegals" but which as a group does not attract anywhere near the level of popular and official concern as unauthorized boundary crossers.

58. As Ho and Marshall (1997: 210) argue, we need to ask not only what constitutes criminality, illegitimacy, illegality, and savagery, but also how and why the powerful have categorized these issues as problematic." If we fail to do so, we run the risk of allowing the powerful to define our "problems" and, thus, our political priorities for us.

59. This trade-off also helps to explain why the INS has dedicated the lion's share of its enforcement resources to efforts along the U.S.-Mexico boundary, rather than on interior (worksite) enforcement.

60. Andreas 2000: 76.

CHAPTER 2

1. Ross 1998: 27.
2. Williams 1981: 156.
3. Knight 1994.
4. Murphy 1991.
5. Vázquez and Meyer 1985: 13–15; and Martínez 1995: 8–10.
6. The United States formally annexed the territory two years later as part of its war with England, as Spain had entered into an anti-Napoleon alliance with Great Britain (Vázquez and Meyer 1985: 16).
7. Vázquez and Meyer 1985: 16; and Griswold del Castillo 1990: 8–11. Proponents of this assertion justified it on the basis of French claims during eighteenth century boundary disputes with Spain (Griswold del Castillo 1990: 11).
8. Ross 1998: 28. Sullivan first employed the term in 1845 (Takaki 1993: 176).
9. Acuña 1988: 6.
10. Vázquez and Meyer 1985: 21. Rodolfo Acuña traces the origins of Manifest Destiny back to the country's Puritan roots, noting, "According to the Puritan ethic, salvation is determined by God. The establishment of the City of God on earth is not only the duty of those chosen people predestined for salvation but is also the proof of their state of grace. Anglo-Americans believed that God had made them custodians of democracy and that they had a mission—that is, that they were predestined to spread its principles. . . . Many citizens believed that God had destined them to own and occupy all of the land from ocean to ocean and pole to pole. Their mission, their destiny made manifest, was to spread the principles of democracy and Christianity to the unfortunates of the hemisphere" (Acuña 1988: 13). Indeed, as Representative David Trimble proclaimed in castigating Secretary of State John Quincy Adams for abandoning U.S claims to Texas, "the Great Engineer of the Universe has fixed the natural limits of our country and man cannot change them!" (Weinberg 1963: 55). For a thorough analysis of manifest destiny as an ideology, see Weinberg 1963.
11. Vázquez and Meyer 1985: 23. According to John Ross (1998: 27), the subtext of the doctrine "was merely the military and mercantile domination of the Americas." Subsequent U.S. behavior toward Mexico would seem to substantiate Ross's contention.
12. Quoted in Takaki 1993: 173.
13. For an account of the war, see Williams 1981, chapter 8. U.S. troops often committed great atrocities (see Takaki 1993: 175).
14. The annexation of California was undoubtedly one of the principle objectives of the U.S. war effort against Mexico. As Ronald Takaki (1993: 172) explains,

    This territory was an important source of raw material for the Market Revolution: it exported cattle hides to New England, where Irish factory laborers manufactured boots and shoes. California was also the site of strategic harbors. Sperm oil from whales was a crucial fuel and lubricant in the economy of the Market Revolution, and the American whaling industry was sending its ships to the Pacific Ocean. The ports of California were needed for repairs and supplies. Moreover, policymakers wanted to promote American trade with the Pacific rim. In a message to Congress, President James K. Polk explained that California's harbors "would afford shelter for our navy, for our numerous whale ships, and other merchant vessels employed in the Pacific ocean, and would in a short period become the marts of an extensive and profitable commerce with China, and other countries of the East."

15. For the full text of the treaty, see Martínez 1996 or Griswold del Castillo 1990.
16. Martínez 1995: 11–14; Ross 1998: 30, 35–36; Takaki 1993: 172–76; and Williams 1981: 148–56; also see map, appendix D. For some U.S. expansionists, however, the gains embodied by the Treaty of Guadalupe Hidalgo were not enough. The United States should, so the argument went, exploit its position of strength and take all of Mexico. As the "all Mexico" idea spread through elite

U.S. opinion, Mexico became increasingly worried and seized the opportunity to sign the treaty, thus keeping at least half of its territory. At the same time, however, serious opposition to the "all Mexico" movement had developed in the United States among Polk's political opponents. Some even opposed it on the basis of race, fearing that the extension of U.S. citizenship to dark-skinned Mexicans would undermine the United States. Furthermore, U.S. efforts to gain more territory from Mexico would have most probably resulted in a continuation of the war (Martínez 1995: 15–16; and Acuña 1988: 19).

17. Vélez-Ibáñez 1997: 57–58. In making this claim, Vélez-Ibáñez cites David J. Weber, *Myth and the History of the Hispanic Southwest*, Albuquerque: University of New Mexico Press, 1988: 117.
18. Sack 1986: 19.
19. The term *pacification* has not always had the negative connotations that it now seems to have. Prior to the rise of European expansionism, for example, the term appeared between 1460 and 1483 in English, French, and Spanish to signify "the ending of war, assuaging of discontented parties and negotiating of settlements" (Dunkerley 1994: 3). European imperialism, however, gave a new meaning to the term. Michael Aung-Thwin, for example, in discussing Sir Charles Crosthwaite's *Pacification of Burma*, argues that the term implied "the forceful, militarily achieved suppression of organized, large-scale, armed resistance to what was defined as British rule" as well as the successful extension of administrative rule throughout the pacified territory (Aung-Thwin 1985: 246).
20. Giddens 1987: 329.
21. Mann 1984: 185–89.
22. Jardine 1996: 398–99.
23. See Carey 1998.
24. Acuña (1988: 6) defines a filibuster as "an adventurer who engages in insurrectionist or revolutionary activity in a foreign country." Much of such activity was aimed at gaining territory for the United States.
25. Martínez 1995: 38–43.
26. With about 160,000 Indians living near the U.S. side of the boundary, many of whom, especially the Apaches and Comanches, having a long history of raiding towns on the Mexican side of the boundary, U.S. control of border Indians was an expensive proposition. The United States placed 8,000 troops in the border area to enforce its obligations under Treaty of Guadalupe Hidalgo. U.S. military expenditures from 1848 to 1853 were $12 million in the territory of New Mexico alone (Griswold del Castillo 1990: 59).
27. The Isthmus of Tehuántepec is the narrowest part of Mexico, south of Veracruz.
28. Martínez 1995: 17–21, 43; and Griswold del Castillo 1990: 55–61; see also the map, appendix D of this volume.
29. Martínez 1995: 44–46, 51. Porfirio Díaz ruled Mexico from 1876 to 1910. For an analysis of his reign, see Ross 1998, chapter 4.
30. Dunn 1996: 6.
31. Dunn 1996: 7.
32. Dunn 1996: 8.
33. Martínez 1995.
34. Many of the U.S. Army forts constructed during this time later became modern military bases (Dunn 1996: 7). Fort Bliss in El Paso is one such example.
35. Martínez 1995: 58–59; and Dunn 1996: 7.
36. Martínez 1995: 60–62.
37. Martínez 1995: 62; see also Nadelmann 1993: 69–76.
38. See Dunn 1996: 9–10.
39. Taylor 1993: 157–59.
40. Nadelmann 1993: 64.
41. Nadelmann 1993: 63.

42. Nadelmann 1993: 62–63.
43. Torpey 2000: 18
44. Torpey 2000; see also Harris 1995 and Herzog 1990.
45. Grebler 1966: 19.
46. Grebler 1966: 19.
47. But as Gerald Neuman (1993) argues, it is incorrect that boundaries of the U.S. were thus open until the late nineteenth century as states attempted to regulate immigration through the implementation of qualitative criteria. U.S. Supreme Court decisions of 1849 and 1875, however, declared all such laws unconstitutional, interpreting them as attempts by states to regulate foreign commerce, a function of the federal government (INS 1991: 4).
48. See appendix E.
49. Perkins 1978: 9.
50. Coppock 1968: 1. The new group of "mounted watchmen" never numbered more than seventy-six; their small numbers combined with their lack of training made the force "woefully inadequate to cope with the illegal entry problem" (Coppock 1968: 2).
51. Commissioner-General of Immigration 1903: 62–63.
52. Gordon 1999: 48.
53. Sánchez 1993: 51.
54. Coppock 1968: 2.
55. Paradoxically, there were occurrences of unprecedented transboundary cooperation during that time. U.S. authorities, for example, authorized Mexican officials in mid-1912 to search passengers (for antigovernment activists) on streetcars leaving El Paso, Texas for Ciudad Juárez across the international boundary. But this practice did not last long as U.S. authorities responded to public outcry against Mexican officials searching U.S. citizens in American territory (Nadelmann 1993: 79).
56. Sánchez 1993: 54–56.
57. Legal immigration thus declined from 90,000 in 1924 to 32,378 the year following the implementation of the 1924 Act (Sánchez 1993: 57).
58. Sánchez 1993: 56–59. The acting supervising inspector of the Immigration Service in El Paso described the ports of entry west of El Paso in 1917 as places "where an imaginary line alone separates the two countries, and where one side of the street is in Mexican territory, and the other in American territory, with people crossing to and fro, practically at all hours, and for all manner of purposes" (NARA file 54261/276, June 6, 1917). Such a situation would hardly seem to facilitate the effective regulation of boundary crossing.
59. Coppock 1968: 1–2 and INS 1991: 23; see also Wixon 1934.
60. Galarza 1964: 61.
61. Coppock 1968: 2.
62. See NARA file 54261/267.
63. Coppock 1968: 2–4, and INS 1991: 9–11.
64. Coppock 1968: 4–6 and INS 1991: 23.
65. See Wixon 1934 for a description by an INS official of the nature of the Border Patrol and the challenges faced by the agency in the early 1930s.
66. Coppock 1968: 9–10; INS 1991: 23; Dunn 1996: 12; and Wixon 1934: 6.
67. See Balderrama and Rodríguez 1995.
68. That said, in all probability the size of the Border Patrol did not increase as quickly as Congress intended. In Fiscal Year 1944, for example, the authorized size of the Border Patrol was around 1,300 officers, but the average actual force only numbered 997 officers "as inductions of patrol inspectors into the armed forces and the increasing difficulty of recruiting qualified personnel made it impossible to keep the force at its authorized strength" (Harrison 1944: 21).
69. Dunn 1996: 13; and Coppock 1968: 11–12.
70. Wixon 1934: 8.

71. Wilmoth 1934: 6.
72. Wilmoth 1934: 6–7, 9.
73. Grebler 1966: 19; see also Pitt 1966.
74. In 1900, Texas had an immigrant population of 71,062; Arizona had 14,172; California had 8,096; and New Mexico had 6,649 Mexican immigrants (McWilliams 1968: 163).
75. Cornelius 1978: 14. See also the map, appendix B of this volume.
76. Sánchez 1993: 39.
77. Cornelius 1978: 14.
78. Sánchez 1993: 39; see also Guerin-Gonzales 1994, chapter 2.
79. Grebler 1966: 8.
80. Dunn 1996: 11.
81. Balderrama and Rodríguez 1995: 6–7.
82. Grebler 1966: 20.
83. Grebler 1966: 20–21, and Cornelius 1978: 14–15.
84. Grebler 1966: 21, and Cornelius 1978: 15.
85. Balderrama and Rodríguez 1995: 7.
86. Cornelius 1978: 15–16.
87. Cornelius 1978: 15–16.
88. Balderrama and Rodríguez 1995: 17; see also Roberts 1928b and 1928c. One grower explained his opposition to the proposed restrictions in 1928 as follows: "We have no Chinamen, we have no Japs. The Hindu is worthless, the Filipino is nothing, and the white man will not do the work" (Balderrama and Rodríguez 1995: 17).
89. Balderrama and Rodríguez 1995: 52–53.
90. Cornelius 1978: 16–17; and Cockcroft 1986: 61. The term *bracero* comes from the Spanish word for "arm," *brazo*. *Bracero* thus refers to a manual laborer.
    According to Kitty Calavita (1992: 1–2), "What came to be called the Bracero Program was in fact a series of programs initiated by administrative fiat, subsequently endorsed by Congress, and kept alive by executive agreement whenever foreign relations or domestic politics threatened their demise."
    From 1942 to 1947, the Bracero Program provided more than 219,000 workers to agricultural employers. California farms employed 63 percent of the braceros during the regular growing season and 90 percent of the braceros in the off-season (January–April) (Calavita 1992: 20–21). The U.S. Congress officially ended the wartime Bracero Program at the end of 1947, but, in tandem with various federal agencies, continued it in various forms until 1964. During the twenty-two years of the Bracero Program, U.S. authorities contracted out five million braceros to growers and ranchers in twenty-four states.
91. See Espenshade 1995, and U.S. GAO 1997b.
92. Grebler 1966: 32.
93. In 1947, for example, a year when relatively few braceros were imported, the INS instituted a de facto legalization program for "illegal" Mexican immigrants discovered working in agriculture, contracting them out to employers as braceros. This informal legalization program continued to be an integral part of the Bracero Program for several years (Calavita 1992: 24–25).
94. Calavita 1992: 28.
95. Calavita 1992: 47–50. Senator Pat McCarran, Chair of the Senate Subcommittee on Internal Security, for example, argued in 1951 that there were as many as five million "illegal aliens" in the U.S., including "vast numbers of 'militant Communists, Sicilian bandits and other criminals'" that could potentially serve as a "fifth column" for an enemy country. A year later, McCarran argued that communists and spies often posed as farmworkers and frequently traveled back and forth across the U.S.-Mexico boundary. Such hysterics were not limited to the far right as liberals such as Hubert Humphrey joined the calls during the

1950s for a crackdown, in the name of national security, on "illegal" immigrants entering from Mexico (Calavita 1992: 47–50).

96. Dunn 1996: 14.
97. Calavita 1992: 50–56.
98. Cornelius 1978: 17–18.
99. The name "Texas Proviso" was a result of the fact that the exemption was a concession to growers in Texas.
100. Calavita 1992: 66–70.
101. See, for example, Cockcroft 1986.
102. The INS did not hide the fact that it assisted in facilitating the employment of "illegal" immigrants. As one INS official testified to Congress in 1951 regarding the process of "drying out" unauthorized immigrants, "We do feel we have the authority to permit to remain in the United States aliens who are here as agricultural workers whether they are here legally or not" (Galarza 1964: 63).
103. Samora 1971: 48. An analysis of the Border Patrol from 1951 relates the following story to illustrate this argument: As Samora quotes, " 'One [INS] Inspector laughingly tells of the reaction of a local farmer to his suggestion that the Border Patrol retire a hundred miles north and allow wetbacks free access to the Valley. 'Don't do that,' the farmer said. 'In a week they'd be overrunning the place, camping on our lawns, swarming everywhere. And there wouldn't be enough local police to handle them. What we want of the Border Patrol is to let in enough wetbacks for us to get our crops harvested and to keep the others out' " (Lyle Saunders and Olen E. Leonard, "The Wetback in the Lower Rio Grande Valley of Texas," Inter-American Education—Occasional Paper 4, University of Texas-Austin, 1951: 82, quoted in Samora 1971: 49).
104. Calavita 1994: 60. Calavita provides some examples in this regard:

> The chief inspector at Tucson reported that he "received orders from the District Director at El Paso each harvest to stop deporting illegal Mexican labor" (Kirstein 1973: 90). During World War II, the INS Director in Los Angeles explained to the Department of Labor that it was INS policy not to check farms and ranches for illegal aliens while harvest work was being done (Calavita 1992: 33). In 1949, the Idaho State Employment Service reported, "The United States Immigration and Naturalization Service recognizes the need for farm workers in Idaho and . . . withholds its search and deportation until such times as there is not a shortage of farm workers" (quoted in President's Commission on Migratory Labor 1951: 76). The implicit message from Congress was consistent with this laissez-faire approach. As one observer put it, Congress was "splendidly indifferent" to the rising number of illegals, reducing the Border Patrol budget just as undocumented migration increased (Hadley 1956: 334).

105. Galarza 1964: 61.
106. Galarza 1964: 61.
107. Calavita 1994: 61.
108. See appendix F.
109. Thus, for example, the Immigration Act of March 20, 1952, made illegal for the first time the transportation of "illegal entrant aliens" and empowered INS officials to enter *private* lands (but not dwellings) within 25 miles of the international boundary "for the purpose of patrolling the border to prevent the illegal entry of aliens" (Coppock 1968: 7–8).
110. Martinez 1995: 125–27.

CHAPTER 3

1. Said 1993: 3.
2. Conversi 1995; Kearney 1991; Manzo 1996; and Paasi 1996.
3. Herzog 1990: 99–101.

4. Herzog 1990: 101–4; see also chapter 5 of this volume. For the definitive history of the marginalization of the Californios, see Pitt 1966.
5. Herzog 1990: 104.
6. Starr 1997: 90–91.
7. Herzog 1990: 114–15.
8. Herzog 1990: 91–92.
9. Herzog 1990: 92–93; and Martínez 1995: 111.
10. Chamberlin 1951: 43.
11. Martínez 1995: 111–13.
12. Herzog 1990: 95.
13. Herzog 1990: 95–97.
14. Proffitt 1988: 259.
15. See map, appendix A.
16. Herzog 1990: 97–98 and Proffitt 1988: 321–29; see also Price 1973: 49–53 and Ruiz 2000: chapter 3.
17. See Balderrama and Rodríguez 1995.
18. Southern Californians depended on Tijuana for more than recreational reasons. World War II led to the rationing and unavailability of all sorts of goods in the United States. For example, many on the U.S. side of the boundary crossed into Tijuana to purchase rationed items such as sugar, meat, gasoline, and tires where they were relatively plentiful. The halt in production of many manufactured goods in the United States during the war also led to many going to Tijuana to purchase such items, including alarm clocks (Martis 1970: 42).
19. Herzog 1990: 98–99; Price 1973: 55–59; Proffitt 1988: 259; Piñera Ramírez 1983: 539–40; and Vázquez and Meyer 1985: 147–49.
20. Martínez 1994: 25.
21. Buffington 1994: 28–31.
22. Arreola and Curtis 1993: 26–27.
23. Sklair 1993; Arreola and Curtis 1993: 28–29; and Herzog 1990: 53. By 1970, the only Mexican border cities whose population growth was due more to migration than natural increase were Reynosa (across the boundary from McAllen, Texas) and Tijuana, the latter a testament to California's tremendous growth (Arreola and Curtis 1993: 30).
24. Herzog 1990: 48–49.
25. Herzog 1990: 52–53.
26. Herzog 1990: 56–57.
27. Price 1973: 175–79.
28. Proffitt 1988: 451.
29. Proffitt 1988: 452–53.
30. Buffington 1994: 30.
31. Buffington 1994: 31.
32. Buffington 1994: 32.
33. Buffington 1994: 37.
34. Buffington 1994: 37–38.
35. The earliest cooperation between the United States and Mexico in environmental matters in the border region was in the early part of the twentieth century. There are now international treaties regulating riparian use and water allocation between the two countries.
36. Water quality—more specifically, sewage emanating from Tijuana—was, until recently, a major issue and point of tension between San Diego and Tijuana (Proffitt 1988: 457–60).
37. Zelinsky 1988: 175.
38. Griswold del Castillo 1990: 187–88.
39. Lesley 1930: 4–5.
40. Lesley 1930: 10–14; see also Davidson 1934a.
41. Lesley 1930: 15. According to a June 19, 1851 report in the *San Diego Herald*, the

commission placed the first boundary monument on the Pacific coast to mark the beginning of the division between the United States and Mexico in June 1851 (Davidson 1934b). Perhaps this monument was the permanent one, as opposed to temporary ones set up during the initial marking of the boundary.

42. Griswold del Castillo 1990: 39.

43. Griswold del Castillo 1990: 39–40.

44. *The San Diego Union* 1871.

45. The main source of customs revenue for the United States was from Mexican cattle stock. Taxes on goods brought by ship through the port of San Diego were also important. Through the late 1800s, smuggling was of serious concern to U.S authorities. Mexican cattle, cigars, tequila, and abalone were among the more noteworthy objects of smuggling (Brown 1991: 10–12).

46. Price 1973: 46, and Martis 1970: 29.

47. Brown 1991: 17–19.

48. Taylor H. 1994: 46–47; this source also discusses the different extralegal methods used by Chinese migrants to enter the United States following the passage of the Chinese Exclusion Act.

49. Proffitt 1988: 422–23.

50. See map, appendix A.

51. Brown 1991: 66.

52. Logan 1969: 72.

53. NARA file 55921/971.

54. There were thirty-five soldiers assigned to the border station in San Ysidro as of January 1918, their duty being "to assist in guarding the border in the vicinity of Tia Juana, Cal., and to temporarily taking care of persons arrested for violations of the draft law, passport regulations, etc." Letter from Inspector in Charge, Tia Juana, California, to Supervising Inspector, Immigration Service, El Paso, Texas, January 9, 1918. Copy of letter on file with author.

55. Martis 1970: 32 and NARA file 54261/276, February 5, 1918.

56. Logan 1969: 72 and NARA file 55853/300. There were two Border Patrol subdistricts in southern California at the time, one centered in Chula Vista (in between San Ysidro and the city of San Diego) and one in El Centro (about 115 miles east of San Diego and just north of the U.S. border town of Calexico) of Calexico. In the case of the Chula Vista subdistrict (today known as the San Diego Sector of the U.S. Border Patrol), there were thirty-two patrol inspectors, one chief patrol inspector, and seven senior patrol inspectors.

57. See NARA file 55853/320, June 5, 1940.

58. NARA file 55853/320, December 2, 1940.

59. Martis 1970: 42.

60. NARA file 55853/320b.

61. It is not possible to know for certain without documentation, but it is probably safe to assume at the very least that, similar to the trend on the national scale (see appendix F), the level of staffing reached by the early 1940s in the San Diego area was roughly the level maintained through the 1960s, with a slight decline during the period of the mid-1940s to the mid-1950s. It is also possible (and perhaps probable) that staffing in the area of San Diego increased at a much more rapid rate than that of the country as a whole as a disproportionately high number (and increasingly so) of the unauthorized immigration crossing the U.S.-Mexico boundary passed through the San Diego section of the boundary.

   According to *The San Diego Union* (1954), the Chula Vista sector had 105 agents just prior to the beginning of "Operation Wetback" in 1954, with another 137 assigned there for the operation.

62. *The San Diego Union* 1936.

63. U.S. Senate Subcommittee on Immigration and Naturalization 1948: 7. At the same hearing, local officials admitted that at that time even a conviction on a

charge of migrant smuggling resulted most often in a very light (suspended) sentence, despite the illegal nature of unauthorized entry into the United States (U.S. Senate Subcommittee on Immigration and Naturalization 1948: 8).

For photos of the boundary fence along the westernmost portion of the boundary in the late 1950s, see Ryan 1958.

64. NARA file 56364/44.15.
65. Cornelius 1978: 18.
66. Doty 1996a and 1996b.
67. Richmond 1994.
68. Sánchez 1993: 59.
69. Ruiz 2000: 21.
70. Sánchez 1993: 61.
71. Sánchez 1993: 62.
72. McWilliams 1968: 60.
73. Bustamente 1973: 269.
74. Bustamente 1972: 708–9. Technically it would seem that an "illegal" would have been anyone that did not pass through an immigration checkpoint along the U.S.-Mexico border and did not meet the qualitative standards imposed by the immigration laws beginning in 1875.
75. U.S. INS 1953: 459–61; see also Gómez-Quiñones 1981: 25.
76. Heyman 1991: 120.
77. Rotella 1998: 26; and Martis 1970: 41.
78. Martínez 1995: 119–21.
79. Martis 1970: 47.
80. See Garcia 1968, Long 1968, and Grant 1970.
81. See Guerin-Gonzales 1994: 84–92.
82. This process of "social spatialization" (Paasi 1995, 1996) often had an overtly racist aspect to it. As Edwin Tilton, the assistant superintendent of San Diego's school system, stated in explaining his opinion that Mexican students were of inferior intelligence, "He is inferior; an inferior race, no doubt. . . . The Mexicans are slow to learn" (Guerin-Gonzales 1994: 69).
83. See chapter 5 for an analysis of media coverage surrounding the operation.
84. Analysis based on author's review of newspaper archives.
85. The actual port of entry into the United States from Tijuana is in San Ysidro, a small community sixteen miles south of downtown San Diego. (San Ysidro remained the only official port of entry into San Diego until the 1980s.) Until 1957, San Ysidro was separate from San Diego, but in that year the city annexed the community. San Ysidro's economic well-being was long tied to that of Tijuana and San Diego, but with the outlawing of gambling in Tijuana in 1936, San Ysidro's economic fortunes declined. The poverty of the area, its proximity to the boundary, and the fact that a solid majority of the population was Mexican American all contributed to an overall negative opinion of San Ysidro by San Diegans. While many in San Ysidro (both Anglos and Mexican Americans) wanted to join San Diego, many in San Diego also wanted to annex the territory. Many San Diegans saw the annexation of San Ysidro as a way of better exploiting the area's tourist potential and gaining greater control over the border region given their concerns with drug trafficking across the border and the crossing of the boundary by U.S. minors into Tijuana (Kurtz 1973: 10). See also Herzog 1990: 180–84 for an historical overview of the development of San Ysidro.
86. *The San Diego Union* 1958; and Martis 1970: 45. Concerns about southern California youths drinking in Tijuana continue today, with U.S. authorities at times policing the boundary to ensure that unaccompanied, underage teenagers do not venture into Tijuana. As a 1998 news report related, "In a flip-flop of usual border enforcement practices, U.S. officials have imposed a high-profile spring

break crackdown on southbound travelers—stopping teenagers under 18 at the border and turning them back by the hundreds" (Ellingwood 1998a: A1).

87. *The San Diego Union* 1959.
88. NARA file 56364/43.1.
89. Gutiérrez 1996: 255–56; see also Ruiz 2000.
90. Efforts by U.S. authorities to stem the flow to Tijuana of American pleasure seekers by closing the boundary at 9:00 P.M. only served to boost demand for overnight accommodations in Tijuana, thus further fueling the Mexican border town's booming economy.
91. Proffitt 1988: 423–27; and Herzog 1990: 97–98; see also Price 1973: 49–53.
92. Barry 1994: 55.
93. See Beckett 1997.
94. Barry 1994: 64.
95. *The San Diego Union* 1957; see also *The San Diego Union* 1960a and 1960b.
96. Long 1968.
97. Barry 1994: 64.
98. McHugh 1969; see also Clance 1969.
99. See O'Connor 1969 and Price 1973: 111–16.
100. Liberal advocacy groups also contributed to this trend. James Lorenz, the associate director of the California Rural Legal Assistance Program, for example, testified to a U.S. Senate subcommittee on August 8, 1969, stating that Nixon's attorney general had "'a law and order crisis right in his own office' because of the Justice Department's failure to stem the flood of illegal alien farmworkers" (Porter 1969). César Chávez and the United Farm Workers also often argued for stronger boundary enforcement measures to stem the influx of unauthorized immigrants who were a seemingly endless source of strikebreakers for growers the UFW was fighting. During farmworker strikes in California and Texas from 1965 to 1970, the UFW often organized demonstrations against the INS, which the union accused of colluding with growers in their use of unauthorized and authorized (green card holders) immigrants as strikebreakers. This position of Chávez and the UFW continued until the mid-1970s when the union and its leaders came under strong criticism from a variety of Chicano and Mexican-American groups. By 1976, the UFW went on record as supporting the rights of unauthorized immigrants and made special efforts to organize them into the UFW (Griswold del Castillo 1992: 36–41; see also Gutiérrez 1995: 196–99).

CHAPTER 4

1. Hall 1988: 21.
2. Letter to the Editor, the *New York Times*, October 15, 1994.
3. This is an example of the process of social spatialization—the process by which the social construction of the spatial takes place within a collective imagination and, physically, on the landscape (Paasi 1995 and 1996).
4. See Sahlins 1989.
5. Edmonston 1990 and Espenshade and Calhoun 1993.
6. The following account illustrates the level of ignorance surrounding the U.S.-Mexico boundary in the 1970s:

> Former El Paso Rep. Richard White remembers it as one of the worst experiences during his eighteen years in the House. He was speaking to the House Armed Services Committee about the needs of El Paso's Fort Bliss when a committee member stopped him.
> The question hurt. "Is El Paso in the United States or Mexico?" the congressman wanted to know. (Bob Duke, "Border Ignored: Congressmen Fight Nationwide Indifference," Special Report on the Border, *El Paso Herald-Post*, Summer 1983, 8–9, reprinted in Martínez 1996.)

White served in Congress from 1965–1983.

7. Dunn 1996: 17–18. U.S. academics such as Arthur Corwin helped raise the specter of irredentism. Corwin sent a letter to Secretary of State Henry Kissinger in 1975 claiming that the United States was becoming a "welfare reservation." Corwin called upon the United States to deploy the military along the boundary and upon Congress to appropriate $1 billion to the INS so that it could hire an additional 50,000 Border Patrol agents. He also advocated the construction of an electrified fence along the boundary (Acuña 1988: 374–75).

8. See Muller 1997.

9. Dunn 1996: 18; Walters 1990: 10; Fernandez and Pedroza 1982; Cardenas 1979: 83; and Lewis 1979: 137–41.

10. Chapman assumed the position of INS commissioner in December 1973.

11. Acuña 1996: 115.

12. Ostrow 1974.

13. Cockcroft 1986: 39.

14. Quoted in Rico 1992: 261.

15. Fernández and Pedroza 1982: 3.

16. Acuña 1988: 374.

17. Cardenas 1979: 72.

18. *New York Times* 1974.

19. Chapman 1976: 190, emphasis in the original. The use of such statistics has great potential for abuse and is often a tool to realize narrow political goals. As Gilbert Cardenas (1979: 79) argues, "The widespread use and flagrant abuse of public data as a means of realizing policy and strategy stand out as a prominent feature of administrative action. Most Americans are not familiar with illegal alien migration, most do not know illegals and most do not feel intimidated by the presence of illegal aliens. Outside of the border region and its communities and specific types of agricultural and industrial enterprises, illegals pose no serious problems to the American people" (1979: 79).

20. Ardman 1974: 6. According to the 1981 final report of the U.S. Select Commission on Immigration and Refugee Policy, "Mexican nationals probably account for less than half of the undocumented/illegal population" (U.S. Select Commission 1981: 36).

21. Walters 1990: 16.

22. Diamond 1996: 159.

23. Calavita 1996: 289.

24. Gutiérrez 1995: 189. California Assemblyman Dixon Arnett sponsored the legislation. Regarding the legislation's effects, see McVicar 1971 and Calavita 1982. By mid-1978, fourteen states and Puerto Rico had passed similar legislation (Lewis 1979: 168).

25. In 1975, the first amnesty provision was attached to the House of Representatives' employer sanctions bill. Public opinion polls have consistently shown that the majority of Americans oppose amnesty for the undocumented. Nevertheless, the provision was instrumental in garnering votes for the reform effort, both from liberal advocates of immigrants' rights and from members of Congress concerned with offsetting the effects of employer sanctions and stabilizing the labor supply (Calavita 1994: 66).

26. Calavita 1994: 65–66.

27. Bernstein 1977.

28. Dunn 1996: 36 and Gutiérrez 1995: 200. Carter's election took place with overwhelming support from Mexican Americans, who expected him to address immigration issues in a manner sympathetic to the perspective of Mexican-American and Chicano civil rights advocates. Thus many of them were shocked when Carter announced his administration's immigration plan in the summer of 1977 based on assumptions that differed little from that of his predecessors and closely resembled that of Rodino (Gutiérrez 1995: 200).

29. Quoted in Gutiérrez 1995: 200.

30. Calavita 1994: 66.
31. U.S. Select Commission 1981: xi. According to Timothy Dunn, the commission conducted its deliberations and investigations largely within the framework of border control and national security. Not surprisingly, the commission framed its final report in terms of the "national interest" and emphasized law enforcement in its final recommendations. Dunn argues that the national interest is "roughly analogous or at least directly related to the concept of national security" (Dunn 1996: 36).
32. The Select Commission's final report did not actually come out until the beginning of the Reagan administration in 1981.
33. U.S. Select Commission 1981: 35.
34. U.S. Select Commission 1981: 339.
35. Also see Martin 1994: 95. This argument would reemerge more than a decade later as an important assumption underlying the immigration and boundary enforcement policies of the Clinton administration.
36. U.S. Select Commission 1981: 46–47.
37. U.S. Select Commission 1981: 60; see also page 82.
38. The Mariel boatlift took place between April 20 and September 26, 1980 (Zucker and Zucker 1996).
39. Dunn 1996: 36–37.
40. Zucker and Zucker 1996: 62–63.
41. Dunn 1996: 37.
42. Calavita 1994: 66–68.
43. Dunn 1996: 36–41.
44. Dunn 1996: 41–42.
45. Quoted in Morganthau 1984: 18.
46. Quoted in Dunn 1996: 2. A report on Reagan's speech in the June 21, 1983 edition of *The Washington Post* contained the quote.
47. Dunn 1996: 42–45.
48. Dunn 1996: 53–61; see also Palafox 1996.
49. Dunn 1996: 91.
50. Dunn 1996: 91–92; see also Kahn 1996: 11–14. Silvestre Reyes, at the time chief Border Patrol agent of the McAllen Sector, which is responsible for the Rio Grande Valley, states that the operation was called Operation Hold-the-Line and was the strategic blueprint for the Operation Hold-the-Line that he launched as chief Border Patrol agent in the El Paso Sector in September 1993 (interview with Reyes 1996; see also Zucker and Zucker 1996: 99).
51. Dunn 1996: 63–64.
52. According to Peter Nunez, who served as U.S. Attorney for southern California from April 1982 through August 1988, the Reagan administration arrived in office with a strong interest in boundary enforcement, largely due to drug trafficking, but this inevitably led to the matter of unauthorized immigration. Reagan's attorney general, Edwin Meese, had spent a number of years in San Diego and would frequently visit the area and bring congresspeople with him. In this manner, the Reagan administration played an important role in raising awareness of boundary enforcement issues (interview with Nunez, 1997).
    At the start of the Reagan administration, a maximum of 450 Border Patrol agents were "directly engaged in activities to stop persons attempting to enter the United States without inspection" at any one particular time, despite an increase between 1969 and 1979 in permanent work years for the Border Patrol of 42.4 percent—a time during which Border Patrol apprehensions increased by 414.5 percent (U.S. Select Commission 1981: 48).
53. Most interestingly, the Bush-Reagan drug war focused its efforts largely on the boundary in between the official ports of entry despite the admission by the Drug Enforcement Agency that about 85 percent of illegal drugs entering the

United States arrived through official ports of entry by land, sea, or air (Dunn 1996: 105).

54. Dunn 1996: 103. The most recent (and ongoing) war on drugs in the U.S.-Mexico border region has its roots in the Reagan administration's South Florida Task Force on Organized Crime, established in 1982. Around that time, drug trafficking was increasing in the U.S.-Mexico border region. Thus, one year later, the administration extended the Florida model to the Southwest border region under the name of the National Narcotics Border Interdiction System (NNBIS), headed by then Vice President George Bush. The NNBIS acted as a coordinating agency between the Department of Defense and civilian law enforcement agencies engaged in anti-drug-trafficking efforts along the U.S.-Mexico boundary (Dunn 1996: 108–11). The border region drug war intensified significantly in 1986 with President Reagan's signing of a secret directive that formally characterized drug trafficking as a "significant threat to national security." In doing so, Reagan authorized a broad expansion of the Pentagon's powers regarding antidrug efforts (Dunn 1996: 103).

The most notable venture of the Reagan-Bush border drug war was Operation Alliance, begun in 1986—the same year Reagan declared drug trafficking a national security threat. Alliance was basically "a more serious attempt to accomplish what the NNBIS had set out to do," and its goal was, according to its senior tactical coordinator, "to interdict the flow of drugs, weapons, *aliens*, currency, and other contraband across the southwest border" (Dunn 1996: 113, emphasis added). Thus, Operation Alliance explicitly blurred the distinction between drug and immigration enforcement activities. Alliance led to a significant increase in the amount of resources and equipment deployed along the U.S.-Mexico boundary and provided much of the organizational infrastructure for law enforcement activities in the border region from 1986 to 1992. Alliance also facilitated increasing cooperation between the U.S. military and civilian law enforcement, thus contributing to the ongoing militarization of the boundary and boundary-related enforcement activities (Dunn 1996: 117; see also pages 118–45).

According to Peter Nunez (interview 1997), Operation Intercept/Operation Cooperation virtually wiped out the growing of marijuana and opium poppies in Mexico. As a result, the number of drug-related border arrests had plummeted in San Diego by 1976. During this time, Columbian drug cartels stepped in and began smuggling through south Florida.

55. Dunn 1996.

56. McVicar 1971; see also Calavita 1982.

57. Interview with Herman Baca 1998; according to Baca, the president of the Committee on Chicano Rights (CCR), there were a variety of issues that the Chicano movement in San Diego took up at the beginning of the 1970s that indicated that matters vis-à-vis the boundary and unauthorized immigration were heating up. At the beginning, most of the issues the Chicano movement took up in the early 1970s focused on individual abuses by immigration authorities, such as the rape of a young woman by a Border Patrol agent in 1972 and other cases of police brutality. The CCR also worked on policy issues, however, one of the first being the Dixon Arnett employer sanctions bill.

According to Baca, the immigration issue began bubbling in the area in 1971. In that year, San Diego County Sheriff Duffy issued a directive to licensed taxi drivers that they had to send a code message to the sheriff's department if they had picked up a "suspected illegal." The CCR put a lot of pressure on Duffy and helped force him to withdraw the directive in 1972. At that time, according to Baca, there was some sort of federal-level decision that the enforcement of immigration laws was the exclusive purview of federal authorities.

All local enforcement agencies in the San Diego area agreed to respect this federal directive except Raymond Hoobler, the chief of the San Diego Police

Department (SDPD), who claimed the right to enforce federal immigration laws. The CCR engaged in a wide variety of activities over a six-year period to compel the SDPD to change its position. Eventually, but for reasons other than the CCR's campaign, Hoobler had to resign in 1978. Some time after that, the SDPD announced that it would not attempt to enforce immigration laws (interview with Baca 1998).

58. See, for example, Parry 1975 and Dillon 1975.
59. *The San Diego Union* 1975.
60. San Diego County Border Task Force 1980.
61. According to Senator Barry Goldwater (R-Arizona), the meeting marked the first time to his knowledge in his 25 years in Congress that a U.S. president had met with members of Congress from the border region (Texas, New Mexico, Arizona, and California) to discuss boundary-related problems (Cary 1977: A-17).
62. Cary 1977.
63. Murphy 1977a.
64. So-called border bandits were usually from Mexico and would attack unauthorized immigrants on the U.S. side of the boundary and then flee back into Tijuana.
65. See Wambaugh 1984 for an account of the brief, one-year history of the SDPD's Border Alien Robbery Force (BARF). The book focuses on: (1) BARF's efforts to combat crime by Mexican bandits (and sometimes Mexican police) against "pollos" on the U.S. side of the boundary; and (2) the devastating effects participation in BARF had on the squad's members. While the book has a certain soap-opera aspect to it, it is valuable for its description of the traumatic experiences faced by migrants who, unprotected, were traveling through the canyons of San Ysidro to reach the United States. In the process, they exposed themselves to ruthless drug addicts, bandits, police, and others who often committed great atrocities against them. In this regard, the book provides further argument for the idea that the very "illegality" of the migrants merely serves to make them vulnerable to a variety of social actors rather than serve as a deterrent to migration. Given the significant changes that have taken place along the boundary since the time of the book, the phenomena it describes no longer apply to the San Ysidro area, although undoubtedly, the exploitation of and violence against unauthorized migrants by unscrupulous individuals and groups continues in other locales on both sides of the U.S.-Mexico boundary.
66. *The San Diego Union* 1977.
67. Williamson 1977.
68. Harrison 1977.
69. Ramos 1978.
70. Murphy 1977b.
71. Murphy 1977c.
72. Ramos 1977.
73. See, for example, Cubbison 1978.
74. Congressman Lionel Van Deerlin of San Diego, for example, opposed the Carter administration's proposal for a new fence (interview with Van Deerlin 1998). Regarding the San Diego City Council, see *The San Diego Union*, 1978.
75. Donner 1979. About 40–50 members from the local branch of the Ku Klux Klan, along with national "grand wizard" David Duke, staged a patrol of the boundary area the following evening. See *The San Diego Union*, 1979.
76. The year 1977 marked the first time Congressman Van Deerlin felt compelled to include questions on unauthorized immigration and boundary enforcement, a strong indication of when public concern in the San Diego area regarding these matters became widespread and noticeable.

   More than 15,000 of Van Deerlin's constituents responded to Van Deerlin's 1977 poll and more than 22,000 answered the 1979 poll. Poll results are taken from the July 1, 1977 and May 21, 1979 editions of Congressman Van Deerlin's "Washington Report," mailed out to his constituents. Congressman Van Deerlin's 42nd district encompassed Imperial Beach, all of south San Diego (which includes the downtown area), National City, Chula Vista, and parts of El Cajon.

77. Lopez 1979: A-4.
78. Interview with Van Deerlin 1998.
79. See *The San Diego Union* 1979.
80. Golden 1980.
81. Samora 1971; and Calavita 1994. Moehring (1988: 292) refers to this phenomenon as a combination of "*de jure* concern" and "*de facto* neglect," and argues that there is a tension between widespread, latent public opinion in favor of reducing illegal immigration and non-latent, organized groups that are opposed to increasing restrictions (such as the U.S. Chamber of Commerce, small business people, and members of the Congressional Hispanic Caucus): "A deft politician can satisfy both parties if he apparently does one thing when he is in fact doing another" (Moehring 1988: 291; see also Harwood 1986: 204). Thus, Moehring contends that anti-illegal immigration legislation, at least in the 1972–1986 period, was a symbolic politics.
82. McMahon 1979.
83. See Standefer and Drehsler 1980a–e.
84. San Diego County Border Task Force 1980.
85. Shore 1986; see also Dillin 1986.
86. Republican Duncan Hunter defeated Lionel Van Deerlin in 1981 and remains in office today. Davis 1986; McDonnell 1986; and Dietrich 1986. The militarization of boundary enforcement in the San Diego region was already underway, however. By April of 1986, for example, U.S. Marines were already working along the boundary in San Diego. While not apprehending unauthorized entrants into the United States, the soldiers were engaging in surveillance. Reportedly, federal authorities sent the marines to the San Diego boundary in response to a request by Congressman Hunter (Dietrich 1986).
87. Braun 1986. Mexican authorities cooperated a number of occasions with U.S. efforts to reduce unauthorized crossings of the boundary. See, for example, Cleeland 1989b and 1989c.
88. Golden and Meyer 1988.
89. Braun, 1987, Briseno and Shore 1989, Cleeland 1989a and 1989d, FAIR 1989, Lait 1989, and Louv 1987.
90. Sahlins 1989: 270–71.
91. I thank Rudy Murillo (1998 interview) for pointing this out to me.
92. Martínez 1994: 48.
93. Chavez 1998.
94. Quoted in Chavez 1998: 17. Quote taken from E. Bailey and H. G. Reza, "An Alien Presence," *Los Angeles Times*, June 5, 1988: 1, 36.
95. See Walker 1988.
96. Wolf 1988: 23.
97. Wolf 1988: 23–24; see also Gorman 1986.
98. Reza 1986.
99. Ott 1986; and interview with Nunez 1997.
100. See *The San Diego Union* 1986.
101. Quoted in Chavez 1998: 20. The quote comes from J. S. Meyer, "Sheriff Urges Posting Marines Along Border," *The San Diego Union*, April 6, 1986: A-3.
102. See map, appendix A.
103. Quoted in Weintraub 1986.
104. Wolf 1988: 13.
105. Chavez 1998.
106. Wolf 1988: 14.

107. Quoted in Wolf 1988: 14–15.
108. Quoted in Hughes 1986.
109. See map, appendix A.
110. Eisenstadt and Thorup 1994: 3–5.
111. Doty 1996a: 185.
112. Chavez 1998: 21, and 74–75; Webster 1990; Portillo 1990c; Novick 1995: 175–81; and Chavira 1990.
113. Shore 1990.
114. Barfield 1989.
115. Portillo 1990a.
116. Quoted in Portillo 1991a: B-2.
117. Interview with De La Viña 1997. There is some disagreement as to whom the credit should go for the establishment of the steel wall/fence. Congressman Duncan Hunter also claims credit (see U.S. Congress 1995: 13–14).
118. Portillo 1991b.
119. Barfield 1991; Portillo 1991b; *The San Diego Union* 1991a; and interview with De La Viña 1997.
120. As Gustavo De La Viña explained in a 1997 interview with the author, Mexican authorities had to be very careful in dealing with the United States on border issues given the sensitivity of the matter in Mexico and a Mexican constitutional ban prohibiting Mexico from impeding its citizens from leaving the country. Thus, Mexican authorities had to avoid giving the impression of working with the Border Patrol to stop migrants and ensure that the focus was on border criminality. For this reason, the San Diego Police Department became the liaison between Grupo Beta and the U.S. Border Patrol.
121. Interview with De La Viña 1997; interview with Olea Garcia 1995; *The San Diego Union* 1991a; see also Rotella 1998.
122. Herzog 1990: 121–22.
123. *Municipios* are the Mexican equivalent of counties in the United States (San Diego Dialogue 1995).
124. San Diego Dialogue 1995: 6, 11.
125. San Diego Dialogue 1995: 11.
126. See, for example, Chaze 1985; Crewdson 1979; Lang 1985; Magnuson 1985; and Starr 1983.
127. Crewdson 1979.
128. Ganster 1997: 261.
129. Showley 1991.
130. Herzog 1990: 183.
131. Showley 1991.
132. Herzog 1990: 183.
133. Martínez 1994: 48.
134. Herzog 1990: 204–205.
135. Tijuana relies far more on San Diego for its economic well-being than does San Diego on Tijuana (Herzog 1990: 145). Indeed, annual per capita income in Tijuana in 1997 was an estimated $3,200 while it was $25,000 in San Diego (Smith and Malkin 1997: 67). The significant power differential between the United States and Mexico undermines simple characterizations of the U.S.-Mexico relationship as one of "interdependency." See Ruiz 2000.
136. See Kubik 1986.
137. Based on interviews I conducted and my review of INS documents and congressional hearings, few U.S. authorities—politicians or INS officials—seem to appreciate the practical contradiction between promoting intensified transboundary economic links and growth and a border region of "law and order." One notable exception is Republican Congressman Duncan Hunter, one of the principle proponents of enhanced boundary enforcement, as demonstrated by this statement:

We have wrestled with the problem of illegal immigration, and what you have across the Southwest is a series of cities, urban areas on both sides of the border, whether it is San Diego, Tijuana, Calexico, Mexicali in my area, El Paso, Juarez in Ron Coleman's district, all the way to Matamoros, Mexico where most smuggling takes place. Where the alien and narcotic smugglers are most effective is where you have two cities on the border.

The reason for that is simple. First, the smuggler has a logistical base. Secondly, he has a major artery that comes down to the border, so you have people in vehicles, and they are on their way into the interstate system. Last, you have what I would call a grand central station atmosphere, lots of people, lots of population, you get lost in the crowd.

It is actually very difficult for the smugglers to move large numbers of people through the desert that intersperses our cities in the Southwest. So what you really have is not a situation of 2,000 miles on the border where you have to have Border Patrol men linking arms across the 2,000 miles; you really have 12 smugglers' corridors. They go all the way to Brownsville, Texas.

Each of these urban areas has what I would call a smugglers' corridor between it. I coined that phrase a few years ago because that is what we had in the San Diego smugglers' corridor. That is where about half of the illegal immigration nationwide takes place and that is where about half in recent years of the cocaine smuggling coming across the land borders has taken place.

So what do you have to do? We have to add up those smugglers' corridors from those 12 areas, which adds up to about 165 miles. We have got about 14 miles in the San Diego-Tijuana corridor. And you have to have sufficient resources. That means a sufficient perimeter, if you will, a border, an established border, to deter illegal crossings (U.S. Congress 1995: 11–12).

Thus, the growth of the border region necessitates "building up" the boundary.

138. Showley 1991.
139. Ruiz 2000: 31.
140. The October 30, 1993 edition of the *El Paso Times* reported that more than 75 percent of the city's Latino population supported Operation Blockade (Vila 1999b: 44).
141. See Gutiérrez 1995.
142. As Pablo Vila demonstrates, the ties of Mexican Americans to Mexico and its people is not a mere "fact," but also a matter of interpretation of what is Mexico (past and present) and who are "true" Mexicans. Such factors often lead third- and fourth-generation Mexican Americans to share many of the negative stereotypes of Mexico and recent immigrants present in mainstream U.S. culture (Vila 1994: 60–63; see also Vila 1997). Thus, their attitudes toward immigrants (legal and unauthorized) share much with those of Anglos in the United States. Such reasons, along with a number of other complex factors, have resulted in a situation in which Mexican Americans share much with the larger U.S. population vis-à-vis matters of immigration and boundary control (see Gutiérrez 1995; see also Hernández 1997). Nevertheless, Mexican Americans— while sharing with Anglos a tendency to favor lower rates of immigration and employer sanctions—do not favor immigration policies as restrictive as those of Anglos. Thus, Mexican Americans—unlike Anglos in general—tend to support the granting of amnesty to unauthorized immigrants and the provision of education to the children of extralegal immigrants (Binder, Polinard, and Winkle 1997).
143. See Vélez-Ibáñez 1997.
144. See Vila 1999a, 1999b, and 2000.
145. See Paasi 1995 and 1996.
146. Sahlins 1989: 271–72.
147. Sjoberg et al. 1991.
148. In the case of sociology, Gideon Sjoberg et al. (1991: 56–58) decry the tendency of sociologists to ignore important historical events and trends, as well as

fundamental patterns relating to complex organizations. Because "secrecy is a fundamental means of sustaining power and influence" of the organizational elite, sociologists need to pay more attention to personal documents and extensive interviews and need to have access to multiple perspectives on social developments. In this regard, sociologists have much to learn from the methods used by investigative journalists. We can apply this critique and prescription to the work of social scientists more generally.

149. Calavita 1994: 68–70.
150. Schrag 1998: 230; see also Chavira 1990.
151. Walker 1995 and 1996; see also Schrag 1998, and Baldassare 2000.
152. Walker 1995: 46; see also Baldassare 2000.
153. Spivak 1991.
154. Muller and Stacks 1991.
155. *The San Diego Union* 1991d.
156. Caldwell 1991.
157. Quoted in *The San Diego Union* 1991c.
158. Mendel 1993. Mountjoy later emerged as the author of California's Proposition 187 as well as the chairman of the Save Our State Committee. "Save Our State" was the nickname given to Proposition 187 by its backers.
159. Quoted in Chavez 1997: 64.
160. Chavez 1997: 64.
161. Van Deerlin 1992; McLaren 1992; Portillo 1992; and *The San Diego Tribune* 1992.
162. Braun 1992.
163. Muller 1997: 112.
164. Muller 1997: 112.
165. Clinton and Gore 1992: 117.
166. Barnes 1993.
167. Interview with Walters 1997.
168. Shore 1992.
169. See Glastris 1993; Conniff 1993; Barnes 1993; and Stacy and Lutton 1990.
170. Schrag 1998: 232.
171. Wilson 1993.
172. Wilson 1993.
173. Stern 1993c and 1994e. This interpretation of the effect of the law proved to be valid when I visited a strawberry farm in Watsonville, California, in 1996. One of the owners informed me that he had not seen the INS on his establishment in over ten years; he speculated that at least 50 percent of his employees were unauthorized immigrants.
174. Jacobs 1995.
175. See King and Foote 1993; Barnes 1993; Conniff 1993; and Murr 1993; see also Money 1997: 697.
176. Barnes 1993.
177. Zucker and Zucker 1996: 114; see also Robinson and Walsh 1993.
178. See Milton 1993.
179. Popkin and Friedman 1993.
180. Once again, California led the way when U.S. authorities discovered a shipload of 198 smuggled Chinese immigrants off the coast of San Diego. Just two weeks prior, Mexican authorities had apprehended a shipload of 306 Chinese immigrants—all of whom reportedly intended to go to the United States—off the coast of Ensenada, south of Tijuana (Lau 1993 and Gross 1993a). Republican congressman Duncan Hunter's office successfully exploited these incidents to heighten media and public attention and concerns in southern California about unauthorized immigration and boundary enforcement (interview with Becks 1998).
181. See Duffy 1993; Liu 1993; and Smolowe 1993.

182. Kwong 1997: 2.
183. Kwong 1997: 3; interview with Nunez 1997; see also Rotella 1998: 73–85.
184. Glastris 1993: 34.
185. U.S. Government, 1994: 1194. At the press conference, Clinton came very close to equating unauthorized immigrants to criminals. His quote later continues: "[T]o treat terrorists and smugglers as immigrants dishonors the tradition of the immigrants who have made our nation great. And it unfairly taints the millions of immigrants who live here honorably and are a vital part of every segment of our society. Today's initiatives are about stopping crime, toughening the penalties for the criminals, and giving our law enforcement people the tools they need to do the job" (U.S. Government 1994: 1194).
186. Barnes 1993.
187. See Mendel 1993.
188. Endicott 1993; Stern 1993a and 1993b; Marelius and Hearn 1993; see also California Senate Office of Research 1994.
189. Marelius 1993. Although whites account for only 57 percent of California's population, they are about 80 percent of the state's voters (Chavez 1997: 63).
190. Morganthau 1993 and Thomas 1993.
191. Kwong 1997: 4.
192. Zucker and Zucker 1996: 105.
193. McDonald 1997: 69.
194. Fried 1994: 15–18.
195. Stern 1993d.
196. Stern 1993e.
197. Alvord 1993.
198. Roletti 1993.
199. Barabak 1993.
200. Interview with Stern 1997.
201. See Fried 1994: 15–18; and Gross 1993b.
202. Interview with Walters 1997. Gustavo De La Viña (interview 1997) made a similar argument regarding Chief Reyes going against some sort of national agreement within the Border Patrol that San Diego would receive a large infusion of resources as the first step in a national strategy of gaining control over the boundary. Silvestre Reyes strongly disputes this argument, contending that, if there had been such a consensus around a national strategy, he certainly was not aware of it. According to Reyes, the INS did officially approve Operation Blockade/Hold-the-Line, but did not provide the funding needed to realize the operation (a de facto rejection of the operation). Reyes was able to negotiate the INS bureaucracy and to obtain funding, nevertheless, through a contact of his within the agency's bureaucracy who accessed funds for overtime pay for Border Patrol agents (Interview with Reyes 1997).

    It does appear, however, that few people in the halls of power in Washington, D.C., knew about Reyes' intention of launching the operation. U.S. Attorney General Janet Reno, for example, reportedly claimed to have no prior knowledge of the operation prior to its launching (see *The San Diego Union-Tribune* 1993b).
203. See, for example, *The San Diego Union-Tribune* 1993a.
204. Stern 1993f and 1993g, and Interview with De La Viña 1997; see also Barabak 1993 and Graham 1996. When pressed, however, administration officials would often admit that the neoliberal agenda embodied by NAFTA would actually lead to an *increase* in Mexican immigration. In testimony to Congress in November 1993, INS commissioner Doris Meissner stated that NAFTA could lead to increased migratory pressure for a period of about 20 years. But she argued that NAFTA was the best way to reduce unauthorized immigration in the long run (Stern 1993h).
205. See, for example, Gross and Sanchez 1994.

206. See Stern 1994a and 1994b.
207. Stern 1994d.
208. See Walczak 1994.
209. Kondracke 1993; and interviews with Aleinikoff 1997, Anbender 1997, and Schenk 1997.
210. U.S. Government 1994: 1194.
211. See Martin 1994.
212. Schrag 1998: 229–33. In early 1992 in response to the post-holiday return by migrants to the U.S., San Diego Sector chief Gustavo De La Viña deployed an unusually high number of agents along the boundary, greatly frustrating the efforts of migrant smugglers. In response, the smugglers organized groups of fifty migrants at a time to charge through the southbound Mexican Customs lane onto the freeway at the San Ysidro port of entry. The Border Patrol dubbed these "banzai runs." The INS did its best to confront these large-scale crossings and to publicize them as a way of pressuring state authorities in both countries to take action. The Border Patrol demanded that Mexican authorities stop the boundary runners and threatened to reduce Tijuana-bound traffic to a crawl by deploying twenty-five agents on the freeway itself. Grupo Beta responded by breaking up groups assembling near the freeway and by arresting smugglers (Rotella 1998: 55).

    While the banzai runs declined significantly due to efforts by both U.S. and Mexican authorities, the image of the banzai runs did not disappear so quickly. Pete Wilson used them quite effectively two years later in his bid for reelection to see the passage of Proposition 187. Wilson's television ads showed unauthorized migrants streaming through the port of entry onto the freeway under a big "Mexico" sign with a narrator warning "They keep coming" (Rotella 1998: 55–56).
213. As Tom Epstein, the special assistant to the president for political affairs (responsible for California affairs) from February 1993 until August 1995, stated, "[T]he idea was that 'Wilson has finger on a hot-button issue, but he's got the wrong solution. So what's the right solution? How do we solve this problem in the appropriate manner?' And I think that is what Gatekeeper was all about. I think no one in the White House wanted to emulate Wilson. But we did want to craft the proper response to what was an issue of great concern in the West" (Interview with Epstein 1998).
214. See Rotella 1998: 125.
215. Wilkie and Marelius 1994.
216. T. J. Walters, the associate chief of the U.S. Border Patrol, made this point during our interview in 1997.
217. Stern 1994a: A22.
218. Money 1997: 693; see Money 1999 for an expansion of this argument.
219. Sontag 1994.
220. Verhovek 1994.
221. I thank an anonymous reviewer of an earlier version of this manuscript for this insight.

CHAPTER 5

1. Steinbeck 1983: 312.
2. Monroy 1999: 106.
3. Doty 1996b: 129.
4. As a 1927 issue of the *Imperial Valley Press* (the precise date of which is not visible on the photocopy) reported, "[T]he large number of arrests of ineligible aliens made by the border patrol prove that it is very much on the job. Occasionally citizens may happen to get through to San Diego or the coast

without being stopped, but it is nearly a safe bet that the border patrol knows they are citizens." (The article is on file with the author.)

5. Neuman 1993: 1899.
6. Mehan 1997: 250.
7. See Wilson and Donnan 1998.
8. Drawing on Max Weber, Emile Durkheim, and Marc Bloch, Michael Mann (1986: 22–23) contends that ideology incorporates concepts and categories of *meaning* (as we cannot understand the world simply through our senses), *norms* ("shared understandings of how people should act"), and *aesthetic/ritual practices.* Mann notes, "In some formulations the terms 'ideology' and 'ideological power' contain two additional elements, that the knowledge purveyed is false and/or that it is a mere mask for material domination. I imply neither. Knowledge purveyed by an ideological power movement necessarily 'surpasses experience' (as Parsons put it). It cannot be totally tested by experience, and therein lies its distinctive power to persuade and dominate. But it need not be false; if it is, it is less likely to spread. People are not manipulated fools. And although ideologies always do contain legitimations of private interests and material domination, they are unlikely to attain hold over people if they are merely this" (1986: 23).

    Out of these concepts and categories emerge two main types of ideological organization. The first type is sociospatially *transcendent* of Mann's four sources of social power and "generates a 'sacred' form of authority" that operates above and apart from more secular authority structures. This type is often dependent on *diffused* power techniques. The second type is "ideology as immanent *morale*," which serves as a maintainer and fortifier of an already established group. The ideologies of class or nation are two of the more obvious examples (Mann 1986: 23–24).

    In addition to utilizing Mann's concept of ideology, I also draw on David Pepper (1984) who understands ideology to contain biases and unexamined assumptions about how the world works, and to represent a particular set of interests. Ideology, Pepper seems to suggest, is similar to a cultural filter which informs how we perceive and thus act upon the material world.
9. I outline Money's argument at the end of chapter 4; see Money 1997.
10. Muller 1997: 105.
11. Feagin 1997: 14.
12. Also see Willoughby 1997: 270.
13. According to the 1990 U.S. Census, only twelve countries (in a world of almost two hundred) were designated by 1 percent or more of the respondents as their country of national or ancestral origin. Those countries were the United Kingdom, Ireland, Canada, Italy, Russia, Poland, France, the Netherlands, Sweden, Germany, Norway, and Mexico (Feagin 1997: 14).
14. As John Higham, author of the classic *Strangers in the Land* defines the term, *nativism* is "intense opposition to an internal minority on the grounds of its foreign (i.e. un-American) connections. Specific nativistic antagonisms may, and do, vary widely in response to the changing character of minority irritants and the shifting conditions of the day; but through each separate hostility runs the connecting, energizing force of modern nationalism. While drawing on much broader cultural antipathies and ethnocentric judgements, nativism translates them into a zeal to destroy the enemies of a distinctively American way of life" (quoted in Perea 1997: 1).
15. Race is a socially constructed concept. There is general agreement among geneticists and biologists that there is no scientific basis for putative "races." While phenotypical characteristics often help to define a race, a variety of characteristics—most often social—define a racialized group. A "race" emerges in situations in which supposedly physical and/or cultural differences are reified or essentialized, usually in situations characterized by social and/or political

conflict, and/or inequality in terms of power relations. It is usually the relatively powerful that racialize the less powerful, designating members of a defined group as a "race." Given that race is a socially constructed concept, it is a dynamic category. Thus, the ascribed characteristics of a particular race, and the justifications given for the group's racialization, can and do change over time and space. See Almaguer 1994, Blaut 1992, Escobar 1999, and Gordon 1999.

16. Calavita 1996: 286.
17. Calavita 1996: 285.
18. In this chapter, I employ the term *Anglo* to describe different groups coming from the British Isles, including the Scottish. More generally, the term describes English-speaking, white Americans of non-Hispanic descent.
19. Feagin 1997: 15–16.
20. Feagin 1997: 16–17.
21. See Neuman 1993.
22. Feagin 1997: 17.
23. Neuman 1993 and 1996. The acts were very unpopular. As a result, the Alien Act expired in 1800 while Congress repealed the Naturalization Act in 1802. The re-establishment of comprehensive federal registration of aliens did not occur until 1940.
24. Calavita 1984.
25. Calavita 1984: 20–21.
26. Quoted in Calavita 1994: 56.
27. Calavita 1984: 26.
28. Calavita 1984: 27.
29. Calavita 1984: 31–34.
30. Calavita 1994: 57–58.
31. Mink 1986: 50. In the first few years after the Civil War, organized labor enjoyed strong unity and growth—trends that were to prove short-lived as business and the government collaborated to promote immigration after the war. While workers sometimes responded with acts of Luddism and frequent antiboss militancy, hostility toward new labor was also common (Mink 1986: 54–56). The influx of immigrants had profound objective and subjective effects on native-born and "old immigrant" workers as their presence helped to facilitate the owners' desire to cut wages. The high levels of immigration led to "desperate economic competition among the newcomers," which often led to anti-immigrant violence whether against Eastern European Jews in New York City or against Chinese laborers in California and Wyoming (Zinn 1990: 259–60).
32. Calavita 1984: 39–40.
33. A further stimulus to this tendency was the development of class-based political movements like the National Labor Union, the Knights of Labor, and the socialist parties. Admittedly, all these organizations made compromises over the immigration question, but the essential point is that in tracing the roots of working-class impoverishment to the financial manipulators and the capitalists, they averted the search for scapegoats for social problems and concentrated attention on the real rather than the symbolic causes of labor's dissatisfaction. . . . [W]hat was necessary was fundamental social and economic reform, which could best be attained by a united movement of all workers, of whatever ethnicity, religion, or culture (Lane 1987: 211).
34. Lane 1987: 210. Contract labor became the major legislative target of organized labor in the latter part of the nineteenth century. Labor's agitation culminated in the passage of the Anti–Contract Labor Law of 1885. Unfortunately for labor, however, private labor exchanges or labor pools had become by that time the primary mechanism through which employers recruited immigrant strikebreakers. Indeed, by that time, it was no longer feasible nor necessary for

most sectors of U.S. industry to import European contract workers—a fact that facilitated congressional passage of the law. In this regard, the Anti–Contract Labor Law required little in terms of sacrifice from capital and was thus largely symbolic (Calavita 1984: 44–66).

35. Zinn 1990: 236.

36. Immigration during the Gilded Age, the heyday of industrial capitalism in the United States, aroused a defensive group consciousness in organizing labor because it coincided with blows dealt more frontally by courts and employers. The new immigration—disproportionately of male peasants and unskilled laborers—roused trade unionists against new workers because demographic changes coincided with technological, political, and economic setbacks to trade union efforts to empower workers through association in the workplace. Most new immigrants went directly into the labor market where, notwithstanding rapid industrial expansion, they came into competition with old labor and its workplace institutions (Mink 1986: 49).

37. Ong and Liu 1994: 47. The first target of organized labor's nativist struggle were Chinese immigrants. The anti-Chinese movement helped to create national labor solidarity despite the geographically limited extent of the "problem"; it foreshadowed a more general anti-immigrant movement and the substitution of an anticapitalist sentiment with an anti-immigrant one.

    The substitution of "race feeling" for "class feeling" greatly enhanced "union feeling" (Mink 1986: 71–72) and thus set the tone for the development of a national labor movement. The movement against the Chinese marked the entrance of organized labor's entrance into the national political arena as they fought to get enacted anti-Chinese legislation. But as their earliest political struggles helped to shape American workers (like workers in other countries), "[t]he prominence of this political goal had enormous and enormously negative consequences for class-based labor politics in the United States" as it promoted and reified ethnic and racial cleavages within the working class (Mink 1986: 73). Whereas U.S. workers fought immigration as their initial struggle on the national level, many European workers first struggled on a national scale to gain suffrage rights. As Gwendolyn Mink explains, "Both European and American labor went on to struggle with state sanctions against working-class activity, but they did so from very different starting points. Suffrage hung on inequality between classes, immigration on racial and ethnic differences within the working class. Labor-based political action reflected this difference: suffrage often required European labor to mobilize outside established political channels where immigration required American unions to mobilize within existing politics" (Mink 1986: 74). While white working-class racism has its roots in slavery, its racism applied to a variety of groups as embodied by labor's "almost universal endorsement of the Chinese Exclusion Act of 1882," helping to set a tone of racism for organized labor at the time when the movement was taking shape in the United States (Moody 1988: 281).

38. Reimers 1992: 4. In terms of the labor movement, the debate, by the early twentieth century, had evolved into one between two sets of restrictionists—the radicals and the moderates. As A. T. Lane argues, "Supporters of the open door in immigration policy had not totally disappeared from the labor movement, but their influence was only marginal by that time" (Lane 1987: 210).

39. See appendix E.

40. Neuman 1993.

41. Neuman 1993: 1833–34.

42. Neuman 1993: 1841–80. In terms of the reasons for the weakness of federal immigration legislation until the 1870s, slavery was one of the keys: "Historians have reasonably suggested that a primary cause of the federal government's

failure to adopt qualitative restrictions on immigration before the Civil War was the slave states' jealous insistence on maintaining power over the movement of free blacks as a states's right" (Neuman 1993: 1866). The geographical aim of some race-based state laws was sometimes outside of U.S. territory. Some states, for example, enacted legislation prohibiting the entry of free blacks following the successful slave uprising in Haiti. Such race-inspired legislation strongly parallels much of the late nineteenth-century immigration law, most notably the Chinese Exclusion Act (Neuman 1993: 1872).

43. Carter, Green, and Halpern 1996: 139.
44. Wyse 1966: D-4.
45. Ironically, this was a time of very little immigration due in part to the disruption of shipping caused by the outbreak of World War I. Immigration to the United States declined by over 80 percent between 1914 and 1918 (Carter, Green, and Halpern 1996: 145).
46. Carter, Green, and Halpern 1996: 142.
47. Carter, Green, and Halpern 1996: 140.
48. Carter, Green, and Halpern 1996: 140.
49. Carter, Green, and Halpern 1996: 146.
50. Wyse 1966: D-5–D-6. For an example of such thinking, see Roberts 1921.
51. Reimers 1992: 6.
52. Wyse 1966: D-6. As the *Los Angeles Times* opined in a May 14, 1924 editorial in support of the proposed legislation, "Limiting immigration tends to increase the cost of living, for it cuts off the supply of cheap foreign labor; but it will also result in the gradual elimination of foreign communities on American soil. There will be no more 'little Germany,' 'little Russia,' 'little Poland' or 'little Italy.'"
53. Carter, Green, and Halpern 1996: 48. The authors draw upon Higham (1975: 309–10) in making this argument.
54. Carter, Green, and Halpern 1996: 149.
55. Reimers 1992: 8.
56. Reimers 1992: 11–16.
57. At the same time, however, Congress applied the quota of one hundred to all colonized territories, whether in Asia or elsewhere. In doing so, Congress—in the name of consistency—effectively and significantly reduced immigration from colonies in the Western Hemisphere, such as Jamaica, which had averaged about one thousand immigrants per year during the 1940s (Reimers 1992: 19).
58. Reimers 1992: 17–20 and López 1996: 1–2. The Nationality Act of 1790 limited citizenship to "free white persons." Congress extended the right of naturalization to persons of African descent in 1870. All Asians were ineligible for citizenship until Congress passed legislation allowing for the naturalization of Chinese immigrants in 1943 (Lee 1996: 92–93).

U.S. authorities often had great difficulty in deciding who was "white." While at one point U.S. court deemed petitioners from Hawaii, Japan, Syria, and the Philippines as nonwhite, courts ruled that applicants from Mexico and Armenia were, indeed, white (Haney-López 1996: 2).
59. Reimers 1992: 25.
60. Reimers 1992: 36.
61. Reimers 1992: 80–84.
62. As Carter, Green, and Halpern (1996: 137) contend, "Through immigration and nationality laws, governments racialize the social relations between native and alien Other, and animate and legitimate popular notions of 'who belongs.'"
63. Manzo 1996.
64. Gordon 1999: 59. See also Vélez-Ibáñez 1997.
65. Gordon 1999: 122. See also Sandrino-Glasser 1998.
66. See Gordon 1999 for an exceptionally compelling account of how this process unfolded in the Arizona border region.

67. Vélez-Ibáñez 1997: 65–66. See also Sánchez 1990.
68. Quoted in Vélez-Ibáñez 1997: 74. Quote taken from David J. Weber, *The Spanish Frontier in North America*, New Haven: Yale University Press, 1992: 339.
69. Calavita 1994: 58. The original citation is as follows: U.S. Congress. Senate. Senate Immigration Commission, *Immigration Commission Report*. Senate Document No. 747, 61st Congress, 3rd Session, 1911: 690–91.
70. Acuña 1996: 110–11 and Calavita 1994: 58–59; see also Gómez-Quiñones and Maciel 1998: 37. The legislation actually exempted the entire Western Hemisphere from the quotas, "largely," according to David Reimers (1992: 7), "because of the legislators' sensitivity to a traditional Pan American liberal immigration policy." Secretary of State Paul Kellogg argued that quotas would hurt U.S. relations with Canada and Mexico.
71. Reisler 1976: 127.
72. McWilliams 1968: 206.
73. Gómez-Quiñones and Maciel 1998: 37.
74. Reisler 1976: 155; see also Takaki 1993.
75. Takaki 1993: 331. Quote taken from "Singling Out Mexico," *The New York Times*, May 16, 1930. For an interesting account of racism, science, and Mexican students in California schools in the early twentieth century, see Monroy 1999: 134–40.
76. Acuña 1996: 111–12.
77. Quoted in Sánchez 1990: 253. According to Sánchez's endnote, quote taken from U.S. Congress, House, Committee on Immigration and Naturalization, *Hearings on Temporary Admission of Illiterate Mexican Laborers*, 69th Congress, 1st session, 1926, 191, and *Hearings on Seasonal Agricultural Laborers from Mexico*, 46.
78. Reisler 1976: 180.
79. Reimers 1992: 7.
80. Reisler 1976: 181.
81. See Almaguer 1994.
82. Kazin 1988: 263; see also Saxton 1971.
83. The class and status structure of Spanish California was very rigid and highly stratified. At the top were the so-called *gente de razón*, or "people of reason." This group included the Spanish Franciscans, Spanish officials, and the Spanish military officers. There was also the prominent California families, supposedly full-blooded Spaniards. Below the gente de razón on the social ladder were Mexicans. The population was largely illiterate, and spoke a different dialect of Spanish. Generally, this population perceived itself as Mexican, not Spanish. And below the Mexicans were Native Americans (McWilliams 1968: 89–90). The social structure of California under Mexican rule had a similar appearance. Nevertheless, while the gente de razón were supposedly of Spanish origin and Castillian-speaking, the category did come to include mestizos who had a formal education (Takaki 1993: 169). As Carey McWilliams describes, "[I]n many respects, the social structure of Spanish [Mexican] California resembled that of the Deep South: the *gente de razón* were the plantation-owners; the Indians were the slaves; and the Mexicans were the California equivalent of 'poor white trash' " (McWilliams 1968: 90).
84. Almaguer 1994: 7–8.
85. Almaguer 1994: 8.
86. Almaguer 1994: 8; see also Pitt 1966.
87. Almaguer (1994: 8) argues that this is why blacks did not become the major target of racist legislation, unlike in other parts of the country.
88. Almaguer 1994: 8.
89. Almaguer 1994: 9.
90. Almaguer 1994: 11. See Gordon 1999 for a fascinating case study illustrating this point.

91. Mexicans in California initially welcomed U.S. immigrants, but as in other Mexican territories to where Americans migrated, tensions soon arose as the newcomers looked down upon the Mexican population and its way of life. As one settler wrote about the Mexican population, "The greater part of them are the most miserable, wretched poor creatures that I have ever seen, poor, petty, thieving, gambling, bullbaiting...." (McWilliams 1968: 131). Of greater concern, however, was the feared intentions of annexation of the American settlers whose numbers rapidly increased, reaching several hundred by 1846. As (Mexican) California Governor Pío Pico wrote in the mid-1840s, "We find ourselves threatened by hordes of Yankee immigrants who have already begun to flock to our country and whose progress we cannot arrest" (Takaki 1993: 172). For a very interesting account of the complex relationships between "Anglos" and Californios in the nineteenth century, see Pitt 1966.
92. Almaguer 1994: 7.
93. Almaguer 1994: 26–28; and Takaki 1993: 178; see also Pitt 1966.
94. Almaguer 1994: 130.
95. Almaguer 1994: 150.
96. Takaki 1993: 178. According to Sandrino-Glasser, "Initially, the term 'greaser' was used exclusively to describe Mexicans in Texas, New Mexico, Arizona, and early California. However, after the arrival of other Latin Americans, especially in the gold fields of California after the Gold Rush of 1849, the term "greaser" was applied to all persons of Latin American origin. Although there four distinct Latino groups in California in 1850—the Californios (originally born in Mexican territory, but then citizens of the United States under the Treaty of Guadalupe Hidalgo), Mexicans, Peruvians, and Chileans—the mining society tended to view them all as one race, generally limping them together under the term 'greaser'" (1998: 117).
97. Takaki 1993: 182.
98. Takaki 1993: 184–87; see also Almaguer 1994: 29–32 and 65–73; and Vélez-Ibáñez 1997. As Carey McWilliams advises, "[I]t is important to remember that Mexicans are a 'conquered' people in the Southwest, a people whose culture has been under incessant attack for many years and whose character and achievements, as a people, have been consistently disparaged. Apart from physical violence, conquered and conqueror have continued to be competitors for land and jobs and power, parties to a constant economic conflict which has found expression in litigation, dispossessions, hotly contested elections, and the mutual disparagement which inevitably accompanies a situation of this kind. Throughout this struggle, the Anglo-Americans have possessed every advantage: in numbers and wealth, arms and machines" (1968: 132).
99. Almaguer 1994: 71.
100. Takaki 1993: 320.
101. McWilliams 1968: 189–90.
102. Quoted in McWilliams 1968: 190; see also Takaki 1993: 321. In 1927, Clements reminded California governor C. C. Young that "the Mexican laborer is an alien possible of deportation should he become indigent or a social menace" (quoted in Monroy 1999: 100).
103. Quoted in McWilliams 1968: 190.
104. Takaki 1993: 323.
105. Quoted in Acuña 1996: 110; *cholos* is a pejorative term for low-status Mexicans. As Rodolfo Acuña explains, "Mexicans were ... easily scapegoated during times of economic hardship. During the 1913 recession, the Commissioner of Immigration, for instance, publicly announced his fear that Mexicans might become public charges, since according to these authorities, Mexicans came to the United States only to receive public relief. This theme was to become a key part of the folklore surrounding Mexican immigration" (Acuña 1996: 110).
106. McWilliams 1968: 190–92; see also Escobar 1999.

107. Quoted in McWilliams 1968: 193.
108. Quoted in Monroy 1999: 108.
109. See Monroy 1999: 108.
110. Quoted in Takaki 1993: 333.
111. Takaki 1993: 334.
112. Acuña 1996: 112.
113. See Monroy 1999: 27–29.
114. Acuña 1988: 254–59; see also McWilliams 1968: 227–58; and Escobar 1999.
115. See Acuña 1988: 258.
116. The June 12, 1954 edition of *Los Angeles Times* described the pending operation in militaristic terms: "An army of border patrolmen complete with jeeps, trucks and seven aircraft will begin moving into El Centro today, dispersing their forces for an all-out war to hurl tens of thousands of Mexican wetbacks back into Mexico."
117. For sections relating to immigration in political party platforms from 1798 to 1964, see Hutchinson 1981. The author conducted the analysis of the Democratic and Republican party platforms from 1968–1996. Copies of these platforms are on file with the author.
118. Nevins 1998.
119. Botts 1997: 11.
120. Botts 1997: 11–13; and McDonald 1997: 84.
121. Based on research by the author. The table that follows represents the actual numbers of articles from *The New York Times* from 1970–1980.

Year	No. of Articles Discussing Unauthorized Immigration	No. of Articles Discussing Unauthorized Immigration from Mexico
1970	5	1
1971	10	2
1972	11	1
1973	21	11
1974	41	21
1975	55	11
1976	43	4
1977	94	40
1978	34	17
1979	66	29
1980	104	32

122. Nevins 1998.
123. Walters 1990: 10–12.
124. Ardman 1974. See also appendix G.
125. Fernández and Pedroza 1982: 4.
126. A February 3, 1975 cover story entitled "Rising Flood of Illegal Aliens: How to Deal With It," for example, asserted that the "illegal flow . . . is raising problems more troublesome than those created many decades ago by the 'huddled masses' waiting docilely on Ellis Island for entry to the promised land" (*U.S. News and World Report*, 1975: 30).
127. Murray Edelman explains how media discourse functions to construct threats to the social order:

    News accounts highlight the dimensions of the spectacle of politics that attract audiences: leaders, enemies, problems, and crises. All of them are social constructions because they are created through gestures and discourse that evoke similar perceptions in people who are important to one another, and also because each of these aspects of the experienced political scene helps create the others. The spectacle assumes different forms for different groups according to their respective concerns and ideologies, so that there are conflicting definitions of problems, enemies, and crises and conflicting meanings for leaders. These constructions make the political spectacle resonate with moral passions and with expectations of danger or amelioration. But because they are social constructions of officials, interest groups, and audiences, they should be understood as symbols rather than facts. They exist to evoke beliefs about particular worlds, with specified or implied histories, heroes, villains, issues, threats, desirable and undesirable courses of action, and prospects for the future. (1985: 202)

128. *Time* 1977: 26.
129. Morris and Mayio 1982: 4.
130. *Time* 1977: 26.
131. Nevins 1998.
132. Calavita 1996.
133. Gamson and Modigliani 1987: 169.
134. Gutiérrez 1995: 207.
135. See Yeh 1994; see also Camarota 1997; and Reimers 1998.
136. Gabriel 1998: 122.
137. Grace Chang (1996 and 2000) contends that anti-immigrant rhetoric increasingly focuses on women, most notably unauthorized immigrant Latinas. Images of them as welfare cheats and indefatigable "breeders" are pervasive.
138. See Gabriel 1998: 117–23.
139. Quoted in Martinez and McDonnell 1994; see also Suro 1996.
140. See Gabriel 1998.
141. According to Sara Diamond, "The paleoconservatives were a group of intellectuals who viewed themselves as heirs to the Old Right, from the decades before the Cold War, when rightists advocated a non-interventionist role for the state in foreign affairs and the capitalist economy, combined with a 'traditionalist' view of society as inherently unequal and antidemocratic. Paleoconservatives, joined by Pat Buchanan, opposed U.S. participation in United Nations-conducted wars (e.g., Iraq, 1991). They also opposed any kind of civil rights legislation to achieve racial and gender equality" (1996: 156).
142. Diamond 1996: 156–58; see also Lewis 1979: 141–44. While groups like FAIR and the AICF succeeded in raising the profile of illegal immigration and boundary control, leading right-wing organizations did not take up the anti-immigrant cause in any sort of significant manner. Instead, it has been numerous small, grassroots groups that have organized to fight against the perceived negative repercussions created in their locales by unauthorized immigrants (Diamond 1996: 158).
143. McDonald 1997: 69.
144. See Schmidt 1997.
145. Kelley 1997: 120–21.
146. Chavez 1997: 63. See Baldassare 2000 for interesting data and analysis about the attitudes of California's principal racial/ethnic groups toward immigration.
147. Gutiérrez 1995 and Binder, Polinard, and Winkle 1997. A tendency toward right-wing authoritarian politics and the holding of negative stereotypes about "illegal" immigrants are important predictors of support for anti-unauthorized immigration measures such as Proposition 187 (Quinton, Cowan, and Watson 1996). Californians tend to have more prorestrictionist positions than Americans in general. And Anglos who self-identify as relatively conservative and view Latinos in a negative light tend to favor more restrictive levels of immigration (Hood and Morris 1997).
148. Buchanan 1994.
149. Below the organization's name on the newsletter's masthead, it reads "Citizenship/Sovereignty/Law."
150. Brimelow has called for a new Operation Wetback to reverse the influx of unauthorized immigrants to reclaim U.S. national sovereignty. He issued this call at the April 25, 1996 meeting of Voice of Citizens Together (VCT) in North

Hollywood, California (see the March 1996 issue of the VCT newsletter—on file with the author).

151. As the VCT newsletter's masthead proclaims, for example, " 'This is not a racial issue. It is an economic, ecological, and social survival issue.' " And Peter Brimelow argues, "I am not prejudiced—in the sense of committing and stubbornly persisting in error about people, regardless of evidence—which appears to me to be the only rational definition of 'racism' " (1995: 11).

152. Lipsitz 1998: 215.

153. Lipsitz 1998: 19.

154. Lipsitz 1998.

155. Blaut 1992.

156. Walker 1995 and 1996; see also Schrag 1998.

157. Muller 1997: 115.

158. Delgado and Stefanic 1992 and Johnson 1997.

159. Neuman 1995: 1429.

160. Not surprisingly, a general suspicion of all Latinos as potential "illegals" informed the thinking of many backers of California's Proposition 187. California state senator William Craven, a Republican from Oceanside, north of San Diego, for example, suggested in October 1994 that "the [California] state legislature should explore requiring all people of Hispanic descent to carry an identification card that would be used to verify legal residence" (quoted in Chavez 1997: 62). (In February 1993, Craven informed a U.S. Senate hearing in San Diego that "migrant workers were on a lower scale of humanity" [quoted in Chavez 1997: 63].) As Leo Chavez (1997: 62) argues, the effect of Craven's call was to define all Latinos as members of a suspect class.

161. See Lee 1996.

162. See, for example, Chavez 1997.

163. See Chang 1996 and 2000; see also Varsanyi 1996 and U.S. GAO 1997a.

164. See Abramovitz 1996.

165. See Beckett 1997. While the mid- and late 1970s were times of dramatically increased rates of drug use (peaking in 1979) and crime, for example, "the percentage of poll respondents identifying crime and drugs as the nation's most important problem remained quite low throughout this period" (Beckett 1997: 23).

166. Beckett 1997: 62, 78.

167. Whitney et al. 1989.

168. Beckett 1997: 65; see also Gamson and Modigliani 1987.

169. Analysis of media coverage supports this claim. See Nevins 1998.

170. See Sassen 1998.

171. Mehan 1997: 264–65.

172. I want to add a cautionary note. In pointing to "the state" as the primary shaper of the "illegal" as a discursive category, I seem to be suggesting that there is a sharp divide between the state and society. Clearly, as the analysis presented in this study demonstrates, the relationship between state actors, the institutions of governance (the state apparatus), and nonstate actors (chapter 1, note 51) is highly complex. The relationships between these social actors are so intertwined that it is very difficult to make analytical distinctions. Thus, I acknowledge that there are multiple causal agents, and that the power that constructs the "illegal" emanates from a whole host of overlapping and mutually constitutive social relations. It follows, therefore, that there are multiple possibilities for actions to counter the production of the "illegal" and that we all are agents in the processes that produce the phenomenon. Similarly, we all have the potential to participate in creating a radically different discursive category (see Yapa 1996). Nevertheless, I want to avoid suggesting that all social actors are equal in terms of their ability to shape social outcomes. Depending on the phenomenon in question, there is almost always a certain level of inequality between social

actors. It is for this reason that it is important to make analytical distinctions between social categories. Doing so allows us to ascertain the differential effects particular social actors have in helping to shape the world.

173. Almaguer 1994: 212.
174. A framework suggesting a crisis is very common in media accounts related to unauthorized immigration. Such accounts usually present "illegals" as a threat to society and/or conflate them with criminals (Coutin and Chock 1995).
175. As U.S. Attorney General Janet Reno stated in arguing for a budget increase for the Department of Justice in fiscal year 1997, "We are making progress in fighting drugs, violent crime, and illegal immigrants. Now we must redouble our efforts and build on our results" (Andreas 1997: 38).
176. Corrigan and Sayer 1985: 3.
177. Corrigan and Sayer 1985: 5–6.

CHAPTER 6

1. Jones 1998.
2. Smith 1997.
3. Corruption is a very serious problem within the INS. See Walth, Christensen, and Read 2000.
4. Unauthorized migrants and their smugglers use a variety of methods to "beat" the Border Patrol and the INS. These range from the employment of false identity documents (such as a fake border crossing card that one can buy—very high-quality ones are available if you have sufficient money—"rent," or borrow from someone whose appearance is reasonably similar) to the use of relatively simple radio devices to jam (from the Mexican side of the boundary) the sensors of the Border Patrol.

   One of the most ingenious methods I heard about was from a Border Patrol agent in the El Paso Sector. Some migrants had reportedly used space blankets to prevent their body heat from escaping, thus inhibiting detection by the infrared scopes. While an experienced camera person can still see shadows, it is reportedly extremely difficult.
5. U.S. INS 1997b: 3.
6. Border Patrol sectors are comprised of stations. The San Diego Sector has seven such stations: Brown Field; Campo (which includes the Boulevard substation); Chula Vista; El Cajon (which includes the San Marcos substation); Imperial Beach; San Clemente; and Temecula. The geographical areas of the stations sometimes change due to the changing flow of unauthorized migrants.
7. See map, appendix A.
8. U.S. INS 1997b: 4.
9. Bersin 1996b: 2.
10. U.S. INS 1997b: 4–5.
11. See O'Connor 1997 and U.S. INS 1997c.
12. U.S. INS 1997b: 6.
13. U.S. GAO 1999.
14. U.S. INS 1997b and O'Connor 1997.
15. *The San Diego Union-Tribune* 1998a.
16. U.S. Border Patrol 1994: 9.
17. See Bean et al. 1994.
18. A quantitative analysis of the number of apprehensions and boundary enforcement hours between 1964 and 1996 found a positive correlation between rising apprehensions and rising enforcement hours, "indicating that there may be increasing returns to scale in border enforcement" (Hanson and Spilimbergo 1999: 1355). Wage levels in the United States and Mexico, however, have a more immediate effect on apprehension levels, suggesting that a reduction in U.S.-

Mexico wage differentials is an effective tool for reducing unauthorized immigration from Mexico.

19. Cornelius 1998: 130.
20. See U.S. Border Patrol 1994: 10.
21. Cornelius 1998: 131.
22. Singer and Massey 1998. The authors draw upon the work of Josiah Heyman (1995) in making this argument.
23. Reyes 1997.
24. Taylor, Martin, and Fix, 1997: 83–84.
25. Cornelius 1998: 131–32.
26. See Espenshade 1995, and U.S. GAO 1997b and 1999
27. U.S. GAO 1999: 2. On the basis of the Border Patrol's own criteria as set out in its 1994 "Strategic Plan," the increase in total apprehensions also calls into question the claimed success of the agency's national strategy, of which Gatekeeper is a central component. As stated in the document, one of its "key assumptions" was that "Alien apprehensions will decrease as Border Patrol increases control of the border" (U.S. Border Patrol 1994: 4).

   Furthermore, preliminary data from the 2000 U.S. Census suggests that the number of unauthorized immigrants arriving and living in the United States increased substantially in the 1990s in response to a rapidly growing economy and, thus, more jobs. As the *Los Angeles Times* reported, "[n]ew data suggest that the United States has nearly twice the number of undocumented immigrants than officials thought—possibly 11 million or more, compared with earlier estimates of 6 million" (Zitner 2001: A–1).
28. See Sanchez and Stern 1996.
29. Graham 1996; and interview with Bonner 1996.
30. Graham 1996: 50.
31. See, for example, Cooper 1997, Hedges 1996 and 1997, Katz 1996, and Stern 1997a–d and 1998b.
32. See Andreas 1998.
33. See, for example, Kopytoff 1999.
34. As one journalist described the situation, "One result of Operation Gatekeeper is certain: The decibel level surrounding illegal immigration in San Diego has fallen as steeply as the arrest numbers. Rapes, killings and robberies along the border are now rare—as is the sight of border jumpers sprinting across freeways at San Ysidro's port of entry. Politicians no longer show up to fulminate about a border that is out of control. Border Patrol commanders who once begged for agents from other zones now lend them out" (Ellingwood 1999a: A35).
35. See Graham 1996.
36. Andreas 1998: 353.
37. Edelman 1985: 20.
38. Zolberg 1978.
39. According to a study by the Banco de México and El Colegio de la Frontera Norte, Mexican residents (authorized and unauthorized) in the United States sent U.S. $3.673 billion in remittances to Mexico in 1995 (Gazcón 1996).
40. McWilliams 1968: 103.
41. Lewis 1979: 48–52. While the Mexican government does not try to prevent its citizens from leaving the country, the smuggling of migrants is a crime in Mexico.
42. Dunn 1996: 94–96.
43. Rotella 1998: 94–95.
44. Dunn 1996: 96.
45. Rotella 1998: 92–93, 114–16.
46. Bersin and Feigin 1998: 309–10. According to Mohar and Alcaraz (2000: 150), there are now six Beta groups along the U.S.-Mexico boundary. The total size of the force is 123 agents, with the largest (45) being in Tijuana. Grupo Beta gener-

ally has a reputation for being very clean—especially in comparison to other Mexican law enforcement agencies. Nevertheless, problems of corruption and brutality seem to have infected Beta somewhat. See Davidson 2000 and Gross 1998.

47. Dunn 1996: 97.
48. See Morgan 1993.
49. Bersin 1996a: 1414. Given this conundrum (from the perspective of U.S. authorities), Bersin argues that the U.S. needs to work to

> center binational attention on the public safety dimensions of these movements [of unauthorized migrants]. We must reach a consensus with our partners in Mexico on the rights and obligations that attach to a border ruled by law [rather] than dominated by lawbreakers. This formulation properly would include unambiguous recognition of a sovereign's right to regulate entry as well as its obligation to afford humane and lawful treatment to those who violate the law. The entire debate over illegal immigration, recognizing those differences that we cannot bridge, would give way in the bilateral context to a single-minded concentration on aspects of pure mutual interest. Recasting the focus in terms of public safety and security for the border region as a whole—resident, migrants and agents alike—could furnish that elusive basis for concrete cooperative action that does not now exist uniformly across the border. (Bersin 1996a: 1414–15)

This, as earlier discussion demonstrates, is what is already taking place—to a certain (but increasing) extent—between the United States and Mexico regarding the border region. Bersin, of course, wants to see the realization of his prescription to a much greater degree than is the present case.

50. Gross 1993c: A-23.
51. U.S. Government 1995: 200.
      This explanation is almost a word-for-word duplication of the argument put forth by the Select Commission on Immigration and Refugee Policy in its 1981 final report (see chapter 4).
52. Bersin 1996c.
53. Robert Bach refers to this policy as the "Meissner doctrine," named after former INS commissioner Doris Meissner and her late husband Charles Meissner (who died in 1996), the former head of international commerce at the U.S. Department of Commerce (Bach 1997).
54. Bach 1997.
55. See U.S. Government 1995: 199–204.
56. Kahn 1997b: 14–15.
57. *Migration News*, November 1998. About two thousand U.S. employers were participating in 1998 in the INS's voluntary Basic Pilot program, under which the Social Security Administration and the INS verify the Social Security and immigration numbers of all newly hired workers. As a reward for cooperation, participating companies are immune from INS raids. Given that many unauthorized immigrants are able to borrow legal documents from friends or relatives or obtain fraudulent documents, the program has the unintended effect of sheltering unauthorized immigrants from INS enforcement (see Cohen 1998).
58. While true as a general statement, there are specific areas of the country where interior enforcement remains active. The areas around meatpacking plants in Iowa and Nebraska, for example, are still subject to sporadic immigration enforcement. In FY 1999, the INS apprehended 2,524 unauthorized immigrants in Iowa and Nebraska. In FY 2000, the figure was 3,242 (*Migration News*, November 2000).
59. Uchitelle 2000. By reducing workplace enforcement in times of low unemployment—ostensibly because of less political pressure to do otherwise—and by threatening unauthorized workers largely only when anti-union

employers want to undermine worker organizing, the INS is serving the interests of capital. While the INS has long served this function to varying degrees depending on time and place, it is a mistake to reduce the role of the INS to one of a regulator of immigrant labor (see Chang 2000: 174–75).

60. Cornelius 1998: 130.
61. Kahn 1997a: M6.
62. Quoted in Kahn 1997b: 15.
63. Nader and Wallach 1996: 95–96.
64. Interview with Cobian 1997.
65. Warnock 1995: 197.
66. See Andreas 1998–99. As Massey and Espinosa argue, "The provisions of NAFTA reinforce the ongoing process of market consolidation in Mexico and help to bring about the social and economic transformations that generate migrants. The integration of the North American market will also create new links of transportation, telecommunication, and interpersonal acquaintance, connections that are necessary for the efficient movement of goods, information, and capital but which also encourage and promote the movement of people—students, business executives, tourists, and ultimately, undocumented workers" (1997: 991–92).
67. At the same time, however, the Clinton administration claimed that the passage of NAFTA would actually help realize the goal of boundary enforcement: by creating better, high-paying jobs in Mexico—so went the argument—NAFTA would lead to less immigration from Mexico to the United States. See, for example, Reno 1993.
68. U.S. Congress 1994b: 36. Nevertheless, upon ending her tenure as INS head in November 2000, Meissner wondered aloud, "What drives people from one place to somewhere else, taking all kinds of risks? It's one of the fundamental questions of our time" (quoted in *Migration News*, December 2000).
69. See Ohmae 1995.
70. Manzo 1996.
71. A number of Clinton administration political appointees voiced such a view to me during interviews.
72. I thank Ben Forest of the Department of Geography at Dartmouth College for explaining this perspective to me.
    Such an analysis, however, assumes a preexisting context of justice that the law serves to strengthen. In this regard the establishment of a regime of "law and order," however, while providing some benefits to unauthorized immigrants in the form of less violence from "border bandits," can actually make matters worse for extralegal crossers by institutionalizing injustice.
73. U.S. Select Commission 1981: 41–42. Such an analysis serves to reinforce wide-spread stereotypes rooted in history equating Mexican immigrants and Mexican-Americans with criminality given the tendency in the United States to associate "illegal" immigration with Mexico (see Gutiérrez-Jones 1995).
74. Blomley 1994.
75. This is a characteristic of what Agnew and Corbridge (1995) call the "territorial trap."
76. Gutiérrez 1995: 211–12.
77. In trying to explain why we have this good/bad distinction, Aleinikoff argues that "[t]he central immigration metaphor of an earlier day—the warm, inviting melting pot—is being replaced by metaphors of impending doom by water: we hear of the steady stream, the rising tide, the waves, the flood of illegal aliens. The Court, it seems, hears the water lapping at its doors" (1987: 48).
78. Aleinikoff 1987: 47.
79. Aleinikoff 1997.
80. U.S. Select Commission 1981: 74.
81. Although changes resulting from the 1986 Immigration Reform and Control

Act (IRCA) made it a crime for employers to employ knowingly unauthorized immigrants, the de facto situation has changed little. More than a decade after IRCA's passage, there is hardly any real sanction for employers who hire "illegal" workers because the federal government must prove that the accused was fully aware of the "illegal" status of the workers, and because of the lack of enforcement resources to investigate and prosecute employers in violation of the law.

82. Aleinikoff 1997: 326. That said, there are efforts to challenge U.S. society's de jure exclusion of unauthorized immigrants. In February 2000, the AFL-CIO officially reversed its long-held immigration restrictionist position, calling for a repeal of the employers sanctions created by IRCA in 1986, for an amnesty for all undocumented immigrants, and for a program to educate immigrant workers about their civil rights. See Bacon 2000.

83. Neuman 1995: 1441.

84. Below are three letters to the editor (in whole or in part) from various newspapers that demonstrate such views.

> Respect has to be earned before it is given. Foreigners do not earn our respect by violating our laws. We should not be respected if we violate the laws of any country we might visit.
> It is a felony to enter the United States illegally. We encourage legal immigration. We assimilate large numbers of immigrants every year. But we cannot permit ourselves to be assimilated. The entire Third World is knocking at our door. (Roland H. Bouchard, San Marcos, *The San Diego Union-Tribune,* October 31, 1993).

> I am sick of hearing Proposition 187 supporters being called racists by those against 187. Try as they might to obfuscate the issue, the real issue involved in Proposition 187 is not one of race, but of whether one supports the Rule of Law.
> Our society is based upon the Rule of Law, and the absence of such would lead to anarchy. When someone is termed an illegal immigrant (of whatever age or national origin), the key word is *illegal.* Those who have come here illegally have broken the law and to reward them is to promote breaking the law. (Jim Swarzman, Senior, Economics, *UCLA Daily Bruin,* November 7, 1994)

> As a legal Latino immigrant I am amazed by what I hear and read about Prop. 187 and illegal immigration in general. . . .
> One of the reasons I wanted to come here was to leave behind the lapsed law enforcement, the corruption, the impunity, the colonial mentality prevalent everywhere in Latin America. I was convinced that this was the country of the rule of law.
> In reality, the laws in this case are not enforced. Illegal immigrants are outside the law, they are outlaws. They infringe on this country's sovereignty. This is plainly unacceptable in any civilized society. Our borders should be defended by any means, including any necessary level of force. (José M. Waechter, Redondo Beach, *Los Angeles Times,* October 11, 1994)

85. The term "illegal alien" is even stronger than "illegal immigrant" in terms of casting the unauthorized immigrant as someone to be feared and rejected. As Hugh Mehan contends in relation to Proposition 187, "The *illegal* alien designation invokes a representation of people who are outside of society. The illegal *alien* designation invokes images of foreign, repulsive, threatening, even extra-terrestrial beings. The proposition was aimed, therefore, not at 'people like us,' who are 'law-abiding' and 'tax-paying citizens.' It was aimed at foreigners, people from outside our world, who are invading and threatening our lives, 'the quality of our life' " (Mehan 1997: 258).

86. I credit Alexander Aleinikoff for pointing this out to me during my interview with him in 1997.

87. See Nevins 1998: chapter 6.

88. Ho and Marshall 1997.

89. Bosniak 1996: 571.
90. Quoted in Graham 1996: 35.
91. Andreas 1998; see also Huspek 1997.
92. See, for example, Skerry and Rockwell 1998.
93. See U.S. Border Patrol 1994.
94. INS anti-smuggling efforts are ever increasing. As part of Operation Global Reach, the INS has opened thirteen new offices abroad dedicated to disrupting migrant smuggling networks. There are now a total of thirty-five such "overseas" offices (Skerry and Rockwell 1998).
95. Andreas 1998: 349; see also Bersin and Feigin 1998.
96. Andreas 1998: 349–50; Bersin and Feigin 1998: 305; and Light 1996.
97. Light 1996.
98. Kahn 1997: 15.
99. See U.S. Border Patrol 1994.
100. See Ortiz Pinchetti 1997.
101. *Migration News*, December 2000.
102. Cleeland 1998.
103. See Cleeland 1998, Stern 1998, and Welch 1996. This practice, however, is increasingly coming under strong attack. On April 10, 2000, a federal appeals court in San Francisco pronounced as illegal the indefinite imprisonment of immigrants convicted of crimes who cannot be deported to their countries of origin due to the lack of an extradition treaty with the United States. But as federal appeals courts in Denver and New Orleans have rendered decisions in support of the federal government's practice, it is likely that the U.S. Supreme Court will hear the case and ultimately decide the legality of the practice. See Weinstein 2000.
104. See Wilgoren and McDonnell 1997, and Hedges 2000.
105. See U.S. INS 1997a.
106. See Beckett 1997.
107. McDonnell 1998, and Palafox and Jardine 1999; see also Ojito 1997a–b.
108. Ortega 1998 and Robbins 1998. Often these deportees are married and have U.S.-born (thus citizen) children. The deportations can only take a big toll on the socioeconomic security of the deportees' families. Thus, federal efforts to reduce crime associated with immigrants is most likely increasing the demand immigrants place on the Social Security net. See also Parenti 1999 and Hedges 2000.
109. See Dunn 1997, Huspek, Martinez, and Jimenez 1998, Martínez 1998, and Ortiz Pinchetti 1997. For a detailed account of one particularly infamous incident, see Davidson 2000.
110. See Parenti 1999.
111. Willoughby 1997: 287.
112. van Dijk 1996: 291; see also Huspek 1997.
113. United States Congress 1994a; see also Stern 1994d. The language authorizing the increase, contained in Title XIII—Criminal Aliens and Immigration Enforcement, Section 130006(b), Improving Border Controls, reads, "Of the sums authorized in this section, all necessary funds shall, subject to the availability of appropriations, be allocated to increase the number of agent positions (and necessary support personnel positions) in the Border Patrol by not less than 1,000 full-time equivalent positions in each of fiscal years 1995, 1996, 1997, and 1998 beyond the number funded as of October 1, 1994."
114. Beckett 1997.
115. Andreas 1997.
116. It is arguably the INS that has benefited from this resource shift more than any other U.S. government agency: as of 1997, the INS had the most armed agents of any federal bureau (*Migration News*, March 1998).
117. Heyman 1999a: 628. See also Heyman 1999b.

118. Tuan 1979.
119. For particularly powerful accounts of the difficulties encountered by immigrants trying to avoid the Border Patrol by crossing in remote areas, see Annerino 1999 and Thompson 2000.
120. See Davis 2000.
121. CRLA 1998 and 2000b; and *The San Diego Union-Tribune* 1998b; see also Ellingwood 1998b.
122. García 1980: 13. See also Annerino 1999.
123. See Curry 1986, and Bailey et al. 1996.
124. See Fineman 1998.
125. See Esbach, Hagan, and Rodriguez 2001. For an excellent series of maps showing the changing geography of migrant deaths along the California-Mexico boundary (1995–2000), see the website of the California Rural Legal Assistance Foundation's Border Project at http://www.stopgatekeeper.org.
126. CRLA 1998, 2000a, and 2000b; and ILEMP 1998. These estimates are conservative. They do not include those who have died in the deserts and mountains on the Mexican side of the boundary while attempting to gain entrance into the United States (CRLA 1998). The undercounting is also compounded by a number of other difficulties associated with researching such a phenomenon. See Bailey et al. 1996.
127. Number 500 was twenty-year-old José Luis Uriostegua of Guerrero, Mexico. Border Patrol agents discovered his frigid body on Mount Laguna in eastern San Diego County, about twenty miles north of the U.S.-Mexico boundary.
128. As one of its "indicators of success" for San Diego and El Paso, the Border Patrol included the "reduction of serious accidents involving aliens on highways, trains, drowning, dehydration (main effort)." See U.S. Border Patrol 1994: 9.
129. Interview with De La Viña 1997. The reason for this, according to INS Commissioner Doris Meissner, is that the smugglers have proven even more nefarious than anticipated. As Meissner explained in a visit to the border region in September 2000, "The geography itself in these very tough places in the mountains and desert should be a deterrent in and of itself. But what's happened is that there have been shifts in the patterns of behavior, largely by the smugglers." Meissner stated that it would take up to five more years to add enough Border Patrol agents and technology to realize "a reasonable level of control" of the rural areas traversed by unauthorized immigrants (*Migration News*, October 2000). In response, Claudia Smith of the California Rural Legal Assistance states that "If you assume that the same migrant flow will continue through the same dangerous areas, there will be at least 2,000 more deaths in the next five years" (see CRLA website: www.stopgatekeeper.org).
130. See Claudia Smith 1997 and 1998.
131. *Los Angeles Times* 1998. A few days earlier, *The San Diego Union-Tribune* editorialized that the fault for such deaths "does not lie, as some immigrant advocates claim, with the U.S. Border Patrol, which has been aggressively policing the border under Operation Gatekeeper. The increasing efficiency of border enforcement has led ruthless and inhuman smugglers to take people into the remote desert and abandon them." The editorial argued for increased penalties for smugglers and called upon the U.S. and Mexican governments to "declare war on immigrant smuggling." While not going as far as the *Los Angeles Times*, the *Union-Tribune* stated that "if an immigrant dies of heat exposure in a smuggler's charge, or after being abandoned, the smuggler should be charged with murder." Interestingly, the paper also assigned (non-criminal) responsibility for migrant deaths to American employers who "knowingly, or negligently hire illegal immigrants" and characterized as "hypocrisy" the fact that "Americans rail against illegal immigrants while enjoying the benefits of those who are debased" (see *The San Diego Union-Tribune* 1998b).
132. Mozingo 1998.

133. See, for example, Thompson 2000 and Annerino 1999. Yet as Annerino points out, there is a fine line between a rescue and an apprehension. In this regard, statistics of "rescues" reported by the Border Patrol are likely somewhat inflated. Mexico's Grupo Beta has also rescued large numbers of at-risk crossers. According to Mohar and Alacaraz (2000: 150, n. 30), there were 550 rescues on both sides of the boundary in 1998, whereas preliminary figures suggest more than 1,500 rescues for 1999.
134. Smith 1998 and *Los Angeles Times* 1998.
135. Smith 1998.
136. The term "alien" is also quite problematic. As Nestor Rodriguez argues, "Promoting perceptions of Mexicans or other national groups as 'aliens,' whether residing in the United States or in their own countries, adds to the social construction of the U.S.-Mexico border by reinforcing the idea that these national groups are incompatible with, and even harmful to, U.S. society and culture. It amounts to a process of villianization of the foreign born, which thus must be kept out with strict immigration policies and a strong southern border" (1997: 232).
137. Gutiérrez 1995: 211.
138. *The San Diego Union-Tribune* 1996.
139. Sack 1986: 33.
140. See Gutiérrez 1995. According to David Manuel Hernández, members of the Congressional Hispanic Caucus, for example, almost unanimously support increased funding for the Border Patrol and stricter immigration and boundary enforcement. While Latino members of Congress have been at the forefront of the fight against the most extreme anti-immigration measures, they have "resorted to 'damage control' maneuvers, indicating a growing tendency to sacrifice the rights of undocumented immigrants in order to protect those of immigrants recognized as legal" (Hernández 1997: 81).
141. Quoted in Holmes 1996.
142. Aleinikoff 1997: 326.
143. See U.S. Congress 1993: 148; see also Bosniak 1996, n. 41.
144. This is not his real name.

CHAPTER 7

1. Sahlins 1989: 285–286.
2. Tuan 1979: 6.
3. Sibley 1988.
4. See Anderson and O'Dowd 1999.
5. Giddens 1987: 51.
6. Giddens 1987: 51.
7. Lucien Febvre makes this argument, contending that "Given a certain type of state, we get a certain type of limit" (1973: 213).
8. Sahlins 1989: 6.
9. Sahlins 1989: 6.
10. Febvre 1973: 213.
11. Murphy 1996: 84.
12. Murphy 1996: 85–86.
13. Febvre 1973: 213–14.
14. Sahlins 1989: 7.
15. As Indonesia specialist Benedict Anderson explains, "Certain frontiers were generally recognized in practice: formidable geographical obstacles like mountains and seas, which, however, tended to be regarded as the abodes of powerful unseen forces. Otherwise the kingdoms were regarded not as having fixed and charted limits, but rather flexible, fluctuating perimeters. In a real

sense, there were no political frontiers at all, the Power of one ruler gradually falling into the distance and merging imperceptibly with the ascending Power of a neighboring sovereign" (1990: 41).

16. Anderson 1990: 41–42.
17. See Zerubavel 1996.
18. Anderson and O'Dowd 1999: 596.
19. Taylor 1993: 158.
20. Taylor 1993: 162–63; see also Torpey 2000.
21. Paasi 1996: 28.
22. Régis Debray (1977) argues that the nation is a sort of natural phenomenon— that it is the logical outgrowth of the family, the "gens," the tribe, etc. By suggesting that the nation is "natural," Debray neglects other possible outcomes (in terms of political geography) and does not at all help us to understand how the present outcome came to be.

    Eric Hobsbawm rejects such ideas in no uncertain terms as he shows when quoting Gellner noting "[W]ith Gellner I would stress the element of artifact, invention and social engineering which enters into the making of nations. 'Nations as a natural, God-given way of classifying men, as an inherent . . . polit-ical destiny, are a myth; nationalism, which sometimes takes pre-existing cultures and turns them into nations, sometimes invents them, and often obliterates pre-existing cultures: *that* is a reality.' . . . Nations do not make states and nationalisms but the other way round (Hobsbawm 1990: 10).

    As Anderson (1990: 94) points out, "most states have genealogies older than those of the nations over which they are now perched." Especially in the colonial context, it would seem logical that the state (whether consciously or not) helped to create "the nation."
23. Benedict Anderson (1990) and Eric Hobsbawm (1991) are two of the better known proponents of this view.

    That said, Anthony Smith is correct to point out that nationalists rely on the pre-national, in the form of myths and symbols, for example, to legitimate their ideology (cited in Conversi 1995: 73–74). But while nationalists draw upon "traditions" to establish a continuous thread with the past, many so-called tradi-tions are recent inventions. As such, the "invention of tradition" is also part of a nationalist project aimed at constructing and reproducing the identity of the national community (Hobsbawm 1993).
24. Giddens 1990: 1–10.
25. Harvey 1990a: 240–49.
26. Harvey 1990a: 250.
27. Harvey 1990a: 258–59.
28. Murphy 1996: 97–98.
29. Anderson 1986.
30. See Ignatieff 1994: 5.
31. Conversi 1995: 78.
32. In making this argument, Conversi draws on Frederick Barth, ed., *Ethnic Groups and Boundaries: The Social Organization of Cultural Difference*, London: Allen and Unwin, 1969.
33. Conversi 1995. In making this argument, Conversi seems to be speaking of boundaries in both the social and territorial or spatial senses of the concept.
34. Paasi 1996.
35. Manzo 1996: 3.
36. Kearney 1991: 54–55.
37. Hobsbawm 1991: 38. Quote taken from B. Porter, *Critics of Empire: British Radical Attitudes to Colonialism in Africa, 1985–1914* (London 1968), 331, citing G. Lowes Dickinson's *A Modern Symposium* (1908).
38. Appadurai 1990.
39. Featherstone 1990.

40. Arnason 1990.
41. Smith 1990.
42. Mann 1984.
43. Mann 1984: 195–96.
44. Mann 1984: 198.
45. Mann 1984.
46. Summary and critique of the Weberian view taken from Mann 1984: 188.
47. Torpey 2000.
48. Scholars often distinguish between "society-centered" and "state-centered" theorists; the first group understand the state as an extension of the will and interests of groups in society while the second group perceives the state as having a significant amount of autonomy. The dominant view of the state in the United States is a society-centered one—more precisely, a pluralist one that sees the state as a neutral arena in which competing interest groups that share underlying values struggle over different issues, eventually reaching a compromise that results in laws and policies. Indeed, this view of the state dominated U.S. social science until the late 1960s (Calavita 1992: 170–71).
49. Neo-Marxists have most forcefully put forth this argument. See Miliband 1969, and Poulantzas 1969. For a good, general overview of debates surrounding the concept of "the state," see Calavita 1992.
50. Calavita 1992: 172–74.
51. Calavita 1992: 175–76, 179. See also Skocpol 1985.
52. Uvin 1998: 163, 167.
53. Mann 1984: 195. In this sense, the state-society boundary is an elusive one in reality (Mitchell 1991).
54. See Mitchell 1991.
55. Mitchell calls the production and reproduction of the appearance of a state-society divide "the essence of modern politics" (Mitchell 1991: 95), but he does not make it clear why this divide is so important.
56. See Appadurai 1990.
57. Doty 1996a: 175.
58. Doty 1996b: 121–23.
59. Quoted in Doty 1996a: 181. Doty quotes Peter H. Schuck, "The Great Immigration Debate," *American Prospect*, Fall 1990, 100–118.
60. Doty 1996a: 182.
61. Doty 1996a: 185.
62. Doty 1996a: 186.
63. Paasi (1995 and 1996) calls this "social spatialization." Paasi borrows this concept from R. Shields, *Places on the Margin: Alternative Geographies of Modernity* (London: Routledge, 1991).
64. Agnew and Corbridge 1995.
65. Drawing on Michael Mann, I define power "in its most general sense . . . [as] the ability to pursue and attain goals through mastery of one's environment." Mann, in turn, draws on Talcott Parsons ("The Distribution of Power in American Society," in *Structure and Process in Modern Societies* [New York: The Free Press, 1960]: 199–225) to distinguish between two different aspects of power: distributive (the power of A over B) and collective ("whereby persons in cooperation can enhance their joint power over third parties or over nature"). The relationship between the two different aspects of power is dialectical in nature (Mann 1986: 6). Power itself is not a resource; rather, "(r)esources are the media through which power is exercised." In other words, it is the organization of resources (of various types) that facilitates the exercise of power (Mann 1986: 4–7).

   According to Mann, social power manifests itself in different forms or, more precisely, has different sources: ideological, economic, military and political. As multiple factors cause social change, we should avoid overarching generalizations about which single source of social power is primary in understanding social change in our contemporary world. It is more important to understand the interrelationships between the ideological, military, economic, and political, than to try to establish singular, determinant factors of social change. This is not to say that we cannot abstract one or more major structural determinants to explain social change; such an approach is unavoidable given the myriad assumptions we bring to any intellectual endeavor. But given that "societies are much *messier* than our theories of them," we need to employ an approach of skeptical empiricism in trying to understand society (Mann 1986: 3–7).

Mann distinguishes between two types of state power: *despotic* and *infrastructural*, the latter being by far the more effective of the two. Both types "flow principally from the state's unique ability to provide a territorially-centralised form of organization" (Mann 1984: 185). *Despotic* power refers to "the range of actions which the elite is empowered to undertake without routine, institutionalised negotiation with civil society groups" (Mann 1984: 188). As the capacity of the state to "actually penetrate civil society" expands, the state can increasingly implement its policies throughout the territory; Mann labels this *infrastructural* power (Mann 1984: 189).

It would seem, however, that the employment of despotic power is often a prerequisite for the establishment of infrastructural power due to frequent popular resistance to the extension of state power. Despotic power can provide a context in which the state can institutionalize power. This is certainly the case in terms of U.S. government control over the border area. Historically, the employment of despotic power was a necessary first step to "pacify" the border area as the successful establishment of a territorial administration requires internal pacification (Giddens 1987).

66. Giddens 1987: 13.
67. See Foucault 1984 and Herbert 1997.
68. Sack 1986: 19.
69. Foucault 1980 and Giddens 1987.
70. Edward Soja distinguishes between two types of space: *contextual* and *created*. *Contextual* space is given or physical space. Soja feels that such objective conceptions that see space as geometrically defined and as mere "containers" are of limited use, noting, "The dominance of the contextual view has so permeated spatial analysis that it distorts even our vocabulary. Thus, while such adjectives as 'social,' 'political,' 'economic,' and even 'historical' generally suggest, unless otherwise specified, a link to human action and motivation, the term spatial typically evokes the image of something physical and external to the social context and to social action, a part of the 'environment,' a context *for* society— its container—rather than a structure created *by* society" (Soja 1980: 210). While space "may be primordially given," its use, organization, and cultural and social meanings are very much socially constructed. It is this meaning of space which I utilize herein.
71. Doty 1996a: 126.
72. Sibley 1988: 411.
73. Sibley 1988: 417.
74. The "other" is at the same time (and, arguably, in shared space) "interior and foreign." It is perhaps for this reason that there is a perceived need within a given culture to exclude the "other" and, thus, "to exorcise the interior danger . . . in order to reduce its otherness" (Foucault 1970: xxiv).
75. Duncan 1993: 39.
76. Paasi 1996: 12.
77. See Duncan 1993. This power-laden discourse is a dialectical one between two languages, that of *difference* and that of *integration*: "The latter aims at homoge-

nizing the contents of spatial experience, the former strives to distinguish the homogenized experience from the Other" (Paasi 1996: 15).

78. Doty 1996b: 127.
79. Doty 1996b: 128.
80. Doty 1996b: 129.
81. Richmond 1994: 10.
82. Wong 1989.
83. Richmond 1994: 10.
84. Corrigan and Sayer 1985: 1–4.
85. Corrigan and Sayer 1985.
86. Heyman and Smart 1999: 10–11.

CHAPTER 8

1. Quoted in Calavita 1992: 6.
2. Rodriguez 1996: 224.
3. Gómez-Peña 1996: 70.
4. Carens 2000: 636.
5. For an interesting discussion of the case, see Chang 2000. According to Chang, "white professional women have historically relied on the 'affordability of immigrant women workers." This explains why "the major women's groups were conspicuously silent during Baird's confirmation hearings"—a manifestation of the racial and class (and nationality) privileges their members enjoy. See Chang 2000: 79–80.
6. What led to public outrage, according to Chang, was more the "resentment that this practice was so easily accessible to the more privileged classes while other working-class mothers struggled to find any child care" than the flouting of the law (Chang 2000: 55). While Chang presents a couple of anecdotes to support this contention, I would surmise that the law—as it relates to unauthorized immigrants—was an important factor in informing public opinion. As this book demonstrates, the nexus of the law, national boundaries, and the unauthorized immigrant is extremely powerful in the public imagination.
7. Chavez and her supporters argued that these tasks did not constitute work, but were the equivalent of chores that members of a household perform for the common good. Many, including a neighbor of Chavez, questioned the nominee's characterization of Mercado's performing of tasks as nonwork. As the National Network for Immigrant and Refugee Rights wrote in a January 9, 2001 press release,

> Linda Chavez is no friend to immigrants, despite her proclaimed habit of reaching out to those in need. Inviting a Guatemalan immigrant woman to clean her house in exchange for occasional "charitable gifts" of some spending money is not friendship. It's exploitation.
>
> Chavez's claim of charity smacks of an attitude all-too-typical of those who say they are "doing a favor" to immigrant women by hiring them as domestic workers. Immigrant women, usually poor women of color, are expected to be grateful for a job any job—even washing someone else's clothes and scrubbing their floors for below minimum wage.
>
> The truth is that these jobs are not so far from the work historically performed by slaves and indentured servants, among our first immigrants. Because of the informality of these jobs, domestic workers' duty usually extends round-the-clock, without formal clock-out times, privacy, or paid time off.
>
> It's work, no matter what Chavez wants to call it. And if her view of labor relations is that benevolent people with money (employers) give out charity to needy people (employees) in exchange for some floor-scrubbing, then workers are in trouble.

8. Holmes and Greenhouse 2001. While appearing on the *MacNeil-Lehrer Newshour* on PBS in December 1993, Chavez stated, "I think most of the American people were upset during the Zoë Baird nomination that she hired an illegal alien. That was what upset them more than the fact the she did not pay Social Security taxes."

9. Anthony Giddens describes globalization "as the intensification of worldwide social relations which link distant localities in such a way that local happenings are shaped by events occurring many miles away and vice versa. This is a dialectical process because such local happenings may move in an obverse direction from the very distanciated relations that shape them" (Giddens 1990: 64).

10. *La Migra* is Spanish-language slang for the enforcement arm of the INS.

11. See Beckett 1997 for an in-depth analysis of the political origins of the federal government's war on crimes and drugs.

12. See Parenti 1999.

13. See Andreas 2000 and Dunn 1996.

14. Chang 2000: 174–75.

15. Chang 2000: 216.

16. See *The Wall Street Journal* 1990: A10.

17. See Chang 2000. Because of a backlash from union, immigration, and human rights activists to INS raids of workplaces—combined with a much stronger national economy and low unemployment (see Uchitelle 2000)—raids appear to have diminished over the last couple of years.

18. Andreas 2000: 7.

19. Andreas 2000: 140.

20. Andreas 2000: 86.

21. Andreas 2000: 140.

22. Andreas 2000: 86–87.

23. Andreas 2000: 141.

24. The *Los Angeles Times* was one of the few papers that had an article on the occasion of Gatekeeper's fifth anniversary, but rather than celebrating the operation, the article suggested that the operation has fallen short of its goals. See Ellingwood 1999a.

25. In a September 2000 Gallup poll, 44 percent of respondents stated that immigrants mostly help the U.S. economy, whereas 40 percent said that they mostly hurt it. In July 1993, only 26 percent responded to the same question in a positive fashion, while 64 percent answered in a negative manner (Schmitt 2001).

26. Ojito 1998.

27. McDonnell and Ellingwood 1998. Latino immigrants—especially in California—registered as citizens in unprecedented numbers in the wake of Proposition 187.

I am not suggesting, however, there are still not efforts to intensify the "war" against "illegals." As this excerpt from a 1999 article of *The Washington Times* illustrates, the image of a U.S.-Mexico boundary "out of control" and of a wave of crime-prone, unauthorized immigrants continues to be present (albeit at a significantly lower level than in the early to mid-1990s):

The streetwise in cities like Chihuahua, Managua, San Salvador and Beijing say sneaking into the United States is a snap.

And they're right.

More than 21,000 illegals infiltrate the United States each month. Among them: petty crooks, drug couriers, mobsters and potential terrorists.

As one high-ranking Border Patrol agent stationed in the Southwest remarks: "They're getting through, and they're headed your way—to places like Washington D.C., New York and other cities in the interior."

Except in the regions around San Diego and Tucson, Ariz., and three areas in

Texas—where the border cops have been reinforced—the nation's relentlessly violated borders are increasingly underprotected and open. (Gribbin 1999)

28. A continuing worrisome development, however, are the efforts by influential individuals to warn of the supposed threat of an "alien invasion" in the form of a flood of immigrants from Mexico. In *The Next War*, for example, former Reagan administration secretary of defense Caspar Weinberger and Peter Schweitzer describe future conflicts that they envision confronting the United States. One is with Mexico after a radical populist—one very critical of the United States—comes to power in 1999. The nationalization of the banking and insurance sectors, and radical land reform lead to an economic crisis and then massive social unrest, resulting in a flood of migrants and drugs across the U.S. boundary. In response, the Pentagon sends more than 60,000 troops to the border region, and then, as tensions between the two countries mount, launches a full-scale invasion of Mexico in 2003. After approximately six months, the U.S. military withdraws, having largely eliminated the threat embodied by the rogue regime and the drug traffickers allied with it (Weinberger and Schweitzer 1996).

Many high-level national security types also continue to paint terrorism as another potential boundary-related threat. Anthony Lake, a former national security advisor in the Clinton administration, warns in a book about future potential dangers the United States could face that terrorists could easily smuggle weapons of mass destruction across the countries boundaries. "Globalization," he argues, "has dramatically multiplied the flows of goods across borders, making it effectively impossible to check what comes in and out of our country" (Lake 2000: 27).

29. Goldsborough 2000: 91. For a discussion of vigilante activity aimed at unauthorized immigrants in Douglas, Arizona, see Palafox 2000.

30. Goldsborough 2000.

31. See Huntington 1993. Huntington's thesis was that, with the end of the Cold War and the relaxing of East-West tensions, the primary source of global difference and, therefore, conflict was and would continue to be civilizational in nature. By "civilization," Huntington was referring to the highest cultural entity ("culture" being implicitly defined in an idealist manner) to which an individual or group of people attach their allegiance. For Huntington, culture has both objective aspects (language, history, and religion, for example) and the subjective aspect of self-identification. In terms of the contemporary world, Huntington identified seven or eight "major" civilizations: Western; Confucian; Japanese; Islamic; Hindu; Slavic-Orthodox; Latin American; and ("possibly") African.

32. Huntington 2000: 22.

33. MALDEF (the Mexican American Legal Defense and Educational Fund), which is hardly a "Mexican" group, describes itself as "a national nonprofit organization whose mission is to protect and promote the civil rights of the more than 29 million Latinos living in the United States" (see www.maldef.org). MALDEF supports important elements of the Washington establishment's agenda for the border region, such as NAFTA. See Hernández 1997.

34. Mann 1993; see also Brenner 1999.

35. Giddens 1990 and Harvey 1995b.

36. Sassen 1998: 7.

37. Sassen 1998: 7–8.

38. U.S. Select Commission 1981: 74.

39. Aleinikoff 1997: 326.

40. Massey et al. (1993) label this mode of analysis a "micro-neoclassical" perspective.

41. See Beckett 1997.

42. There is nothing automatic about international norms leading to more open immigration regimes. As Gurowitz (1999) demonstrates, a variety of outcomes

are possible given the complex interplay of national and international factors. While international norms provide a useful tool for those trying to liberalize national immigration regimes, myriad national factors significantly inform the potential effectiveness of this international "tool." See Gurowitz 1999 for a very interesting analysis of the effectiveness of pro-immigrant activism employing international norms in the case of Japan.

43. Sassen 1998: 8–18.
44. *Migration News*, June 1997.
45. Mitchell 1991; and Doty 1996a and 1996b.
46. Sassen 1998: 20.
47. Doty 1996a.
48. Sassen 1998: 10.
49. Giddens 1990: 3.
50. Giddens 1990: 6.
51. Giddens 1990: 7–10.
52. Giddens 1990: 175.
53. See Giddens 1990: 65. As Saskia Sassen (1996: 59) states, "Economic globalization denationalizes national economies; in contrast, immigration is renationalizing politics."
54. Richmond (1994) calls this sense of individual security "ontological security." Drawing on R. D. Laing (*The Self and Others: Further Studies in Sanity and Madness* [New York: Pantheon, 1960]), Richmond defines ontological security "in terms of an individual's self-confidence, derived from a sense of the permanency of things." It involves a disruption of the routines necessary for everyday life (Richmond 1994: 19).
55. Immigrants and refugees are often innocent victims in this struggle, "caught in this countervailing effort to combat the onslaught of a global system on the sovereignty of states" (Richmond 1994: 34).
56. Huysmans 1995: 53–59; see also Teitelbaum and Weiner 1995.
57. Manzo 1996: 19.
58. Indeed, even supposed liberals like President Bill Clinton construct a fear of the "other" in the name of the national interest. In arguing for support for a financial aid package to Mexico in the aftermath of the collapse of the peso, for example, Clinton warned that the package was necessary to prevent Mexico's economy from worsening which would lead to the influx of an additional one million unauthorized immigrants into California and Texas in 1995 (Willoughby 1997: 271).
59. Manzo 1996: 220.
60. Andreas 1998 and 2000.
61. Manzo 1996: 38. Quote within the quote taken from Geoffrey Bennington, "Postal Politics and the Institutions of the Nation," in Bhaba 1990: 121
62. See Peck and Tickell 1994.
63. Harvey 1995b: 10.
64. Harvey 1995b: 11.
65. See Beckett 1997 and Andreas 1997. See also Parenti 1999.
66. See Lewis 1979: 182–84.
67. See, for example, Ohmae 1995.
68. Anderson 1996: 190. Regarding transnational "flows," see Appadurai 1990.
69. Taylor 1993.
70. See Anderson and O'Dowd 1999.
71. Anderson 1996: 190–91.
72. See Anderson 1996: 191.
73. Massey 1998, Sassen 1998, and Zolberg 1978.
74. Sassen 1998; see also Harris 1995.
75. *Migration News*, November 1998.
76. The Border Patrol hired 1,100 new agents in FY 1999, but because of a high

turnover among Border Patrol agents, the net increase was only 369 agents, short of the 1,000-a-year increase mandated by Congress (*Migration News*, February 2000).

77. Andreas 1998 and 2000.
78. Agnew and Corbridge 1995.
79. See Rouse 1995.
80. Bosniak 1996: 607–10.
81. See Rosen 1998. See also Hathaway 2000.
82. See Moody 1997.
83. Anderson 1996: 191.
84. See Davis 2000, chapter 8, for a fascinating discussion of transnational communities in the United States and Mexico.
85. From *Democracy Now!* radio show, Pacifica Radio, December 29, 2000 (available online at www.pacifica.org).
86. At other times, however, Clark seems to suggest that too much entho-linguistic diversity/racial diversity in a geographically defined area—especially among the socioeconomically disadvantaged—leads almost automatically to conflict as groups struggle over political power and the crumbs of the economic pie. Clark's call for a far greater public investment in education "from a California perspective" entails "a critical need for greater federal recognition of the special role of California as the immigrant entry port" (1998: 195). Because of the high proportion of immigrants in California, the costs of educating immigrant children are highly localized, necessitating, in Clark's estimation, a significant increase in federal funding for education.
87. Stoll 1997.
88. See Stoll's letter to the editor in *NACLA Report on the Americas*, November–December 1993.
89. Carens 2000: 642.
90. Chang 2000.
91. See Barry and Goodin 1992 for a presentation of a variety of philosophical perspectives on freedom of movement.
92. See, for example *The Wall Street Journal* 1990. For an interesting critique of some studies informed by such logic, see Chang 2000.
93. See Isbister 2000.
94. See Carens 2000.
95. See, for example, Ingram, Laney, and Gillian 1995: 3. See Walzer (1984) as it is probably the best known example promoting such a view.
96. Bosniak 1996. Of course, many have already done so. In southern Arizona, for example, church-affiliated and other humanitarians provide assistance to unauthorized migrants as they make the dangerous trek across the state's harsh terrain. In doing so, some of these "good Samaritans" are running significant risks as their actions sometimes are in violation of immigration laws. See Ellingwood 2000.
97. See Bosniak 1996, Castles and Davidson 2000, Flores 1997, Jonas 1996, and Lee 1996.
98. Galeano 2000: 31.
99. Along many of these boundaries—as in the United States—unauthorized immigrants often meet their untimely deaths in their efforts to avoid state authorities. An estimated 360 persons, for example, died in 2000 trying to cross the sea from Morocco to Spain (Lennon 2000–2001). See also Stanley 2000. Regarding the criminalization of foreigners in Europe, see Wacquant 1999.
100. Regarding South Africa, see, for example, Magardie 2000.
101. Anderson 1996. Heyman (1999: 621) argues that immigration interdiction "maintains the distinction between the two [significantly unequal in a socio-economic sense] polities that undegirds their different social wages." For an interesting discussion of the relationship of enhanced boundary enforcement,

economic development in the border region, and socioeconomic inequality between the United States and Mexico, see Dunn 1996, Chapter 5.

102. Falk 1993: 629. See also Bendaña 1994. Anthony Richmond (1994) interrogates this phenomenon in greater depth, demonstrating how perceived threats to the territorial integrity and privileged lifestyles in wealthy countries (which are predominately white) have led them to increase measures to prevent unwanted immigration by largely poor and nonwhite peoples.

Descriptions of the world economic order as apartheid-like are not limited to progressive analysts. In trying to imagine the outlines of a constitutionally based "new world order" in which a reduction in national sovereignty would be the trade-off for "a more effective legal structure," conservative scholar Thomas Schelling suggests that the outcome would be "stunning and depressing" in that it would probably resemble apartheid-South Africa:

> We live in a world that is one-fifth rich and four-fifths poor; the rich are segregated into the rich countries and the poor into the poor countries; the rich are predominately lighter skinned and the poor darker skinned; most of the poor live in "homelands" that are physically remote, often separated by oceans and great distances from the rich.
>
> Migration on any great scale is impermissible. There is no systematic redistribution of income. While there is ethnic strife among the well-to-do, the strife is more vicious and destructive among the poor.
>
> [W]e have defined national security as "preserving the U.S. as a free nation with our fundamental institutions and values intact." "Values" is a wonderfully ambiguous word. I believe it must include what we *possess* as well as what we *appreciate*. It includes our material standard of living. We protect those institutions and values by, among other things, protecting our national boundaries. (Schelling 1992: 200)

103. In this respect, it is time to resurrect the debate among progressive geographers regarding whether inequality across space is merely an inevitable outcome or is a necessary aspect to the production, reproduction, and maintenance of the capitalist mode of production (see Browett 1984). Whether or not we see inequality across space as a necessary condition for capitalism or as an epiphenomenon of capitalism that capitalists exploit has important implications for social theory as well as progressive politics.

104. Gilbert Cardenas (1979) differentiates between two epistemological approaches to studying the question of immigration: the "dominant political paradigm" and what he champions, a "critical-scientific paradigm." The critical-scientific approach does not take political economic relations as a given, and "unlike the dominant political paradigm, it is not necessary for a critical-scientific paradigm to limit crucial questions and suggest practical solutions that are directly linked to its survival [that of the paradigm]" (Cardenas 1979: 89). The critical-scientific paradigm seeks to pose questions and offer solutions that go beyond the boundaries of the dominant political paradigm. But first, "the social sciences must also struggle themselves away from political consciousness (political knowledge) before they can make significant advances under the problematics of science." Only in this way can social science serve all of humanity, rather than the interests of powerful groups (Cardenas 1979: 89–90).

105. Pacific Council on International Policy 1999. Signatories to the piece included: Alan Bersin, the former United States Attorney General's Special Representative for Southwest Border Issues (and currently the head of the San Diego public school system); Kathleen Brown, the California Democratic Party's gubernatorial nominee in 1994 and current president of Private Bank West, Bank of America; Susan Golding, then mayor of San Diego; Antonia Hernandez, president, Mexican American Legal Defense Fund (MALDEF); and Julie Meier Wright, CEO, San Diego Development Corporation.

106. Pacific Council on International Policy 1999.

107. Pacific Council on International Policy 1999.

Bibliography

BOOKS, ARTICLES, AND REPORTS

Abramovitz, Mimi. 1996. *Regulating the Lives of Women: Social Welfare Policy from Colonial Times to the Present* (revised edition). Boston: South End Press.

Acuña, Rodolfo. 1988. *Occupied America: A History of Chicanos.* New York: Harper-Collins.

———. 1996. *Anything But Mexican: Chicanos in Contemporary Los Angeles.* New York: Verso.

Adler, Jerry and Tim Padgett. 1995. "Selena Country," *Newsweek,* October 23: 76–79.

Agnew, John and Stuart Corbridge. 1995. *Mastering Space: Hegemony, Territory and International Political Economy.* New York: Routledge.

Aleinikoff, T. Alexander. 1987. "Good Aliens, Bad Aliens and the Supreme Court." In Lydio F. Tomasi (ed.), *In Defense of the Alien* (Volume IX), Proceedings of the 1986 Annual National Legal Conference on Immigration and Refugee Policy, vol. 9. New York: Center for Migration Studies, 46–51.

———. 1997. "The Tightening Circle of Membership." In Juan F. Perea (ed.), *Immigrants Out! The New Nativism and the Anti-Immigrant Impulse in the United States.* New York: New York University Press, 324–32.

Almaguer, Tomás. 1994. *Racial Fault Lines: The Historical Origins of White Supremacy in California.* Berkeley and Los Angeles: University of California Press, 1994.

Alter, Jonathan. 1984. "Games Illegals Play." *Newsweek,* June 25: 24–26.

Alvord, Valerie. 1993. "County Sending Clinton Tab for Immigrants." *The San Diego Union-Tribune,* September 29: A-1+.

Anderson, Benedict. 1990. *Language and Power—Exploring Political Cultures in Indonesia.* Ithaca: Cornell University Press.

———. 1991. *Imagined Communities—Reflections on the Origin and Spread of Nationalism.* London: Verso (original edition, 1983).

Anderson, James. 1986. "Nationalism and Geography." In James Anderson (ed.), *The Rise of the Modern State.* Brighton (U.K.): Wheatsheaf.

Anderson, James and Liam O'Dowd. 1997. "Borders, Border Regions and Territoriality: Contradictory Meanings, Changing Significance," *Regional Studies* 33, no. 7: 593–604.

Anderson, Malcolm. 1996. *Frontiers: Territory and State Formation in the Modern World.* Cambridge: Polity Press.

Andreas, Peter. 1994. "The Making of Amerexico: (Mis)Handling Illegal Immigration." *World Policy Journal,* summer: 45–56.

———. 1996. "U.S.–Mexico: Open Markets, Closed Borders." *Foreign Policy* 103: summer: 51–69.

———. 1997. "The Rise of the American Crimefare State." *World Policy Journal,* fall: 37–45.

———. 1998. "The U.S. Immigration Control Offensive: Constructing an Image of Order on the Southwest Border." In Marcelo Suárez-Orozco (ed.), *Crossings: Mexican Immigration in Interdisciplinary Perspectives.* Cambridge, Mass.: Harvard University Press, for the David Rockefeller Center for Latin American Studies: 343–56.

———. 1998–99. "The Escalation of U.S. Immigration Control in the Post-NAFTA Era." *Political Science Quarterly* 113, no. 4: 591–615.

———. 2000. *Border Games: Policing the U.S.-Mexico Divide*. Ithaca: Cornell University Press.

Andreas, Peter and Timothy Snyder (eds.). 2000. *The Wall Around the West: State Borders and Immigration Control in North America and Europe*. Lanham, Md.: Rowman and Littlefield.

Annerino, John. 1999. *Dead in Their Tracks: Crossing America's Borderlands*. New York: Four Walls Eight Windows.

Appadurai, Arjun. 1990. "Disjuncture and Difference in the Global Cultural Economy." *Theory, Culture & Society* 7, nos. 2–3: 295–310.

Ardman, Harvey. 1974. "Our Illegal Alien Problem." *The American Legion Magazine* 97, no. 6: 6–9+.

Arnason, Johann P. 1990. "Nationalism, Globalization and Modernity." *Theory, Culture and Society* 7, nos. 2–3: 207–36.

Arreola, Daniel D. and James R. Curtis. 1993. *The Mexican Border Cities: Landscape Anatomy and Place Personality*. Tucson: The University of Arizona Press.

Aung-Thwin, M. 1985. "The British 'Pacification' of Burma: Order Without Meaning." *Journal of Southeast Asian Studies* 16, no. 2: 245–61.

Bach, Robert. 1997. Talk at Immigration Control Panel at workshop entitled "Perspectives on U.S.-Mexico Border Policy." Center for U.S.-Mexican Studies, University of California, San Diego, October 17, 1997.

Bacon, David. 2000. "Labor's About-Face." *The Nation*, March 20: 6–7.

Bailey, Stanley R., Karl Eschbach, Jaqueline Maria Hagan, and Nestor Rodriguez. 1996. "Migrant Deaths at the Texas-Mexico Border, 1985–1994." Center for Immigration Research, University of Houston, January.

Baird, Peter and Ed McCaughan. 1979. *Beyond the Border*. New York: North American Congress on Latin America.

Baldassare, Mark. 2000. *California in the New Millenium: The Changing Social and Political Landscape*. Berkeley and Los Angeles: University of California Press.

Balderrama, Francisco E. and Raymond Rodríguez. 1995. *Decade of Betrayal: Mexican Repatriation in the 1930s*. Albuquerque: University of New Mexico Press.

Barabak, Mark Z. 1993. "Wilson Urges Expanded Border Blockade." *The San Diego Union-Tribune*, December 21: A-1+.

Barfield, Chet. 1989. "Flood Lamps Shedding Light on Illegal Activity along Border." *The Tribune* (San Diego), September 29: A-1+.

———. 1991. "Border Patrol on Guard as Smugglers Foil Huge Project to Fence Them Out." *The San Diego Tribune*, June 21: A-1+.

———. 1992. "Border Patrol Seeks Help of Top Mexico Cops." *The San Diego Tribune*, January 25: B-+.

Barker, Jeff and Mark Shaffer. 1998. "Troops on Border." *The Arizona Republic*, June 14.

Barnes, Fred. 1993. "No Entry: The Republicans' Immigration War." *The New Republic*, November 8: 10+.

———. "Crime Scene: Republicans With a Cause." *The New Republic*, September 5: 30+.

Barry, Brian and Robert E. Goodin (eds.). 1992. *Free Movement: Ethical Issues in the Transnational Migration of People and of Money*. University Park: Pennsylvania State University Press.

Barry, Tom with Harry Browne and Beth Sims. 1994. *Crossing the Line: Immigrants, Economic Integration, and Drug Enforcement on the U.S.-Mexico Border*. Albuquerque: Resource Center Press, 1994.

Bean, Frank D., Ronald Chanove, Robert G. Cushing, Rodolfo de la Garza, Gary P. Freeman, Charles W. Haynes and David Sponer. 1994. *Illegal Mexican Migration and the United States/Mexico Border: The Effects of Operation Hold-The-Line on El Paso/Juarez*. Austin: Population Research Center, University of Texas at Austin (prepared for the U.S. Commission on Immigration Reform).

Beckett, Katherine. 1997. *Making Crime Pay: Law and Order in Contemporary American Politics*. New York: Oxford University Press, 1997.

Bendaña, Alejandro. 1994. "The 'New World Order'—Neither New, Global nor Orderly." *Links* (New South Wales, Australia) no. 2: 37–59.

Berger, John. 1980. *Ways of Seeing*. Harmondsworth, U.K.: Penguin.

Berman, Marshall. 1982. *All That Is Solid Melts into Air: The Experience of Modernity*. New York: Simon and Schuster.

Bernstein, Harry. 1977. "Panel to Deal With Illegal Aliens Is Established by Administration." *The Washington Post*, February 22.

Bersin, Alan D. 1996a. "El Tercer País: Reinventing the U.S./Mexico Border." *Stanford Law Review* 48: 1413–20.

———. 1996b. "Statement of Alan D. Bersin, United States Attorney, Southern District of California, Concerning Operation Gatekeeper." Committee on Government Reform and Oversight, Subcommittee on Government Management, Information and Technology, U.S. House of Representatives, Imperial Beach City Hall, August 9, 1996.

———. 1996c. "Reinventing the U.S./Mexico Border" (op-ed). *The San Diego Union-Tribune*, August 25.

Bersin, Alan D. and Judith S. Feigin. 1998. "The Rule of Law at the Margin: Reinventing Prosecution Policy in the Southern District of California." *Georgetown Immigration Law Journal* 12, no. 2: 285–310.

Best, Natalie. 1960. "Halt Border Dope Traffic, VFW Asks." *The San Diego Union*, June 24: A–17.

Bhabha, Homi K. 1990. *Nation and Narration*, New York: Routledge.

Binder, Norman E., J. L. Polinard, and Robert D. Winkle. 1997. "Mexican American and Anglo Attitudes toward Immigration Reform: A View from the Border." *Social Science Quartely* 78, no. 2: 324–37.

Blaut, James M. 1992. "The Theory of Cultural Racism." *Antipode* 24, no. 4: 289–99.

Blomley, Nicholas K. *Law, Space, and the Geographies of Power*. New York: Guilford Press.

Borjas, George. 2000. "The Case for Choosing More Skilled Immigrants." *The American Enterprise* 11, no. 8: 30–31.

Bosniak, Linda S. 1996. "Opposing Prop. 187: Undocumented Immigrants and the National Imagination." *Connecticut Law Review* 28, no. 3: 555–619.

Botts, Gene. 1997. *The Border Game: Enforcing America's Immigration Laws*. Phoenix: Quest.

Brady, Mary Pat. 2000. "The Fungibility of Borders." *Nepantla: Views from the South* 1, no. 1: 179–99

Braun, Gerry. 1986. "Wilson Would Close Border If . . ." *The San Diego Union*, August 22: A-1+.

———. 1987. "Area Lawmakers Differ on Beefing Up Fence at Border." *The San Diego Union*, February 14: A-3.

———. 1992. "75% See U.S. Seriously Off Track." *The San Diego Union*, February 10: A-1+.

Brenner, Neil. 1999. "Beyond State-Centrism? Space, Territoriality, and Geographical Scale in Globalization Studies." *Theory and Society* 28: 39–78.

Brimelow, Peter. 1995. *Alien Nation: Common Sense About America's Immigration Disaster*. New York: Random House.

Briseno, Olga and Benjamin Shore. 1989. "Border Trench Plan Cuts Swath of Controversy." *The San Diego Union*, January 26: A-1+.

Browett, John. 1984. "On the Necessity and the Inevitability of Uneven Spatial Development Under Capitalism." *International Journal of Urban and Regional Research* 8, no. 2: 155–75.

Brown, Jim. 1991. *Riding the Line: The United States Customs Service in San Diego, 1885–1930*. Washington, D.C.: Department of the Treasury, United States Customs Service.

Buchanan, Patrick J. 1994. "What Will America Be in 2050?" (op-ed). *Los Angeles Times*, October 28.

Buchanan, Ruth. 1995. "Border Crossings: NAFTA, Regulatory Restructuring, and the Politics of Place." *Indiana Journal of Global Legal Studies* 2, no. 2: 371–93.

Buffington, Robert. 1994. "Prohibition in the Borderlands: National Government-Border Community Relations." *Pacific Historical Review* 63, no. 1: 19–38.

Burawoy, Michael (ed.). 1991. *Ethnography Unbound: Power and Resistance in the Modern Metropolis*. Berkeley and Los Angeles: University of California Press.

Burgess, Robert G. 1982. "The Unstructured Interview as a Conversation." In Robert G. Burgess (ed.), *Field Research: A Sourcebook and Manuel*. London: Allen and Unwin.

Bustamente, Jorge A. 1972. "The 'Wetback' as Deviant: An Application of Labeling Theory." *American Journal of Sociology* 77, no. 4: 706–18.

———. 1973. "The Historical Context of Undocumented Mexican Immigration to the United States." *Aztlan* 3, no. 2: 257–81.

———. 1990. "México-Estados Unidos: Migración Indocumentada y Seguridad Nacional." In Sergio Agauayo Quezada and Bruce Michael Bagley (eds.), *En Busca de la Seguridad Perdida: Aproximaciones a la Seguridad Nacional Mexicana*. Mexico City: Siglo Veintiuno Editores: 340–66.

Calavita, Kitty. 1982. *California's "Employer Sanctions": The Case of the Disappearing Law*. Research Report Series 39. San Diego: Center for U.S.-Mexican Studies, University of California, San Diego.

———. 1984. *U.S. Immigration Law and the Control of Labor: 1820–1924*. Orlando, Florida: Academic Press.

———. 1992. *Inside the State: The Bracero Program, Immigration, and the I.N.S.* New York: Routledge.

———. 1994. "U.S. Immigration and Policy Responses: The Limits of Legislation." In Wayne Cornelius, Philip L. Martin, and James F. Hollifield (eds.), *Controlling Immigration: A Global Perspective*. Stanford: Stanford University Press, 55–82.

———. 1996. "The New Politics of Immigration: Balanced-Budget Conservatism and the Symbolism of Proposition 187." *Social Problems* 43, no. 3: 284–305.

Caldwell, Robert J. 1991. "Washington Is Shirking the Costs of Immigration" (op-ed). *The San Diego Union*, September 29: C-1+.

California Rural Legal Assistance Foundation. 1998. Press release regarding migrant deaths, Oceanside, California, September 11.

———. 2000a. "Migrant Deaths from San Diego to Yuma, 1995–2000." Oceanside, California, February 21.

———. 2000b. Press release regarding migrant deaths, Oceanside, California, April 5.

California Senate Office of Research. 1994. "Addressing Immigration Issues in California." Briefing paper on California immigration issues prepared for Senator Bill Lockyer, March.

Camarota, Steven A. 1997. "Reducing Greenhouse Gases: The Vital Immigration Angle" (op-ed). *The San Diego Union-Tribune*, November 28.

Cardenas, Gilbert. 1979. "Critical Issues in Using Government Data Collected Primarily for Non-Research Purposes." In Stephen R. Crouch and Roy Simón Bryce-Laporte (eds.), *Quantitative Data and Immigration Research*. Washington, D.C.: Research Institute on Immigration and Ethnic Studies, Smithsonian Institution: 55–98.

Carens, Joseph H. 1999. "Reconsidering Open Borders: A Reply to Meilander." *International Migration Review* 33, no. 4: 1082–97.

———. 2000. "Open Borders and Liberal Limits: A Response to Isbister." *International Migration Review* 34, no. 2: 636–43.

Carey, Ryan. 1998. "The Geography of Chaos: William H. Emory's Images of the Texas Borderlands." *Paisano* 1, no. 1 June 1998 (online journal: http://ccwf.cc.utexas.edu/~paisano/).

Carr, Matthew. 1997. "Policing the Frontier: Ceuta and Melilla." *Race and Class* 39, no. 1: 61–66.

Carter, Bob, Marci Green, and Rick Halpern. 1996. "Immigration Policy and the Racialization of Migrant Labour: The Construction of National Identities in the USA and Britain." *Ethnic and Racial Studies* 19, no. 1: 135–57.

Cary, James. 1977. "Carter Discusses Border Problems." *The San Diego Union*, February 10: A-1+.

Castles, Stephen and Alastair Davidson. 2000. *Citizenship and Migration: Globalization and the Politics of Belonging.* New York: Routledge.

Castles, Stephen and Mark J. Miller. 1993. *The Age of Migration: International Population Movements in the Modern World.* New York: Guilford Press.

Chamberlin, Eugene Keith. 1951. "Mexican Colonization versus American Interests in Lower California." *Pacific Historical Review* 20, no. 1: 43–55.

Chang, Grace. 1996. "Disposable Nannies: Women's Work and the Politics of Latina Immigration." *Radical America* 26, no. 2: 5–20.

———. 2000. *Disposable Domestics: Immigrant Women Workers in the Global Economy.* Cambridge: South End Press.

Chapman, Leonard F. 1976. "Illegal Aliens: Time to Call a Halt!" *The Reader's Digest*, October: 188–92.

Chavez, Leo R. 1997. "Immigration Reform and Nativism: The Nationalist Response to the Transnationalist Challenge." In Juan F. Perea (ed.), *Immigrants Out! The New Nativism and the Anti-Immigrant Impulse in the United States.* New York: New York University Press: 61–77.

———. 1998. *Shadowed Lives: Undocumented Immigrants in American Society*, 2d. ed. New York: Harcourt Brace Jovanovich College Publishers.

Chavira, Ricardo. 1990. "Hatred, Fear and Violence." *Time*, November 19: 12+.

Chaze, William L. 1985. "On El Main Street, U.S.A., The Birth of a New Nation." *U.S. News and World Report*, August 19: 32–35.

Church, George J. 1993. "Send Back Your Tired, Your Poor . . . " *Time*, June 21: 26–27.

Clance, Homer. 1969. "U.S. Will Inspect All Border Traffic." *The San Diego Union*, September 18: A-1+.

Clark, William A. V. 1998. *The California Cauldron: Immigration and the Fortunes of Local Communities.* New York: Guilford Press, 1998.

Cleeland, Nancy. 1989a. " 'Sunken Wall' Is Among Group's Tough Border Control Measures." *The San Diego Union*, January 27: B-1+.

———. 1989b. "Flood of Aliens Dwindles to Trickle." *The San Diego Union*, February 19: B-1+.

———. 1989c. "Mexico, U.S. Join in Sweep of Border." *The San Diego Union*, February 24: B-1+.

———. 1989d. "INS Plan for Ditch as Border Barrier Is Castigated at Hearing." *The San Diego Union*, March 23: B-3+.

———. 1998. "Waits, Crowding Worsen Tensions in INS Centers." *Los Angeles Times*, March 14: A-1+.

Clinton, Bill and Al Gore. 1992. *Putting People First: How We All Can Change America.* New York: Times Books.

Cockcroft, James D. 1986. *Outlaws in the Promised Land: Mexican Immigrant Workers and America's Future.* New York: Grove Press.

Cohen, Laurie P. 1998. "Free Ride: With Help From INS, U.S. Meatpacker Taps Mexican Work Force." *The Wall Street Journal*, October 15: A1+.

Condon, George E. and Dana Wilkie. 1993. "U.S. Must Gain Control of Border, Clinton Says." *The San Diego Union-Tribune*, October 4: A-1+.

Commissioner-General of Immigration. 1903. *Annual Report of the Commissioner-General of Immigration for the Fiscal Year Ending June 30, 1903.* Washington, D.C.: Government Printing Office.

Conniff, Ruth. 1993. "The War on Aliens." *The Progressive*, October 22: 22–29.

Conversi, Daniele. 1995. "Reassessing Current Theories of Nationalism: Nationalism as Boundary Maintenance and Creation." *Nationalism and Ethnic Politics* 1, no. 1: 73–85.

Cooper, Marc. 1997. "The Heartland's Raw Deal: How Meatpacking is Creating a New Immigrant Underclass." *The Nation* 264, no. 4: 11–17.

Coppock, Donald R. 1968. "History: Border Patrol." Unpublished manuscript, available in the library of the INS Historian, Washington, D.C. .

Cornelius, Wayne A. 1978. *Mexican Migration to the United States: Causes, Consequences, and U.S. Responses.* Cambridge, Mass.: Center for International Studies, Massachusetts Institute of Technology.

———. 1998. "The Structural Embeddedness of Demand for Mexican Immigrant Labor: New Evidence from California." In Marcelo Suárez-Orozco (ed.), *Crossings: Mexican Immigration in Interdisciplinary Perspectives.* Cambridge, Mass.: Harvard University Press, for the David Rockefeller Center for Latin American Studies: 115–44.

Corrigan, Philip and Derek Sayer. 1985. *The Great Arch: English State Formation as Cultural Revolution.* Oxford: Basil Blackwell.

Coutin, Susan Bibler and Phyllis Pease Chock. 1995. "'Your Friend, the Illegal:' Definition and Paradox in Newspaper Accounts of U.S. Immigration Reform." *Identities* 2, nos. 1–2: 123–48.

Crewdson, John M. 1979. "Border Region Is Almost a Country unto Itself, Neither Mexican Nor American." *The New York Times,* February 24: A22.

Cubbison, Gene. 1978. "Park with Flimsy Fence Leads Border Patrol's Trouble List." *The San Diego Union,* July 24: B-1+.

Curry, Bill. 1986. "Hunt for Better Life Leads Aliens to 'Season of Death.' " *Los Angeles Times,* June 16: 1.

Daniels, Stephen. 1993. *Fields of Vision: Landscape Imagery and National Identity in England and the United States.* Cambridge: Polity Press.

Davidson, Miriam. 2000. *Lives on the Line: Dispatches from the U.S.-Mexico Border.* Tucson: The University of Arizona Press.

Davidson, Winifred. 1934a. "Famous 'Firsts' of San Diego, No. 49—First Activities of the Mexican Line Runners." *The San Diego Union,* August 5.

———. 1934b. "Famous 'Firsts' of San Diego: no. 50—The First Boundary Monument." *The San Diego Union,* August 12.

Davis, Don. 1986. "Troops Are Proposed for Border." *The San Diego Union,* March 22: B-3.

Davis, Mike. 2000. *Magical Urbanism: Latinos Reinvent the U.S. City.* London: Verso.

Debray, Régis. 1977. "Marxism and the National Question." Interview. *New Left Review,* no. 105: 25–41.

Delgado, Richard and Jean Stefanic. 1992. "Images of the Outsider in American Law and Culture: Can Free Expression Remedy Systemic Social Ills?" *Cornell Law Review* 77, no. 6: 1258–97.

DePalma, Anthony. 1996. "U.S.-Mexican Border: A Shifting Line in the Mud." *The New York Times,* May 7.

Diamond, Sara. 1996. "Right-Wing Politics and the Anti-Immigration Cause." *Social Justice* 23, no. 3: 154–68.

Dietrich, Robert. 1986. "Marines Manning Border Sites." *The Tribune* (San Diego), April 24: A-1+.

Dillin, John. 1986. "Illegal Aliens Flood Across U.S. Border." *The Christian Science Monitor,* February 21: 1+.

Dillon, Patrick. 1975. "Border Area Emerges As Heroin Hub." *The San Diego Union,* April 10: B-1.

Donner, John. 1979. "1,300 Protest 'Tortilla Curtain.' " *The San Diego Union,* February 12: A-3.

Doty, Roxanne L. 1996a. "The Double-Writing of Statecraft: Exploring State Responses to Illegal Immigration." *Alternatives* 21: 171–89.

———. 1996b. "Sovereignty and the Nation: Constructing the Boundaries of National Identity." In Thomas J. Biersteker and Cynthia Weber (eds.), *State Sovereignty as Social Construct.* Cambridge: Cambridge University Press: 121–47.

Driessen, Henk. 1998. "The 'New Immigration' and the Transformation of the European-African Frontier." In Thomas M. Wilson and Hastings Donnan (eds.), *Border Identities: Nation and State at International Frontiers*. Cambridge: Cambridge University Press: 96–116.

Drogin, Bob. 1996. "Post-Apartheid S. Africa Targets Illegal Migrants." *Los Angeles Times*, October 7: A1+.

Duffy, Brian. 1993. "Coming to America." *U.S. News and World Report*, June 21: 26–29+.

Duncan, James. 1993. "Sites of Representation: Place, Time, and the Discourse of the Other." In James Duncan and David Ley (eds.), *Place/Culture/Representation*. New York: Routledge: 39–56.

Dunkerley, J. 1994. *The Pacification of Central America*. New York: Verso.

Dunn, Timothy J. 1996. *The Militarization of the U.S.-Mexico Border, 1978–1992: Low-Intensity Conflict Doctrine Comes Home*. Austin: Center for Mexican American Studies, University of Texas at Austin, 1996.

———. 1999. "Border Enforcement and Human Rights Violations in the Southwest." In Chris G. Ellison and W. Allen Martin (eds.), *Race and Ethnic Relations in the United States: Readings for the 21st Century*. Los Angeles: Roxbury, 443–51.

Edelman, Murray. 1985. *The Symbolic Uses of Politics*. Urbana: University of Illinois Press.

Edmonston, Barry, Jeffrey S. Passel, and Frank D. Bean. 1990. "Perceptions and Estimates of Undocumented Migration to the United States." In Frank D. Bean, Barry Edmonston, and Jeffrery S. Passell. *Undocumented Migration to the United States: IRCA and the Experience of the 1980s*. Washington, D.C.: The Urban Institute Press: 11–31.

Eisenstadt, Todd A. and Cathryn L. Thorup. 1994. *Caring Capacity versus Carrying Capacity: Community Responses to Mexican Immigration in San Diego's North County*. San Diego: The Center for U.S.-Mexican Studies, University of California, San Diego.

Ellingwood, Ken. 1998a. "A Border War on Boozing." *Los Angeles Times*, April 9: A1+.

———. 1998b. "Activists in Tijuana Mourn Dead Migrants." *Los Angeles Times*, November 3: A3+.

———. 1999a. "Data on Border Arrests Raise Gatekeeper Debate." *Los Angeles Times*, October 1: A3+.

———. 1999b. "Border Trade Boom Gives Rise to New Ports of Entry." *Los Angeles Times*, December 28: A28.

———. 2000. "Humanitarians Drive to Aid Migrants Gains Momentum." *Los Angeles Times*, December 19: A1+.

Endicott, William. 1977. "Carter Tells of Concern Over Illegal Aliens Issue." *Los Angeles Times*, February 10: I, 3.

———. 1993. "Immigration: The Issue for '94" (op-ed). *The San Diego Union-Tribune*, August 4.

Esbach, Karl, Jacqueline Hagan, and Nestor Rodriguez. 2001. "Causes and Trends in Migrant Deaths along the U.S.-Mexico Border, 1985–1998." Houston: Center for Immigration Research, University of Houston.

Escobar, Edward J. 1999. *Race, Police, and the Making of a Political Identity: Mexican Americans and the Los Angeles Police Department, 1900–1945*. Berkeley: University of California Press.

Espenshade, Thomas J. "Using INS Border Apprehension Data to Measure the Flow of Undocumented Migrants Crossing the U.S.-Mexico Frontier." *International Migration Review* 29, no. 2: 545–565.

Espenshade, Thomas J. and Maryann Belanger. "Immigration and Public Opinion." In Marcelo Suárez-Orozco (ed.), *Crossings: Mexican Immigration in Interdisciplinary Perspectives*. Cambridge, Mass: Harvard University Press, for the David Rockefeller Center for Latin American Studies: 365–403.

Espenshade, Thomas J. and Charles A. Calhoun. 1993. "An Analysis of Public Opinion toward Undocumented Immigration." *Population Research and Policy Review* 12: 189–224.

Falk, Richard. 1993. "Democratising, Internationalising, and Globalising: A Collage of Blurred Images." *Third World Quarterly* 13, no. 4: 627–40.

Featherstone, Mike. 1990. "Global Culture: An Introduction." *Theory, Culture and Society* 7, nos. 2–3: 1–14.

Feagin, Joe R. 1997. "Old Poison in New Bottles: The Deep Roots of Modern Nativism." In Juan F. Perea (ed.), *Immigrants Out! The New Nativism and the Anti-Immigrant Impulse in the United States.* New York: New York University Press: 13–43.

Federation for American Immigration Reform (FAIR). 1989. *Ten Steps to Securing America's Borders.* Washington, D.C.: FAIR.

———. 1995. *Ten Steps to Ending Illegal Immigration,* Washington, D.C.: FAIR.

Febvre, Lucien. 1973. "*Frontière*: The Word and the Concept." In Peter Burke (ed.), *A New Kind of History: From the Writings of Febvre.* London: Routledge and Kegan Paul, 208–18.

Fernandez, Celestino and Lawrence R. Pedroza. 1982. "The Border Patrol and News Media Coverage of Undocumented Mexican Immigration during the 1970s: A Quantitative Content Analysis in the Sociology of Knowledge." *California Sociologist* 5, no. 2: 1–26.

Fineman, Mark. 1998. "Dominican Bones Line Pathway to States." *Los Angeles Times,* May 12: A1+.

Flores, William V. 1997. "Citizens vs. Citizenry: Undocumented Immigrants and Latino Cultural Citizenship." In William V. Flores and Rina Benmayor (eds.), *Latino Cultural Citizenship: Claiming Identity, Space, and Rights.* Boston: Beacon Press: 255–90.

Foucault, Michel. 1970. *The Order of Things: An Archaeology of the Human Sciences.* New York: Pantheon Books.

———. 1978. *The History of Sexuality.* Translated by R. Hurley. New York: Pantheon Books.

———. 1979. *Discipline and Punish, The Birth of the Prison.* New York: Vintage Books.

———. 1980. "Questions on Geography." In Michel Foucault, *Power/Knowledge: Selected Interviews and Other Writings, 1972–1977.* Edited by Colin Gordon. Brighton: Harvester Press, 1980.

———. 1984. "Space, Knowledge, and Power." In Paul Rabinow (ed.), *The Foucault Reader.* New York: Pantheon.

Frendreis, John and Raymond Tatalovich. 1997. "Who Supports English-Only Laws? Evidence from the 1992 National Election Study." *Social Science Quarterly* 78, no. 2: 354–69.

Fried, Jonathan. 1994. *Operation Blockade: A City Divided.* Report from the American Friends Service Committee's Immigration Law Enforcement Monitoring Project (ILEMP). Houston: ILEMP, July 1994.

Friedmann, John. 1994. "Borders, Margins, and Frontiers: Myth and Metaphor." Unpublished keynote address for the international conference Regional Development: The Challenge of the Frontier, Ben Gurion University, Israel, December 28–30, 1993, revised September 1994.

Gabriel, John. 1998. *Whitewash: Racialized Politics and the Media.* New York: Routledge.

Galarza, Ernesto. 1964. *Merchants of Labor: The Mexican Bracero Story.* Santa Barbara: McNally and Loftin.

Galeano, Eduardo. 2000. "A World Gone Mad." *The Progressive* 64, no. 12, December: 30–32.

Galtung, Johan. 1994. "Coexistence in Spite of Borders: On the Borders in the Mind." In Werner A. Gallusser (ed.), *Political Boundaries and Coexistence* (Proceedings of the IGU-Symposium, Basle/Switzerland, 24–27 May 1994.) Bern, Switzerland: Peter Lang: 5–14.

Gamio, Manuel. 1930. *Mexican Immigration to the United States.* Chicago: The University of Chicago Press.

Gamson, William A. 1992. *Talking Politics.* Cambridge: Cambridge University Press.

Gamson, William A. and Andre Modigliani. 1987. "The Changing Culture of Affirmative Action." *Research in Political Sociology* 3: 137–77.

Ganster, Paul. 1997. "On the Road to Interdependence? The United States–Mexico Border Region." In Paul Ganster, Alan Sweedler, James Scott, and Wolf Dieter-Eberwein (eds.), *Borders and Border Regions in Europe and North America.* San Diego: San Diego State University Press and Institute for Regional Studies of the Californias: 237–66.

Garcia, Aurelio. 1968. "Trip To Mexico Out for Hippies." *The San Diego Union,* February 2: B-1.

García, Juan Ramon. 1980. *Operation Wetback: The Mass Deportation of Mexican Undocumented Workers in 1954.* Westport, Conn.: Greenwood Press, 1980.

Gazcón, Felipe. 1996. "Envían emigrantes Dls. 3,673 millones." *Reforma* (Mexico), May 27.

Giddens, Anthony. 1979. *Central Problems in Social Theory—Action, Structure, and Contradiction in Social Analysis.* Berkeley and Los Angeles: University of California Press (reprinted 1986).

———. 1984. *The Constitution of Society, Outline of the Theory of Structuration.* Berkeley and Los Angeles: University of California Press.

———. 1987. *The Nation-State and Violence: Volume Two of a Contemporary Critique of Historical Materialism.* Berkeley and Los Angeles: University of California Press.

———. 1990. *The Consequences of Modernity.* Stanford: Stanford University Press.

Glastris, Paul. 1993. "Immigration Crackdown: Anxious Americans Want New Restrictions and Tougher Enforcement." *U.S. News and World Report,* June 21: 34+.

Golden, Arthur. 1980. "Gaping Holes Ripped In New Fence At Border." *The San Diego Union,* June 26: A-1+.

Golden, Arthur and J. Stryker Meyer. 1988. "Nunez Would Deploy Troops Along Border." *The San Diego Union,* June 27: A-1+.

Goldsborough, James. 2000. "Out-of-Control Immigration." *Foreign Affairs* 79, no. 5: 89–101.

Gómez-Peña, Guillermo. 1996. *The New World Border: Prophecies, Poems and Loqueras for the End of the Century.* San Francisco: City Lights Books.

Gómez-Quiñones, Juan. 1981. "Mexican Immigration to the United States and the Internationalization of Labor, 1848–1980: An Overview." In Antonio Rios-Bustamente (ed.), *Mexican Immigrant Workers in The U.S.* Los Angeles: Chicano Studies Research Center Publications, Anthology No. 2. University of California, Los Angeles: 13–34.

Gómez-Quiñones, Juan and David R. Maciel. 1998. "What Goes Around, Comes Around: Political Practice and Cultural Response in the Internationalization of Mexican Labor, 1890–1997." In David R. Maciel and María Herrera-Sobek (eds.), *Culture across Borders: Mexican Immigration and Popular Culture.* Tucson: The University of Arizona Press, 27–65.

Gordon, Linda. 1999. *The Great Arizona Orphan Abduction.* Cambridge, Mass.: Harvard University Press.

Gorman, Tom. 1986. "Rising Illegal Alien Crime a Touchy Issue." *The San Diego Union,* February 17: A-1+.

Graham, Wade. 1996. "Masters of the Game: How the U.S. Protects the Traffic in Cheap Mexican Labor." *Harper's,* July: 35–50.

Grant, Lee. 1970. "Mexicans Bar Long-Haired Men." *The San Diego Union,* March 25: A-1.

Grebler, Leo. 1966. *Mexican Immigration to the United States: The Record and Its Implications.* Mexican-American Study Project, Advance Report 2, University of California, Los Angeles.

Grebler, Leo, Joan W. Moore, and Ralph C. Guzman. 1970. *The Mexican-American People*. New York: The Free Press.

Gribbin, August. 1999. "Border Patrol Too Small to Do Job." *The Washington Times*, June 7: A1+.

Griswold del Castillo, Richard. 1990. *The Treaty of Guadalupe Hidalgo: A Legacy of Conflict*. Norman: University of Oklahoma Press.

———. 1992. "César Chávez, the United Farm Workers and Mexican Immigration." *Río Bravo* 2, no. 1: 32–53.

Gross, Gregory. 1993a. "300 from China Found in Ensenada." *The San Diego Union-Tribune*, April 28: A-1+.

———. 1993b. "Mexico, U.S. Border Dance Is Long, Wary." *The San Diego Union-Tribune*, October 2: A-1+.

———. 1993c. "San Diego, Tijuana Grow Closer Together." *The San Diego Union-Tribune*, December 5: A-1+.

———. 1998. "Elite Mexican Border Unit Showing Signs of Tarnish." *The San Diego Union-Tribune*, August 17.

Gross, Gregory and Leonel Sanchez. 1994. "Big Lights Brighten Border for Two Miles." *The San Diego Union-Tribune*, February 18: B-1+.

Guerin-Gonzales, Camille. 1994. *Mexican Workers and American Dreams: Immigration, Repatriation, and California Labor, 1900–1939*. New Brunswick, N.J.: Rutgers University Press.

Gurowitz, Amy. 1999. "Mobilizing International Norms: Domestic Actors, Immigrants, and the Japanese State." *World Politics* 51, no. 3: 413–45.

Gutiérrez, David G. 1995. *Walls and Mirrors: Mexican Americans, Mexican Immigrants, and the Politics of Ethnicity*. Berkeley and Los Angeles: University of California Press.

Gutiérrez, Ramón. 1996. "The Erotic Zone: Sexual Transgression on the U.S.-Mexican Border." In Avery F. Gordon and Christopher Newfield (eds.), *Mapping Multiculturalism*. Minneapolis: University of Minnesota Press, 253–262.

Gutiérrez-Jones, Carl. 1995. *Rethinking the Borderlands: Between Chicano and Legal Discourse*. Berkeley and Los Angeles: University of California Press, 1995.

Hadley, Eleanor. 1956. "A Critical Analysis of the Wetback Problem." *Law and Contemporary Problems* 21: 334–57.

Hall, Douglas Kent. 1988. *The Border: Life on the Line*. New York: Abbeville Press.

Haney López, Ian F. 1996. *White by Law: The Legal Construction of Race*. New York: New York University Press.

Hanson, Gordon and Antonio Spilimbergo. 1999. "Illegal Immigration, Border Enforcement, and Relative Wages: Evidence from Apprehensions at the U.S.-Mexico Border." *The American Economic Review* 89, no. 5: 1337–57.

Harris, Nigel. 1995. *The New Untouchables: Immigration and the New World Worker*. New York: I. B. Tauris.

Harrison, Donald H. 1977. "Military Area Urged At Border." *The San Diego Union*, April 29.

Harrison, Earl G. 1944. *Annual Report of the Immigration and Naturalization Service* (for the year ended June 30, 1944). Washington, D.C.: U.S. Immigration and Naturalization Service.

Harvey, David. 1974. "Population, Resources, and the Ideology of Science." *Economic Geography* 50, no. 3: 256–78.

———. 1995a. *The Condition of Postmodernity*. Cambridge: Blackwell (first published, 1990).

———. 1995b. "Globalization in Question." *Rethinking Marxism* 8, no. 4: 1–17.

Harwood, Edwin. 1986. *In Liberty's Shadow: Illegal Aliens and Immigration Law Enforcement*. Stanford, Ca.: Hoover Institution Press, Stanford University.

Hastrup, Kirsten. 1990. "The Ethnographic Present: A Reinvention." *Cultural Anthropology* 5, no. 1: 45–61.

Hathaway, Dale. 2000. *Allies across the Border: Mexico's "Authentic Labor Front" and Global Solidarity*. Cambridge, Mass.: South End Press.

Hedges, Chris. 2000. "Condemned by Past Crimes: Deportation Law Descends Sternly." *The New York Times*, August 30.

Hedges, Stephen J. 1996. "The New Jungle." *U.S. News and World Report*, September 23: 34–45.

———. 1997. "Illegal Aliens on the Cutting Edge." *U.S. News and World Report*, 123, 16, October 27: 8.

Herbert, Steve. 1997. *Policing Space: Territoriality and the L.A.P.D*. Minneapolis: University of Minnesota Press.

———. 1999. "The End of the Territorially-Sovereign State? The Case of Crime Control in the United States." *Political Geography*, 18, 2: 149–172.

Hernández, David Manuel. 1997. "Divided We Stand, United We Fall: Latinos and Immigration Policy." *Perspectives in Mexican American Studies* 6: 80–95.

Herzog, Lawrence A. 1990. *Where North Meets South—Cities, Space, and Politics on the U.S.-Mexico Border*. Austin: Center for Mexican American Studies, University of Texas at Austin.

———. 1992. "Changing Boundaries in the Americas: An Overview." In Lawrence A. Herzog (ed.), *Changing Boundaries in the Americas: New Perspectives on the U.S.-Mexican, Central American, and South American Borders*. San Diego: Center for U.S.-Mexican Studies, University of California, 3–24.

———. 1999. "Urban Planning and Sustainability in the Transfrontier Metropolis: The San Diego-Tijuana Region." In , Mark J. Spalding, (ed.), *Sustainable Development in San Diego-Tijuana: Environmental, Social, and Economic Implications of Interdependence*. San Diego: Center for U.S.–Mexican Studies, University of California, San Diego, 1–15.

Heyman, Josiah McC. 1991. *Life and Labor on the Border: Working People of Northeastern Sonora, Mexico, 1886–1986*. Tucson: The University of Arizona Press.

———. 1995. "Putting Power in the Anthropology of Bureaucracy: The Immigration and Naturalization Service at the Mexico-United States Border." *Current Anthropology* 16, no. 2, April 1995: 261–87.

———. 1999a. "Why Interdiction? Immigration Control at the United States—Mexico Border." *Regional Studies* 33, no. 7, 1999a: 619–30.

———. 1999b. "United States Surveillance over Mexican Lives at the Border: Snapshots of an Emerging Regime." *Human Organization* 58, no. 4: 429–37.

Heyman, Josiah McC. and Alan Smart. 1999. "States and Illegal Practices: An Overview." In Josiah McC. Heyman (ed.)., *States and Illegal Practices*. New York: Berg: 1–24.

Higham, J. 1975. *Strangers in the Land: Patterns of American Nativism 1860–1925*. New York: Atheneum.

Hing, Bill Ong. 1998. "The Immigrant as Criminal: Punishing Dreamers." *Hastings Women's Law Journal* 9, no. 1: 79–96.

Hinojosa, Raul and Peter Schey. 1995. "The Faulty Logic of the Anti-Immigration Rhetoric." *NACLA Report on the Americas* 29, no. 3: 18–23.

Ho, Karen and Wende Elizabeth Marshall. 1997. "Criminality and Citizenship: Implicating the White Nation." In Judith Jackson Fossett and Jeffrey A. Tucker (eds.), *Race Consciousness: African-American Studies for the New Century*. New York: New York University Press, 208–26.

Hobsbawm, Eric J. 1991. *Nations and Nationalism since 1780: Programme, Myth, Reality*. Cambridge: Press Syndicate of the University of Cambridge.

———. 1993. "Introduction: Inventing Traditions." In Eric Hobsbawm and Terence Ranger (eds.), *The Invention of Tradition*. Cambridge: Cambridge University Press (first published in 1983): 1–14.

Holmes, Steven A. 1996. "Census Sees a Profound Ethnic Shift in U.S." *The New York Times*, March 14: A-8.

Holmes, Steven A. and Steven Greenhouse. 2001. "Bush Choice for Labor Post

Withdraws and Cites Furor of Illegal Immigrant Issue." *The New York Times*, January 10.

Hood, M. V. and Irwin L. Morris. 1997. "Amigo o Enemigo? Context, Attitudes, and Anglo Public Opinion toward Immigration." *Social Science Quartely* 78, no. 2: 309–23.

Hughes, Joe. 1986. "Seizure of Aliens Set Record." *The Tribune* (San Diego), October 3: A-1+.

Huntington, Samuel P. 1993. "The Clash of Civilizations?" *Foreign Affairs* 72, no. 3: 22–49.

Huntington, Samuel. 2000. "The Special Case of Mexican Immigration: Why Mexico Is a Problem." *The American Enterprise* 11, no. 8: 20–22.

Huspek, Michael. 1997. "Discourse and the Treatment of Illegal Aliens." *Discourse and Society* 8, no. 2: 283–85.

———. 1998. "Law and Lawlessness in San Diego" (op-ed). *The San Diego Union-Tribune*, February 26.

Huspek, Michael, Roberto Martinez, and Leticia Jimenez. 1998. "Violations of Human and Civil Rights on the U.S.-Mexico Border, 1995 to 1997: A Report." *Social Justice* 25, no. 2: 110–30.

Hutchinson, Edward P. 1981. *Legislative History of American Immigration Policy, 1798–1965.* Philadelphia: University of Pennsylvania Press.

Huysmans, Jef. 1995. "Migrants as a Security Problem: Dangers of 'Securitizing' Societal Issues." In Robert Miles and Dietrich Thanhardt (eds.), *Migration and European Integration: The Dynamics of Inclusion and Exclusion.* London: Pinter, 53–72.

Ignatieff, Michael. 1994. *Blood and Belonging: Journeys into the New Nationalism.* New York: Farrar, Straus and Giroux (originally published London: BBC Books, 1993).

Immigration Law Enforcement Monitoring Program (ILEMP) of the American Friends Service Committee. 1998. "The Migrant Count has Grown to 345." (press release), November 20.

Ingram, Helen, Nancy K. Laney, and David M. Gillilan. 1995. *Divided Waters: Bridging the U.S.-Mexico Border.* Tucson: The University of Arizona Press.

Isbister, John. 2000. "A Liberal Argument for Border Controls: Reply to Carens." *International Migration Review* 34, no. 2: 629–35.

Jacobs, Paul. 1995. "Wilson Often Battled INS, Letters Show." *Los Angeles Times*, September 25: A3.

Jardine, Matthew. 1996. "Pacification, Resistance, and Territoriality: Prospects for a Space of Peace in East Timor." *GeoJournal* 39, no. 4: 397–404.

———. 1998. "Operation Gatekeeper." *Peace Review* 10, no. 3, September: 329–35.

Johnson, Kevin R. 1997. "The New Nativism: Something Old, Something New, Something Borrowed, Something Blue." In Juan F. Perea (ed.), *Immigrants Out! The New Nativism and the Anti-Immigrant Impulse in the United States.* New York: New York University Press, 165–89.

Johnston, David. 1992. "Border Crossings Near Old Record; U.S. to Crack Down." *New York Times*, February 9: 1+.

Johnston, R. J. 1991. *A Question of Place: Exploring the Practice of Human Geography.* Oxford: Blackwell.

Jonas, Susanne. 1996. "Rethinking Immigration Policy and Citizenship in the Americas: A Regional Framework." *Social Justice* 23, no. 3: 68–85.

Jones, Robert A. 1998. "It's Quiet—Too Quiet." *Los Angeles Times*, March 22: B7.

Kahn, Robert. 1996. *Other People's Blood: U.S. Immigration Prisons in the Reagan Decade.* Boulder: Westview.

———. 1997a. "Keeping Illegal Workers Male, Young and Fit" (op-ed). *Los Angeles Times*, July 6: M1+.

———. 1997b. "Operation Gatekeeper." *Z Magazine*, 10, no. 12: 14–16.

Katz, Jesse. 1996. "1,000 Miles of Hope, Heartache." *Los Angeles Times*, November 10: A1+.

Kazin, Michael. 1988. "A People Not a Class: Rethinking the Political Language of the Modern U.S. Labor Movement." In Mike Davis and Michael Sprinkler (eds.), *Reshaping the US Left: Popular Struggles in the 1980s*. New York: Verso, 257–86.

Kearney, Michael. 1991. "Borders and Boundaries of State and Self at the End of Empire." *Journal of Historical Sociology* 4, no. 1, March 1991: 52–74.

Kelley, Robin D. G. 1997. *Yo' Mama's Disfunktional! Fighting the Culture Wars in Urban America*. Boston: Beacon Press.

King, Neil. 1998. "A New Era for European Immigrants: Coping With Europe's Immigration Wave Is Nearly On a Par With Common Currency." *The Wall Street Journal*, May 4.

King, Patricia and Donna Foote. 1993. "Across the Borderline." *Newsweek*, May 31: 25.

Kirstein, Peter Neil. 1973. "Anglo over Bracero: A History of the Mexican Worker in the United States from Roosevelt to Nixon." Ph.D. Dissertation, St. Louis University.

Kligman, David. 1999. "Emphasis on San Diego Area Cuts Border Patrol's Manpower Elsewhere." *St. Louis Post-Dispatch*, February 19: A11.

Knight, David. 1994. "People Together, Yet Apart: Rethinking Territory, Sovereignty, and Identities." In George J. Demko and William B. Wood (eds.), *Reordering the World: Geopolitical Perspectives on the Twenty-First Century*. Boulder: Westview Press: 71–86.

Kolossov, Vladimir and John O'Loughlin. 1998. "New Borders for New World Orders: Territorialities at the *fin-de-siecle*." *GeoJournal* 44, no. 3: 259–73.

Kondracke, Morton M. 1993. "Immigration to Be Demagogues' Next Issue After NAFTA." *Roll Call*, November 18: 6.

Kopytoff, Verne G. 1999. "A Silicon Wall Rises Along the Border." *The New York Times*, January 14: D1+.

Kristof, Ladis K. D. 1959. "The Nature of Frontiers and Boundaries." *Annals of the Association of American Geographers* 49, no. 3, September: 269–82.

Kubik, Agnes. 1986. "Officials Split on Sale of U.S. Border Land." *The Tribune* (San Diego), July 26: C-1+.

Kurtz, Donald V. 1973. *The Politics of a Poverty Habitat*. Cambridge, Mass.: Bollinger.

Kwong, Peter. 1997. *Forbidden Workers: Illegal Chinese Immigrants and American Labor*. New York: The New Press.

Lait, Matt. 1989. "At the Border, Deep Concern About a Shallow Ditch." *The Washington Post*, March 2: A3.

Lake, Anthony. 2000. *Six Nightmares: Real Threats in a Dangerous World and How America Can Meet Them*. Boston: Little, Brown.

Lane, A. T. 1987. *Solidarity or Survival? American Labor and European Immigrants, 1830–1924*. Westport, Conn.: Greenwood Press.

Lang, John S. 1985. "The Disappearing Border." *U.S. News and World Report*, August 19: 30–31.

Lattimore, Owen D. 1968. "The Frontier in History." In Robert A. Manners and David Kaplan (eds.), *Theory in Anthropology: A Sourcebook*. Chicago: Aldine, 374–86.

Lau, Angela. 1993. "Boatload of Chinese Seized Here." *The San Diego Union-Tribune*, May 13: A-1+.

Lee, Susan K. 1996. "Racial Construction through Citizenship in the U.S." *Asian American Policy Review* 6: 89–116.

Lennon, Peter. 2000–2001. "Sun, Sea, Sand and Beached Corpses." *Manchester Guardian Weekly*, December 28, 2000-January 3, 2001: 4.

Lesley, Lewis B. 1930. "The International Boundary Survey from San Diego to the Gila River, 1849–1850." *Quarterly of the California Historical Society* 9, no. 1: 3–15.

Lewis, Sasha G. 1979. *Slave Trade Today: American Exploitation of Illegal Aliens*. Boston: Beacon Press.

Light, Julie. 1996. "Baiting Immigrants: Women Bear the Brunt." *The Progressive*, September: 21–24.

Lipsitz, George. 1998. *The Possessiveness of Whiteness: How White People Profit from Identity Politics*. Philadelphia: Temple University Press.

Liu, Melinda. 1993. "The New Slave Trade." *Newsweek*, June 21: 34–36+.

Logan, Michael H. 1969. "Immigration and Relative Deprivation: The Tijuana-San Ysidro Border Station." Master's Thesis, Department of Anthropology, San Diego State College.

Long, Bill. 1968. "Mexico Bars 200 Hippies At Border." *The San Diego Union*, February 4.

Lopez, Michael D. 1979. "Border Fence Plans Appear Doomed." *The San Diego Union*, March 17: A-1+.

Los Angeles Times. 1994. "Illegal Immigration: Ideas Worth Trying" (editorial). *Los Angeles Times*, October 5: B6.

———. 1998. "Hard Line on Human Coyotes" (editorial). *Los Angeles Times*, August 20: B8.

Louv, Richard. 1987. "Controversy Flourishes Over Elusive Border Wall." *The San Diego Union*, March 8: A-3.

Lyman, Rick. 1998. "Heat Making Illegal Border Crossings Deadlier." *The New York Times*, August 5: A1+.

Magardie, Khadija. 2000. "Victims of Xenophobia." *BBC Focus on Africa* 11, no. 4: 28–30.

Magnuson, Ed. 1985. "Symbiosis along 1,936 Miles." *Time*, July 8.

Mann, Michael. 1984. "The Autonomous Power of the State: Its Origins, Mechanisms and Results." *European Journal of Sociology* 25: 185–213.

———. 1986. *The Sources of Social Power*, vol. I. Cambridge (U.K.): Cambridge University Press.

———. 1993. "Nation-States in Europe and Other Continents: Diversifying, Developing, Not Dying." *Daedalus* 122, no. 3: 115–40.

Manson, Bill. 1993. "A Soft Border: Ease Tension, End Waste with Buffer Zone" (op-ed). *The San Diego Union-Tribune*, October 28.

Manzo, Kathryn A. 1996. *Creating Boundaries: The Politics of Race and Nation*. Boulder and London: Lynne Rienner.

Marcus, George. 1992. "Past, Present and Emergent Identities: Requirements for Ethnographies of Late Twentieth-Century Modernity Worldwide." In Scott Lash and Jonathan Friedman, *Modernity and Identity*. Oxford: Basil Blackwell: 309–30.

Marden, Peter. 1997. "Geographies of Dissent: Globalization, Identity, and the Nation." *Political Geography* 16, no. 1: 37–64.

Marelius, John. 1993. "Illegal Immigration Hurts State, 74% Say." *The San Diego Union-Tribune*, August 19: A-1+.

Marelius, John and Lorie Hearn. 1993. "Border Woes Seen Close Up by Reno." *The San Diego Union-Tribune*, August 18: A-1+.

Martin, Philip L. 1994. "The United States: Benign Neglect toward Immigration." In Wayne Cornelius, Philip L. Martin and James F. Hollifield (eds.), *Controlling Immigration: A Global Perspective*. Stanford: Stanford University Press, 83–99.

Martinez, Gene and Patrick J. McDonnell. 1994. "Prop. 187 Backers Counting on Message, Not Strategy." *Los Angeles Times*, October 30: A1+.

Martínez, Elizabeth. 1998. *De Colores Means All of Us: Latina Views for a Multi-Colored Century*. Cambridge, Mass.: South End Press.

Martínez, Oscar J. 1994. *Border People: Life and Society in the U.S.-Mexico Borderlands*. Tucson: The University of Arizona Press, 1994.

———. 1995. *Troublesome Border*. Tucson: The University of Arizona Press.

———, (ed.). 1996. *U.S.-Mexico Borderlands: Historical and Contemporary Perspectives*. Wilmington, Del.: Scholarly Resources.

Martis, Kenneth Charles. 1970. "United States International Land Border Crossings, San Ysidro, California." Master's Thesis, Department of Geography, San Diego State College.

Massey, Douglas S. 1998. "March of Folly: U.S. Immigration Policy After NAFTA." *The American Prospect*, March-April: 22–33.

Massey, Douglas S. and Kristin E. Espinosa. 1997. "What's Driving Mexico-U.S. Migration? A Theoretical, Empirical, and Policy Analysis." *American Journal of Sociology* 102, no. 4: 939–99.

Massey, Douglas S. et al. 1993. "Theories of International Migration: A Review and Appraisal." *Population and Development Review* 19, no. 3: 431–66.

Mazón, Mauricio. 1975. "Illegal Alien Surrogates: A Psychohistorical Interpretation of Group Stereotyping in Time of Economic Stress." *Aztlán* 6, no. 2: 305–24.

McDonald, William F. 1997a. "Crime and Illegal Immigration: Emerging Local, State, and Federal Partnerships." *National Institute of Justice Journal* 232: 2–10.

———. 1997b. "Illegal Immigration: Crime, Ramifications, and Control (The American Experience)." In William McDonald (ed.), *Crime and Law Enforcement in the Global Village*. Cincinnati: Anderson, 65–86.

McDonnell, Patrick J. 1986. "Hunter Asks for National Guardsmen Along Border." *Los Angeles Times*, San Diego County edition, June 24: 2–3.

———. "Deportation Shatters Family." *Los Angeles Times*, March 14: B-1+.

McDonnell, Patrick J. and Ken Ellingwood. 1998. "Immigration—the Big Issue of '94—Disappears From '98 Debate." *Los Angeles Times*, October 23: A3+.

McHugh, Ray. 1969. "Nixon Launches U.S.-Mexican War On Drugs." *The San Diego Union*, September 14: A-1.

McLaren, John. 1992. "500-Foot-Wide 'DMZ' Proposed at Border." *The San Diego Tribune*, January 18: A-1+.

McMahon, Eston. 1979. "Border Tension Called 'Potentially Explosive.'" *The San Diego Union*, June 11: B-3.

McNeil, Eddy and James V. Grimaldi. 1986. "Border Emerges as War Zone." *The Tribune* (San Diego), September 16: A-1+.

McVicar, Jim. 1971. "Law Bans Hiring of Illegal Aliens." *The San Diego Union*, November 15: B-1+.

McWilliams, Carey. 1939. *Factories in the Field: The Story of Migratory Farm Labor in California*. Boston: Little, Brown.

———. 1968. *North from Mexico: The Spanish-Speaking People of the United States*. New York: Greenwood Press (originally published in 1949).

Mehan, Hugh. 1997. "The Discourse of the Illegal Immigration Debate: A Case Study in the Politics of Representation." *Discourse and Society* 8, no. 2: 249–70.

Meilander, Peter C. 1999. "Liberalism and Open Borders: The Argument of Joseph Carens." *International Migration Review* 33, no. 4: 1062–81.

Mendel, Ed. 1993. "Both Parties Seek High Ground in Battle to Contain Illegal Immigrants." *The San Diego Union-Tribune*, September 6.

Migration News (online version), various issues, current and back issues available via Internet on the *Migration News* home page (http://migration.ucdavis.edu).

Miliband, Ralph. 1969. "Reply to Nicos Poulantzas." *New Left Review* 58.

Milton, Pat. 1993. "Trade Center Plotters May Have Left U.S." *The San Diego Union-Tribune*, March 6: A-1+.

Mink, Gwendolyn. 1986. *Old Labor and New Immigrants in American Political Development: Union, Party, and State, 1875–1920*. Ithaca: Cornell University Press.

Mitchell, Timothy. 1991. "The Limits of the State: Beyond Statist Approaches and their Critics." *American Political Science Review* 85, no. 1: 77–96.

Moehring, H. B. 1988. "Symbol versus Substance in Legislative Activity: The Case of Illegal Immigration." *Public Choice* 57: 287–94.

Mohar, Gustavo and Maria-Elena Alcaraz. 2000. "U.S. Border Controls: A Mexican Perspective." In Peter Andreas and Timothy Snyder (eds.), *The Wall Around the West: State Borders and Immigration Control in North America and Europe*. Lanham, Md.: Rowman and Littlefield, 139–150.

Money, Jeannette. 1997. "No Vacancy: The Political Geography of Immigration Control in Advanced Industrial Countries." *International Organization* 51, no. 4: 685–720.

———. 1999. *Fences and Neighbors: The Political Geography of Immigration Control*. Ithaca: Cornell University Press.

Monroy, Douglas. 1999. *Rebirth: Mexican Los Angeles from the Great Migration to the Great Depression.* Berkeley and Los Angeles: University of California Press.

Moody, Kim. 1988. *An Injury to All: The Decline of American Unionism.* New York: Verso.

————. 1997. *Workers in a Lean World: Unions in the International Economy.* New York: Verso.

Morgan, Neil. 1993. "Mexico Boosts Role in Fighting Border Crime." *The San Diego Union-Tribune,* December 28: A-2.

Morganthau, Tom. 1984. "Closing the Door?" *Newsweek,* June 25: 18–24.

————. 1993. "America: Still a Melting Pot?" *Newsweek,* August 9: 16–23.

Morris, Milton D. and Albert Mayio. 1982. *Curbing Illegal Immigration* (a staff paper). Washington, D.C.: The Brookings Institution.

Mozingo, Joe. 1998. "A Tragic Journey Home." *Los Angeles Times,* August 21: B1+.

Muller, Henry and John F. Stacks. 1991. "Wilson Decries State's Welfare Magnetism." *The San Diego Tribune,* November 11: A-1+.

Muller, Thomas. 1997. "Nativism in the Mid-1990s: Why Now?" In Juan F. Perea (ed.), *Immigrants Out! The New Nativism and the Anti-Immigrant Impulse in the United States.* New York: New York University Press, 105–118.

Murphy, Alexander B. 1991. "Territorial Ideology and International Conflict: The Legacy of Prior Political Formations." In Nurit Kliot and Stanley Waterman (eds.), *The Political Geography of Conflict and Peace.* London: Belhaven Press, 126–41.

————. 1996. "The Sovereign State System as Political-Territorial Ideal: Historical and Contemporary Considerations." In Thomas J. Biersteker and Cynthia Weber (eds.), *State Sovereignty as Social Construct.* Cambridge: Cambridge University Press, 81–120.

Murphy, Vi. 1977a. "Van Deerlin Hits at Illegal Aliens." *The San Diego Union,* February 17: A-4.

————. 1977b. "New Fence May Rise On Border." *The San Diego Union,* March 26: A-1+.

————. 1977c. "U.S. Erects New Line of Defense." *The San Diego Union,* May 29: A-1+.

Murr, Andrew. 1993. "A Nasty Turn on Immigrants." *Newsweek,* August 23: 28.

Nadelmann, Ethan A. 1993. *Cops across Borders: The Internationalization of U.S. Criminal Law Enforcement.* University Park: Pennsylvania State University Press.

Nader, Ralph and Lori Wallach. 1996. "GATT, NAFTA, and the Subversion of the Democratic Process." In *The Case Against the Global Economy: And For a Turn toward the Local.* San Francisco: Sierra Club, 92–107.

Neuman, Gerald L. 1993. "The Lost Century of American Immigration Law (1776–1875)." *Columbia Law Review* 93, no. 8: 1833–1901.

————. "1995. Aliens as Outlaws: Government Services, Proposition 187, and the Structure of Equal Protection Doctrine." *UCLA Law Review* 42, no. 6: 1425–52.

————. 1996. *Strangers to the Constitution: Immigrants, Borders, and Fundamental Law.* Princeton, N.J.: Princeton University Press.

Nevins, Joseph. 1998. "California Dreaming: Operation Gatekeeper and the Social Geographical Construction of the "Illegal Alien" along the U.S.-Mexico Boundary." Ph.D. dissertation, Department of Geography, University of California, Los Angeles.

————. 2000a. "The Law of the Land: Local-National Dialectic and the Making of the U.S.-Mexico Boundary in Southern California." *Historical Geography* 28: 41–60.

————. 2000b. "The Re-Making of the California-Mexico Boundary in the Age of NAFTA." In Peter Andreas and Timothy Snyder (eds.), *The Wall Around the West: State Borders and Immigration Control in North America and Europe,* Lanham, Md.: Rowman and Littlefield, 99–114.

————. 2000c. "How High Must Operation Gatekeeper's Death Count Go?" *Los Angeles Times,* November 19.

————. 2000d. "Borderline Justice," review essay of Peter Andreas's *Border Games:*

Policing the U.S.-Mexico Divide and Grace Chang's *Disposable Domestics: Immigrant Women Workers in the Global Economy. The Nation* 271, no. 6: 33–38.

The New York Times. 1974. "Job Rise Is Linked to Curb on Aliens." *The New York Times,* September 22.

Novick, Michael. 1995. *White Lies, White Power: The Fight Against White Supremacy and Reactionary Violence.* Monroe, Maine: Common Courage Press.

O'Connor, Anne-Marie. 1997. "INS Crackdown Expands into Imperial Valley." *Los Angeles Times,* October 8: A1+.

O'Connor, Michael. 1969. "U.S., Mexico Agree To Modify 'Intercept.'" *The San Diego Union,* October 11: A-1+.

Ohmae, Kenichi. 1995. *The End of the Nation State: The Rise of Regional Economies.* New York: The Free Press.

Ojito, Mirta. 1997a. "New Law Resurrects an Old Crime." *The New York Times,* October 15.

———. 1997b. "U.S. Releases Man Jailed For a 1974 Misdemeanor." *The New York Times,* October 25.

———. 1998. "Once Divisive, Immigration Is Muted Issue." *The New York Times,* November 1: 28.

Ong, Paul and John M. Liu. 1994. "U.S. Immigration Policies and Asian Migration." In Paul Ong, Edna Bonacich, and Lucie Cheng (eds.), *The New Asian Immigration and Global Restructuring.* Philadelphia: Temple University Press.

Ortega, Bob. 1998. "Last Call: Texas Agents Spark Outcry in Roundup of Legal Immigrants." *The Wall Street Journal,* October 12: A1+.

Ortiz Pinchetti, Francisco. 1997. "Como si fueran criminales, menores indocumentados mexicanos son confinados en prisiones estadunidenses." *Proceso* (Mexico City), May 11: 18–24.

Ostrow, Ronald J. 1974. "Saxbe Calls Illegal Aliens a U.S. Crisis." *Los Angeles Times,* October 31: 1+.

Ott, Bill. 1986. "Smuggler Tells of Plan to Shift Drug Traffic to San Diego." *The San Diego Union,* October 23: B-5.

Paasi, Anssi. 1995. "The Social Construction of Peripherality: the Case of Finland and the Finnish-Russian Border Area." In Heikki Eskelinen and Folke Snickars (eds.), *Competitive European Peripheries.* Berlin: Springer, 236–58.

———. 1996. *Territories, Boundaries and Consciousness: The Changing Geographies of the Finnish-Russian Border.* New York: John Wiley.

Pacific Council on International Policy. 1999. "Strengthen Ties Between California and Mexico" (op-ed). *Los Angeles Times,* May 18: B7.

Palafox, José. 1996. "Militarizing the Border." *Covert Action Quarterly,* Spring 1996: 14–19.

———. 2000. "Arizona Ranchers Hunt Mexicans." *Z Magazine* 13, nos. 7–8: 28–30.

Palafox, José and Matthew Jardine. 1999. "Hardening the Line: The Growing American War on 'Illegals.'" *ColorLines* 1, no. 3: 20–22.

Parenti, Christian. 1999. *Lockdown America: Police and Prisons in the Age of Crisis.* New York: Verso.

Parry, Bill. 1975. "Patrol Force Cuts Hurt Effectiveness." *The San Diego Union,* March 24: A-6.

Peck, Jamie and Adam Tickell. 1994. "A Jungle Law Breaks Out: Neoliberalism and Global-Local Disorder." *Area* 26, no. 4: 317–26.

Pennell, Susan, Christine Curtis, and Jeff Tayman. 1989. "The Impact of Illegal Immigration on the Criminal Justice System." San Diego Association of Governments, Criminal Justice Research Unit, July 1989.

Pepper, David. 1984. *The Roots of Modern Environmentalism.* New York: Routledge (reprinted 1990).

Perea, Juan. 1997. "Introduction." In Juan F. Perea (ed.), *Immigrants Out! The New Nativism and the Anti-Immigrant Impulse in the United States.* New York: New York University Press, 1–10.

Perkins, Clifford Alan. 1978. *Border Patrol, With the U.S. Immigration Service on the Mexican Boundary 1910–1954*. El Paso: The University of Texas at El Paso. Texas Western Press.

Piñera Ramírez, David and Jesús Ortiz. 1983. "Panorama de Tijuana." In David Piñera Ramírez (ed.), *Panorama Histórico de Baja California*. Tijuana: Centro de Investigaciones Históricas, UNAM-UABC, 535–48.

Pitt, Leonard. 1966. *The Decline of the Californios: A Social History of the Spanish-Speaking Californians, 1846–1890*. Berkeley and Los Angeles: University of California Press.

Popkin, James and Dorian Friedman. 1993. "Return to Sender—Please." *U.S. News and World Report*, June 21: 32.

Portillo, Ernesto. 1990a. "Permanent Lights Put In Along Tijuana River." *The San Diego Union*, May 5.

———. 1990b. "Added Border Agents, Lights Set." *The San Diego Union*, June 21: B-1+.

———. 1990c. "Protests at Border Turn 1 Year Old." *The San Diego Union*, November 16: B-3.

———. 1991a. "Border Patrol Chief Takes on the Bandits." *The San Diego Union*, June 24: B-1+.

———. 1991b. "Border 'Metal Wall' Stirs Anger in Mexico." *The San Diego Union*, September 2: B-1+.

———. 1992. "Bill Would Override Landowner's Objection to Border Fence." *The San Diego Union*, January 25: B-7.

Poulantzas, Nicos. 1969. "The Problem of the Capitalist State." *New Left Review*, no. 58: 119–33.

Prescott, J. R. V. 1987. *Political Frontiers and Boundaries*. London: Allen and Unwin.

President's Commission on Migratory Labor. 1951. *Migratory labor in American Agriculture*, Report of the President's Commission on Migratory Labor. Washington, D.C.: U.S. Government Printing Office.

Price, John A. 1973. *Tijuana: Urbanization in a Border Culture*. Notre Dame, Ind.: University of Notre Dame Press.

Proffitt, Thurber Dennis. 1988. "The Symbiotic Frontier: The Emergence of Tijuana Since 1769." Ph.D. Dissertation, Department of History, University of California, Los Angeles.

Quinton, Wendy J., Gloria Cowan, and Brett D. Watson. 1996. "Personality and Attitudinal Predictors of Support of Proposition 187—California's Anti-Illegal Immigrant Initiative." *Journal of Applied Social Psychology* 26, no. 24: 2204–23.

Ramos, George. 1977. "Border Patrol Swears In 100 Agents." *The San Diego Union*, October 4: B-1+.

———. 1978. "Illegal Alien Tide Continues to Rise." *The San Diego Union*, January 1: B-3.

Reimers, David M. 1992. *Still the Golden Door: The Third World Comes to America*. New York: Columbia University Press.

———. 1998. *Unwelcome Strangers: American Identity and the Turn Against Immigration*. New York: Columbia University Press.

Reisler, Mark. 1976. *By the Sweat of their Brow: Mexican Immigrant Labor in the United States, 1900–1940*. Westport, Conn.: Greenwood Press.

Reno, Janet. 1993. "Consider NAFTA a Border Control Tool." *Los Angeles Times*, October 22: B11.

Reyes, Belinda I. 1997. *Dynamics of Immigration: Return Migration to Western Mexico*. San Francisco: Public Policy Institute of California.

Reza, H. G. 1986. "Golding Wants U.S. to Pick Up Alien Tab." *Los Angeles Times* (San Diego County edition), May 13: 1+.

Richmond, Anthony. 1994. *Global Apartheid: Refugees, Racism, and the New World Order*. Oxford: Oxford University Press.

Rico, Carlos. 1992. "Migration and U.S.-Mexican Relations, 1966–1986." In

Christopher Mitchell (ed.), *Western Hemisphere Immigration and United States Foreign Policy*. University Park: Pennsylvania State University Press, 221–83.

Robbins, Maro. 1998. "500 Facing Deportation Due to DWI." *San Antonio Express-News*, September 3.

Roberts, Kenneth L. 1921. "Plain Remarks on Immigration for Plain Americans." *The Saturday Evening Post*, February 12: 21+.

———. 1928a. "Wet and Other Mexicans." *The Saturday Evening Post*, February 4: 10–11+.

———. 1928b. "Mexicans or Ruin." *The Saturday Evening Post*, February 18: 14–15+.

———. 1928c. "The Docile Mexican." *The Saturday Evening Post*, March 10: 39+.

Robinson, Linda and Kenneth T. Walsh. 1993. "Riding a Tide of Hope." *U.S. News and World Report*, January 18: 47–49.

Rodriguez, Richard. 1996. "Pocho Pioneer." In Bobby Byrd and Susannah Mississippi Byrd (eds.), *The Late Great Mexican Border: Reports from a Disappearing Line*. El Paso: Cinco Puntos Press: 211–24.

Rohter, Larry. 2000. "Dancing Across an Imaginary Line in the Jungle." *The New York Times*, November 28: A4.

Rojas, Aurelio. 1997. "Most Mexicans Don't Stay in U.S." *The San Francisco Chronicle*, January 29: A1.

Roletti, Agnes. 1993. "Three Top Cops Cite Needs in Battle at Border." *The San Diego Union-Tribune*, October 9: B-1+.

Rosen, Fred. 1998. "Breaking Away: Mexican Workers Rebel against Government-Dominated Trade Unionism." *In These Times* 22, nos. 4–5: 25–27.

Ross, John. 1998. *The Annexation of Mexico: From the Aztecs to the I.M.F.* Monroe, Maine: Common Courage Press.

Rotella, Sebastian. 1998. *Twilight on the Line: Underworlds and Politics at the U.S.-Mexico Border*. New York: W.W. Norton.

Rouse, Roger. 1995. "Thinking through Transnationalism: Notes on the Cultural Politics of Class Relations in the Contemporary United States." *Public Culture* 7: 353–402.

Ruiz, Ramón Eduardo. 2000. *On the Rim of Mexico: Encounters of the Rich and Poor*. Boulder: Westview Press.

Russell, George. 1985. "Trying to Stem the Illegal Tide." *Time*, July 8.

Ryan, John A. 1958. "Lonely Monument on the Border." *Westways*, June.

Sack, Robert David. 1986. *Human Territoriality: Its Theory and History*. Cambridge: Cambridge University Press.

Sahlins, Peter. 1989. *Boundaries: The Making of France and Spain in the Pyrenees*. Berkeley and Los Angeles: University of California Press.

Said, Edward W. 1993. *Culture and Imperialism*. New York: Alfred A. Knopf.

Samora, Julian. 1971. *Los Mojados: The Wetback Story*. Notre Dame, Ind.: University of Notre Dame Press.

San Diego County Border Task Force. 1980. "San Diego County Border Task Force Final Report." San Diego: San Diego County Board of Supervisors, May 1980.

San Diego Dialogue. 1995. *Demographic Atlas San Diego/Tijuana Atlas Demográfico*. San Diego: The San Diego/Tijuana Planning for Prosperity Fund.

The San Diego Tribune. 1992. "Border Needs This Buffer" (editorial). *The San Diego Tribune*, January 21: B8.

The San Diego Union. 1871. "Smuggling from Lower California." *The San Diego Union*, January 26: 3.

———. 1936. "New Fencing along Mexican Border Begun by CCC Boys to End Smuggling Activity." *The San Diego Union*, January 8: II: 6.

———. 1954. "Patrol Drive on Wetbacks Starts Soon." *The San Diego Union*, June 11: A-7.

———. 1958. "Officers at Border Bar 26,133 Youths." *The San Diego Union*, January 19: 23.

———. 1959. "Utt, Agriculture Officials Confer on Border Fence." *The San Diego Union*, January 31: A15.

———. 1960a. "Judge Urges Border Ban to Halt Dope." *The San Diego Union*, January 8: A-22.

———. 1960b. "Border Dope Menace Cited By Senate Unit." *The San Diego Union*, July 5: A-1+.

———. 1961. "Federal Aid Urged for Border Fence." *The San Diego Union*, March 21: 14.

———. 1975. "Mexico Aid Sought for Border Fence." *The San Diego Union*, November 23: B-9.

———. 1977. "Border Peril Escalating" (editorial). *The San Diego Union*, February 11: B-10.

———. 1979. "Border Fence Works, Debate Continues." *The San Diego Union*, August 14.

———. 1986. "Drug War Must Be Won . . . Starting at the Border" (editorial). *The San Diego Union*, September 17: B-6.

———. 1991a. "Q and A with Gustavo De La Viña." *The San Diego Union*, October 15: C-6.

———. 1991b. "Hands Across the Border" (editorial). *The San Diego Union*, November 10: C2.

———. 1991c. "Former INS Official Urges Crackdown on Illegal Immigrants." *The San Diego Union*, November 21.

———. 1991d. "The Cost of Immigration" (editorial). *The San Diego Union*, November 27: B8.

The San Diego Union-Tribune. 1993a. "Misnamed and Futile" (editorial). *The San Diego Union-Tribune*, September 30: B-12.

———. 1993b. "The INS Stepchild" (editorial). *The San Diego Union-Tribune*, October 12, 1993b.

———. 1994. " . . . What a difference: Enforcement on the Line Nets Dividends" (editorial). *The San Diego Union-Tribune*, October 4: B6.

———. 1996. "Two Kinds of Immigration" (editorial). *The San Diego Union-Tribune*, April 1: B6.

———. 1998a. "Gatekeeper Works: Despite Charges, Border Has Been Secured" (editorial). *The San Diego Union-Tribune*, July 17: B6.

———. 1998b."Death in the Desert" (editorial). *The San Diego Union-Tribune*, August 17: B6.

Sánchez, George J. 1990. "'Go After the Women': Americanization and the Mexican Immigrant Woman, 1915–1929." In Ellen Carol DuBois and Vicki L. Ruiz (eds.), *Unequal Sisters: A Multicultural Reader in U.S. Women's History.* New York: Routledge: 250–63; originally published in the Stanford University Center for Chicano Research Working Paper Series vol. 6, 1984.

———. 1993. *Becoming Mexican American: Ethnicity, Culture, and Identity in Chicano Los Angeles, 1900–1945.* New York: Oxford University Press.

Sanchez, Leonel and Marcus Stern. 1996. "INS Probe Can't Find Evidence of False Reports." *The San Diego Union-Tribune*, July 7: A-1+.

Sandrino-Glasser, Gloria. 1998. "Los Confundidos: De-Conflating Latinos/as' Race and Ethnicity." *Chicano-Latino Law Review* 19, no. 69: 69–161.

Sassen, Saskia. 1996. *Losing Control: Sovereignty in an Age of Globalization.* New York: Columbia University Press.

———. 1998. *Globalization and Its Discontents: Essays on the New Mobility of People and Money.* New York: The New Press.

Saxton, Alexander. 1971. *The Indispensable Enemy: Labor and the Anti-Chinese Movement in California.* Berkeley and Los Angeles: University of California Press.

Schatzman, Leonard and Anselm L. Strauss. 1973. *Field Research: Strategies for a Natural Sociology.* Englewood Cliffs, N.J.: Prentice-Hall.

Schelling, Thomas C. 1992. "The Global Dimension." In Graham Allison and Gregory

F. Treverton (eds.), *Rethinking America's Security: Beyond Cold War to New World Order*. New York: W. W. Norton.

Schmidt, Samuel. 1997. "Stereotypes, Culture, and Cooperation in the U.S.-Mexican Borderlands." In Paul Ganster, Alan Sweedler, James Scott, and Wolf Dieter-Eberwein (eds.), *Borders and Border Regions in Europe and North America*. San Diego: San Diego State University Press and Institute for Regional Studies of the Californias, 299–314.

Schmitt, Eric. 2001. "Americans (a) Love (b) Hate Immigrants." *The New York Times*, January 14.

Schneider, Julie. 2000. "NAFTA and Transportation: Impacts on the U.S.-Mexico Border." *Borderlines* 8, no. 5, June.

Schrag, Peter. 1998. *Paradise Lost: California's Experience, America's Future*. New York: The New Press, 1998.

Shore, Benjamin. 1986. "Cross-border Flow of Aliens Becomes Flood." *The San Diego Union*, February 21: A1+.

———. 1990. "Poll Shows Most Americans Object to More Immigrants." *The San Diego Union*, June 5: A2.

———. 1992. "Low-key Attitude Shift Favors Getting Tough on Immigration." *The San Diego Union-Tribune*, September 26: A3.

Showley, Roger M. 1991. "A Tale of Two Cities Slowly, Inexorably, Inextricably Linked." *The San Diego Union*, November 3: A-1+.

Sibley, David. 1988. "Purification of Space." *Environment and Planning D: Society and Space* 6: 409–21.

———. 1995. *Geographies of Exclusion: Society and Diffference in the West*. New York: Routledge.

Simon, Rita J. 1985. *Public Opinion and the Immigrant: Print Media Coverage, 1880–1980*. Lexington, Mass.: Lexington Books.

Singer, Audrey and Douglas Massey. 1998. "The Social Process of Undocumented Border Crossing Among Mexican Migrants." *International Migration Review* 32, no. 3: 561–92.

Sjoberg, Gideon, N. Williams, T. R. Vaughan, and A. F. Sjoberg. 1991. "The Case Study Approach in Social Research." In J. R. Feagin, A. M. Orum, and G. Sjoberg, *A Case for the Case Study*. Chapel Hill: University of North Carolina Press: 27–79.

Skerry, Peter and Stephen J. Rockwell. 1998. "The Cost of a Tighter Border: People-Smuggling Networks" (op-ed). *Los Angeles Times*, May 3: M2.

Sklair, Leslie. 1993. *Assembling for Development: The Maquila Industry in Mexico and the United States*, San Diego: Center for U.S.-Mexican Studies, University of California, San Diego.

Skocpol, Theda. 1985. "Bringing the State Back In: Strategies of Analysis in Current Research." In Peter B. Evans, Dietrich Rueschemeyer, and Theda Skocpol (eds.), *Bringing the State Back In*. Cambridge: Cambridge University Press, 3–37.

Smith, Anthony D. 1990. "Towards a Global Culture?" *Theory, Culture and Society* 7, nos. 2–3: 171–91.

Smith, Claudia. 1997. "Operation Gatekeeper's Darker Side" (op-ed). *The San Diego Union-Tribune*, October 16.

———. 1998. "Is America Losing Its Soul in Its Attempt to Control the Border?" (op-ed). *The San Diego Union-Tribune*, September 10: B-9.

Smith, Geri and Elisabeth Malkin. 1997. "The Border." *Business Week*, May 12: 64–70+.

Smollar, David. 1984. "Four Marines to Stand Trial in Raids on Illegal Aliens." *Los Angeles Times* (San Diego County edition), April 14: 2,1+.

Smolowe, Jill. 1993. "Where's the Promised Land?" *Time*, June 21: 29–30.

Soja, Edward W. 1980. "The Socio-Spatial Dialectic." *Annals of the Association of American Geographers* 70, no. 2: 207–25.

Sontag, Deborah. 1994. "New York Officials Welcome Immigrants, Legal or Illegal." *The New York Times*, June 10: A1.

Spivak, Sharon. 1991. "Wilson Blames Budget Woes on Unchecked Immigration." *The San Diego Tribune*, April 12: A-1+.

Stacy, Palmer and Wayne Lutton. 1990. *Why Not Defend America's Borders?* Monterey, Va.: Americans for Immigration Control, 1990.

Standefer, Jon and Alex Drehsler. 1980a. "'Border Country' Has Own Culture, Laws, Lawlessness." *The San Diego Union*, January 6: A-1+.

———. 1980b. "At Times, 'Border Country' Is Law Unto Itself." *The San Diego Union*, January 7: A-1+.

———. 1980c. "'Border Country' Smuggling Flows Both Ways." *The San Diego Union*, January 8: A-1+.

———. 1980d. "'Illegal Aliens Become 'Invisible' Residents." *The San Diego Union*, January 9: A-1+.

———. 1980e. "'Secession By Hispanics: A Reality in Year 2000?" *The San Diego Union*, January 10: A-1+

Stanley, Alessandra. 2000. "Bodies of 6 Remind Italy of Migrants' Plight." *The New York Times*, October 19: A13.

Starr, Kevin. 1997. *The Dream Endures: California Enters the 1940s*. New York: Oxford University Press.

Starr, Mark. 1983. "The Border: A World Apart." *Newsweek*, April 11: 36–40.

Steinbeck, John. 1983. *The Grapes of Wrath*. New York: Penguin Books, 1983 (originally published in 1939).

Stern, Marcus. 1993a. "Boxer Urges National Guard Use at Border." *The San Diego Union-Tribune*, July 30, 1993a: A1+.

———. 1993b. "Border Lures the Lawmakers." *The San Diego Union-Tribune*, August 11: A3.

———. 1993c. "Back in '89, Pete Wilson Wasn't So Adamant About Migrant Issue." *The San Diego Union-Tribune*, September 4: A3.

———. 1993d. "U.S. Blockade Halts El Paso Migrant Flow." *The San Diego Union-Tribune*, September 27: A-1+.

———. 1993e. "Crackdown Is Successful in El Paso; More Planned." *The San Diego Union-Tribune*, September 29: A-1+.

———. 1993f. "INS Nominee Eyes 'Balance' on Blockades." *The San Diego Union-Tribune*, October 1: A-1+.

———. 1993g. "Border Blockade: Simple—And Complicated." *The San Diego Union-Tribune*, October 7: A-1+.

———. 1993h. "Congress Warned: NAFTA No Fix for Migrant Influx." *The San Diego Union-Tribune*, November 4.

———. 1994a. "Border Control Plan to Slowly Shut Door." *The San Diego Union-Tribune*, January 27: A1+.

———. 1994b. "$540.5 Million Plan to Tighten Border Control." *The San Diego Union-Tribune*, February 4: A1+.

———. 1994c. "Democrats Resist Quick Border Fix." *The San Diego Union-Tribune*, August 6.

———. 1994d. "Crime Bill Gives Border Control a Big Lift." *The San Diego Union-Tribune*, August 30: A-1+.

———. 1994e. "In '83, Wilson Helped Curb INS Searches." *The San Diego Union-Tribune*, September 17: A-1+.

———. 1994f. "Reno to Tell New Border Plans Here." *The San Diego Union-Tribune*, September 17: A-1+.

———. 1997a. "The Border Fences are Stronger and the Number of Guards has Grown. Yet Undocumented Immigrants to Find Their Way into the United States. They Come for Jobs. And They're Getting Them." *The San Diego Union-Tribune*, November 2.

———. 1997b. "Labor Contractors Contribute to Illegal Immigration's Spread throughout U.S." *The San Diego Union-Tribune*, November 2.

———. 1997c. "Low-Skill Labor Markets Full of Illegal Workers, but Employers are Seldom Fined." *The San Diego Union-Tribune*, November 2.

———. 1997d. "Legislators Put Focus on Fences, Not Jobs." *The San Diego Union-Tribune*, November 3.

———. 1997e. "Illegal-Immigration Bill Weakened by Unlikely Alliance." *The San Diego Union-Tribune*, November 4.

———. 1997f. "Labor-Union Split Helps Kill Worker-Verification Proposal." *The San Diego Union-Tribune*, November 4.

———. 1998a. "In Teeming INS Cells, Many Face Prospect of Life Term." *The San Diego Union-Tribune*, March 13.

———. 1998b. "A Semi-Tough Policy on Illegal Workers" (op-ed). *The Washington Post*, July 5: C2.

Stoll, David. 1997. "In Focus: The Immigration Debate." *Foreign Policy in Focus* 2, no. 31, March.

Suro, Roberto. 1996. *Watching America's Door: The Immigration Backlash and the New Policy Debate*. New York: The Twentieth Century Fund Press.

Takaki, Ronald. 1993. *A Different Mirror: A History of Multicultural America*. Boston and New York: Little, Brown.

Tatalovich, Raymond. 1997. "Official English as Nativist Backlash." In Juan F. Perea (ed.), *Immigrants Out! The New Nativism and the Anti-Immigrant Impulse in the United States*. New York: New York University Press, 78–102.

Taylor, J. Edward, Philip L. Martin, and Michael Fix. 1997. *Poverty amid Prosperity: Immigration and the Changing Face of Rural California*. Washington, D.C.: The Urban Institute Press.

Taylor, Peter J. 1993. *Political Geography: World-Economy, Nation-State and Locality*. Essex: Longman Group/New York: John Wiley and Sons.

———. 1994. "The State as Container: Territoriality in the Modern World-System." *Progress in Human Geography* 18, no. 2: 151–62.

Taylor H., Lawrence Douglas. 1994. "El contrabando de chinos a lo largo de la frontera entre México y Estados Unidos, 1882–1931." *Frontera Norte* 6, no. 11: 41–57.

Teitelbaum, Michael S. and Myron Weiner (eds.). 1995. *Threatened Peoples, Threatened Borders: World Migration and U.S. Policy*. New York: W. W. Norton.

Tesfahuney, Mekonnen. 1998. "Mobility, Racism and Geopolitics." *Political Geography* 17, no. 5: 499–515.

Thomas, Rich. 1993. "The Economic Cost of Immigration." *Newsweek*, August 9: 18–19.

Thompson, Ginger E. 2000. "The Desperate Risk Death in a Desert." *The New York Times*, October 31: A13.

Time. 1977. "Getting Their Slice of Paradise." *Time*, May 2: 26+.

Torpey, John. 2000. *The Invention of the Passport: Surveillance, Citizenship and the State*. Cambridge: Cambridge University Press.

Tuan, Yi-Fu. 1979. *Landscapes of Fear*. Minneapolis: University of Minnesota Press.

Turque, Bill. 1993. "Why Our Borders Are Out of Control." *Newsweek*, August 9: 25.

U.S. Border Patrol. 1994. "Border Patrol Strategic Plan: 1994 and Beyond" (National Strategy). Washington, D.C.: U.S. Border Patrol, July.

U.S. Commission on Immigration Reform. 1995. "Staff Report on Border Law Enforcement and Removal Initiatives in San Diego, CA." Washington, D.C.: U.S. Commission on Immigration Reform, November.

U.S. Congress. 1994a. "Violent Crime Control and Law Enforcement Act of 1994" (Public Law 103–322, September 13, 1994). Washington, D.C.: United States Congress.

———. 1994b. Subcommittee on International Law, Immigration, and Refugees of the Committee on the Judiciary, House of Representatives, 103rd Congress. "Immigration-related Issues in the North American Free Trade Agreement" (November 3, 1993). Washington, D.C.: U.S. Government Printing Office.

———. 1995. Subcommittee on Immigration and Claims of the Committee on the

Judiciary, House of Representatives, 104th Congress. "Border Security" (March 10, 1995). Washington, D.C.: U.S. Government Printing Office.

U.S. General Accounting Office (U.S. GAO). 1997a. *Illegal Aliens: Extent of Welfare Benefits Received on Behalf of U.S. Children* (report number GAO/HEHS-98–30). Washington, D.C.: U.S. General Accounting Office, November.

———. 1997b. *Illegal Immigration: Southwest Border Strategy Results Inconclusive; More Evaluation Needed* (report number GAO/GGD-98–21). Washington, D.C.: U.S. General Accounting Office, December.

———. 1999. *Illegal Immigration: Status of Southwest Border Strategy Implementation* (report number GAO/GGD-99–44). Washington, D.C.: U.S. General Accounting Office, May 1999.

U.S. Government. 1994. *Public Papers of the Presidents of the United States: William J. Clinton, 1993, Book I-January 20 to July 31, 1993*. Washington, D.C.: U.S. Government Printing Office.

———. 1995. "Memorandum on Illegal Immigration" and "Remarks on the Immigration Policy Initiative and an Exchange with Reporters" (February 7, 1995), *Weekly Compilation of Presidential Documents*. Vol. 31, No. 6, Washington, D.C.: United States Government Printing Office, Monday, February 13: 199–204.

U.S. Immigration and Naturalization Service (U.S. INS). 1953. *Laws Applicable to Immigration and Nationality*. Washington, D.C.: U.S. Government Printing Office.

———. 1991. *An Immigrant Nation: United States Regulation of Immigration, 1798–1991*. Washington, D.C.: Immigration and Naturalization Service, U.S. Department of Justice, June 18, 1991.

———. 1996. "Border Patrol Division." Washington, D.C.: The Office of Public Affairs, U.S. Immigration and Naturalization Service, revised as of February 28, 1996.

———. 1997a. "INS Removes Record Number of Criminal and Illegal Aliens in Second Quarter" (Press Release). Washington, D.C.: The Office of Public Affairs, U.S. Immigration and Naturalization Service, May 13, 1997a.

———. 1997b. *Operation Gatekeeper: 3 Years of Results*. Washington, D.C.: The Office of Public Affairs, U.S. Immigration and Naturalization Service, October 1997b.

———. 1997c. "INS Launches Next Phase of Operation Gatekeeper" (Press Release). Washington, D.C.: The Office of Public Affairs, U.S. Immigration and Naturalization Service, October 7, 1997c.

———. 1998. "Operation Gatekeeper: New Resources, Enhanced Results" (Fact Sheet). Washington, D.C.: The Office of Public Affairs, U.S. Immigration and Naturalization Service, July 14, 1998.

U.S. News and World Report. 1971. "Why 'Wetbacks' Are So Hard to Control." *U.S. News and World Report*, October 18: 50.

———. 1972. "Surge of Illegal Immigrants Across American Borders." *U.S. News and World Report*, January 17: 32–34.

———. 1973. "'Invasion' by Illegal Aliens, and the Problems They Create." *U.S. News and World Report*, July 23: 32–35.

———. 1975. "Rising Flood of Illegal Aliens: How to Deal With It." *U.S. News and World Report*, February 3: 27–30.

U.S. Select Commission on Immigration and Refugee Policy. 1981. *U.S. Immigration Policy and the National Interest* (final report of the commission). Washington, D.C.: U.S. Select Commission on Immigration and Refugee Policy.

U.S. Senate Subcommittee on Immigration and Naturalization. 1948. Unpublished hearing held in San Ysidro, California, U.S. Senate Subcommittee on Immigration and Naturalization of the Senate Committee on Judiciary, September 24, 1948 (available on microfiche at the U.S. Library of Congress).

Uchitelle, Louis. 2000. "I.N.S. Is Looking the Other Way As Illegal Immigrants Fill Jobs." *The New York Times*, March 9: A1+.

Uvin, Peter. 1998. *Aiding Violence: The Development Enterprise in Rwanda*. West Hartford, Conn.: Kumarian Press.

Van Deerlin, Lionel. 1992. "Buchanan is a Kook, Not a Conservative" (op-ed). *The San Diego Tribune,* January 3: B7.

van Dijk, Teun A. 1996. "Illegal Aliens" (editorial). *Discourse and Society* 7, no. 3: 291–92.

Varsanyi, Monica W. 1996. "Proposition 187: Xenophobia, the Feminized Immigrant, and Public Spaces of Reproduction in a Transnational Era." Masters Thesis, Department of Geography, University of Washington, June 1996.

Vázquez, Josefina Zoraida and Lorenzo Meyer. 1985. *The United States and Mexico.* Chicago and London: The University of Chicago Press.

Vélez-Ibáñez, Carlos G. 1997. *Border Visions: Mexican Cultures of the Southwest United States.* Tucson: The University of Arizona Press.

Verhovek, Sam Howe. 1994. "Texas and California: Two Views of Illegal Aliens." *The New York Times,* June 26: A12.

Vila, Pablo. 1994. "The Construction of Social Identities on the Border: Some Case Studies in Ciudad Juarez and El Paso." In Howard C. Daudistel and Cheryl A. Howard (eds.), *Sociological Explorations: Focus on the Southwest.* Minneapolis/St. Paul: West: 51–64.

———. 1997. "Narrative Identities: The Employment of the Mexican on the U.S.-Mexican Border." *The Sociological Quarterly* 38, no. 1: 147–83.

———. 1999a. "Constructing Social Identities in Transnational Contexts: The Case of the Mexico-U.S. Border." *International Social Science Journal* 51, no. 159: 75–88.

———. 1999b. "Identity and Empowerment on the Border." *NACLA Report on the Americas* 33, no. 3: 40–45.

———. 2000. *Crossing Borders, Reinforcing Borders: Social Categories, Metaphors and Narrative Identities on the U.S. –Mexico Border.* Austin: University of Texas Press.

Wacquant, Loic. 1999. "'Suitable Enemies': Foreigners and Immigrants in the Prisons of Europe." *Punishment and Society* 1, no. 2: 215–22.

Walczak, Lee. 1994. "Why Clinton Can't Keep His Eyes off California." *Business Week,* June 13: 51.

Walker, Richard. 1996. "California Rages Against the Dying of the Light." *New Left Review,* no. 209: 42–74.

———. 1996. "California's Collision of Race and Class." *Representations,* no. 55: 163–183.

Walker, S. L. 1988. "Residents, Migrants, Are Uneasy Neighbors." *The San Diego Union,* December 22: A-1+.

Wall Street Journal. 1990. "The Rekindled Flame." *Wall Street Journal,* July 3: A10.

Walters, Jana. 1990. "Illegal Immigration: The Making of Myth." Unpublished paper, in sociology, University of Texas at Austin.

Walth, Brent, Kim Christensen and Richard Read. 2000. "INS One of the Most Corrupt Federal Law-Enforcement Agencies." *The Oregonian,* December 11.

Walzer, Michael. 1984. *Spheres of Justice: A Defense of Pluralism and Equality.* New York: Basic Books.

Wambaugh, Joseph. 1984. *Lines and Shadows.* New York: William Morrow.

Wang, Peter H. 1975. *Legislating "Normalcy": The Immigration Act of 1924.* Saratoga, Calif.: R and E Research Associates.

Warnock, John. 1995. *The Other Mexico: The North American Triangle Completed.* Montreal: Black Rose Books.

Waterman, Stanley. 1994. "Spatial Separation and Boundaries." In Werner A. Gallusser (ed.), *Political Boundaries and Coexistence.* Proceedings of the IGU-Symposium, Basel, Switzerland, May 24–27, 1994. Bern, Switzerland: Peter Lang: 395–401.

Webb, Eugene, Donald Campbell et al. 1981. *Nonreactive Measures in the Social Sciences.* Boston: Houghton Mifflin.

Webster, Katherine. 1990. "Marchers Demand Strong Measures to Control Border." *The San Diego Union,* October 7: B-3.

Weeks, John R. 1999. "Demographic Dynamics of the San Diego-Tijuana Region." In Mark J. Spalding (ed.), *Sustainable Development in San Diego-Tijuana:*

Environmental, Social, and Economic Implications of Interdependence. San Diego: Center for U.S.-Mexican Studies, University of California, San Diego, 17–33.

Weinberg, Albert K. 1963. *Manifest Destiny: A Study of Nationalist Expansionism in American History.* Chicago: Quadrangle Books (originally published in 1935 by Johns Hopkins Press).

Weinberger, Caspar and Peter Schweitzer. 1996. *The Next War.* Washington, D.C.: Regnery Publishing, Inc.

Weinstein, Henry. 2000. "Court Bans the Indefinite Detention of Immigrants." *Los Angeles Times,* April 11: A3+.

Weintraub, Daniel M. 1986. "Telegram on Illegal Aliens by Romney Is Condemned." *Los Angeles Times* (San Diego County edition), October 15, sec. 2, p. 1.

———. 1994. "Crime, Immigration Issues Helped Wilson, Poll Finds." *Los Angeles Times,* November 9: A-1+.

Welch, Michael. 1996. "The Immigration Crisis: Detention as an Emerging Mechanism of Social Control." *Social Justice* 23, no. 3: 169–84.

Whitney, D. Charles et al. 1989. "Geographic and Source Biases in Network Television News 1982–1984." *Journal of Broadcasting and Electronic Media* 33, no. 2: 159–74.

Wilgoren, Jodi. 1998. "INS' Border Focus Is Shifting to Other States." *Los Angeles Times,* March 11: A1+.

Wilgoren, Jodi and Patrick J. McDonnell. 1997. "INS Deportations Soar as Crackdown Proceeds." *Los Angeles Times,* October 31: A1+.

Wilkie, Dana and John Marelius. 1994. "Brown Backs Blockade of Border at San Diego." *The San Diego Union-Tribune,* September 14: A-1+.

Williams, T. Harry. 1981. *The History of American Wars: From 1745 to 1918.* New York: Alfred A. Knopf.

Williamson, Jennifer. 1977. "Davis Urges Tight Fence, Patrols All Along Border." *The San Diego Union,* March 4: A-1.

Willoughby, Randy. 1997. "Immigration, Race, and Security on the California-Mexico Border." In Paul Ganster, Alan Sweedler, James Scott, and Wolf Dieter-Eberwein (eds.), *Borders and Border Regions in Europe and North America.* San Diego: San Diego State University Press and Institute for Regional Studies of the Californias, 267–92.

Wilmoth, G. C. 1934. "Mexican Border Procedure." Lecture no. 23, 2d. series, November 19, 1934. Washington, D.C.: Immigration and Naturalization Service, U.S. Department of Labor.

Wilson, Pete. 1993. "Why Does the U.S. Government Continue to Reward Illegal Immigration . . . At Such Cost to the American People?" (paid advertisement). *The New York Times,* August 10: A11.

Wilson, Thomas M. and Hastings Donnan. 1998. "Nation, State and Identity at International Borders." In Thomas M. Wilson and Hastings Donnan (eds.), *Border Identities: Nation and State at International Frontiers.* Cambridge: Cambridge University Press: 1–30.

Winichakul, Thongchai. 1994. *Siam Mapped: A History of the Geo-Body of a Nation.* Honolulu: University of Hawaii Press.

Wixon, I. F. 1934. "Immigration Border Patrol." Lecture no. 7, March 19, 1934. Washington, D.C.: Immigration and Naturalization Service, U.S. Department of Labor.

Wolf, Daniel. 1988. *Undocumented Aliens and Crime: The Case of San Diego County.* San Diego: Center for U.S.-Mexican Studies, University of California, San Diego.

Wong, Diana. 1989. "The Semantics of Migration." *Sojourn* (Singapore) 4, no. 2: 275–85.

Wyse, Ronald. 1966. "The Position of Mexicans in the Immigration and Nationality Laws." In Leo Grebler, *Mexican Immigration to the United States: The Record and Its Implications.* Mexican-American Study Project, Advance Report 2, University of California, Los Angeles.

Yapa, Lakshman. 1996. "What Causes Poverty? A Postmodern View." *Annals of the Association of American Geographers* 86, no. 4: 707–28.

Yeh Ling-Ling. 1994. "The Welcome Mat Is Threadbare" (op-ed). *Los Angeles Times,* April 13.

Zelinsky, Wilbur. 1988. *Nation into State: The Shifting Symbolic Foundation of American Nationalism.* Chapel Hill: University of North Carolina Press.

Zerubavel, Eviatar. 1996. "Social Memories: Steps to a Sociology of the Past." *Qualitative Sociology* 19, no. 3: 283–299.

Zinn, Howard. 1990. *A People's History of the United States.* New York: Harper Perennial.

Zitner, Aaron. 2001. "U.S. Tallies More Illegal Workers." *Los Angeles Times,* March 10: A-1+.

Zolberg, Aristide R. 1978. "International Migration Policies in a Changing World System." in William H, McNeil and Ruth S. Adams (eds.), *Human Migration: Patterns and Policies.* Bloomington, Ind.: Indiana University Press, 241–86.

Zucker, Norman L. and Naomi Flink Zucker. 1996. *Desperate Crossings: Seeking Refuge in America.* Armonk, N.Y.: M. E Sharpe.

FILES FROM THE NATIONAL ARCHIVES AND RECORDS ADMINISTRATION (NARA) IN WASHINGTON, D.C.:

Subject/Description of File	Date(s)	File Number
Request for additional immigration inspectors	June 5, 1907	55921/971
General border patrol activities, El Paso	June 6, 1917	54261/276
Enforcement along the Mexican border	February 5, 1918	54261/276
Proposal to establish an immigration patrol service on the land boundaries	April 29, 1918	54261/267
Border Patrol employees by class and subdistrict	March 16, 1934	55853/300
Authorized Border Patrol force	June 5, 1940	55853/320
Memorandum on Border Patrol in Tecate	December 2, 1940	55853/320
Authorized Border Patrol force	December 2, 1943	55853/320b
Letter from Commissioner Swing regarding boundary fences	March 29, 1956	56364/44.15
Intelligence report, Chula Vista Sector	August 6, 1956	56364/43.1

INTERVIEWS

Aleinikoff, T. Alexander. General counsel for the U.S. Immigration and Naturalization Service, March 1994–June 1995; executive associate commissioner for programs, INS, June 1995–1996; Carnegie Endowment for International Peace, 1996–present. May 8, 1997, Washington, D.C.

Anbender, Julie. Deputy director of public affairs, U.S. Department of Justice, 1993–1995; Acting Director of Media Services, March–July 1995; Director of Public Affairs at Immigration and Naturalization Service, March 1997– . May 30, 1997, Washington, D.C.

Baca, Herman. President, Coalition for Chicano Rights (San Diego), 1970–present. June 2, 1998, National City, California (via telephone).

Becks, Gary. Special assistant to Congressman Duncan Hunter (Republican, El Cajon, California). April 30, 1998, San Diego.

Bonner, T. J. President of the Border Patrolman's Association. October 3, 1996, San Diego.

Braniff, William. U.S. Attorney for the Southern District of California, 1988–1992. September 22, 1997, San Diego.

Cobian, Ana. Special assistant to the United States Attorney General's Special Representative for Southwest Border Issues. September 23, 1997, San Diego.

De La Viña, Gustavo. Regional Director, Western Region of the Immigration and Naturalization Service. September 11, 1997, Laguna Niguel, California.

Epstein, Tom. Special assistant to the president for political affairs (responsible for California affairs). February 1993–August 1995. April 29, 1998, Washington, D.C. (via telephone).

Martínez, Roberto. Head, U.S./Mexico Border Program of the American Friends Service Committee. February 18, 1995 (and on numerous subsequent occasions), San Diego.

Murillo, Rudy. Administrative assistant, Washington, D.C. office of Congressman Lionel Van Deerlin, November 1972–October 1978; press officer for the Immigration and Naturalization Service, Southern District of California, 1988–1994; Special assistant to the district director of the Immigration and Naturalization Service, Southern District of California, 1994 to July 8, 1998, San Diego (via telephone).

Nunez, Peter. U.S. Attorney for Southern California, 1982–1988; assistant secretary of the treasury for enforcement, January 1990–January 1992; currently president of Americans for Responsible Immigration, and member of the advisory boards of the Federation of American Immigration Reform, the Border Solution Task Force, and American Patrol. September 24, 1997, San Diego.

Olea Garcia Coronel y Licenciado, Alejandro. Coodinador General, Grupo Beta. February 20, 1995, Tijuana.

Reyes, Silvestre. Chief Border Patrol agent, El Paso Sector, 1993–1996; U.S. Representative, 1996–present (Democrat, El Paso). April 5, 1996, El Paso, and November 13, 1997, Washington, D.C.

Schenk, Lynn. U.S. Representative 1993–1994 (Democrat, Imperial Beach, California). September 23, 1997, San Diego.

Simmons, Matthew. Legislative aide for Congressman Duncan Hunter (Republican, El Cajon, California). May 12, 1997, Washington, D.C.

Smith, Claudia. Director of Border Office, California Rural Legal Assistance. August 21, 1997, Oceanside, California.

Smith, Marian. Historian, U.S. Immigration and Naturalization Service. May 19, 1997, Washington, D.C.

Spencer, Glenn. Cofounder and president, Voice of Citizens Together. September 8, 1997, Sherman Oaks, California (via telephone).

Stern, Marcus. Reporter responsible for immigration and border-related issues in the Washington, D.C., bureau of Copley News Service. May 14, 1997, Washington, D.C.

Van Deerlin, Lionel. U.S. Representative 1963–1981 (Democrat, Chula Vista, California). June 5, 1998, San Diego (via telephone).

Walters, T. J. Associate chief, United States Border Patrol. Immigration and Naturalization Service Headquarters, Washington, D.C., June 2, 1997.

Index